FINANCIER

FINANCIER

The Biography of ANDRÉ MEYER
*A Story of Money, Power, and the
Reshaping of American Business*

CARY REICH

WILLIAM MORROW AND COMPANY, INC.
New York / 1983

Library of Congress Cataloging in Publication Data

Reich, Cary.
    Financier, the biography of André Meyer.

    1. Meyer, André, 1898–   . 2. Capitalists and
financiers—United States—Biography.   3. Investment
banking—United States—History.   I. Title.
HG172.M49R44   1983   332′.092′4 [B]   83-8291
ISBN 0-688-01551-4

Printed in the United States of America

    2   3   4   5   6   7   8   9   10

BOOK DESIGN BY ELLEN LO GIUDICE

*To my mother
and
to Karen*

Acknowledgments

Any serious biography involves an enormous amount of legwork. For their help in library, courthouse and schoolhouse research, I would like to thank Hillary Potashnick and A. Dennis White in New York, and Veronika Hass and Esther Eder in Paris.

Many of the interviews for this book were taped. Unfortunately, tapes must be transcribed, an arduous and tedious process under even the best of circumstances. My thanks, in that regard, to Herman Jaffee and his associates for their assistance.

I am deeply grateful to Gilbert Kaplan and Peter Landau at *Institutional Investor* for their understanding and patience during the long leave of absence that this book necessitated.

Finally, for his constant enthusiasm during every stage of the project, and his wise and perceptive comments along the way, I am indebted to Harvey Ginsberg at William Morrow and Company.

Contents

FINANCIER

CHAPTER ONE

A Tale of Two Financiers

On May 23, 1969, the gates of the Federal House of Correction in Danbury, Connecticut, swung open, and out into the sunshine walked forty-seven-year-old Edward Gilbert. His release, after serving two years in Danbury and Sing Sing for embezzlement, went unheralded and unnoticed; his was just another routine discharge from the federal penitentiary system. Yet only seven years before, the misdeeds that sent Gilbert to prison were headlined in newspapers across the country. In 1962, Gilbert was nothing less than the most famous white-collar criminal in America—a one-time Wall Street boy wonder who had plunged swiftly, dizzyingly into notoriety.

Eddie Gilbert had always played for big stakes, and almost always been a winner. In the late 1950s and early 1960s, he had gained renown as a gutsy stock market speculator who had come out of nowhere to engineer the takeover of the country's leading manufacturer of hardwood flooring, E. L. Bruce & Company. Courted by the high and mighty of the financial world, he slipped effortlessly into a Gatsbyish life-style. His ten-room Fifth Avenue apartment was decorated with paintings by Monet, Fragonard, and Canaletto; his eleven-bedroom summer villa in Roquebrune in the south of France was a favorite jet-set watering hole, with a jazz band entertaining guests at poolside in the afternoons and a dance orchestra doing the honors in the evenings. Occasionally, there were some embarrassing nouveau riche incidents, such as the time Cartier filed suit against his wife when she failed to return $732,000 worth of diamonds she had "borrowed" for inspection. But for the most part, Eddie Gilbert lived the life of someone who had arrived.

Then, in early 1961, Gilbert mapped out his biggest deal yet: the takeover of another big building-materials company, Celotex. Aiming to acquire 500,000 Celotex shares on the open market, he had purchased 250,000 shares on margin (loans from stockbrokers) when the stock market suddenly nose-dived in May 1962. Besieged by margin calls—demands by the brokers for more collateral—and unable to come up with the $1.9 million out of his own pocket, Gilbert took the money out of the coffers of E. L. Bruce. When he was unable to bail himself out through a last-minute sale of his Celotex holdings, Gilbert purchased a one-way airplane ticket to Brazil. "I just can't face people," he told reporters on his arrival in Rio de Janeiro.

The fall and flight of Eddie Gilbert—a classic riches-to-rags saga—captured the American imagination as few business stories ever do. The *New York Times* dispatched one of its top financial journalists, Murray Rossant, in search of the fugitive financier. He found Gilbert in a small Rio beachfront apartment, eager to tell his tale to a waiting world, and the story was given full-blown page-one treatment.

The life of a Brazilian exile, however, soon palled on Gilbert, and in late October he returned to the United States and surrendered to federal authorities. Two years later he pleaded guilty to embezzlement, and in May 1967 Eddie Gilbert was sent to prison.

During his two years of incarceration, Gilbert had plenty of time to brood upon his fate. And what he brooded upon most was the unfairness of it all. Someone else, he was convinced, should have been sitting in Sing Sing alongside him. Someone who had helped him hatch the Celotex scheme, who had agreed to bankroll it, and who had then pulled the rug out from under him. Someone who had left him dangling as the margin calls closed in, and who had then hidden himself behind an impregnable wall of wealth and power. Someone *very big.*

Someone named André Meyer.

On the thirty-third floor of New York's swank Carlyle Hotel, in a two-bedroom suite crammed with rare Louis XIV furniture and adorned with an imposing collection of Monets, Chagalls, and Picassos, the man who was Eddie Gilbert's obsession was ensconced.

He was a slight, bespectacled, owlish-looking Frenchman in his early seventies, one of that small band of elegant expatriates whose natural habitats were the galleries and museums of Madison Avenue north of Sixtieth Street. Impeccably dressed in a carefully tailored three-piece suit, his close-cropped, slicked-back hair betraying hardly a trace of gray, he seemed incredibly spry for someone who, by his own constant admission, was perennially at death's door. He would customarily arise at four or four-thirty each morning—he couldn't sleep, he would insist—and work nonstop until six or seven in the evening. During those hours he would wheedle, flatter, cajole, soothe, bargain with, and bully some of the world's most important people, and make staggering amounts of money for himself and his associates.

When Gilbert walked out of Danbury, his nemesis was, in the words of *Fortune* magazine a year earlier, "the most important investment banker in the Western world." As senior partner of the very private firm of Lazard Frères, André Meyer spun a web of wealth and influence over two continents. Having built a personal fortune reckoned in the hundreds of millions of dollars, he was revered as a twentieth-century Midas, a man with an awesome gift for financial success. His advice on everything from personal investments to politics was eagerly sought by the great and near-great, who came trooping to the Carlyle like supplicants to a shrine. He was a friend, confidant, and escort of Jackie Kennedy, and a valued adviser to the rest of the Kennedy family. Lyndon Johnson would often seek his counsel, as would French president Georges Pompidou. He could count among his intimates numerous other statesmen, politicians, and tycoons, including David Rockefeller, RCA chief David Sarnoff, CBS chairman William Paley, and Fiat king Giovanni Agnelli.

André Meyer was one of the most outrageously successful venture capitalists of the postwar era, coming in on the ground floor of such companies as Warner-Lambert, Avis, and Holiday Inns. He financed many of the biggest real estate deals of the fifties and sixties, putting his money into everything from oil wells to avocado farms, from Texas ranchland to Haitian plantations. Through his firm, he became the world's most prolific corporate marriage broker, setting the stage for the great wave of mergers and consolidations that goes on, unabated, to this day. On Wall Street, where praise of one's competitors is the rarest commodity of all, he was universally hailed as the one true genius in the investment-banking profession. In the gilt-edged world in which he dwelled, the world of charity balls and benefits, he was celebrated for his philanthropy: for the hospitals he built, for the laboratories he donated, for the schools he supported.

But Eddie Gilbert remembered him differently.

The André Meyer he remembered was an old man he would pick up at the Carlyle early in the morning. As they bundled into Gilbert's

Rolls-Royce for the drive down to Wall Street, Meyer would say, "I wish I could afford a car like this." And Gilbert would say, "Are you kidding?" The two would have breakfast with Meyer's young partner Michel David-Weill, whose family had a principal ownership position in Lazard, and they would talk about what the old-line investment firm and the hungry young hotshot could do together. In the fall of 1961, they talked about Celotex.

The way Gilbert recalled the conversations, Meyer was enthusiastic about the takeover idea and eager to help. Meyer offered to have Lazard and some investment-banking partners buy 250,000 shares of Celotex; when the time came for Gilbert to close the deal and merge Celotex into E. L. Bruce, Lazard and partners would trade their Celotex shares for Bruce debentures for at least a 50 percent profit. Confident of Meyer's backing, Gilbert went ahead with his own purchase of Celotex—only to find, less than seven months later, that the benevolent old man was tightening the screws on him. Back in 1960, Lazard had lent E. L. Bruce $2 million in exchange for debentures that were convertible into Bruce stock. Now Lazard demanded that before it purchased any Celotex shares, half of that loan had to be repaid. And because the value of Bruce shares had doubled since the loan was made, Lazard wanted $2 million, not $1 million. Anxious to keep the deal going, Gilbert paid Lazard out of his own pocket and went on with the Celotex campaign.

Then, in May 1962, with the prices of Bruce and Celotex shares sliding, and with worried brokers who had sold Gilbert stock on credit starting to squeeze, Gilbert got another call from Lazard. The firm, which at that point had only purchased 87,000 Celotex shares, refused to buy any more unless it received immediate repayment of the other half of that 1960 note—again at more than twice its face value. Once more, Gilbert came up with the money. But with his personal finances already extended to the breaking point, the Lazard demand was nothing less than a *coup de grace*. A month later, Gilbert was on his way to Brazil.

As if all this weren't bad enough, what was equally galling to Gilbert was what happened after he returned to face justice. Using the shares it had already acquired in Celotex as a lever, Lazard was able to arrange a takeover of Celotex by the Jim Walter Corporation in August 1964. Jim Walter stock subsequently rose from $20 a share to $120, and Gilbert was convinced the gain was largely because of Celotex. The big payoff had come in, just as he had foreseen—but for someone else's benefit. And there on the sidelines, cheering the deal on, was his old friend, his old partner, André Meyer.

Every time Gilbert recalled these events, he seethed: " 'My dear boy,' that's what he used to call me. 'Such a nice young man,' he used to say. That son of a bitch. He put his arm around me and squeezed my balls off at the same time."

That was Eddie Gilbert's André Meyer. It was not at all the same André Meyer whom Jackie Kennedy and David Sarnoff and Lyndon Johnson knew.

CHAPTER TWO

The Picasso of Banking

In many ways, André Meyer was not a nice man.

He was greedy, vindictive, domineering, and often quite sadistic. His constant browbeating and temper tantrums made life unbearable for his business associates and his family. No matter how wealthy he became—and he became *very* wealthy—he could not stop plotting and scheming to build an even bigger fortune. He would allow nothing and no one to get in his way. Once, a Lazard colleague gave some investors the right of first refusal on a deal, after they had given Lazard first-refusal rights on one of *their* transactions. After all, this Lazard partner explained, it was a two-way street. Meyer was furious. "Where is it written there is a two-way street?" he demanded.

"He could be brutal, and he *enjoyed* being brutal," says his old friend Andrea Wilson, who worked for Meyer as a securities analyst. "When he was through with somebody, when he wanted to get rid of you, it was something to behold." But Wilson readily recognized what others only grudgingly acknowledged: that Meyer could not have come as far as he did—specifically, from obscure lower-middle-class origins—by relying solely on gentility and charm. "For him to break through to the extent that he did, and to achieve the position that he did, that took something," she says.

What it took was the ruthlessness of the totally self-made man, writ large. And leaving aside his methods and his personality, there can be little doubt that André Meyer did accomplish great things. "What Horowitz is to the piano," said a friend, "what Picasso was to painting, André Meyer was to banking." David Rockefeller called him "the most creative financial genius of our time in the investment-banking field." Former defense secretary and World Bank president Robert McNamara hailed Meyer as "a giant. Absolutely unique."

The son of a struggling Paris printing salesman, Meyer left school in 1914, when he was sixteen years old, to become a messenger on the

Paris Bourse. By the time he reached thirty, he was a partner in the eminent private banking firm of Lazard Frères. By the age of forty, he had helped save the foundering auto giant Citroën, had founded France's first consumer finance company, and was awarded the Legion of Honor. Forced into exile as a Jew by the Nazi occupation, he resettled in the United States, took over Lazard's New York operation, and built it into the most venturesome investment bank in America. He became the financial guru of the postwar power elite, an awesome repository of wisdom, contacts, and influence.

He was also one of the world's savviest individual investors. No one, save his immediate family, knew the exact extent of his fortune—of his many secrets, it was the one he kept best—but close associates reckon that it was at *least* $300 million, and possibly as much as $800 million. When he died in 1979 at age eighty-one, he left an estate valued at $90 million—and that was after he had spent the better part of a decade stripping it down by means of various family trusts to avoid the predations of the Internal Revenue Service.

A Lazard colleague once dubbed Meyer "a genius in the art of acquisitiveness." What set him apart, says David Rockefeller, was "his creativity and judgment, combined with great skills as a negotiator. It's those things that people who were trying to put together a difficult deal involving hundreds of millions of dollars needed, and he had all three to an extraordinary degree." Better than any man alive, he could strip a deal to its essence, to the underlying values that did or didn't make it worthwhile. Then, with the intuitive skill of a painter dabbing from his palette, he would give that essence a form, a structure that somehow enabled him to wring all he could out of the deal with a minimum amount of risk. This he called "financial engineering," and the term became the byword for Meyer's artistry.

He also was a masterful, habitual bargainer. "André negotiated with everyone," comments a former Lazard subordinate. "His partners, his secretaries. He spent all day long negotiating. He found it difficult to stop." Meyer's skill as a negotiator was rooted in his astute, acerbic appraisal of human motivations; as his protégé Felix Rohatyn (no mean bargainer himself) puts it, "André could peel people like bananas." He displayed the rare ability that all the truly great negotiators have: getting what he wanted, while making the other side believe that they were getting what *they* wanted.

The other essential ingredient in Meyer's success was his sheer capacity for work. He regularly toiled from four or five in the morning

to six or seven at night, and his seemingly social weekends and evenings, in the company of the Rockefellers and the Agnellis and the
Sarnoffs, were actually devoted to the accumulation of information
and contacts that were vital lubricants of his business. He never took
vacations as such. "Holidays mean the chance to recuperate," says his
son Philippe, "and he didn't need or want to recuperate. His attitude
was that you don't recuperate from breathing." Adds Robert McNamara, "The only man I knew who worked as hard as André was President Johnson."

"Life is a discipline," Meyer would admonish his colleagues. And
no one was more disciplined than André Meyer himself. "He had a
phenomenal ability to control his own actions," remarks an ex-
Lazard partner. "He didn't lift a fork and move it without a purpose."
One oft-cited example of his calculation was his handling of cocktail
party invitations; he would customarily accept them, then not show
up, and at the last minute send the host a telegram expressing his re-
grets. Inevitably, the missive left a bigger impression on the host than
all the guests who *had* shown up.

Such image building was second nature to Meyer; few financiers
have ever been so assiduous in crafting their personae, and that of
their firms. In the words of one Wall Street contemporary, "André
understood Escoffier's principle: that presentation is nine-tenths of
the battle." Deliberately, Meyer created an aura of mystery for himself, and of a certain snobbishness for his firm; the less accessible they
were, he correctly reasoned, the more the world would seek them out
and prize their advice. He built a firm that was of, by, and for the
elite. The general public's business was no more welcome at Lazard
than it was at J. P. Morgan & Company.

But all this calculation and self-discipline also served a larger
purpose: to rein in and conceal the more unsavory aspects of Meyer's
personality. Indeed, to those who were closest to Meyer, his greatest
achievement was overcoming his rages, his insecurities, his paranoia.
Says his son: "For me it has always been very difficult to understand
how such an emotional and extreme person could have dealt with
business."

Meyer was prone to most unbankerlike explosions, sometimes
quivering so much and turning so pale that his associates were convinced he was about to have a heart attack on the spot. By the same
token, he was a soft touch for the shallowest, most transparent forms
of flattery, even though something within him told him he shouldn't

believe a word of it. He was forever in need of reassurance—about his friends, about his business decisions, about his health, about his place in the world.

His relationships—business and personal—were often marked by violent fallings-out and passionate reconciliations. "If you had a peaceful relationship with him for two weeks, I think he got worried," remarks Michel David-Weill, Meyer's successor as Lazard senior partner. He would fire partners, dismiss friends, and throw family members out of the house for the flimsiest of reasons—then, just as suddenly, welcome them back to his bosom.

He was needlessly cruel in dressing down subordinates, shredding their egos so methodically that several became human wrecks. He called his partners "clerks" and sought to dominate every waking moment of their lives. At the slightest whim he would phone them on weekends, summon them back from vacations, and force them to work on New Year's Eve.

André Meyer took secretiveness—within certain limits, not an undesirable trait in a banker—to grand, almost pathological extremes. He arranged his personal financial affairs in such a byzantine, convoluted way that no one (with the possible exception of his son, in whom he confided) could piece together the full extent of his activities. One Lazard partner might know about his involvement in oil drilling, another in real estate, but none saw the complete picture. Nearly all his business was transacted in person or over the telephone; he was careful not to leave a trail of memos and documents behind that would, after his death, reveal the secrets he had guarded so zealously in his lifetime.

For all the powerful friends he made, for all the homage that was paid him, Meyer could never shake the feeling of being an outsider, an interloper, an émigré in American society. As successful as he was, he could not stop fretting about such trivialities as his command of English (which, while hardly flawless, was actually quite good). It was no accident, intimates say, that during almost forty years in the United States, he never lived anywhere but a hotel. Explains Felix Rohatyn, "He wanted to be able to go downstairs on any day and check out and leave—to just shut the door, turn in the key, pick up his airplane ticket, and go."

His greed was insatiable. A prominent banker who was Meyer's contemporary still marvels at his "almost erotic attachment to money. Just to have it, to feel it, to be in possession of it gave him an enormous kick. Money was the symbol of success, and it was the symbol that attracted him, and not the practical use of it." Money wasn't there for spending but for keeping score, to assure him that he was winning.

André Meyer's insecurity was total. When his friends didn't call or visit when they said they would, he immediately concluded that they had abandoned him. Some of his partners described him as the most unhappy man they had ever met. At the same time, many of these same partners admired and even loved him.

What they appreciated, above all, was that André Meyer was an original. "In twenty-five years in the business, I've never seen anyone as single-minded as he was," says ex-partner Raymond Troubh. "When he wanted something, he *willed* it to happen." André Meyer was a man who could boast, all his life, that "all you need to succeed is a yellow pad and a pencil," and *prove* it. He was regarded by his competitors as "the world's greatest schemer," a man who savored the most complex plots and intrigues—"the more complicated the better," is the way one partner put it. Yet in the exclusive circles in which he moved, he was a beloved, grandfatherly figure, someone who would always remember to send Lady Bird Johnson roses, someone who would unstintingly spend hours at the Carlyle helping John-John and Caroline Kennedy with their homework.

"I remember once, when my son David was around twelve, we were up at André's apartment," says Andrea Wilson's husband Fred, himself a longtime Lazard partner. "This was David's first exposure to André, and I told him beforehand that this would be an historic occasion. When we walked out of there, David said to me, 'Dad, you let this guy with the squeaky voice buffalo all you guys? What's the matter with you?' Well, his dominance certainly didn't come across to this twelve-year-old. But it was there. I can't describe it very well, except to say that the air turned into ozone when André walked into a room."

Schemer, counselor, grand wizard of finance—that, and more, was André Meyer.

CHAPTER THREE

Up and Coming

André Benoit Mathieu Meyer was born September 3, 1898, in Paris. He was the first child of Jules Meyer, but the second of Lucie Cerf Meyer, who had a daughter, Edmáe, by a first husband who had died five years earlier. Both Jules and his bride came from the thriving Jewish community in Strasbourg. No one in the family can recall whether they met in Strasbourg and migrated to Paris, or whether they met after both had resettled in the French capital. During the early years of their son's youth, they lived at 41 Boulevard Beaumarchais, at the edge of the city's old Jewish quarter, near the Bastille. While hardly the most elegant district of Paris, the neighborhood— and the Meyers' residence—was respectably bourgeois.

André Meyer was often vague when asked exactly what his father did for a living. He would describe Jules Meyer as having been "a businessman" or "a printer." Michel Weill, the son of André Meyer's half-sister, believes his stepgrandfather was some sort of printing salesman. In any event, Jules made enough to give his family the comforts of the lower bourgeoisie. At least, until he began to indulge his passion for gambling. Unable or unwilling to devote as much attention to his job as he did to the card table, Jules left a vacuum at the head of the household. The family looked to young André to fill it.

While hardly a model student, André was doing well enough in school. At the Collège Rollin, an old public secondary school he attended from 1909 to 1913, he won honors in recitation and various honorable mentions in history and geography. But for every teacher who commented on the boy's "conscientiousness and assiduousness," there were several more who were put off by some aspect of his behavior. A history and geography instructor wrote that "he understands well, but does not know how to develop an idea. Confines himself to what is strictly necessary." Another found "little attention to work, very weak." Perhaps the one truly prophetic comment was this one from his 1911–1912 history and geography teacher: "Too noisy and fidgeting, his work suffers."

His performance was also hurt by long and frequent absences from school. At the Lycée Charlemagne, which he attended before Rollin, he dropped out during the 1906–1907 term and was forced to repeat the year's work. During his first term at Rollin, a math teacher wrote that "prolonged absence from the class nullified his progress." Never the most robust specimen, he apparently was suffering from various minor maladies. But it wasn't illness that led him to quit school for good in July 1913, before he could complete the requirements for a diploma. It was the need to provide for his family.

Already, he was showing an affinity for the financial markets. At the age of fifteen, it was said, he could recite by heart all the prices on the Paris Bourse. So no one in the family was surprised when he promptly found employment as a Bourse messenger. And then André Meyer fell into his first great piece of luck. Edmáe had just married a young man named Edouard Weill, who, through a family connection, was employed at a small Paris bank, Baur & Sons. When war broke out in the summer of 1914, Weill joined the army. His ambitious brother-in-law applied for, and obtained, the vacated position.

The war, in many ways, was more an opportunity than a crisis for André Meyer. Not only did it give him a chance to break into banking (thanks to Weill's absence), but the vast depletion of manpower in the financial district gave him free rein to learn all he could about his trade, and practice it, at a tender age. Deferred from military service because of what the doctors said was a "weak heart," and because he was already the sole support not only of his mother and father, but his half-sister and her infant son Michel, the young man had a clear field ahead of him.

The French financial market in which Meyer apprenticed was a chaotic maelstrom whose tone was set by the wartime government's timidity and ineptitude. "A worse financial administration it would be difficult to conceive," wrote one commentator. While the French state was quick to take a dominant role in the economy—fixing prices, rationing supplies, nationalizing the railroads, snatching men from their jobs—it was strangely shy about developing the means to pay for all this. The French income tax, which was enacted in March 1914, did not become operative until 1916 and even then had limited effect. To finance itself, the government borrowed and borrowed—from the banks, from the public, and to a huge extent from its Allies.

War contractors were paid with government IOUs, which the contractors then cashed in at the banks for some percentage of their face value. The banks, in turn, made an active market in these IOUs. The result of this massive buy now-pay later program was rampant inflation—the French wholesale price index more than quadrupled between 1913 and 1918—and a back-breaking foreign debt of 43 billion francs, or almost $4 billion. Yet for the banks there was a silver lining: with both the government and the war contractors utterly dependent on them for financing, their business boomed.

For a small bank like Baur, considerable money could be made trading all the government obligations, IOUs, and corporate paper floating around. And trading was a side of the business that attracted André Meyer almost immediately. It called for a quick mind, which the teenager certainly had; a hardheaded sense of values, which he was fast acquiring; and boundless energy, a prerequisite that the nervous, fidgety boy had no problem fulfilling. Already as a youth he was awakening daily at four in the morning to study the financial tables of the newspaper and plot out his moves of the day. During family meals in the cramped apartment, he would put his telephone on the dinner table and chatter away about the market between bites.

In 1918, while still in the army, his brother-in-law contracted the Spanish grippe and died. Edmáe was pregnant with her second child at the time, and when the baby (another son) came along, Meyer continued to support her family as well as his mother and father. His sense of familial responsibility was already very strong: "My uncle was almost a father to us," says Michel Weill. Barely twenty years old, and already with five dependents, the young man drove himself mercilessly at Baur to keep the family afloat. And soon, word about Baur's sharp fledgling trader spread.

Meyer was also coming along on another front. As someone of promise in the stock market, he was able to wangle invitations to the social gatherings of Paris' upper-bourgeois Jewish elite. At one of those parties he met "the little Lehmans," five very lovely and very popular daughters of a wealthy banker who died when they were still children. The Lehmans lived in a spacious apartment on the Avenue Victor Hugo in the fashionable sixteenth arrondissement. Their social standing was, at the very least, two or three cuts above André Meyer's. But that didn't stop him from first admiring, and then coveting, the prettiest and youngest of the little Lehmans, Bella.

Meyer was not going to let Bella get away. When he heard that she was going off on vacation to Switzerland, Meyer told his cousin Léon to follow the girl and keep an eye on her. Just to set things straight, Meyer gave this warning to Léon before he left: "Fool around with whomever you want, but don't fool around with the little one."

The courtship began in earnest upon Bella's return. But one obstacle to marriage remained: Bella's older sisters, with the exception of the eldest, weren't yet married, and for Bella to wed before the second oldest, Ida, was out of the question. (Ida, it was said, almost had a nervous collapse when she heard it was Bella whom André was after, and not she.) Bella's suitor, however, was nothing if not resourceful: he told cousin Léon to marry Ida. And Léon did.

So the way was cleared for André and Bella to marry on December 20, 1922. Within two years, their first child, Francine, was born, and a year later they had a son, Philippe. By then, Meyer was doing well enough at Baur to move his parents to a nicer apartment on the Square Montholon, off the Rue La Fayette in the ninth arrondissement, while continuing to support his widowed half-sister and her two small sons. Meanwhile, he installed his own new family in thoroughly *haute-bourgeois* surroundings on the Avenue George V, just up from the Pont de l'Alma on the Right Bank of the Seine.

It was not hard to see why Meyer was so prosperous. The French franc in the early 1920s was buffeted repeatedly by currency crises; in just a few weeks in 1924 the currency lost nearly half its value. Since currencies were traded on the Bourse between 1:00 and 3:15 every weekday, the market was made to order for speculators who could move in and out of the franc quickly and benefit from the enormous swings in price. An agile trader could sell francs on the floor of the Bourse, dash upstairs to a phone and buy the same amount of francs in London, benefiting from the arbitrage, or price differentials, between Paris and London.

As one observer of the 1924 Bourse scene, a *New York Times Sunday Magazine* correspondent, wrote, "With a clear head, alertness, and quick action a foreign exchange broker in Paris can, by manipulation of a very few million francs routed via London and America, drop the Paris currency several points. He can as quickly in a few short rounds jack it up to his eventual profit."

One of the shrewdest and most nimble of these traders was the young sharpshooter at Baur. And in the hushed corridors of the elite Paris banking firm of Lazard Frères, the partners were beginning to take notice.

* * *

Despite its impeccable reputation, Lazard Frères was something of an oddity in French financial circles: a thoroughly French bank that had not been founded in France, but in the United States, and that had got its start not as a bank, but as a dry-goods business. The creation of Alexandre, Simon, and Lazare Lazard, three brothers who had emigrated from Sarreguemines in the French province of Lorraine to New Orleans, Lazard Frères opened its doors in 1848 with $9,000 in capital—$3,000 from each brother. Within a year, however, the firm was wiped out by a fire that destroyed a large section of New Orleans. Undaunted, the brothers packed their gear and moved to San Francisco.

They couldn't have picked a better place to set up a dry-goods business. Gold had just been discovered nearby at Sutter's Mill, and a horde of prospectors and settlers descended on San Francisco, desperately in need of everything from gold pans to overalls. The Lazards bought an interest in a fabric house making woolen yard goods and also made a small investment in a retail store. Business was so good that they sent for a cousin, Alexandre Weill, to come to the United States as their bookkeeper.

Nevertheless, it didn't take the brothers long to figure out that the real money in 1850s San Francisco wasn't in provisioning gold miners, but in dealing in the metal itself. They began shifting their trading skills from woolens to gold ingots and foreign exchange. By 1852 they had opened a Paris operation, Lazard Frères et Cie., and in 1864 became full-fledged bankers, reorganizing their San Francisco office as the London, Paris and American Bank, Ltd. With the opening of a New York office by Alexandre Weill in 1880, and the establishment of a London arm three years earlier, Lazard became the largest shipper of gold to and from Europe, and the biggest U.S. trader of commercial bills.

In 1908, the original San Francisco bank was sold to a group of California businessmen (the institution later became the Crocker National Bank, one of the state's biggest), thus leaving the three-headed New York-Paris-London structure that exists, intact, to this day. While the three had certain elements in common—notably a devotion to a very select, very private banking business—each evolved into a freestanding, independently managed entity, whose only tie to the others was a common ownership. And even that link was weakened during the First World War, when the Bank of England forced Lazard to sell the London bank to British interests.

By 1925, the one still-tangible bridge beween the American Lazard and the French was David David-Weill, Alexandre's son. Raised in the United States, he spoke English with a broad Far Western twang, yet he was every bit the compleat, cultivated *homme d'affaires français*. As a regent (director) of the Banque de France, he sat at the pinnacle of the French banking establishment; as a collector of great art, few if any in France were his equal. It was said that he bought one *objet* or painting every day of his life. And his generosity was such that he would buy for French museums as often as he bought for himself. Along with André Lazard, the last of the Lazards at the bank, he ran the Paris firm.

Someone who knew David-Weill well described him as "extremely amiable, courteous and modest, but someone who also had an extraordinary sense of the value of people. He knew who would work out and who wouldn't." And in 1925, David-Weill's unerring instincts told him that André Meyer was one of those who would.

David-Weill summoned the twenty-seven-year-old trader and asked him if he would like to join Lazard. Meyer was interested, but he had one question: how quickly could he be made a partner? David-Weill was noncommittal. Meyer told him in that case he wasn't interested and left.

A year later, David-Weill contacted Meyer again. This time David-Weill had a proposition: Meyer would be hired on a one-year trial. If he was as successful as David-Weill thought he would be, he could become a partner at the end of that period. If he didn't work out, he would leave the firm. Meyer instantly accepted.

In 1927, a year after he joined, André Meyer became a partner of Lazard Frères.

Although it was his trading skill that brought him to the attention of Lazard, Meyer already had his eye on a higher calling. He wanted to be a banker, in the old-fashioned sense of the term: someone who counsels companies, who arranges deals and financings, and who at the same time is on the lookout for lucrative investment opportunities for the bank. Banking, in that sense, was the principal activity of the firm; trading, while important, was decidedly out of the mainstream. Meyer wanted to be a banker in the mold of Raymond Philippe, the Lazard deal-maker who was instrumental in saving the franc from disaster in 1926. There was not a trader in France who was lionized as Philippe was, who commanded the prestige and influence he had at his fingertips. Trading stocks and bonds and currencies, for André Meyer, was simply not enough.

Nevertheless, during that first trial year at Lazard, he did what he knew best. But no sooner did he have his partnership in hand than he began restlessly searching for a broader métier. Then, in 1928, his chance came, thanks to the Citroën auto company.

Citroën then was still very much under the sway of its founder, André Citroën, a flamboyant innovator who consistently confounded the skeptics who mocked his grand designs. When the first Citroën rolled off the assembly line in 1919 and he announced plans to manufacture 30,000 of the vehicles, he was told there was no way he could sell them all; Citroën not only sold them, but did so before they were even manufactured. When he made known his ambition to produce 100 automobiles a day, the critics said he was dreaming; but by 1924, he was turning out 300 a day. Nothing seemed beyond Citroën's grasp. He even was once able to persuade the Paris city fathers to allow him to put his name up in lights along the side of the Eiffel Tower by means of 250,000 electric lamps.

One of the many firsts Citroën brought to the French auto industry was the sale of cars on credit, through a Citroën subsidiary known as the Société pour la Vente à Crédit d'Automobiles, or SOVAC for short. Patterned after the credit arms of the big American automakers, SOVAC introduced the concept of consumer finance to the French public. But while André Citroën merely viewed the company as a mechanism for promoting the sales of his automobiles, André Meyer saw the possibility of something bigger. If SOVAC could finance cars, he reasoned, why couldn't it also finance major household appliances, or even apartments and houses?

Since Lazard had just become a major shareholder of the auto company, Meyer had no trouble bringing his idea to the attention of André Citroën himself. What he proposed to the carmaker was a buyout: Lazard, along with two other banks, would take over SOVAC and turn it into a broad-based consumer finance company, the first in France. It would continue to finance Citroën purchasers— in fact, it would agree not to finance any other make of car—but would also branch out into other areas. The advantage for Citroën was that the SOVAC takeover would relieve it of the burden of funding and operating the equivalent of a bank, no small consideration in view of the company's already strained resources. At the same time, SOVAC would still be fulfilling its main role, as far as André Citroën was concerned: encouraging the French public to buy his cars.

Citroën was agreeable. At the age of thirty, Meyer had masterminded his first big deal.

Of course, there were still some important elements to be worked out, including the question of just who the other investors would be. Meyer aimed high and somehow landed two of the most potent backers in the business. One was Commercial Investment Trust, then one of the biggest consumer credit companies in the United States. The other was J. P. Morgan & Company, the world's most prestigious private bank. Each accepted a one-third interest in the new organization. Then, to line up commercial clients who would use SOVAC as their financing arm, Meyer turned to Georges Gay, an old friend of Bella's family. Meyer told Gay he would have to first go to Germany and the United States to learn the business. After a month in Berlin, Gay got a call from Meyer: enough with the learning. It was time to get moving.

Gay went out and almost immediately signed up Kelvinator, one of the best-known U.S. appliance-makers. And SOVAC was off and running. It churned out a consistent stream of profits, even in the worst days of the Depression, and its success led numerous other French companies, both before and after the Second World War, to try their hand at consumer finance. SOVAC became what Meyer dreamed it would be: "a model of the genre." (It remains profitable and powerful to this day.)

Meyer's achievement with SOVAC served notice on his Lazard colleagues, and on the Paris financial community, that he was more than just a canny trader. Not only did he have the imagination to visualize a grand design, but he displayed a relentless determination to bring the scheme to life. A cousin of Gay's who first met Meyer at a dinner party in 1928 gasped afterward to Gay, "My, he is a prodigious man!" Many others in Paris were coming to the same conclusion.

Meyer did not forsake the trading arena: each morning, for instance, he reviewed the firm's huge foreign-exchange positions. It was said that Lazard would not have been such a big player in the treacherous foreign-exchange market if the partners were not confident that Meyer was around to ride herd over the activity. But more and more,

Meyer was preoccupied with the broader concerns of the gentleman banker. And his biggest concern, as he moved into the early 1930s, was Citroën.

Refusing to heed the warnings of skeptics had served André Citroën well in the 1920s. But as the Depression set in, his stubbornness and almost willful disregard for financial considerations proved to be his undoing. Despite the faltering market for cars, and for just about everything else, Citroën went on running his company as though the Great Depression was a mere hiccup. In mid-1933, while scores of companies collapsed all around him, Citroën launched a vast 150-million-franc retooling program to speed up production. His debts mounted, and by early 1934 he owed some 2,100 creditors, including the French government, more than $20 million. Desperately trying to trim costs, Citroën cut wages by 10 percent. But all that came of it was a strike that paralyzed his factories and put him in an even deeper hole.

In early March 1934, Citroën's impatient creditors finally stepped in and asked Lazard to find some way of salvaging the company. At first, Pierre David-Weill, David's son, spearheaded the effort, but as the crisis deepened, Meyer was called in. He was elected to the Citroën board and immediately went about slowing the Citroën machine, reducing overhead, and assessing the company's true financial shape. By December 1934, he and the others overseeing Citroën's affairs concluded that the situation was far from hopeless; if its debt load could be reduced to under $13 million, and if sufficient new credit could be raised for restricted operations, Citroën could once again be profitable. Accomplishing all that, however, would be a long, uphill slog. What would be far simpler, and quicker, would be a takeover of Citroën by another company—preferably a major creditor, prepared to wipe its own debt off the books and infuse new capital into the company.

Meyer approached the Michelin tire company, which with $6.6 million in loans outstanding was Citroën's single largest creditor. And, to the collective sighs of relief of the banks, the French government, and the Citroën work force, Michelin agreed to take a controlling interest. One of France's greatest industrial crises of the Depression had at last been resolved.

If the concept of SOVAC was the first sign that Meyer was more than just a trader, his work in the Citroën crisis clearly was an affirmation that he had come of age as a banker. His growing confidence in his skills was translated into an air of crisp authority. Peering out at the world from behind his wire-rimmed glasses, the slender banker with the closely cropped hair seemed far older than his years. His advice was now sought by the cream of French industry, and foreign bankers visiting Paris often made a point of stopping by Lazard for a chat with its rising young star. Banker Perry Hall, who first encountered Meyer during a swing through Europe as a young J. P. Morgan partner in the 1930s, remembers that "he was very self-contained and definite when he was talking about something. And he had a very electric type of mind. You could tell just by talking to him that he was a coming young man."

His restlessness, often verging on the frenetic, was as pronounced as ever. The four-in-the-morning starts, the telephone on the dining room table—none of that had changed since his early days at Baur more than a decade before. Once, in the late 1930s, Gay returned home at two in the morning and was startled to find the phone ringing. He picked it up, and on the other end was André Meyer. "You're lucky to have reached me," Gay told him. "I just came in a minute ago." Meyer grumbled that luck had nothing to do with it—he had been ringing Gay every fifteen minutes since eight o'clock.

Meyer was also already an intimidating force. In 1937, Gay was walking down the boardwalk in Deauville with his girl friend Irene when he bumped into Léon Lehman, Bella's brother. The Meyers had rented a summer home in Deauville, and Léon suggested that Gay and his friend join them for dinner. Gay was agreeable, but, he recalls, "Irene trembled with fear. She knew André Meyer by reputation and she was scared." As it turned out, Gay may have had more to fear from Meyer than Irene did. Upon his return to Paris, Meyer stormed into Gay's office and barked, "OK, then, you're getting married, right? Don't hesitate! I'm telling you, get married!"

So Gay married Irene. (Forty-five years later, they are still married. "You see," says Gay, "he gave good advice.")

He was an equally imposing figure to his own family. His half-sister, according to her son Michel, "was very attached to him. But at the same time, there was always this impression, this feeling of fear. She was grateful to him for all he had done for her, for such a very, very long time, and she esteemed him greatly. But I never felt, at bottom, there was a total intimacy between them."

His relationship with Bella, meanwhile, was showing signs of strain. A beautiful, pampered woman, Bella was not used to being neglected—and what with his incessant telephoning and his single-minded obsession with business, André was neglecting her quite a bit.

Still, there were many material consolations. Aside from the house in Deauville, there was an apartment on the Cour Albert Premier, in one of the poshest parts of the Right Bank, overlooking the Seine. Decorated by a leading Paris designer, it was furnished in the classic, sober style that both Meyer and his wife preferred. A few pieces of fine art, including a Flemish landscape, enlivened the decor; Meyer had just begun collecting. "André was not a rich man then," says an old friend, industrialist Francis Fabre, "but he was a man in a very good situation."

Indeed he was. Not only was he a success in business, but he was forging some impressive connections in the political world. He could number among his friends Georges Bonnet, the minister of foreign affairs, and Bonnet's successor, Paul Baudouin, the former president of the Banque de l'Indochine. Meyer's involvement in public affairs dated back to 1930, when he was a member of the French delegation to the Young Plan negotiations on German reparations—a rare distinction for a youthful, comparatively inexperienced banker. By the late 1930s he was prominent enough and had achieved enough, to be decorated with the Legion of Honor by the French government.

Few bankers in France had ever come so far, so quickly. The possibilities for him in Paris seemed limitless. Perhaps, some day soon, a directorship of the Bank of France, following in the footsteps of David David-Weill. Perhaps more.

And then the Germans came.

When Nazi troops marched on Poland in September 1939, André Meyer took no chances. He immediately sent Bella and the children to Bordeaux, in western France. There, Philippe and Francine could continue their schooling in relative safety. He himself would remain with the firm in Paris for the time being.

Meyer had no illusions about his situation. He was a prominent Jewish banker working for a prominent Jewish bank. What was more, he had been active in a committee formed by his friend Baron Robert de Rothschild in November 1938 to help Jewish refugees from Nazi Germany. If the Nazis came, Lazard would most likely be shut down, and he would probably be sent to a concentration camp.

Yet as long as danger was not at his doorstep (and in September 1939 it wasn't yet), he felt duty-bound to remain with his colleagues.

But by the last week of May 1940, with Dunkirk besieged and Belgium on the verge of surrender, the time of decision had come. Meyer locked up the apartment on the Cour Albert Premier for the last time, ordered up a car and driver, and headed for Bordeaux. Once there, he dallied only a day or two; Bordeaux, he reasoned, would not be safe for long either. He piled his family into the car and told the chauffeur to head for the Spanish border.

The roads were clogged with refugees, and when the Meyers arrived at the Spanish border "there were queues everywhere," remembers Philippe Meyer. "Everything was disrupted. It was completely disorganized. We had to queue for hours." Once they reached the Spanish border station, however, the family was whisked through, since they had valid visas, which Meyer had obtained during their last two days in Bordeaux. "It wasn't easy to get visas in such a short time," says Philippe. His father's pull, he concedes, probably helped.

They took a train to Santander, stayed there a night or two, and then moved on to Portugal. By that time, Meyer had made up his mind about their ultimate destination: the United States. This time, though, visas were not so easily obtained. The Meyers waited in Portugal a month for them to come through. Finally, in July 1940, their U.S. visas in hand, the Meyers boarded a transatlantic clipper flight in Lisbon, bound for New York. By then, the swastika was flying from the Eiffel Tower.

In February 1941, Lazard Frères was one of twenty-nine Jewish banking firms placed under "Aryan" direction by the Vichy government. But for the absent André Meyer, a far more dramatic event happened some months earlier, shortly after he departed. Along with numerous other prominent French refugees, including Charles de Gaulle, he was formally stripped of his citizenship by the Vichy government, and all his property in France was confiscated. (Later, in October 1940, his Legion of Honor decoration was also taken away, along with those awarded de Gaulle, Eve Curie, and nine other well-known émigrés.) As jarring a blow as this was, far more shattering to Meyer was the identity of the man who signed the decree: his old friend Paul Baudouin.

"André never forgot that," says Francis Fabre, who later surreptitiously looked after Lazard's interests in France during the war. "All the fellows who had not been—" here Fabre stops and searches for the proper word—"*correct* with André during that period he never forgot."

As Meyer came to terms with his new life, the decree served as a bitter reminder of the limits of trust and friendship.

CHAPTER FOUR

Starting Over

When the Meyers arrived in New York, their first stop was a luxury hotel, the Stanhope. Then, after a short stay, they moved on to another luxury hotel, the Delmonico. After a brief while, they moved on to another, and then another, before finally settling into one of the poshest of them all, the Carlyle. "We were in all sorts of hotels," remembers Philippe Meyer. "Some were too big, some were too small."

The Meyers' life as well-heeled nomads had more to do with André's state of mind than with the family's living requirements. During those initial months in the United States he was uncertain and unstable, alternating between his natural restlessness to *do* things and an acute torpor that prevented him from doing *anything*. For days on end he would lie on his hotel suite sofa in his pajamas, mired in depressed contemplation of his plight. "It was all a great shock for him—Nazism, the war, France's defeat," says Philippe. "On the personal side, he had been a great, great success, and suddenly everything collapsed, and he had to start all over again. And he didn't know if he had the strength or the courage to do it."

Suddenly, he was adrift in a world whose language he barely knew; whose ways were strange and unfathomable; whose movers and shakers were, for the most part, merely names to him, nothing more. The sureness and self-confidence with which he had cut such a quick, broad swath through the French banking world were now denied him; in their place were the fumbling and groping of someone stumbling across a darkened room. His mastery of the Bourse and his hard-won roster of Paris contacts were of little use to him now.

It was not that he and his family were starving. He had discreetly transferred enough of his wealth to accounts outside of France in the months before the war to assure them of a comfortable existence. But for André Meyer, to be denied his métier was virtually to be deprived of life itself.

He lay on the sofa awhile longer. And then he steeled himself and went to work.

Not at Lazard, though; the New York firm was an entity that functioned independently of Paris, and while he was welcome to hang his hat there, he didn't really fit. Instead, he rented an office of his own in the same Wall Street-area office building that housed Lazard, 120 Broadway. He would be on the thirty-second floor, while Lazard was down on the ground floor and the fifth. As his secretary, he hired another recent French-Jewish émigré, Simone Rosen. Not only did they share a common heritage, but also a common penchant for secretiveness. Soon after she started working for Meyer, Baron Robert de Rothschild sauntered into the office and tried to charm her, but Rosen remained impassive. "That one doesn't talk," Rothschild grumbled to Meyer.

Meyer was immensely pleased. "He says you are very trustworthy," a beaming Meyer told Rosen afterwards.

From his perch, Meyer gradually began to master the workings of American business and American banking. He was far enough away from Lazard to be totally detached from its activities—yet close enough to watch what was happening. And watch he did.

Lazard Frères New York was then run by Frank Altschul. Few men could have brought to the job a more impressive pedigree.

Altschul's father, Charles, was the eighth employee hired by Lazard Frères and spent his entire business life there, rising to one of the highest positions in the San Francisco bank. Upon moving to New York in 1901, when Frank was fourteen, the Altschuls became members in good standing of the "Our Crowd" network of German-Jewish banking families. In the best Our Crowd tradition, the Altschuls soon became securely intertwined by marriage with another prominent banking family, the Lehmans; Frank's sister Edith became the wife of Herbert Lehman, the future governor of New York, and Frank himself married Herbert Lehman's niece, Helen Lehman Goodhart. After graduating from Yale in 1908, Frank joined his father at Lazard New York; and when Charles Altschul stepped down as a partner in 1916, Frank took his place.

Frank soon rose to be one of Wall Street's grand dukes, both in style and influence. In the 1930s, he served on the governing board of the New York Stock Exchange and became a director of the Rockefeller family bank, the Chase National. During the 1920s, while

André Meyer was speculating on the rise and fall of the French franc, Altschul was advising the French government on how to steady the currency and was awarded a Legion of Honor. One of the world's most prominent rare-book collectors, Altschul set up his own small printing plant, Overbrook Press, at his 450-acre Connecticut estate to turn out exquisitely printed and illustrated limited editions. And, faithfully each fall, Altschul would ride to hounds in the Fairfield and Westchester hunts.

It was Frank Altschul who guided Lazard across the shoals of the 1933 Glass-Steagall Act, which mandated the separation of securities underwriting (the issuing and sale of securities to the public) from normal commercial banking activities. All across the country, financial institutions were caught up in the fateful decision of whether to become investment bankers or commercial bankers. Altschul and his colleagues chose the investment-banking route. The firm quickly climbed to the top rung of underwriting syndicates, but, says one man who was with Lazard then, "It wasn't a major money-making proposition." Far more profitable was General American Investors Corporation, a $25 million investment trust (an early predecessor of today's mutual funds) that Lazard managed.

The Lazard that Frank Altschul ran was every bit the epitome of the old-line, prewar Wall Street firm. It did a little of this and a little of that. Aside from bond underwriting and General American, it still had its old franchise in the gold business, shipping millions of dollars' worth of the metal to France during the drastic 1934 run on the dollar. And Lazard was also involved in the retail stockbrokerage business, with branch offices in Boston, Chicago, and Philadelphia. The partners still worked at rolltop desks in a big old-fashioned partners' room. In one corner, behind a battery of four telephones on his mahogany desk, sat Altschul, the smoke of his pipe lazily floating past the rare prints hanging on the walls.

The firm's business took a turn for the worse with the outbreak of the Second World War. Bond underwritings were few and far between. "People weren't building factories, they weren't building city halls," remarks a veteran of the period. "There was very little damn business." With the exception of General American, Lazard's other activities weren't doing terribly well either. But Altschul and the four other partners weren't panicking. Business had been good before, and it would be good again. All it took was a little time and a little patience, and everything would be as it was.

* * *

In the meantime, Altschul was doing his best to help the émigré partner who arrived on his doorstep in the summer of 1940.

Virtually from the moment the Meyers stepped off their clipper, Altschul had been in the wings offering aid, advice, and companionship. He helped them find a hotel. He suggested private schools for the children. He invited them to spend their weekends at his Connecticut estate.

It was on one of those weekend outings that socialite Marietta Tree first met Meyer. "We had a very large lunch," she says, "and I remember spotting this man I didn't know. He looked incredibly foreign to me, because he was dressed so differently from Americans. He had on crocodile shoes—which no American would ever have worn, especially then—very, very thick horn-rimmed glasses, and, of course, he was wearing a three-piece suit in the country. He was introduced to me as 'Monsieur Meyer, a partner at Lazard's.' I really didn't have a chance to talk with him, particularly, but I had great sympathy for him. He looked *so* foreign, and he must have felt very foreign himself."

Then, in 1942, Frank Altschul found himself with another uprooted Paris partner on his hands: Pierre David-Weill, newly arrived in New York. The urbane, aristocratic crown prince of Lazard Paris, however, needed far less handholding than Meyer, having long since acclimated himself to American ways and customs; from 1926 through 1939 he had visited the United States at least one or two months a year. David-Weill's attitude toward Meyer at this point was an ambivalent one. Tree, who became a close friend of David-Weill during those years (they would have dinner two or three times a week), remembers that "Pierre used to refer to André always very correctly. But I had a feeling that although he admired him, he trusted him, he counted on him, I'm not sure that he liked him." With his air of jaunty, moneyed self-assurance, David-Weill had far more in common with Altschul than he did with his old partner. And, indeed, David-Weill and Altschul soon became fast friends.

In view of all this, Meyer definitely seemed to be the odd man out. Yet, unaccountably, he was starting to show signs of his old bounciness. To some of his new friends—chiefly fellow French émigrés—he was positively cocky, with the ebullience of someone bursting to tell them a wondrous secret. To a few, he confided what it was: "In one year," he told these friends, "I will be the boss."

Coming from someone so out of place, someone who barely spoke English, it was a rather bizarre prophecy. But that is exactly what happened.

In the December 16, 1943, *New York Times* appeared this announcement:

ALTSCHUL RETIRING
FROM LAZARD FIRM

WILL QUIT DEC. 31—PARIS HOUSE
RESIDENTS AND 2 OTHERS TO
BE ADMITTED THEN

Frank Altschul will retire from partnership in Lazard Frères & Co., investment bankers here, on Dec. 31, the firm announced yesterday. He will continue as a member of the New York Stock Exchange and will remain president of the General American Investors Company, Inc.

Pierre David-Weill and André Meyer of the Paris firm of Lazard Frères et Cie., residents in New York for several years, will be admitted as resident partners of the New York firm. The French firm also will continue as a partner in the house here.

Frank Altschul, in essence, was sent packing—with General American Investors bestowed upon him in the manner of a going-away present.

How did Meyer and David-Weill do it? How did they manage to unseat a man who had been a dominant force in the New York firm for over thirty-five years, whose family had been part of Lazard almost from the beginning, whose power and connections in the financial world and in New York society were so formidable?

The short answer is that while he ran Lazard New York, Frank Altschul never actually had voting control of it. That power had always remained in the hands of the David-Weill family—as the sole blood relations of the Lazards still in the banking empire in the early forties—and to a lesser extent in the hands of the other partners in the French house, including Meyer, who were given shareholdings by the David-Weills over the years. Asked about the takeover almost forty years later, Altschul's son Arthur says simply that "I don't think the control was *ever* in my father's hands. I believe it was always in the hands of the French partners. And anytime the French wanted to take control, they had it in their power to do so all along."

Meyer, it was now clear, had simply been biding his time during those first three years, watching and waiting in his aerie for the right moment to strike. And when he felt he knew enough, he did what he had had the power to do all along, secure in the knowledge that David-Weill would back him up. Because for David-Weill, too, the demands of the times—namely, the need to secure a beachhead for himself in the only major nation unscarred by the war—outstripped the demands of friendship. And given the choice, David-Weill preferred to hitch his family's fortune to André Meyer rather than to Frank Altschul. David-Weill and Meyer would share control of the New York house, but from the outset David-Weill let Meyer dominate its affairs.

The man they displaced, meanwhile, went on to successfully run General American Investors until his retirement in 1961, while continuing his rare-book collecting and publishing and his myriad philanthropic activities. But he never forgave André Meyer. "To the best of my knowledge," says someone who knew both Meyer and Altschul, "André and Frank never spoke to each other again." Having done so much to help the bewildered immigrant get started in his new life, Altschul felt betrayed.

If André Meyer felt any remorse over the turn of events, he never revealed it. As far as he was concerned, Lazard was simply not big enough for both him and Frank Altschul.

George Ames, a young assistant in Lazard's corporate underwriting department, had quit the firm in 1942 to join the navy. When he came back in 1946 to pick up where he left off, he was amazed by what he found. The old rolltop desks were gone. The old partners' room was gone. And the old partners were gone, too.

And running the firm was the awkward, mysterious Frenchman from the thirty-second floor.

What André Meyer had in mind, from the start, was the total gutting and rebuilding of Lazard Frères. Lazard's mix of business—which was typical for a firm of its size—he regarded as an unstructured, unprofitable hodgepodge. And Lazard's partners and staff, as far as he was concerned, were largely a bunch of lazy mediocrities. In both areas, he wasted no time forcing through major upheavals.

By 1945, all the old partners had been dismissed. By 1948, the firm had shut down its Boston, Philadelphia, and Chicago offices, and had become, once again, a one-office house. "The closings came as a bombshell," says James Satterthwaite, Jr., who was then working in the municipal-bond department. "I remember making conversation with the Chicago guy the day he came into the office and got the word. Afterward, he came up to me and said, 'My God, it's all being closed down.' "

The branches were anathema to Meyer on two counts: first, they built up overhead, and he intended to run as bare-bones an operation as he possibly could. Second, they were largely in the retail stock-brokerage business, which meant they dealt with the general public. André Meyer did not want Lazard to deal with the general public. He wanted the New York firm to be what the French firm was: a very private, very elite house whose customers were corporations, financial institutions, and a few wealthy friends of the proprietor. Exclusivity, even a certain snobbishness, were to be encouraged.

Fred Wilson, who began with Lazard in 1946, says that Meyer then was "very ambitious for the firm. He wanted to make this *the* leading firm in the business, not in terms of size, but in terms of excellence. He said this many times, that this was his ambition for Lazard."

But, at the same time, Meyer was acutely conscious of his own shortcomings. He knew few of the powerhouses of corporate America, few of the bankers who made the financial system tick. To gain the sort of clientele he sought, he needed someone who could open the right doors, and who was as well known and respected in America as he had been in France. Fortunately, he found such a person almost immediately. His name was George Murnane.

By the time he joined forces with André Meyer, Murnane was already something of a legend in the investment-banking business. As one of the top partners in Lee, Higginson & Company, he had gained a reputation as a superb deal-maker whose determination and grittiness were second to none. The story is told about the time he arranged the purchase of the Nash Company by Kelvinator. At the signing, the Nash president suddenly got cold feet. "I can't do it," he said. "It's my company. I can't sell it." The diminutive Murnane, furious, walked up to the man, grabbed him by the lapels, shook him, and shouted, "You son of a bitch. You sit down and sign those papers, right here, right now, or I swear to God I'll kill you with my bare hands." The man signed.

Murnane's string of successes, however, was abruptly cut short by the troubles that dogged his firm. Lee, Higginson had been the leading bankers for Swedish match king Ivar Kreuger, and when Kreuger's empire collapsed after his suicide in 1932, Lee, Higginson was buried in the rubble. Virtually wiped out, Murnane started from scratch again in a partnership with a French financier, Jean Monnet. Their firm, Monnet & Murnane, thrived, thanks to both men's extensive international connections. But when another world war loomed, Monnet quit to work on building up the Allied defensive forces, and Murnane was on his own again. He was not someone who enjoyed being a lone wolf. And so, when Meyer asked him in the fall of 1944 if he was interested in helping rejuvenate Lazard, Murnane leaped at the opportunity.

He brought with him, as Meyer knew he would, a network of contacts that was the envy of almost every investment banker in America. He was a director of Allied Chemical & Dye and American Steel Foundries, and was the main American adviser for Belgium's great industrial dynasties, the Solvays and the Boëls. What's more, he was the key investment banker for many of America's leading glass companies. His prestige was such that wherever he went, this business followed. So Lazard suddenly fell into a block of clients it had never had before—and Meyer had his instant entrée to corporate America.

Murnane, in fact, was the only other individual at Lazard, other than Pierre David-Weill, whom Meyer could or would accept as a peer. He needed George Murnane, a lot more than Murnane needed him. As Murnane's son, George Jr. (who later became a partner at Lazard himself), puts it, "My father was one of the few people whom André could not dominate."

Still, there were limits to what even a Murnane could do for Meyer. Lazard also required someone who could serve as a liaison to Wall Street, particularly to the syndicate managers, the tightly knit group of brokerage-house executives who controlled the allocation and flow of new stock and bond issues. Theirs was a world of patrician after-hours camaraderie, a world whose inner circle was closed to foreigners, or for that matter to anyone who hadn't gone to a select handful of Ivy League schools. The only way Meyer could gain access to it was to hire one of *them*.

After making some discreet inquiries around the Street, Meyer came up with just the man he was looking for: Edwin Herzog, late of Shields & Company and the United States Army Air Corps. Still in uniform, his discharge papers in his pocket, he met with Meyer and Murnane at Meyer's summerhouse in Ossining, New York, in 1945. Outwardly gregarious but inwardly flinty, Herzog seemed perfectly suited for the demands of the job. Meyer told him he could take charge not only of syndication, but of securities sales and trading. His first task, Herzog recalls, was to "clean out a lot of the deadwood that was sitting here, trading and pretending to be bond dealers."

As logical as the acquisitions of Murnane and Herzog were, in view of Meyer's own limitations, Meyer's other key personnel move must have seemed to Lazard-watchers eminently *illogical*. That was to bring on board, as a partner involved in investment strategy, Albert Joseph Hettinger, Jr. The lanky, quiet, pipe-puffing Hettinger was a rather unlikely soul to be spending his time in the hurly-burly of Wall Street, let alone in the company of the hustling, impatient André Meyer. A former Harvard Business School professor, Hettinger had ambled into the securities business in the mid-1920s and, in 1935, found a position at General American Investors. When Meyer offered him a partnership upon taking over Lazard, Hettinger was still what he had been for most of his career: a scholarly, often absentminded, and slow-moving observer of the securities markets.

But Meyer saw something in Hettinger that eluded nearly all his contemporaries: that behind the philosophical facade was a man with a unique gift for ferreting out investment opportunities. It was a talent that Meyer cherished. The hiring of Hettinger, in fact, said more about the direction in which Meyer was moving than anything else he did during those first few years at the helm.

By the mid-forties, the term "investment banking" had evolved into a classic misnomer, since most of its practitioners were neither investors nor bankers. Banking in the traditional sense—the gathering of deposits and the making of loans—had been ruled off limits for these firms by the Glass-Steagall Act. And investing of the sort done by such hallowed figures as Jacob Schiff and J. Pierpont Morgan at the turn of the century—putting one's own and one's bank's money into potentially lucrative new ventures—was virtually an extinct art form.

The role investment bankers now played was almost strictly that of financial intermediaries. They would advise companies on financing strategy, and when the time came for the companies to raise money in the market, the investment bankers would underwrite the stock or bond issues. Investment-banking underwriters did not really keep the stocks and bonds on their own books; they would purchase the issue from the company and then resell it to institutions such as pension funds or insurance companies, or to individual investors, at a spread, or commission.

That, in a nutshell, was what Lazard New York did before Meyer came along. And as his hiring of Murnane and Herzog showed, it was a business he still very much wanted to pursue.

But with the Second World War drawing to a close and America girding itself for recovery, the people Meyer closeted himself with most weren't Murnane and Herzog, but Al Hettinger and Fred Wilson, the young man Meyer had also just brought over from General American Investors. Hettinger and Wilson weren't corporate advisers or new-issue specialists. They were securities analysts, men who specialized in finding intriguing investment opportunities.

The message was clear. André Meyer didn't want Lazard to be only an investment banker. He wanted Lazard to be an *investor.*

Meyer could see a postwar boom coming, and he wanted to be in on it—not just as an intermediary but as a principal. Relates Wilson, "André had a realization at the end of the war that values in all the markets were unlimited. He could see this, and he could hardly contain himself from putting all his money into all the things that were out there."

He didn't have to wait long. In April 1946, the U.S. Supreme Court upheld the Securities and Exchange Commission's power to break up the giant public-utility holding companies. The decision sent the stock prices of such holding companies as Electric Bond & Share into a tailspin. Meyer, Hettinger, and Wilson concluded that the inherent values of the holding-company shares—even assuming forced breakups—were well in excess of what the shares were selling at. So they bought and bought and bought—for Lazard and for themselves.

"There was a lot of stuff selling for practically nothing at the time," recalls Wilson. "But if you did the work, you could see that they were selling for fifty cents to the dollar of value. So we traded them to a fare-thee-well."

When the utilities were broken up, the Lazard partners' perceptions were proven correct. The liquidation values of the shares were far above what the market had foreseen. "It was about the easiest money I've ever made," says Wilson. "It's still hard to believe, it was so easy."

André Meyer had had his first taste of the opportunities the postwar economy offered. It only whetted his appetite for more.

At Lazard, other changes were afoot.

Each year, in the old days, the firm would have a big, raucous Christmas party. In 1944, Meyer attended his first one and was flabbergasted by the amount of alcohol that was consumed. He was even more upset the next day, when he heard that one inebriated soul had driven his car through a store window on Nassau Street—with a Lazard secretary alongside him in the front seat.

The next year, there was no whiskey at the party, only champagne. And even that, says Satterthwaite, "was measured out with some care."

It was now, truly, André Meyer's Lazard Frères.

CHAPTER FIVE

Gold Under the Asphalt

For fifteen years Wall Street had slept. First there was the crash of 1929, scarring many, destroying some, and laying waste to a generation's faith in the value of investments. Then there was the Second World War, siphoning off the cream of American industry for the war effort, yanking some of the Street's savviest, most energetic young traders off the stock exchange floor and onto the battlefield.

But now the war was over, and so was the great slumber. Flush with wartime savings, buoyant in their hopes for the future, investors plunged into the market with a passion and a naive single-mindedness that hadn't been seen since the final palmy days of the Roaring Twenties. Unable to sate their craving for still-scarce consumer goods, the public turned to the stock market as a substitute. "Instead of buying shirts," sighed one pundit, "they're buying stocks."

Speculative fever was once again in the air. A $53 million stock issue for a new auto company, Kaiser-Frazier Corporation, was snapped up instantly—even though Kaiser-Frazier had yet to produce a single car. (The *Bawl Street Journal*, the investment-banking business's satirical house organ, took note of the phenomenon by publishing this spoof ad for Kaiser-Frazier: "While you wait for our cars—take a ride in our stock!") Eager to tap this abundant new source of capital for their postwar retooling, industrial companies large and small raced to the market in droves. It was a rare week in 1946 when Wall Street underwriters weren't called upon to distribute $100 million or more of new securities. Almost overnight, these new issues soared to as much as a 25 percent premium over their offering prices.

As helter-skelter as the market was, the burst of euphoria could hardly be considered unfounded. The country truly was heading into a boom period, with industrial profits in the late forties climbing 25 percent and more a year. In some parts of the country, heavy industries would need up to four years of full-tilt production to catch up with demand. And most blue chips were grossly undervalued; the mighty Standard Oil of New Jersey, for instance, was selling at a mere five times earnings. As *Time* magazine put it in June 1948, "It was a good bet that Wall Street's baby bull would put on some real meat before the bull-throated roar of the U.S. economy dies down."

None of this, needless to say, was lost on André Meyer. As well as anyone, he could see the awesome potential of corporate America, the veins of gold that lay just beneath the asphalt. He knew that corporations' hunger for capital would be unabated for years to come, and that many bankers would become rich as underwriters, middlemen marketing corporate securities to financial institutions and the public. Meyer had always detested securities underwriting, dismissing it with a wave of his hand as a "silly," mindless business. One reason why he disliked it so much were the margins; in the words of one associate, "It was against his mentality to take a hundred-million-dollar position and make a one-million-dollar profit on it. He would rather take a ten-million-dollar position and make a twenty-million-dollar profit on it."

Nevertheless, the new Lazard senior partner realized that a healthy flow of underwriting commissions could provide Lazard with a nest egg that would give the firm the leeway to go off on its wilder investing sprees. It was a necessary, and potentially very lucrative, evil. Yet he also recognized that to truly cash in on the boom, to get his fair share of the huge volume of new stock issues that were pouring out of corporate suites, he had to reach some sort of accommodation with the mandarins of Wall Street who controlled those issues. And that would not be easy.

Wall Street underwriting—indeed, Wall Street in general—was dominated then by nine houses, with another eight or so occasionally cracking the inner circle. These firms, all old, prestigious names, sliced corporate America up like a giant Thanksgiving turkey; competition among them for clients was, for all intents and purposes, *verboten*. Because the quality of underwriting expertise was so uniform among these houses, the system worked well, and corporations rarely complained. Still, that didn't stop the Justice Department from filing a landmark antitrust suit against the firms in 1947, charging them with conspiracy to monopolize the securities business. (The government eventually lost the case.)

Lazard was not one of these favored few—and Meyer's arrival on the scene seemed to ensure that it never would be. The patriarchs of these firms took an instant dislike to him. Not only was he an outsider, a Frenchman, but he had the effrontery to force out one of their own, Frank Altschul. What's more, in his willy-nilly dismissals of the other old Lazard partners and his shutdown of the Lazard branch offices, he seemed hell-bent on wrecking a perfectly good securities-distribution outlet. Meyer's alienation from the Establishment was compounded by his utter refusal to engage in the ritualistic hobnobbing—the luncheon clubs, the golf outings—that was such an essential lubricant of Wall Street life. Such chores were left to Ned Herzog. As for Meyer himself, he didn't play golf and he rarely went out to lunch, and that was all there was to it. Instead of building bridges, the secretive Lazard boss appeared intent on constructing a moat.

This course of action was a strange one for a firm that ostensibly sought to win friends and influence people on Wall Street. But even more bizarre was the strategy Meyer settled upon to make his mark on the underwriting business. Lazard, he decreed, would become even *more* standoffish. It would be known as a firm that *turned down* underwritings.

He told Herzog to refuse participations in any underwriting syndicate in which Lazard wasn't invited into the so-called "major bracket."

In the well-ordered world of Wall Street underwritings, the syndicate of firms brought together to handle a new issue is divided into clearly defined tiers, known as brackets. At the top rung are the lead managers, the firm or firms that oversee the syndicate and negotiate with the issuer. Next come the "majors," the firms that by dint of power or prestige are granted places of honor in the underwriting; after that group comes all the rest of the underwriters. These brackets are more than theoretical concepts. They are there for all the world to see in the newspaper advertisements known as "tombstones" that announce the deal. True, the average newspaper reader can make neither hide nor hair of the bewildering list of securities houses in these ads. But to the Wall Street cognoscenti, each tombstone ad is a veritable hieroglyphic manuscript, revealing to the initiated who is up and who is down, who has jostled the way to the top and who has been rebuffed.

More is at stake in these brackets than just prestige. Majors tended to get larger chunks of the underwritings, and heftier commissions. Furthermore, presence in the major bracket tended to be self-perpetuating; once a firm had broken through, it was likely to remain a major in nearly every deal henceforth.

Naturally, everyone aspired to be a major, but precious few were chosen. Those who made it had often waited in the wings for years, consolidating their clout and building up their client lists. How in the world could André Meyer expect to make the great leap overnight?

Simple, he said. He would just be obstinate.

Deal after deal came Lazard's way, and deal after deal Herzog refused. The municipal bond issues that the firm agreed to were so few and far between that eventually it dropped out of that business entirely. This was hardly a great blow to Lazard, income-wise; municipal issues then had coupons in the low single digits (New York City long-term bonds were yielding a mere 2 percent in 1946), and commissions were meager. But the firm's diminished profile did not augur well for the future. Still, Herzog refused.

And when obstinacy didn't suffice, Meyer would resort to browbeating. Meyer would phone the head of a firm that had denied Lazard a major-bracket invitation and complain about the "shabby treatment of Lazard."

"André would be insulted, outraged about his syndicate position," recalls the head of one big firm. "He would bawl you out unbelievably for having offended the great firm of Lazard." The impression was left that this was a firm and a man who should not be trifled with—even if neither the firm nor the man had done much so far to justify such an apprehension.

It all seemed like the sort of bluff the hard-nosed sages of Wall Street had called so many times before. But this time, they didn't. No one believed for a minute that Lazard had the capabilities of a major-bracket underwriter—the sales clout, the wide-ranging client list. Yet as the years went by, Lazard received more and more major-bracket invitations. The aura of exclusivity and snobbishness that Meyer had created was starting to take hold.

But it was more than just a matter of a well-orchestrated illusion triumphing over reality. There was also a certain amount of personal public relations involved.

The men who dominated Wall Street in the late 1940s were hardly the homogenous, money-grubbing, white-shoe lot that the public took them to be. Closest to the stereotype were the kingpins of Morgan Stanley—Henry Morgan, Harold Stanley, and Perry Hall—who had successfully spun off the investment-banking side of the House of Morgan in the mid-thirties without any diminution of its pervasive influence. Morgan Stanley was, just as J. P. Morgan & Company had been before it, the godhead of securities underwriting, in total control of the bluest of blue chip issuers. And the men who ran it were, in the best tradition of Pierpont Morgan, stubborn, hardheaded, and imperious; accustomed to leadership, unaccustomed to challenge.

Robert Lehman of Lehman Brothers, however, was a far different sort. A quiet, unfailingly polite aristocrat who had amassed one of the world's great art collections, he seemed more at home among his Goyas and Gothic tapestries than in the airless canyons of the financial district. And Sidney Weinberg, the dominant force at Goldman, Sachs, was yet another type, a fast-talking, self-made dynamo whose first job at Goldman was as assistant to the janitor. Through sheer grit, Weinberg rose to become an adviser to presidents and a man of awesome power in corporate America. At one point he served on thirty-one different corporate boards.

As much as he shunned the hail-fellow-well-met side of Wall Street, Meyer knew that friendships with at least a few of these titans would be essential if Lazard was to make any inroad at all into the Establishment. And so he set out to cultivate them—not in an overt, backslapping way, but with quiet, measured gestures that took into account the personalities and proclivities of each individual.

At Morgan Stanley, he had to contend with crusty, indomitable Perry Hall. Meyer had first met Hall back in Paris in the 1930s, and he knew of the pride Hall took in his fund raising for various charities. Hall, in fact, was one of those Wall Streeters who immediately dismiss their business lives as trivial and uninteresting, preferring to talk instead about the hospitals they have supported and the colleges they have bankrolled. In Hall's case, the institutions in question were New York's Presbyterian Hospital and Princeton University, from which Hall had graduated in 1917.

One day Meyer was visiting Hall when a call came from Robert Tyson, financial vice-president of the U.S. Steel Company. Tyson, who was vice-chairman of the Princeton fund-raising campaign that Hall headed, thought that a Christmas present to the school was in order. "How much should I give?" he asked Hall. "It's up to you," the banker answered. "I think I can give a hundred thousand dollars," Tyson said.

As dumbfounded as he was by the size of the gift, Hall was even more startled when he put down the phone and heard Meyer say, "Perry, I admire you so much for what you do for Princeton and the Presbyterian Hospital. Put me down for fifty thousand dollars."

Hall told Meyer how grateful he was and asked the Frenchman if he was interested in going to a Princeton football game. Meyer accepted, and for the first and probably only time in his life attended an American sporting event. "He loved it," Hall remembers. "The cheering, the bands playing—it fascinated him. He didn't understand it, but it was a total revelation to him." Every year after that, Meyer made a gift to Princeton, and Hall was so appreciative that he arranged for the Lazard senior partner to become an honorary member of the class of '17.

And every once in a while, Meyer would call Hall to ask for a very small favor of his own. "Perry, my dear Perry," he would say, his voice taking on a tone of greatest intimacy, "you must have been *away*, not *knowing*. Do you realize in your absence they are offering Lazard Frères this undignified position in your underwriting? There must be something wrong here." And Hall would do his best to set the matter right.

With Bobbie Lehman, the approach was a bit different. As Meyer built his own art collection, he would ask Lehman for advice. During visits to Meyer's apartment in the Carlyle, Lehman would nod approvingly. "You know, André," he would say, "you have a beautiful collection." And Meyer, in turn, would protest, "It's *nothing*. It's *nothing* compared to yours." In the words of Lehman Brothers partner Herman Kahn, "André never failed to seek Bobbie's approbation."

The feeling soon came to be mutual. Lehman instinctively was wary of Meyer—"Bobbie felt that André would take advantage of every opportunity that was offered to him," points out Kahn—but this was soon overridden by Lehman's admiration for Meyer's business acumen. Despite his long and successful stewardship of Lehman Brothers, investment banking did not come naturally to Bobbie Lehman; according to one longtime associate, "Bobbie did not look upon himself as a professional banker." He stood in awe of someone like Meyer, a total banking animal.

Lehman was also swept up by the sheer cyclonic force of Meyer's personality. A gentle man who would apologize profusely after berating a secretary—the apology would always last longer than the scolding—Lehman was no match for his hypertensive French colleague. "Bobbie was a much more complacent man," notes Kahn. "He would never argue over money with anyone. He either paid the price or he didn't. But André," Kahn adds, "was never that way."

At first, the Lehman-Lazard relationship was one of an old established bank taking an up-and-coming one under its wing. But it soon evolved into something more: Lehman began giving Lazard a fifty–fifty share of its deals, with Lazard agreeing to reciprocate. That Lehman had many clients and Lazard precious few was almost beside the point; this was the way Bobbie Lehman wanted it, and no one was in any position to argue. Lazard gained a foothold at some of Lehman's most cherished corporate clients, including Radio Corporation of America, Chase Manhattan Bank, and Massey Ferguson, much to the dismay of Lehman's junior partners. As one of them, Frank Manheim, puts it, "It was considered a terrible blow when Lazard got half the RCA business."

Anyone at Lehman who neglec ed to pull Lazard into a deal he was putting together lived to regret the oversight. After Kahn omitted Lazard from a Massey Ferguson financing, he found himself on the receiving end of a blistering phone call from Meyer. "He was in an absolute frenzy," Kahn remembers. "He found it difficult to articulate his anger. I tried to explain to him why this should be a Lehman sole financing, but he insisted I had a responsibility to look after his interests, just as he looked after ours in his deals." Kahn relented, and when he arrived at his office the next morning he found a dozen American Beauty roses waiting for him—a peace offering from the senior partner of Lazard.

"On one deal," adds Kahn, "André hadn't done much, but Bobbie suggested he be offered half the fee. A couple of us bet that André would be too proud to take it, that he would feel he didn't deserve it. Well, not only did he take it, but he felt he deserved it!"

In time, some Lehman partners came to use the term "terrified" to describe Bobbie Lehman's reaction to André Meyer. Another top Lehman partner, Paul Mazur, was said by his underlings to be "haunted" by Meyer. "Paul lay awake nights thinking about André," says one of his subordinates. "In his mind, André became the guy who invented everything. He couldn't possibly have done as many things as Paul Mazur gave him credit for."

Younger Lehman partners and associates began to refer derisively to Meyer as "Captain Andy." But no one ever dared use the term around Bobbie Lehman.

At the same time that Meyer was carefully crafting a role for Lazard on Wall Street, he was also busy renewing his contacts in the country he left behind.

Now that the war was over, Meyer was free to return to his native land. But when he came back to Paris he came as a visitor, staying at the Georges V Hotel, just as any well-heeled visitor would. He was a U.S. citizen now, a resident of New York; and having had his first taste of the opportunities America offered, Meyer had no desire to resettle in a France that would, once more, be starting from scratch, economically and politically. Yet, for all that, he was still a Frenchman, and he remained vitally interested in French affairs. Furthermore, as a Frenchman in New York, a Frenchman on Wall Street, he felt he had some special role to play.

So it was that beginning in the late 1940s, Meyer's Carlyle apartment became a way station for visiting French officials. Somehow, the word had gone out in French government circles that atop a hotel in New York resided a financial genius, a Frenchman at that, someone who could fill them in on what was happening in American business and politics—all from a Gallic viewpoint, of course. He would even send his car to pick them up at the airport (the visiting French government people usually accepted the ride).

The dignitaries who paid court at the Carlyle included such rising stars as Maurice Couve de Murville, Georges Pompidou, and Louis de Guiringaud; each visit with Meyer seemed to make the next official's visit with Meyer that much more imperative. In 1949, former French prime minister Paul Reynaud visited the United States for the first time, and among the first people he saw in New York was André Meyer. Recalls Reynaud's assistant, Claude de Kamouleria, "André Meyer gave a lunch for him, and before going to see him Paul Reynaud talked to me about him. He said to me that in his opinion—and Paul Reynaud's opinion was very important—André Meyer was *un génie financier,* a financial genius."

De Kamouleria, who later became a banker himself, remembers the André Meyer he encountered then as "not a warm man. He was a little cold. You could see he was somebody hard, somebody tough, probably somebody *extremely* difficult to deal with. But remarkably well informed, and you could see he was not only a banker, but an entrepreneur. And at the same time, he was a man who knew what political power could do for him."

The power that Meyer was accumulating was not brute force; it was influence, in the finest and most delicate shading of the term. A word here, a raised eyebrow there, an idea casually lofted over tea. But such as his power was, he did not hesitate to use it. And one of the first beneficiaries was the new state of Israel. On the eve of the climactic United Nations vote on Israel in 1948, Meyer was on the phone until the early-morning hours, urging his French government contacts to support the founding of the new country.

Meyer's fervent support for Israel might have come as a surprise to those who knew him as, at best, indifferent to his religion. His way of observing the sabbath, it was said, was to refrain from smoking cigars, and his idea of observing Yom Kippur was to walk to work. When he was asked once for his father's Hebrew name, in connection with a $50,000 gift to a Jewish organization, he could not supply it. Nevertheless, Meyer prayed every morning—in French—and always carried what friends described as "small religious objects." Admittedly, the line between religion and superstition can be a fine one; along with the "small religious objects" in his pocket was the pencil Meyer used when he first was employed at the Paris Bourse.

But if Meyer lacked great depth of religious feeling, his sense of Jewishness, as one colleague put it, "was never more than an eighth of an inch from his consciousness." He could not forget *why* he and his family were forced to flee their native country, nor could he shake the feeling of being a perennial outsider in any society to which he belonged. Perhaps it was this sense that led him to ardently support the creation of the state of Israel.

But there was also a question of friendship: this time with Chaim Weizmann, Israel's first president. Meyer and Weizmann had become acquainted through Philippe Meyer, who had first met the Zionist leader during a boyhood tour of the Middle East in the 1930s. When Philippe was stationed in London during the war with the Free French, the Weizmanns, also living in London at the time, were especially hospitable. After the war, Weizmann would meet from time to time with the elder Meyer at the Carlyle, undoubtedly doing his best to convince the banker of the need for a new Jewish homeland.

Whether Meyer's backing of Israel was motivated more by his belief in the country and the concept, or by his friendship with Chaim Weizmann, no one could ever say.

As the decade drew to a close, André Meyer and his partners were getting restless. "The trouble with Wall Street today," George Murnane was heard to moan, "is not that it is snobbish or predatory, but that it is dull. So much of it is just plain dull." Squabbling over syndicate position had its moments, but it was hardly an activity to which one could devote an entire workday. As for the rest—routine securities underwriting, stock and bond trading, and the like—it was all formularized stuff, businesses that offered little in the way of adventure or reward.

The firm had just made its first forays outside the stock market, buying a Philadelphia warehouse and trucking company and a Cleveland limestone concern that was also in the shipping business. But these ventures would take time to pay off (Lazard planned to liquidate both) and, in any case, were far too small to warrant much attention. The big play that Meyer hungered for had yet to come along.

Then one day, it walked through the door—in the person of Jean Lambert. Lambert was a high-powered young investment banker who ran his own small firm, Lambert & Company, bankrolled largely by his in-laws, the Bronfman whiskey family. (Lambert made no secret of the source of his wealth; after his wedding to Phyllis Bronfman he exulted to everyone within earshot, "I just married seven million dollars.") He was a man of ideas, and of obsessions. And one of his chief obsessions was André Meyer. He talked constantly about Meyer and at one point was convinced that he would be Meyer's heir apparent.

Lambert came to Meyer with an idea, and like many of Lambert's ideas it seemed utterly divorced from reality. He told Meyer about a vast ranch in Texas, 800,000 acres, so big that a cowboy could ride fifty-six miles without leaving the property, so big that it sprawled over seven different counties. Only the 950,000-acre King Ranch was larger. At least 50,000 head of beef cattle grazed on this spread, known as the Matador Ranch, and there was the possibility of oil somewhere on the huge tract; Humble Oil was already drilling. Matador was controlled by a company based in Dundee, Scotland, and had been for almost seventy years. But Lambert had a feeling the Scots were willing to deal.

He suggested that André Meyer join him in buying the Matador Ranch.

As crazy as the idea sounded at the outset—what did a bunch of investment bankers know about running a cattle ranch?—upon further reflection, it sounded even crazier. The deal would have to be steered through a mind-boggling legal maze, what with U.S. and British tax laws, British investment rules, and Texas land laws all coming into play. And if Lazard and its coinvestors bought the ranch and then tried to sell it off in chunks—the most likely course, given the ranch's size—they ran the risk of being deemed real estate dealers by the Internal Revenue Service, with all their profits becoming ordinary income, not capital gains. Given the huge disparity between the maximum capital gains tax—25 percent—and the maximum ordinary tax—90 percent—this development could wring nearly all the profit out of the deal.

Meyer mulled it over—the legal complications, the accounting roadblocks, the formidable dilemma of how he would ever be able to dispose of the property. And he decided to go ahead.

He pulled together a buying group—which, besides Lazard and Lambert, included Lehman Brothers and the arbitrage firm of Model, Roland—and in December 1950 began talking to the Scots. The shares of Matador were traded on the London Stock Exchange at $7, but the hard-bargaining Dundee directors wanted a lot more. They also insisted on retaining a hefty share of the oil and mineral rights on the property. And they wanted assurances from the British Treasury that they could reinvest the proceeds of the sale in other U.S. securities.

After six months of transatlantic talks, Meyer gave them everything they wanted. He offered $23.70 a share, or a total of just under $19 million, for Matador. He gave the shareholders half the mineral rights on the land. And, with the help of Lazard Brothers in London, he arranged the British Treasury dispensation.

Still, there was the thorny tax question hanging over the deal. How could the new owners avoid being deemed real estate dealers when they sold off pieces of Matador?

The solution that Meyer came up with was as simple in its conception as it was horrendously complex in its execution. When Matador was purchased, it would *already* be broken up. Matador would be divided into sixteen pieces, and sixteen different corporations would be set up to buy each one. Then each parcel of land could be resold separately, just as though they were sixteen different ranches. There would be no central corporation, hence no central dealer.

Of course, to put this plan into action would require one of the most awesomely complicated real estate closings of all time. "It was a monster of its kind," remembers George Ames, one of the key Lazard people on the deal. "It started in Edinburgh, kept going in New York, and wound up in Amarillo." But by August 1951, it was done.

And through it all, André Meyer was the unquestioned hub around which the whole transaction revolved. It may have been Jean Lambert's idea, but from the outset Meyer insisted that if he was involved, he would run the show. "He was never able to sit in a meeting without running it," says someone who was in on the deal. "It was against his nature." Through all the ups and downs, it was Meyer's pile driving, tenacity, and ingenuity that powered the deal and drove it to its conclusion.

As Ames recalls, "If it came to a stopping point because we couldn't get around this, this, and that, well, that was the kind of thing he really enjoyed. Figuring out a way to maneuver around the roadblock. He was restless. He always had to get mixed up in an idea, churn it around, do something to it, and then get involved in the process of putting it together.

"The important thing to remember is that when he became involved in that kind of stuff, he wouldn't stop. He would keep bulling his way through it until he got what he wanted to get."

But getting what he wanted in Matador proved far more elusive than Meyer had bargained for. He had only disposed of a few of the sixteen parcels when a drought struck the Southwest. The land sale had to be put on hold and the Matador cattle shipped from Texas to rented ranges from Florida to the Dakotas. No one in the ranching business was about to bail Lazard and friends out of their dilemma. Says Ames: "A lot of those guys from the Southwest were only too happy to see those smart alecks from New York get stuck."

Meyer would pace the corridors of Lazard, complaining that there wasn't any brave notion by which he could solve this problem—by which he meant he couldn't make it rain. The drought persisted, and it wasn't until some six years later that the land sales could resume. Finally, on Christmas Eve 1959, the last Matador Ranch plot was unloaded. All told, the Lazard group pocketed a profit of between $10 and $15 million on the $18 million-plus investment. But, as Ames points out, "It took us the better part of ten years before we got through it. That's a slow way to get rich."

In 1951, however, this was something André Meyer could not foresee. What he did see, as he peered across the financial landscape, were other Matadors, other situations he could bend to his will, other companies he could manipulate and massage until they yielded the profit he sought.

CHAPTER SIX

André and Ferd

Ferdinand Eberstadt had had a life of sterling achievement. A successful Wall Street lawyer, he switched to the investment-banking business in 1923 with Dillon, Read; five years later he helped bring about the merger of Dodge Brothers Inc. into the Chrysler Corporation. Striking out on his own in the early thirties, he was a pioneer in the mutual-fund business, founding the Chemical Fund (specializing in, naturally enough, chemical investments) in 1938. And his public-service record was equally glowing: an assistant to Owen D. Young at the 1929–1930 European Reparations Conference (the same conference in which young André Meyer participated as a member of the French delegation), vice-chairman of the War Production Board during World War Two, an architect of the postwar reorganization of the armed forces, a co-delegate (with Bernard Baruch) to the United Nations Atomic Energy Commission in 1946.

Yet for all that he had accomplished, Ferdinand Eberstadt in his sixties was still a restless and hungry man. And what he was hungry for, most of all, was money. Not because he needed it; his worldly needs could easily be taken care of by the tidy sum he had made doing public stock issues for small and medium-sized companies during the Depression. For Ferdinand Eberstadt, the creation of wealth was simply the most intellectually and emotionally stimulating exercise on earth. "Eberstadt enjoys the hunt," wrote a contemporary. "His eyes take on the intense look of a man in the midst of an absorbing game." In short, he had a lot in common with André Meyer.

The two were alike in other ways. Despite their many business and social contacts, both men were regarded as loners by Wall Street's clubbier circles. Neither man had any use for the Street's traditional ways of doing business. Rather than join the rest of the horde in competing for Fortune 500 clients, for instance, Eberstadt's firm, F. Eberstadt & Company, went after promising smaller companies, the ones he called "the little blue chips." Eberstadt, like Meyer, was constantly chided for not being a good sport in the syndicate game, for driving overly hard bargains, and for going to extraordinary lengths to protect himself when he brought an issue public. His response to these complaints was characteristically caustic: "I don't want to stick anyone else, and I damn well don't want to get stuck myself."

Eleven years Meyer's senior, the gruff, ruddy-faced Eberstadt was someone the French financier could justifiably look up to. Yet he was also someone who was every bit as eager for the big plunge as Meyer was. It was not hard to see, then, why the two became the closest of business associates.

Meyer was always anxious to find coventurers. He needed their capital, he needed their connections, and, above all, he needed their ideas. "The world thought he sat there and came up with great ideas," a Lazard partner said years later. "But he didn't. His genius was in commanding the energy and instincts of other people."

There were others Meyer turned to besides Ferd Eberstadt. One was Louis Green, an avid buyer and seller of companies who was chairman and a major stockholder of the Grand Union supermarket chain (his son, William Green, is today congressman for Manhattan's fifteenth district). Green and Meyer became substantial shareholders in the Parke-Bernet Galleries and were instrumental in the sale of the auction house to Sotheby's in 1964. Meyer also joined Green in a major investment in Loews in the fifties, before Loews became a major conglomerate with holdings in the tobacco industry, hotels, and a host of other companies. Green, however, did not find Meyer to be the most steadfast of partners. When Green tried to engineer a spin-off of the Metro-Goldwyn-Mayer studios, which were then controlled by Loews, Meyer backed out. According to Green's son-in-law, Justin Colin, who later worked for Meyer at Lazard, "While no one was looking, André sold his stock; and when push came to shove, Lou didn't have André's stock to back him up." If Green was upset about Meyer's hasty retreat, he didn't show it; the pair remained amicable coinvestors for years afterwards.

Another financier whom Meyer sought out in the early fifties was Arthur Ross, the young chairman of Central National Corporation, a large diversified trading and investment company. Their first encounter hardly got the relationship off on the right foot; Meyer wanted to take over Central National, and Ross rebuffed him. "I thought it was better to have him as a close associate than have him running the enterprise," explains Ross mildly. Once that bit of bad blood was behind them, the two settled into a lucrative business partnership. And Ross quickly learned the rules of the game.

"After one or two skirmishes with André," he says, "I realized that if our business relationship was to be rewarding, we had to agree that he would be first among equals." Once Ross had committed himself to a deal, Meyer would keep his partner informed of things "up to a point, but not excessively. That was part of the mystique—not to keep you too well informed. It was done in a very nice way, and you didn't feel you were a loser for not having the information. If you asked him about something, he'd say something like, 'Maybe I can tell you about it next Wednesday.'" Sometimes Meyer did, and sometimes he didn't.

That wasn't how it was with Ferd Eberstadt. Meyer and Eberstadt treated each other as equals—as well they might, considering the stature both men had when they met. That isn't to say they were the best of friends. "It was not a sort of 'let's have a drink together' relationship," says Eberstadt's son-in-law, Peter Cannell. "Neither of them were very warm people. They got along because of their cerebral uniqueness. They were like a pair of Russian chess players who develop a relationship that is quite special."

They were sufficiently wary of each other to insist on putting every aspect of their business relationship in writing. Nelson Loud, a top deal-making partner at the Eberstadt firm, makes it clear that "we started out that way with the first deal, when we didn't know each other very well, and we never to my recollection departed from the practice of writing out what our respective rights, privileges, and purposes were." As far as Meyer and Eberstadt were concerned, when it came to business, good fences really did make good neighbors.

With these precautions in place, Meyer and Eberstadt went through twenty years of deal making together without once, as far as anyone associated with them can recall, having a serious argument. "They respected each other's territory," notes another old F. Eberstadt & Company partner, Robert Porter. "Today *nobody* on Wall Street respects anyone else's territory. But André and Eberstadt would rather do a piece of business together than take one away from each other. They used to bring other people into their deals, but they would always wind up saying, 'We can't work with those people.' But they could always work out their own differences."

When it came to the art of making money in the fifties, Meyer and Eberstadt saw things exactly eye to eye. Neither liked the conventional stock-brokerage and underwriting business of Wall Street; as profitable as it might be, it wasn't where the real money was in the postwar economic boom. What they preferred to do was find small companies in a position to ride the boom, invest in them, and then use their influence as investors to meddle with their futures. They wanted to expand the companies and push them into new businesses, preferably through the acquisition of other small companies. "During the fifties," says Nelson Loud, "there were a lot of people who bought companies at bargain-basement prices, for less than current assets, figuring they could always liquidate them. And in many cases they did. They liquidated them. But we were not liquidators. We were builders."

On the other hand, Meyer and Eberstadt had no intention of passing those shareholdings on to their children and grandchildren. They would stay in for as long as it took to build the company into something substantial, and then they would unload their shares and move on to something else. True, they might have made a lot more if they held on to the stock for another five or ten years—but, as they saw it, they might have lost it all, too. "André's attitude," says one of his Lazard partners, "was that if you've made some money, put it in your pocket. Don't be a wise guy." Meyer and Eberstadt were classic examples of aggressive buyers and nervous holders. Says this Lazard partner, "André wanted to make sure he could sell it. And how did he make sure? He sold it."

Eberstadt once remarked, "When I start out on a new venture, I want to be sure I know how much a return ticket will cost"—in other words, how much it would cost to get out if the venture didn't pan out as he had hoped. Neither Eberstadt nor Meyer was a gambler in the true sense of the word; they were only interested in betting on sure things. (If Jules Meyer had taught his son nothing else, it was that.) Yet they also insisted on not the possibility, but the *probability* of huge gains on their investment.

Here is how ex-Eberstadt partner Loud sums up the Meyer-Eberstadt investment philosophy: "You'd take a quick glance and say, 'Is this an attractive situation or isn't it?' If it was attractive, you'd say, 'Well, let's find out how attractive it is.' In that case, you'd want to assure yourself that (a) you'll be able to get out, and (b) that you're going to get out at a profit. You're not just buying it to hold it and have it sit there. It had to have great potential. Otherwise, forget it.

"That's the rule of almost any person who invests risk capital. If I can't double my money in a year and geometrically thereafter, to hell with it."

Meyer and Eberstadt's special gift was their ability to look beyond the state of a company as it was when they bought it and see what could be made of it. To see, for example, that a small proprietary drug company could be built into a major drug conglomerate. Or to realize that a tiny company whose only assets were some Georgia clay deposits could be transformed into a huge worldwide mineral trading and refining operation. Obviously, they couldn't foresee just how big these companies would become. But they were able to figure out how various pieces could be fitted together to make the whole structure bigger and more attractive. And, furthermore, they knew they had the wherewithal, and the company's management the willingness, to put those pieces into place.

In a way, the best description of André Meyer the investor is one of André Meyer the cook, provided by his granddaughter, Marianne Gerschel. "We used to shudder when he made *homard américaine.* Grandfather in the kitchen was rather like seeing the Mad Professor in the laboratory—everything went in. Nutmeg, pepper, you name it. But somehow," she concluded, "he instinctively knew the right combinations."

Here is a sampling of some of the dishes that André and Ferd served up in the fifties.

How do you kick out a ninety-three-year-old chief executive?

That was the dilemma André Meyer faced in early 1951, after he and others from Lazard had bought into a little company called Minerals Separation North America. Its sole business was to collect royalties on various mineral-extraction processes on which it held patents. Minerals Separation's ancient chairman, Dr. Seth Gregory, was content to sit every day in his splendid office on 11 Broadway in lower Manhattan, take in the view of lower Manhattan, log in the royalty checks, and train his various female "protégés."

If this was Dr. Gregory's idea of a good business, it was not André Meyer's. He wanted to *do something* with all those patents, perhaps capitalize on Minerals Separation's process for extracting iron ore through flotation in partnership with a big steel company. But he was strangely reluctant to push the old man. "We are kind people," he told one of his associates, "and we do not want to throw out old Dr. Gregory."

Meanwhile, David E. Lilienthal had appeared on the Lazard scene. A former Tennessee Valley Authority and Atomic Energy Commission chairman, Lilienthal joined forces with André Meyer because, quite bluntly, he wanted to make a fortune. As Lilienthal later put it in his diary, "It is good to be on such cordial and increasingly relaxed terms with so remarkable a man in the art of acquisitiveness." Meyer, for his part, thought that Lilienthal's contacts and technical expertise could be useful, though he wasn't quite sure exactly how. Then the thought dawned on the banker: why not put Lilienthal in charge of Minerals Separation?

Of course, there was still Dr. Gregory to consider. For months the otherwise daring partners of Lazard hemmed and hawed, wary of approaching the feisty old tycoon. Finally, partner James Adams screwed up the nerve. Would you, he asked Gregory, be willing to turn over the reins to Lilienthal?

To everyone's astonishment, the answer was a simple, unqualified yes.

At almost the same time, Ferdinand Eberstadt got a call from an old acquaintance, Francis B. Davis, the former head of the U.S. Rubber Company. Standard Oil of New Jersey was interested in unloading its 50 percent interest in something called the Attapulgus Clay Company. Could Eberstadt help in finding a buyer?

The more Eberstadt studied the Georgia company, the more intrigued he was. Attapulgus was the country's leading producer of fuller's earth, a type of clay used for petroleum refining and oil-well drilling. What's more, it held a 50 percent interest in another company, Filtrol, which was the largest U.S. producer of natural cracking catalysts for oil refining—cracking catalysts being chemicals that break heavy crude oil down into lighter substances, such as gasoline. Eberstadt decided that he wanted to buy Attapulgus himself. But at that point he didn't have the $4.5 million that Standard Oil sought for its half of the company. So he went to see André Meyer.

Meyer was interested—so interested that after the first few discussions he wanted to put up all the money himself. But Eberstadt insisted on going in fifty–fifty. So he borrowed the $2.25 million from Chase, and on April 22, 1952, Lazard and Eberstadt bought their half-interest in Attapulgus Clay.

No sooner did Eberstadt and Meyer step into the picture than their investment was threatened by Myron Bantrell, a former Rochester, New York, chemist who was chairman of Filtrol of California, an offshoot of Filtrol. Bantrell's company owned the other 50 percent of Filtrol, and now that Standard Oil had bowed out, he wanted control of the whole thing. Most investors would have been apoplectic at the prospect of giving up a major portion of a company so soon after they acquired it. But Eberstadt and Meyer were overjoyed, since they saw the Filtrol maneuver as an opportunity to completely recoup their initial investment while holding on to their Attapulgus interest. In effect, they would be purchasing Attapulgus for nothing. But as they calculated it, the only way they could instantly recoup (and avoid the possibility of being taxed twice on their gains) was to liquidate Attapulgus. They would break up the company, sell off the Filtrol interest, pocket the money, and then reorganize what was left of Attapulgus into another company. All they needed was a company that could absorb the Attapulgus assets. And that company could be Minerals Separation.

Accordingly, on the day before Thanksgiving 1952, the Attapulgus Clay Company was liquidated. On the day after Thanksgiving 1952, the remaining assets of Attapulgus Clay were merged into Minerals Separation (two weeks later the company's name was changed to Attapulgus Minerals & Chemicals Company). In between—presumably just as they were sitting down to their turkey and cranberry sauce—Eberstadt and Meyer made $5.5 million on the sale of their Filtrol shares.

As gratifying as this was, it didn't stop André Meyer from worrying endlessly about the fate of his investment (an investment that now cost him nothing). He flew into a rage when the management of the new enterprise forecast lower sales in 1953 than had been recorded in 1952. As Lilienthal describes the scene in his journals, "He was in a lather. I'd never seen a man more upset, or who expressed his distress and chagrin in such an extreme way. I had myself been disappointed with the estimates. I had sent them to him saying they seemed 'conservative.' He said they were not only bad in the sense that they indicated a soggy business (in which case we had all been misled and stupid) but a management that was more interested in justifying its estimates than in making a hard effort to do a bang-up aggressive job." His advice to Lilienthal was succinct: "Hammer these fellows and make them understand what's what." Badly shaken by Meyer's "intemperate" attitude, Lilienthal wandered the halls of Lazard, wondering, "What am I doing here?" In his words, "I had mental pictures of walking into André's office and telling them what they could do with all this clay."

The badgering from Meyer went on through the next year. "André is insatiable for figures," Lilienthal recorded. "If this is carried too far it will rob us of any real focus." Earnings continued to sag, although they took a turn for the better in early 1954. It was then that Meyer and Eberstadt pulled off the coup that would seal the company's success: a merger with Edgar Brothers, which produced kaolin, another form of clay used in the coating of paper. A combination of two clay companies hardly seemed destined to fire the imagination, but for some reason the new company—now renamed Minerals & Chemicals Company—caught Wall Street's eye. (Perhaps it was the fact that aside from coating the pages of *Life* magazine, kaolin could also be used as a petroleum-cracking catalyst.) By late October 1954, just four months after the merger had been consummated, M&C stock had soared to $22 a share, or 40 times earnings; it had been just $5 a share when Meyer and Eberstadt bought into the company.

Now that the stock had climbed, the two bankers were eager to cash in on the market's bountiful assessment of M&C's prospects. They arranged, in great haste, a February 1955 public offering of 436,000 Minerals & Chemicals shares at $22.75 a share. "André has driven through the public offering by sheer willpower on a time basis that everyone said just couldn't be made," wrote Lilienthal. "But it appears that it will be." When the offering was completed, it became clear why Meyer was in such a rush. Of the 436,000 shares, 234,000 were sold by Lazard Frères and F. Eberstadt & Company. (Meyer and Eberstadt had made their investments through their firms.) That meant that Lazard made $3 million in the offering and Eberstadt $2.2 million. What's more, Lazard held on to another 200,000 shares (worth $4.5 million) and Eberstadt another 150,000 shares (worth $3.4 million). In short, when the $5.5 million they took in on the Filtrol deal was added in, Lazard and Eberstadt had managed to quadruple their money on the $4.5 million investment they had made two years before.

But that was only the beginning.

In the late 1950s, Meyer struck up a friendship with the principals of an international metals-trading firm, Philipp Brothers. They were men he could understand: gruff, German-Jewish immigrants who had leveraged their superb trading instincts and impeccable international contacts into a $200 million business. While their operation was regularly churning out profits of $5 million and $6 million a year, they knew full well that their personal net worth could be immeasurably increased if they took the company public. So they went to André Meyer for advice.

"He was a very convincing man," recalls one of those Phillip Brothers principals, Ludwig Jesselson. "He had so much clout, this man, so much prestige. And" says Jessclson, "he liked to earn a commission."

André Meyer the adviser thought the matter over and came up with a brilliant idea. Why not bring Philipp Brothers public by merging it with an already publicly owned company? In fact, he had just the company for Philipp Brothers—something called Minerals & Chemicals.

The fact that this brainstorm of André Meyer the adviser might also handsomely benefit André Meyer the investor did not seem to bother Jesselson and his colleagues very much. All they cared about, in Jesselson's words, was that "it was a vehicle to get on the exchange and go public." Accordingly, in July 1960, Minerals & Chemicals Corporation was merged with Philipp Brothers to form Minerals & Chemicals Philipp Corporation.

For Meyer, what happened afterward was a gratifying replay of the Edgar Brothers coup six years earlier. The Minerals & Chemicals stock, which had traded at around 20 at the time of the deal, jumped to 28 within a year. Jesselson and Siegfried Ullmann, the other top Philipp Brothers principal, were each now worth over $20 million. Lazard came out of the deal with 300,000 shares (including the M&C shares it had held previously) worth at least $8.4 million. Eberstadt, meanwhile, ended up with $3.6 million worth of Minerals & Chemicals shares.

Enough? Not yet. Even as he was mapping out the Philipp Brothers deal, Meyer had bigger objectives in mind—namely a merger with yet another company, Engelhard Industries, the world's largest refiner and fabricator of precious metals. Meyer was on the best of terms with its chairman, portly forty-three-year-old Charles Engelhard; in fact, his friendship with Engelhard's wife, Jane, dated back to Paris in the thirties. And Meyer's dream of a grand amalgam of metals and minerals companies was bound to appeal to Engelhard's well-developed taste for the flamboyant. In less than two decades he had transformed a modest $20 million family business into a worldwide $150 million family empire. He reportedly was the inspiration for Ian Fleming's Goldfinger; amused by the comparison, Engelhard for a while called a stewardess on his company plane Pussy Galore.

The owner of a 150-acre estate in Far Hills, New Jersey, a mansion in Johannesburg, a lodge in the lion country of the eastern Transvaal, and a salmon-river camp in Gaspé, Quebec—to name just a few of his residences—Engelhard lived, played, and worked like the mogul he was. "He ran the company like Louis the Fourteenth," recalls Robert Zeller, a former F. Eberstadt partner and longtime member of Engelhard's board. "He would hold meetings in Palm Beach propped up in bed, just like the Sun King, with his retinue all around him."

Sometime in 1963 Meyer visited Ferd Eberstadt, sat down, and sketched out on a yellow piece of paper his idea for a global alliance of Minerals & Chemicals Philipp, Engelhard Industries, and Harry Oppenheimer's Anglo-American mining empire. The synergy was awesome. Because Anglo-American had an iron grip on most of South Africa's gold and diamond mining, the partnership would control much of the world's precious-metal and mineral production, refining, marketing, and trading.

The plan laid out by Meyer called for Engelhard and Minerals & Chemicals Philipp to merge, with Anglo-American then buying out Charlie Engelhard's position in the newly formed combination. But Engelhard hesitated. His splashy life-style notwithstanding, he was a cautious man when it came to corporate matters. As he once put it, "I play hunches in poker or horse racing, but not in business." So instead of an immediate, all-out merger with M&C Philipp, Engelhard opted to buy merely a 19 percent stake in that company. The shareholding was enough to get him elected chairman of M&C Philipp, but Engelhard adamantly insisted to reporters that he had no interest in a full-scale merger. "They're doing all right on their own," he said of M&C Philipp.

By mid-1967, however, Engelhard had changed his mind. And just as Meyer had foreseen, everyone benefited handsomely from the merger. For starters, the stock multiple zoomed upward. Before the merger, M&C Philipp stock was selling for 14 times its earnings per share, and Engelhard at 20 times earnings. By early 1968, the new company was commanding a multiple of 24 times earnings. This was especially good news for Meyer, other Lazard partners, and their clients, who, all told, wound up with 223,000 common shares of the new company (called Engelhard Minerals & Chemicals), worth $10.7 million in early 1968, and another 36,000 of convertible preferred, worth $5.2 million. (At this point there was no longer any public record of how many shares Eberstadt held.) On top of all that, Lazard was paid a fee of $1.1 million for arranging the merger, 25 percent of which was kicked back to Eberstadt for "assistance" in the deal. The assistance was probably more symbolic than real. Most likely it was André Meyer's way of thanking Ferd Eberstadt for introducing him to the Attapulgus Clay Company sixteen years before.

The rest of the story takes on something of a bittersweet tone. Anglo-American did indeed become a substantial shareholder of the new entity, but, says Jesselson, "they never had any direct impact on the firm. They were just a shareholder like anybody else." Meyer's grand design of a marketing link between Anglo-American and Engelhard did not come off, either. Nevertheless, Engelhard Minerals & Chemicals prospered mightily, its revenues growing from $1.4 billion at the time of the merger to $10.2 billion a decade later. Ninety percent of those revenues were produced by Philipp Brothers, whose oil-trading activities reaped huge gains from the global energy crisis. Unfortunately, Charlie Engelhard didn't live to share the wealth; he died of a heart attack in March 1971, a victim, apparently, of an obesity that was fueled by his addiction to Hershey Kisses and six-packs of Coca-Cola.

And, in the end, the powerful minerals and metals conglomerate that André Meyer forged didn't quite stand the test of time. In 1981, Philipp split off from Engelhard Minerals & Chemicals, largely because the trading operation had become so big and so successful that it was totally dwarfing the industrial end of the empire. "We felt you cannot do justice to an industrial complex if you want to do trading at the same time," explains Jesselson. "You need to do one thing in order to do it well."

So the complicated enterprise that Meyer and Eberstadt built, having yielded millions in profits for the bankers and their associates, is uncomplicated once more.

The company was a modest little drug manufacturer whose main products were the Richard Hudnut line of cosmetics and fading home remedies like Sloan's Liniment. But by the time Ferd Eberstadt and André Meyer got through with it, the firm was making Bromo-Seltzer and Anahist nasal mist and Listerine and Chiclets, and was ringing up sales of over $200 million a year. Its name was Warner-Lambert.

Warner-Lambert—or the William R. Warner Company, as it was originally known—had been controlled by the Pfeiffer family since the 1880s. Traditionally, it brought in a steady income from what are known in the trades as "milkers," assorted nonprescription medicines that your mother said were good for you because *her* mother said they were good for *her*. But by the early 1950s the milkers were fading, and so was the family patriarch, Gustavus Pfeiffer. Fearful that he was losing his faculties, he put his stock in what was by then Warner-Hudnut into a foundation, with one important stipulation: that after he died the stock would be sold and the proceeds donated to medical research.

Pfeiffer's death in 1953, then, presented complications for the Warner-Hudnut Company. The seriousness of them became apparent soon afterward when Nelson Loud at Eberstadt got a call from Alfred Driscoll, an ex-governor of New Jersey who was then president of Warner-Hudnut. Loud was used to taking calls from Driscoll; after all, Eberstadt had taken Warner-Hudnut public a few years earlier, and Ferdinand Eberstadt himself served on its board. But this time, all Driscoll would say on the phone was, "We've got to come and see you."

"What's it all about?" asked Loud.

"Wait till we get there," answered Driscoll.

When Driscoll arrived, he was accompanied by Elmer Bobst, a veteran drug-industry executive who had come out of retirement in 1945 to take over the Warner Company chairmanship. "They came in," recalls Loud, "and their eyes were wild and their hair was on end. Ferd and I sat down and said, 'Now, what's the problem?' And they said, 'A gentleman came up to see us today and offered to buy the Pfeiffer Foundation's stock in Warner-Hudnut.'

"And we said, 'That's kind of a difficult spot. You're trustees of the foundation. You can't not entertain the proposal.' They said, 'We're scared to death of it.' And we said, 'Who is it?' They answered, 'The man who came to see us said he was representing Charles Revson.' "

Revson, of course, was the crude, tyrannical genius who ran Revlon. He was not someone for whom Bobst and Driscoll cared to work. As Loud puts it, "It just scared the living hell out of them.

"So they said, 'What'll we do?' And we said, 'You've got to talk to him. In the meantime, let us make a study of the business and see what should be done. Maybe we can find someone else to buy it.' And as soon as they left, at the wink of an eye, we were in touch with André Meyer."

Eberstadt and Meyer looked at the situation and decided to go ahead and buy the stock—but not on their own. This time, in an effort to spread the risk, they enlisted several other Wall Street firms, including Lehman Brothers, Wertheim, and White Weld. Together, they purchased 558,000 shares—44.5 percent of the company's outstanding stock—for $11.5 million. The deal was hardly the hottest investment on Wall Street at the time; a number of brokerage firms turned down offers to join the syndicate, some pleading poverty, others balking at Meyer and Eberstadt's imperious but customary insistence that they be given full power to buy and sell on behalf of the entire syndicate. (André Meyer did not view such syndicates as democratic institutions.) "It just didn't sit very well with me to turn a thing over to André without any right to withdraw, or veto, or discuss things," relates the former head of a major Wall Street firm. "So I just declined the participation. And I don't think," he chuckles, "that had ever happened to André before. Quite probably because of that, I don't think we had another offer of one of these Lazard syndicates."

The other significant aspect of this syndicate was that Bobst and Driscoll were part of it—at Meyer and Eberstadt's insistence. "They already had some stock in the company," says Loud, "but we wanted them to have some more." Meyer was a firm believer in the thesis that chief executives who were also shareholders did better jobs than chief executives who weren't. As Meyer once put it to an associate, "It doesn't matter if his investment is important to the company. What matters is that it is important to *him.*" Meyer was unmoved by corporate officers' complaints about how much they personally stood to lose on the stock if the company's performance turned sour. One executive who grumbled that he might lose *millions* was greeted with a hard stare. "So," an unimpressed Meyer told him, "I write you a check."

Meyer and Eberstadt didn't wait too long to assert themselves in other ways. Remembers Loud, "We sat down amongst ourselves and thought, 'Well, now, what direction should this company go in?' I remember we wrote down thirteen things we wanted to do. I thought of it as Eberstadt and Meyer's thirteen points," he laughs, "sort of like Woodrow Wilson's fourteen points."

The direction they decided upon, simply put, was to make Warner-Hudnut bigger and bigger by buying other companies. It was the same get-rich-quick formula they were then employing with Attapulgus. Ideally, they wanted to acquire companies that were heavily involved in so-called ethical drugs—unique prescription items that generated, as prescription drugs are wont to do, huge profit margins. Eberstadt at the time was investment banker for Pfizer and had seen how that company had prospered with such items as penicillin and streptomycin. If Warner-Hudnut could be built into not only a big drug company, but a big *ethical*-drug company, its stock would be worth a fortune.

These designs suited Elmer Bobst very well. He would have liked nothing better than to build another Hoffmann-La Roche, the giant international drug company whose U.S. arm Bobst had headed before joining Warner. Comments a former Eberstadt partner, "Elmer Bobst had many good qualities, but humility was not one of them." (In his later years, Bobst began to expect formal recognition of his many contributions to humanity and, accordingly, was feted at numerous testimonial dinners in his honor. So frequent were these dinners that Ferdinand Eberstadt one day remarked wearily to an associate, "Last night I walked down memory lane once again with Elmer. I have walked down memory lane with Elmer so many times that I think the grass must be worn down by now.")

While Bobst took center stage as the master builder of the company, there was little doubt among Eberstadt and Meyer's subordinates about what was going on behind the scenes. "The initial impetus," says Loud, "came from André and Ferd, and then we would talk to management and say, 'Well, how about it? What do you think of this?' We bankers brought them the deals, figured out how to do them, negotiated them, made everybody happy, and did 'em."

The company had already taken one step in the right direction before Eberstadt and Meyer came on the scene by acquiring Chilcott Laboratories, an ethical-drug firm that had done quite well with anti-allergy medications. But Meyer and Eberstadt quickly came up with more acquisition targets. The first was the Napara Chemical Company. It wasn't an ethical-drug company, but it did make Anahist nasal spray, and by that point Bobst and the others reasoned that if they couldn't find ethical-drug manufacturers, they would settle for the next best thing: companies that made brand names.

That rationale also resulted in the purchase of the Lambert Company, makers of Listerine. Lambert was represented in the negotiations by none other than Sidney Weinberg of Goldman, Sachs. There was no love lost between Weinberg and Ferd Eberstadt; the two had served inharmoniously together on the War Production Board and had refused to speak to each other ever since. Perhaps for that reason, Weinberg drove a hard bargain: each Warner-Hudnut share, valued at $36, could be exchanged for a share in the new Warner-Lambert Company, but so could each Lambert share, valued at only $28. But the chance to bring Listerine into the fold was too good to pass up.

With the nose and throat attended to, what more fitting place to turn to next than the stomach? Thus it was that Bromo-Seltzer was added to the Warner-Lambert line soon afterward, through the purchase of the Emerson Drug Company. One antacid, though, wasn't enough for Eberstadt, Meyer, and Bobst. They wanted more. They wanted Rolaids. And they got it, through the purchase of the American Chicle Company, which also made Chiclets chewing gum, Dentyne, Trident sugarless gum (for those who had sworn off Chiclets), and Clorets breath mints.

By this time (October 1962), Warner-Lambert had blossomed into a $200-million-a-year company, and it had done it all by adhering to the Meyer-Eberstadt philosophy: merger, merger, merger. "The interesting thing," says Loud, "was how we kept buying bigger and bigger companies. The first one we bought was about one-fourth or one-fifth the size of Warner-Hudnut. The next one we bought was about half the size of the combined companies, and so on. We started with a company with two million three in earnings and ended up ultimately with a hundred times that."

And still, Eberstadt and Meyer kept prodding it into bigger and bigger mergers. The company held talks with the mammoth R. J. Reynolds tobacco company, but the deal came unglued over a dispute over just who was to run the combined show. As Loud tells it, "Mr. Bobst one day told the head of Reynolds, 'When we get this company together, I'm going to do this and I'm going to do that.' And the head of Reynolds just said, 'The hell you are.' " Not long afterward, discussions began with another industry giant, Minnesota Mining & Manufacturing. A long delay in getting Justice Department approval scotched that one, however.

Inevitably, Meyer and Eberstadt's influence began to weaken. "It was one of those evolutionary things," notes Frank Markoe, Jr., former chief financial officer of Warner-Lambert. "The company became more professionally managed, and when these things happen very often the role of an investment banker gets smaller." Warner-Lambert's new management was much less under the sway of Meyer and Eberstadt than Bobst and Driscoll were, much less inclined to seek their advice and consent.

The final rupture came when new Warner-Lambert president Stuart Hemsley called Bob Zeller at Eberstadt to tell him the company had decided to use another investment-banking firm, Morgan Stanley, as the lead manager of its next issue. Eberstadt could be a comanager, Hemsley said, but Warner-Lambert was dropping Lazard. Zeller walked into Ferd Eberstadt's office to break the news. "No problem," Eberstadt said. "Call him back, and tell him to forget it. We're partners with Meyer, and if he's not in it, we're not in it." To this day Zeller does not know why Warner-Lambert insisted on dropping Lazard completely.

But what happened to that huge block that Meyer and Eberstadt controlled? Wasn't it big enough to bludgeon even the most adamant chief executive? The slightly astonishing fact of the matter is it wasn't, and hadn't been for years. In May 1955, just two months after the Lambert merger and less than a year after they had acquired the stock, Meyer and Eberstadt unloaded 325,000 of the 558,000 shares.

The stock fetched a handsome price—$33 a share, compared to the $20.60 they had paid for it eleven months earlier. But in their rush to bag the bird in the hand, Meyer and Eberstadt had missed the opportunity to truly cash in on Warner-Lambert's explosive growth—the growth for which they themselves had been largely responsible.

They realized $10.7 million on the sale of that block. If they had held it to the early 1970s, it would have fetched $152 million.

When André Meyer and Ferdinand Eberstadt weren't busy forging corporate colossuses they were treating themselves to some quick killings. Such as the time they owned—briefly—the entire northern coast of Haiti.

What they owned, actually, was the world's largest sisal plantation, 35,000 acres in size, which had previously belonged to a group of American investors. (Sisal is a fiber used to make rope, paperboard, and craftboard.) After one of the investors died, his widow and the other partners asked Nelson Loud to appraise the property, since the U.S. government had challenged an earlier appraisal.

Loud went to Eberstadt and asked him about the assignment. Said Eberstadt, "I think the only way you'll make the appraisal really stand up is if we make it and then have the opportunity to buy it at that price." The owners, willing at that point to sell the property, agreed, and Loud and another Eberstadt partner promptly flew down to Haiti to make their inspection.

"It was the middle of August, hotter 'n hell," he remembers. "But we found several intriguing things about the plantation: first, that it was a successful enterprise in itself; and secondly, that it owned several million dollars' worth of foreign securities which were sitting in a vault in the Chemical Bank in New York." The discovery led Loud to up the valuation from $4 million to $6.6 million. "What are we going to do?" he asked Eberstadt on his return. "Let's go see André," Eberstadt shot back.

Eberstadt and Meyer talked it over and decided once again to organize a syndicate to spread the risk. The high-powered group they put together consisted of Vincent Astor and the Rockefeller brothers. But soon problems arose. Astor, whose real estate investments were showing signs of overextension, pulled out early; and in the middle of the planning work, the Rockefellers dropped out, too. Laurence Rockefeller told Meyer and Eberstadt that the Haitian investment, coming on top of the family's already extensive South American holdings, would cause problems for brother Nelson's New York gubernatorial bid.

So Meyer and Eberstadt were left to decide whether they wanted to go ahead on their own. Meyer brought in a sisal expert to study the plantation, and one day, over lunch at India House in downtown Manhattan, the expert made his report to Eberstadt and Loud. Eberstadt had no interest in a long, technical dissertation. "Is this thing any goddamn good?" he barked. The expert, who in earlier conversations with Lazard and Eberstadt people had praised the sisal operation, nervously replied, "It's too big, and it's going to be very hard to handle."

Meyer wasn't at that meeting, and right after it ended Eberstadt phoned him. After a few minutes' conversation, they decided to call the whole thing off.

Loud and another Eberstadt partner who had worked on the deal were flabbergasted. Here was an investment that, by their reckoning, was as close to riskless as they had ever seen. By liquidating the securities portfolio alone, they could have the plantation for nothing. And they could certainly realize *something* on the plantation itself.

So they went to see Ferd Eberstadt again. "Mr. Eberstadt," said Loud, "do you mind if we do that deal ourselves?"

Eberstadt was startled. "Nelson," he replied, "do you want to be an investment banker, or do you want to be in the sisal business?"

But Loud wasn't going to be brushed off so easily. "Answer my question first," he said.

Eberstadt was silent for a minute. Then he reached over for the telephone, dialed Lazard, asked for André Meyer, and said, "André, we're going to go it alone." Meyer didn't hesitate. "OK," he told Eberstadt, "I'm with you."

The investment fully lived up to Loud's expectations: it was some of the easiest money Meyer and Eberstadt ever made. They bought the plantation for $6.6 million, and within a few months turned around and resold it to the Haitian-American Sugar Company. That sale, plus the securities they liquidated, brought in over $10 million.

The deal, in fact, was one of those rare transactions where everyone came out a winner. The former owners received the full appraised value of the plantation. The Haitian-American Sugar Company ended up with a highly profitable sisal operation, plus a surprise windfall of $1 million, the proceeds of some Haitian government bonds in the plantation's portfolio that no one had ever thought would be paid off. And Eberstadt and Meyer made over a 50 percent return on their money in a matter of months.

For all their shrewdness, even Meyer and Eberstadt made their share of mistakes. Perhaps the closest call they had stemmed from their abortive and surprising involvement in the production of television programs.

Neither Eberstadt nor Meyer could say they were uninitiated in the ways of the entertainment business. Eberstadt had worked on the organization of United Artists in the 1920s, had been involved with RKO Pictures as an investment banker in the 1930s, and in the late 1950s had arranged Howard Hughes's sale of the entire RKO film library to United Artists. Both Eberstadt and Meyer were close to Robert Benjamin and Arthur Krim, the two lawyers who controlled United Artists, and at one point even offered to buy out UA co-founder Mary Pickford's remaining interest in the film company— until Krim and Benjamin decided to do so themselves. Later, Eberstadt led United Artists' initial public offering; even though Lazard stayed out because of its involvement at the time with MGM, Krim says, "I thought of the two of them as having taken us public." Afterward, Meyer arranged several private financings for UA. Notes Krim, "When it came to dealing with the Prudential Insurance Company or the U.S. Steel pension fund, our contact was always through André."

But none of this fully prepared Meyer and Eberstadt for Ziv Television. Ziv produced such fifties TV staples as "Sea Hunt," "Highway Patrol," "I Led Three Lives," and "Meet Corliss Archer." It seemed like a flourishing business, and when founder Fred Ziv told Eberstadt he was interested in retiring, Eberstadt wasted no time making Ziv an offer. He and Meyer agreed to pay $18 million for the company, $14 million of which was financed by a loan from Chemical Bank. (One of Meyer and Eberstadt's guiding investment principles was always to put up a bank's money rather than their own.)

No sooner had the purchase been completed than they were approached once more by Fred Ziv and his partner, John Sinn, who were still running the operation. The company, Ziv and Sinn explained, was in the middle of producing that season's series and needed an extra infusion of capital to complete the programs. How much was needed? Ziv and Sinn were asked. Oh, they said, about $6 or $7 million. "When we heard that," says Loud, "everyone just turned pale."

Having borrowed to the hilt to finance the acquisition, Meyer and Eberstadt were in no position to go back to the banks for another $7 million. Nor were they about to furnish the cash from their own pockets. Because, somewhere along the line, they began to realize something else: the television production business was changing, and networks were becoming less and less inclined to buy the output of independent syndicators like Ziv. The networks wanted to finance the shows themselves, to tap into the huge flow of income from reruns that up to then was accruing largely to the syndicators. So Ziv's market over the next few years was likely to be drastically curtailed. Meyer and Eberstadt were stuck with a very glamorous lemon.

Desperate to get out of the situation as fast as they could, they turned to their old friends Benjamin and Krim at United Artists. "There was a lot of pressure on us to get them out of the deal," says Krim. Bowing to that pressure, UA agreed to take Ziv off their hands, on terms that, remarkably, allowed Meyer and Eberstadt to break even on the deal. UA assumed responsibility for the $14 million bank loan, and paid another $4.75 million in notes and debentures.

Over the next several years, United Artists paid even more dearly for its largesse. "We took a financial beating," comments Krim, "because the projections of the value of the series made by Ziv did not hold up. We lost ten to twelve million on it in the five years after the deal." Eventually, UA did manage to recoup most of this, as reruns of the old series brought in more and more income. But Ziv remained, on balance, a United Artists loser.

Yet when, a few years later, United Artists was acquired by Transamerica, to whom did Krim and Benjamin turn for advice?

F. Eberstadt & Company and Lazard Frères.

"The relationship," explains Krim, "remained warm."

CHAPTER SEVEN

Friends

In early November 1951, when former Tennessee Valley Authority chief David Lilienthal was thinking of joining forces with André Meyer, he sought the advice of the legendary advertising man Albert Lasker. Lasker had put him in touch with Meyer, but Lilienthal was still apprehensive, and over lunch at the Cloud Club in Manhattan the adman tried to reassure him.

"André is a financial genius, the outstanding genius of Wall Street today," Lasker told his nervous lunch partner. The only reason the world at large didn't know that, he said, was André's intense dislike for publicity. Then Lasker, with the adman's instinct for the final flourish, added the clincher. "Anyone who sticks around that fellow," he declared, "will get rich."

Already an aura was beginning to envelop André Meyer—the golden aura of the consummate moneymaker, the spinner of fortunes. The aura not only captivated the would-be rich like Lilienthal but the already well-to-do, who sought to keep what they had and, with luck, multiply their wealth. One after another, they trekked to the thirty-third floor of the Carlyle Hotel, to be consoled, teased, flattered, lectured, and advised by the enigmatic Frenchman in the three-piece suit.

And Meyer, for his part, relished every moment of it. To Meyer, friendships with the high and mighty were as indispensable to his business as his ability to put together complicated deals. He had a very European sense that *who* you knew was equally if not more important than *what* you knew. And as he struggled to build his fortune in postwar America, he worked as hard on his friendships as he worked on everything else. As one investment banker put it, "André always had a sense of who was important and how to get his hooks into them."

But it was always done with the utmost subtlety. Meyer may have bullied and screamed at his family and subordinates and some of his business partners. But when it came to the Very Important People, he positively oozed charm and gentility, abstaining from any hint of the hard sell. Always, there were the little things. Taking the wife of the visiting French president out early one morning to visit an automat and a Walgreen's drugstore. Exchanging chitchat with *Washington Post* chairman Katharine Graham over coffee at the Carlyle. Says Graham: "The thing about André was that he was a tremendously gifted high-level gossip. He tended to be very interested in people: who is doing what to whom; is he good or isn't he good? I mean, he would *grill* me about that kind of thing."

Meyer also had a knack for being there when people needed him most. In the words of a former Lazard executive, "He had an ability to relate to people at times of distress in a way that created loyalty and exposed him to grand opportunities in the future." A classic example of this was his relationship with the Boëls and the Solvays, the families that controlled Belgium's giant Solvay industrial empire. During the Second World War, because of an introduction from their old adviser George Murnane, they entrusted management of their assets to Meyer, and his impeccable handling of the situation helped forge a lifelong bond between them. Even in the 1970s, with other bankers competing aggressively for Solvay's business, Lazard was reaping huge dividends from the relationship. A one-time Lazard associate remembers an instance in the mid-seventies when Solvay was buying a factory in the United States. "The financing was easily arranged, and then they called us in at the end and said, 'What do you think of this?' and paid us a giant fee," he recalls. "The fee was a gift. It was their way of paying Meyer off."

Shuffling through his Brussels duplex, the patriarch of the family, Count René Boël, speaks of Meyer as "a man whose line was tackling difficult problems." But he did notice something odd about the relationship—when there weren't any problems to be solved, Meyer made himself scarce. "I used to tease him, 'Why don't you come see me anymore?' And he would say, 'But you and your wife are happy. You have everything. . . .' "

Meyer was particularly drawn to wealthy women in trouble, women such as Katharine Graham, Jackie Kennedy, Jane Engelhard. "I have to see men for business reasons," he remarked late in life. "But I don't like men. They have no courage. All my friends are now women. They have more courage."

One reason why so many rich, elegant women may, in turn, have gravitated toward Meyer was that he was ever so slightly feminine himself. "Physically there was nothing really masculine about him at all," comments one man who worked closely with him. "His hands were soft, and sports or athletics obviously never entered his mind." Another reason was that he *noticed* women, in a way that other men rarely did. His old friend Andrea Wilson points out that "he saw all these things—if I had a new dress, if I changed my hair, or if I was particularly upset about something, he would notice in an instant. There is something tremendously attractive about a man who is so responsive that he notices all these aspects of you. It could also be negative. One time I came to the Carlyle in a particularly nice dress, and he said, 'You look marvelous. You should always look like that—not the way you *sometimes* do.'" Says Wilson: "He liked women who didn't just sit around, who weren't patsies. On the other hand, he liked the other kind, too—women who were just pieces of jewelry."

Just how useful were these friendships—male and female—for Meyer? Some of them added substantially to his fortune, and to the success of Lazard Frères. Others didn't bring him much in the way of direct business but gave him something equally precious: information, the kind of information that not only produces business ideas but that tends to churn up more ideas in its wake. As Meyer knew well, when it came to information, the rich really do get richer—the more you have, the more you are likely to be attractive to people who can give you an even greater supply of it.

The constant parade of personages at the Carlyle also served a purpose less explicitly related to business: the procession filled a deep psychological craving. "It reassured him of his importance," says Michel David-Weill. "He was not a sure man: he was absolutely unsure of himself and of others."

And, for that reason, deep friendship with Meyer sometimes took on hellish aspects. To reassure himself, he played an incessant game of brinksmanship with his friends, morbidly pouncing on any indication that they were less loyal and steadfast than they said they were. "If you didn't come to see him enough," says Katharine Graham, "he would whine. He was always whining if you didn't pay enough attention to him."

The fallings-out Meyer had with his friends could usually be ascribed not to business dealings, but to their failure to visit or call him as often as he felt proper. Take the case of Albert Lasker's socially prominent widow, Mary. "André would take great pride in the fact that Albert Lasker called him every day. That was very precious to him," relates New York public-relations woman Anna Rosenberg Hoffman, a close friend of both Meyer and the Laskers. "After Albert Lasker died, he felt that Mary didn't telephone him enough. That was what caused the falling-out: nothing else. And when Mary said to him, 'You're a man, you can call *me,*' he thought that was terrible. It was almost childish. I used to say to him, 'It wouldn't hurt you to call her.' 'Why should I?' he would say. 'Albert called me every day.' "

Yet for every Mary Lasker who didn't pay Meyer proper homage, there were any number of fashionable people who did. Some came to him for advice about their companies. Others hung around Meyer in the hope that he would allow them to participate in one of his deals. And others just because, in Graham's words, he was "interesting, funny, warm, companionable, interested. He was tremendous good value."

Radio Corporation of America founding father and chairman David Sarnoff gravitated to André Meyer in the early 1950s for a very simple reason. Sarnoff needed money.

Despite having single-handedly built RCA into a (then) $450 million global communications empire, Sarnoff had never accumulated much personal wealth. On his death in 1971, his estate was valued at a mere $1 million. And in early 1951, when he was given his first RCA stock option, for 100,000 shares, he had to borrow from a bank to pay for the stock.

On Yom Kippur 1953, Sarnoff stood outside Temple Emanu-El in Manhattan chatting with Louis Strauss, an RCA director, and Meyer Goldstein, a pension-planning executive. Strauss and Goldstein both painted a gloomy picture of the prospects for RCA stock, then around $20 a share, and Sarnoff became alarmed. What if the stock fell below his option price of $17.75 a share? How would he pay the bank loans off then? Frantic, Sarnoff phoned an old friend, attorney John Cahill. Cahill listened to Sarnoff's tale of woe and told "the General" (as Sarnoff was usually called) that he knew someone who he thought would take the stock off his hands at $21 a share. That someone was André Meyer.

The deal was consummated, and the relationship between Sarnoff and Meyer quickly blossomed. Meyer brought Sarnoff in as an investor in some of his deals, Avis being the most prominent example.

Sarnoff, in turn, made Meyer an RCA director and opened the door to RCA's lucrative investment-banking business to Lazard Frères, with the assent of Bobbie Lehman.

Often, the two tycoons could be seen strolling the streets of the Upper East Side on Sunday morning (Sarnoff's townhouse at 44 East Seventy-first Street was practically next door to the Carlyle). Usually that was the only recreation either man got all week. "The General and André got along, basically, because they were both all business," points out RCA executive vice-president Kenneth Bilbey, an old confidant of Sarnoff's. "I don't think they were renaissance-type men."

Not that all was sweetness and light between the two. For one thing, the General's wife, Lizette, couldn't stand Meyer, perhaps because she was a native of France herself and saw something in Meyer that eluded her husband. "She never completely trusted André," says Bilbey. "I think she thought he was using the General." And Sarnoff himself complained now and then that Meyer never did make him the kind of money that the General hoped he would. "I love André," he would say to friends, "but he sure as hell didn't do anything for my account."

And the two were not immune to violent rifts. One such disagreement, in the midst of an RCA board meeting, prompted Meyer to stalk out of the room and declare he was resigning. Sarnoff looked as though he couldn't care less. "If that's the way he acts, so be it," Sarnoff said. "He has a quick temper." RCA counsel Robert Werner, on his own initiative, visited the Carlyle to try to make peace—and was told by Meyer that he couldn't care less, either. "I spent the weekend shuttling back and forth between their respective homes, against the advice of both of them," says Werner. "The upshot of it was that after eight or ten days of this, in which both parties were very annoyed at me, they cooled off and got back together again."

Indeed, despite their periodic spats, Sarnoff and Meyer remained close. And as the years went by, this relationship, with all its twists and turns, would have a profound impact not only on RCA, but on Sarnoff's son and successor, Robert.

Meyer's close ties to David Sarnoff didn't stop the banker from also cultivating Sarnoff's arch-rival, CBS chairman William Paley.

"We talked about politics quite a bit, and about art sometimes, and about family matters," relates Paley. "A lot of small talk, you know, and big talk, too." And sometimes the big talk focused on where Paley should put his own copious fortune. On occasion, Meyer would invite Paley into one of his real estate deals. "He'd call me up and say, 'I'm sending over something for you to look at,' " recalls Paley. "He never pressured me, you know—it was just 'something to look at.' I'd send it down to my people, and each time they said, 'Oh, my goodness, this is wonderful,' and then we'd go into it." Meyer also suggested that Paley invest in oil stocks—fortunately, well before the big run-up in oil prices. "Every time I followed his advice," says Paley, "I made money."

All this advice apparently came with no strings attached; Meyer did not even press Paley to become CBS's investment banker. (Since Lehman Brothers was CBS's banker, perhaps Meyer feared that a move on the company would be too much for even the low-key Bobbie Lehman to take.) "I never had any indication that André wanted to profit in any way from my friendship," notes Paley. "If anything, I was using him more than he was using me." Paley, however, did notice that "André had a lot of curiosity. He would milk you for information."

Paley managed to patiently put up with Meyer's assorted eccentricities—such as his habit of keeping a telephone next to him on the table during lunch. "He was on that goddamned telephone all day long," snorts Paley. "He couldn't talk to you for ten minutes without being interrupted five times." Every once in a while, though, Paley wouldn't be able to stand it any longer and would growl at Meyer, "Shut it off for a while." Even Paley, though, couldn't get Meyer to do *that*.

But more often, Paley was deferential to Meyer—and, sometimes, afraid. Remarks Meyer's partner and protégé Felix Rohatyn, "Bill told me how nervous he was when he was a half-hour late at André's. I mean, Bill Paley doesn't have to be nervous about *anybody.*"

Paley recalled the time he came back from the country and completely forgot about a late-afternoon appointment he had with Meyer at the Carlyle. Three days later Meyer phoned. "What have I done now?" he asked the CBS boss. Confused, Paley replied, "What do you mean, what have you done?" "Well, obviously, I've done something to hurt you," Meyer answered. "Dear André," said Paley, "I just adore you and there's nothing in the world that you have done that has hurt me." Suddenly, Paley realized what Meyer was alluding to—the forgotten appointment. He immediately raced over to the Carlyle to apologize.

Paley knew better than to stand André Meyer up again.

David Rockefeller, international banking's most celebrated globe-trotter, may have the world's largest Rolodex reportedly, there are some 35,000 names and phone numbers encased within. And one of the things David Rockefeller can tell you from his files is how often, in the course of their thirty-year relationship, he and André Meyer met. One hundred thirty-nine times, to be exact.

They would meet at Rockefeller's bank, the Chase Manhattan; or at the Carlyle; or at the Rockfeller family estate in Pocantico Hills, New York. They would dine with up-and-coming European politicians like James Callaghan (the future British prime minister) and Valéry Giscard d'Estaing (the future French president). Once, Rockefeller was even able to coax Meyer into attending a golf outing with other investment bankers near the Rockefeller estate.

And the frequency of their encounters gives only the barest hint of how close they actually were. "There's nothing on earth I wouldn't do for David," Meyer once told the *New Yorker*. "It's not because he's a Rockefeller, but because he's the kind of human being you want to do something for. I've never seen him mean; I've always seen him acting with poise and class and greatness. In this financial jungle, you have all kinds of animals. He's the best." And the feeling was definitely mutual. As early as 1955, Rockefeller was spreading the word at dinner parties that "Mr. Meyer is the most remarkable man on Wall Street, a real genius." And he went on fervently extolling Meyer's greatness for as long as the financier lived. Says one friend of Rockefeller's, "André had David under his spell."

Their business dealings together were extensive. They joined forces to finance such mammoth real estate projects as L'Enfant Plaza in Washington and the Embarcadero Center in San Francisco. They formed a syndicate to obtain mineral concessions in Tanganyika. They worked together to organize development banks in Iran and the Ivory Coast. Along with Paley, John Hay Whitney, and David's brother Nelson, they purchased Gertrude Stein's art collection. And Lazard became investment bankers for Chase.

Rockefeller repeatedly turned to Meyer for advice whenever a critical decision had to be made. When Rockefeller was offered the post of secretary of the treasury by the Nixon administration, he went to Meyer and was advised not to take it (he didn't). "I felt that on issues of a serious nature involving either public affairs or finance, his judgment was apt to be very reliable," says Rockefeller. "Some people you just feel confidence in."

To those who knew both men, the reason for their close ties was obvious. In the words of one intimate adviser to the Rockefeller family, "Each of them saw something in the other that he didn't have, but wanted to have." For Meyer, what was attractive was not just the Rockefeller money but the Rockefeller name, a name that opened doors and lent an aura of permanence and respectability to any project they were involved in. As for Rockefeller, one aide explained Meyer's allure this way: "David admired people with great magnetism, intuition, and drive, because he had so little of those things himself. And David always had a penchant for things French."

In later years, Rockefeller's staunch support of Lazard as Chase's prime investment banker came under fire from officers at the bank who felt Lazard was taking Chase for granted. According to a former top Chase executive, "David had completely lost the support of people at the higher levels of the bank in terms of their satisfaction with Lazard. The Chase business was held largely by the sheer force of André's personality on David." But Rockefeller continued to stand by his old friend—at least until the mid-seventies, when even Rockefeller was powerless to stem the drift away from Lazard.

As Rockefeller looks back on their relationship, about the only thing that surprises him is that Meyer, in all those years, never blew up at him once. "Given the number of things that we did together, I would have thought that he might," says Rockefeller, who really *does* seem surprised by this. "After all, he did with everyone else."

In the years after the war, Meyer kept in touch with George Murnane's old partner, Jean Monnet. And when Monnet moved onto the world stage as the main architect of the European Economic Community, Meyer emerged as one of Monnet's key behind-the-scenes sounding boards. Monnet's former aide, Jean Guyot (who was later lured by Meyer to Lazard Paris), recollects, "Every time Jean Monnet had an important decision he would say, 'I really would like to talk to André. From him I will get an unprejudiced opinion.' "

When Monnet was negotiating the EEC's first big loan in 1954—$100 million from the U.S. Export-Import Bank—he talked it over with Meyer. Meyer asked him what interest rate he expected to pay, and Monnet said 3.5 percent. Bah, retorted Meyer, you can knock it down to 3 percent *sans problème.* "That's very easy for *you* to say," Monnet sighed, and Meyer answered, "I'll try to discuss it with some of my friends." His "friends" were high officials at the U.S. Treasury; after calling them, Meyer told Guyot, "The way is prepared. You may go and see them." The EEC got 3 percent.

This little favor was repaid manyfold by Monnet in the years to come. In most of the Community's subsequent financings, Lazard was designated as one of the lead managers, an honor reaping a rich harvest of underwriting commissions.

Of Giovanni Agnelli, a friend once said: "He took up pleasure at rather an early age, and finally he decided that power was more interesting." Throughout his youth, into his twenties, Agnelli played the part of the jet-setting European voluptuary, content to leave Fiat, the giant Italian automaker his grandfather founded, in the hands of other men. But after he turned thirty, the playboy's life began to pall on him; the exercise of power—specifically, power over Fiat—became compelling. And at this stage of his life, as Agnelli metamorphosed into an industrial magnate, he came to rely on the counsel of André Meyer.

"He knew *everything* that was involved in finance, and he knew *everybody,*" explains Agnelli. "His connections were infinite, and at the top level. And of all the bankers in the States, he was the most European. Which meant he was extremely discreet. Other bankers, they like to talk, discuss things with the press. But with him, it was always secret diplomacy." And as Agnelli rose to the top of Fiat, he sought Meyer's advice even more. When Agnelli mapped out his international business plans, he admits, "André was always the main architect, the last judge, and the last word."

Together, they engineered an enormous expansion of Agnelli's and Fiat's interests overseas. There was the merger of Fiat and Citroën; the acquisition of Bantam Books by IFI, the Agnelli family holding company; the sale of Ferrania, an Agnelli-owned manufacturer of photographic material, to Minnesota Mining & Manufacturing. Meyer put some of Agnelli's spare cash into various real estate ventures, including several shopping centers; on Saturday afternoons he and Agnelli would often journey out to the Roosevelt Field Mall on Long Island to check on how their investment was faring.

For all the renown Agnelli eventually attained as an international industrial statesman, he was forever a student in Meyer's presence, perennially in awe of Meyer's ability to get things done. When Agnelli encountered problems getting French government approval of Fiat's takeover of Citroën from Michelin (undoing the merger Meyer had engineered some thirty years before), he turned to Meyer for help. Meyer obliged by calling up one of his old French contacts, Maurice Couve de Murville—who by that time was the prime minister of France. Negotiating the new ownership structure directly with Couve de Murville, Meyer pushed the deal through.

Agnelli also came to appreciate Meyer's thoroughness. The automaker was often intrigued by the perfect condition of the soufflés served at the Lazard dining room; no matter how long he and Meyer dawdled before sitting down to eat, the soufflé would always arrive in perfect condition. Then one day, Meyer confided the secret; he had ordered that a soufflé be slipped into the oven every five minutes.

Still, they were an odd couple: Agnelli, tall, athletic, and perpetually tanned; Meyer, short, determinedly unathletic, and as pale as his cheese soufflés. "He thought it was completely odd to enjoy skiing, to enjoy traveling," says Agnelli. "I think he hardly ever went to Rome. In fact, I think he never saw Rome. I once suggested he go to Venice, and he said, 'I'm sure it's very beautiful.' " Meyer, for his part, was horrified that Agnelli, whose right leg was left virtually immobile by a 1952 auto crash, would choose to spend his time whizzing down the slopes of Saint Moritz. "Isn't it enough for you with your leg?" he would scream at Agnelli. "Do you need more?"

Once in a while, Agnelli's stylish inclinations ran head-on into Meyer's hidebound conservatism. On one occasion, Agnelli was thinking of buying the Cartier boutique line, Les Musts de Cartier, but Meyer vetoed the deal because he thought it was "a cheap business." Then there was the time the Agnellis and the Meyers decided to go to the Broadway theater together. Agnelli's wife Marella asked her good friend Truman Capote for advice, and Capote told her they simply *had* to see something called *Lenny*. What he didn't tell her was that the stage biography of comedian Lenny Bruce featured an abundance of four-letter words and full frontal nudity. His blood boiling at the notion of having to sit through such trash, Meyer indignantly stormed out of the theater at the end of the first act.

And Agnelli, as usual, followed right behind.

When Philip Graham killed himself in August 1963, his wife Katharine suddenly found herself in control of two of America's most powerful news organizations, the *Washington Post* and *Newsweek* magazine. She groped for help; while her family, the Meyers (no relation to André), owned those organizations, she had always left running them to Phil. One of the people she turned to was a little man she had met at a dinner party named André Meyer.

As Graham herself tells the story, "I was very unsure of myself, and *most* unsure of myself in the business world at that point. And so it was nice to have this tycoon friend who would talk business with me. It helped build my ego—the fact that André liked me and invited me to lunch and sort of treated me as an equal. You know, if you've always lived your whole life with a very dominant personality, and you think everybody likes you because of him—well, it's quite reassuring to find some people who actually *do* like you. Especially men."

Meyer would invite her to lunch at Lazard five or six times a year. They would talk about the *Post,* and about her investments. Once, he asked Graham and her close personal adviser, Frederick Beebe, if they needed tax shelters. Relates Graham: "I was so naive at that point that after we left, I said, 'What's a tax shelter?' " She gave Lazard half her personal portfolio—outside her *Post* holdings—to manage. "It did OK. Nothing spectacular, but I think they did pretty well with it," she says. When the *Post,* after much soul-searching by Graham, went public in 1971, Lazard managed the offering. Aware of the Graham family's concern about losing control of the company, Meyer set up a system of "A" and "B" shares, with the family holding most of the "A" shares—which had all the voting power. Says *Washington Post* director Richard Paget, "The way he's got it set up, *nobody* can take the company over."

In many ways, Meyer played the role of mother hen for Kay Graham and her family. He was irate when one of the country's most successful private investors, Warren Buffet, took a substantial position in *Post* shares. As someone who had done that sort of thing himself, Meyer was naturally suspicious of Buffet's motives. "André thought he was one of these guys who was out there with a scalpel," says Paget.

"André kept warning me about Warren Buffet," recalls Graham. "He regarded all people who bought into companies uninvited as threats. But I checked Warren out rather carefully and decided that we were quite lucky, in that he was a very hands-off and honorable man." Graham, in fact, wound up inviting Buffet onto the board and has enjoyed an amicable relationship with him ever since. Meyer, however, continued to twit her on the subject. "How is your boss?" he would ask her.

Meyer also served as an avuncular adviser to Graham's children. He was especially close to her daughter, Elizabeth "Lally" Weymouth, a free-lance writer, and would regale her for hours with his life story. Once he settled a serious row between Weymouth and the rest of the family over her reservations about her brother Donald's ability to run the Post Company. When Donald became increasingly influential in corporate affairs, she threatened to sell her stock, but Meyer stepped in and calmed her down. According to a close family friend, "She went to talk to Mr. Meyer, and that clinched it. He told her not to sell. He was the determining voice in that decision."

Meyer's protectiveness toward the Grahams reached its peak during the period when the *Post* was making its sensational Watergate disclosures. Graham remembers that "he didn't much understand what we were doing, because most European people didn't, and he was pretty sympathetic to Nixon and indeed had given a large sum in that [1972] campaign. And I think he was worried about me and the paper."

One day he summoned her to the Carlyle. "Be very careful not to be alone," he told her. "Come on, André," she said, "you're joking." "No, I'm not joking," Meyer insisted. "I am telling you seriously, be very careful about yourself."

"He was worried about my personal safety," relates Graham. "And he obviously knew *something.*"

Graham was never physically threatened. And she never did find out where and how Meyer obtained his information.

Jane Engelhard's life was torn apart twice. And both times, André Meyer was there to help her put it back together.

The first time was in 1939. The tall, striking daughter of a Brazilian diplomat, she had just been married, at twenty-one, to one of the world's leading financiers, Fritz Mannheimer. On their wedding day, Mannheimer suffered a heart attack; eight weeks later, another heart attack killed him. He was forty-nine. The day after he died, the bank he ran, Mendelssohn & Company, collapsed. Bewildered, in need of help, financial and otherwise, she turned to André Meyer.

With Meyer's help, she made her way in the business world. For a time she worked for John J. Raskob, the General Motors and Du Pont magnate. Then she operated a microfilm library that copied

U.S. war records and material for the Library of Congress. Not long after the war ended, she met Charles Engelhard, the high-spirited heir to a precious-metals company founded and run by his father. In 1947 they were married.

As the years went by, Charlie Engelhard's business empire prospered, with no small amount of assistance from André Meyer. Charlie and Jane became social mainstays of three continents, throwing lavish parties for Lynda Bird Johnson, Ethel Kennedy, and other luminaries in one of their many grand homes. Jane was a fixture on the lists of the Ten Best-Dressed Women and was known in New York society as "Our Mother Superior." In 1968, when *Vogue* magazine wanted to know, "What are the Beautiful People doing?" it went to Jane Engelhard for the answer. Charlie, meanwhile, built one of the world's biggest racing stables, investing over $15 million in thoroughbred horses.

Then in 1971, at age fifty-four, Charlie Engelhard died. Once again, Jane was adrift, this time with five young daughters to worry about. And once more, she turned to André Meyer for help.

With Meyer by her side, she sorted out her husband's complex estate. "The advice André gave her was mostly financial," says Fred Wilson, himself a close friend of the Engelhards. "He recommended lawyers, and whatever talents she happened to need. But he also advised her on family matters." Meyer's close, confidential relationship with the oldest daughter, Annette, in particular, became virtually a carbon copy of the one he had with Lally Weymouth. As a friend puts it, "I never heard Annette refer to anyone with such reverence."

Jane's dependence on Meyer increased, rather than lessened, over the years—though not without a few minor instances of rebellion. Meyer would lay down rules for her to follow, and she would say, in a naughty-little-girl voice, "Well, I'm not going to do *that.*" She insisted, for example, on keeping her husband's stable of racehorses, much to Meyer's obvious annoyance. Relates Fred Wilson, "André advised her to sell the stable each time she saw him after Charlie died. He thought it was wasteful, that she was pouring her money down the drain. The horses just didn't fit André's sense of discipline."

But Jane kept the horses. And the stable ended up making more money for her than all the carefully screened, shrewdly thought-out investments that André Meyer put her into. "Charlie," Fred Wilson notes with a trace of awe, "had a touch for horses, just as he had a touch for gold."

* * *

André Meyer also made some friends in the U.S. Senate. One was Jacob Javits, the senior senator from New York. Javits regarded Meyer as "one of the important personalities of my life" and would visit the financier at the Carlyle every three weeks or so. Sometimes they would talk about the world's finances, and sometimes they would talk about Javits's own.

Meyer persuaded Javits to invest in Lazard's new real estate investment vehicle, Corporate Property Investors. "It took a while, but that one turned out very very well," says the senator. Meyer steered European business clients, such as France's Machines Bull, to Javits's law firm. He was one of five Javits friends who put up between $10,000 and $20,000 apiece to help finance the research and writing of the senator's memoirs. He even backed a play that Javits's wife Marion was producing.

Meyer, in turn, acquainted Javits with *his* problems, such as legislation affecting the investment business. "I gave him the benefit of my thinking from the Washington point of view," explains Javits. "We spent many warm and happy hours in this pursuit."

Meyer's relationship with the senior senator of Illinois, Charles Percy, went even farther back than his friendship with Javits. The banker and Percy had first become acquainted in the mid-fifties, when Percy was the ambitious young chief executive of Bell & Howell. Percy wanted to resuscitate Bell & Howell by buying a film manufacturer, and the company he had his eye on was Ansco, a division of General Aniline & Film. But a rather daunting obstacle stood in his way: General Aniline had been seized as German property by the U.S. government during the Second World War, and the government still hadn't decided when and how it would dispose of the property. What's more, the fledgling industrialist would have to contend with wily, well-connected Sidney Weinberg, who was pressing the government to simply sell all of General Aniline in a big public share offering—managed, naturally, by Weinberg's firm, Goldman, Sachs.

So what Percy needed, most of all, was an investment banker who was, as he put it, "Just as smart as, if not even smarter than, Sidney Weinberg." He phoned his banker for advice. And the banker, David Rockefeller, put him in touch with Meyer.

Percy went over to Meyer's office late one afternoon to explain the situation. So engrossed did the two men become that soon the room was virtually pitch-black; they had forgotten to turn any lamps on. As they talked in the darkness, Meyer began spinning out his strategy. First, he told Percy, they would have to hire the best lawyers they could find; maybe Sullivan & Cromwell. Then they would have to line up a company in a position to absorb General Aniline's chemical business, since the film division surely would not be sold alone. And, finally, they would have to expand Bell & Howell to make it big enough to swallow Ansco. And that meant Meyer's favorite expedient: acquiring other companies.

Percy followed Meyer's advice to the letter. He hired Sullivan & Cromwell, lined up Dow Chemical to take over the chemical business, and went on an acquisition spree that built Bell & Howell from a company with $13 million in sales to one pulling in revenues of $700 million. The expansion helped Percy achieve his ultimate goal, which was to diversify Bell & Howell away from the photographic-equipment area, where it was most vulnerable to foreign competition. Yet, ironically, by the time Percy achieved this, he was no longer interested in Ansco. "Government ownership had so debilitated General Aniline that it wasn't worth the kind of money that would have to be paid for it," notes Percy.

But, meanwhile, Meyer's strategy had helped Percy make his mark on American industry. Soon Percy was eyeing the U.S. Senate. He went to see Meyer about his Senate bid and found his old financier friend dead set against it. "Bell & Howell will fall apart if you leave," Meyer snapped at him. "It all depends on you. And if you do leave, then we will resign our seat on the board, and we will resign as investment bankers for Bell & Howell." Meyer said he had no faith in Percy's chosen successor, Peter Peterson. When Percy went ahead anyway, ran for the Senate and won, Meyer was true to his word. Lazard resigned from the board and resigned as the company's investment banker.

Meyer suddenly became very frosty to Chuck Percy. He told Percy he should never have left Bell & Howell to fool around with politics. But as time went on, Meyer became reconciled to Percy's new role. Eventually, he became one of his biggest boosters, contributing to his campaigns and telling Percy what the government needed was more people with a grounding in the business world.

And as Percy had foreseen, Peterson succeeded admirably at Bell & Howell. He even went into government himself, first as an assistant to President Nixon on international economic affairs, and then as commerce secretary. And when he decided to return to private life, one of the first to make him an offer was André Meyer of Lazard Frères. (Peterson chose to go to Lehman Brothers instead.)

"I think that was André's way of saying to me that maybe my judgment on Peterson was right, after all," says Percy. "Of course," he adds, "André never said it to me directly. André *never* acknowledged a mistake."

CHAPTER EIGHT

The Women in His Life

In the world that André Meyer was building for himself—the world of high-powered deal making and high-level friendships—Bella Meyer just didn't fit.

Despite her own semiaffluent upbringing, Bella never seemed quite able to acclimate herself to the *grande dame* role. It wasn't that the trappings of wealth didn't attract her—they did, up to a point. But she was never able to acquire that unerring, almost unconscious sense of the *right* thing to do and say and wear that people of easy affluence were supposed to have.

She would tell friends about the time she and André were invited to an affair at the David Rockefellers'. Bella was delighted; here was a chance to show herself off in a fancy designer dress, a chance to wear her most expensive jewelry. But when she arrived at the party, she was mortified to find the guests wearing the most dowdy clothes, while she stood out in all her overdressed splendor. Then, two weeks later, she was invited to a party at New York University thrown by the president, James Hester. (Her husband had become a major contributor to NYU.) It will be an intellectual gathering, Bella said to herself; she mustn't put on anything too showy. So she arrived in her simplest dress, and was shocked to find the most magnificent array of gowns and jewels she had ever seen in one room—while she, Bella Meyer, looked like something the cat had dragged in. "So you see," Bella would sigh, "I can't win."

Recalls Andrea Wilson, "She was full of stories like that. Once she met the Hesters at the airport, and they were all going to Paris on the same flight; and as they get to the plane she realizes that the Hesters are flying first-class and she's flying tourist. So on the return trip back to New York she decided to change her ticket from tourist to first-class; and as she was at the Paris airport, about to leave, she bumped into one of the Rothschilds, who was on the same flight. And Bella said, 'It's marvelous, we can talk together on the plane.' And the

Rothschild said, 'But listen, I'm not flying first-class; I'm flying tourist, because these flights are usually empty and you can lie down and sleep across three seats.' So Bella thought that was very intelligent, and she went back to tourist the next time she flew. And that's when she ran into the Hesters *again* at the airport, again flying first-class."

"So you see," Bella would say again, "I can't win."

In her husband's presence, she never played, nor sought to play, any role but that of the old-fashioned, dutiful French wife, staying discreetly in the background, emerging from the shadows only when she was summoned. "I didn't get to know Bella for years," observes Katharine Graham, "because when I would see André, she would be sort of kept out of sight. It was only after I began meeting her at dinner parties that I started to seek her out. Then later, the more I got to know André, the more I went to the apartment, the more I got to see Bella. And the more I saw Bella, the more I loved her. But I had to seek her out.

"She would be so tough and warm and wonderful in enduring this business of being dismissed when I would be there. And I would always try to not have that happen. But she was so tactful. If she thought he wanted to talk to you alone, she'd disappear."

Yet for all her reticence and uneasiness, Bella could hardly be considered a washed-out old *hausfrau*, minding the stew while husband was in the front room entertaining visiting dignitaries. To begin with, she retained her classic, aristocratic beauty, ravishing even in middle age. Furthermore, she was notably undomestic. "I don't think she ever cooked a meal in her life," says one woman who knew her well.

What her quiet, self-effacing demeanor masked was an iron determination that was every bit a match for her husband's. During the latter stages of the Second World War, she enlisted in the WACs (along with daughter Francine), mainly so the story goes, because she wanted to see her son Philippe, who was fighting for the Free French somewhere in Alsace. Philippe remembers well the call he got on the field phone from his cousin Michel Weill, who was in the same division. "I have a package for you," Weill told him. When Philippe came by later to pick it up, there was Bella.

Realizing that in her husband's world she would always be in the background, she worked hard to carve out a large measure of independence for herself. While he was going about his business in New York, she would spend at least six months a year in Europe. Part of the time she stayed at the house they had bought in the Swiss mountain resort of Crans-sur-Sierre, where she would indulge in all the diversions her husband shunned: swimming, golfing, rolling around town in her Fiat 600. The rest of the time she spent in Paris, first at hotels, then in an apartment they rented on the Quai des Orfèvres, overlooking the Seine. She had her own friends, her own whirl of activities—in short, her own world.

Bella had little reason to hurry back home. Obsessive about his work, incurably restless, her husband left little time for quiet, intimate moments *à deux*. There was never *any* time for vacations. In the early years in New York, some distraction was provided by the country house in Ossining, where on a sunny summer weekend, Meyer would imitate a suburban bourgeois and don a chef's apron to barbecue some steaks. But after he gave up the house, his life in the city became almost exclusively centered on his office at 44 Wall Street and his home at the Carlyle. For Bella, a vigorous woman with a love of outdoor sports, it was a stultifying existence.

When she was with André, she also had to put up with the relentless outpourings of nervous energy, which often took the form of chronic hypochondria. He constantly complained about his intestines and his stomach, and visited a doctor almost every week. Wherever he went, he left a trail of expended pill bottles. "His collection of pills and medications of many kinds was about the largest I've ever seen," says Fred Wilson. "He had certain pills for certain times of the day, and they were always lying around on his desk." Some of his colleagues, awed by his hyperactivity, were convinced that a few of those pills must have been amphetamines.

And if all that wasn't enough to justify Bella's semi-independent life-style, there was something else. The other women in André Meyer's life.

"Oh, yes, André had a wandering eye," says one of his oldest and dearest friends. "And he made no secret of it. Even to his wife. They were almost members of the family. It was taken for granted. If the women wanted it, and he wanted it, and Bella didn't object—who could make a big deal out of it?"

If the situation sounds terribly Gallic, it was. There was no slinking about, no surreptitious rendezvous, none of the sinister intrigue that surrounds most Americans' extramarital relationships. Everything was very much out in the open: even the women's husbands knew and didn't make a scene. And while these relationships may have caused Bella a certain amount of inner anguish (as some of her friends surmise), she never allowed her facade of quiet dignity to crack. Not only was she totally forgiving, but over the years she herself became fast friends with these women.

"Sometimes my mother learned to live with it, and sometimes she didn't," reflects Philippe Meyer. "She saw through my father completely; nothing he did surprised her. But she knew she was important to him; she knew she was the most important thing in his life. And that was enough for her to put up with all that."

Yet to hear André Meyer himself tell the tale, it was hardly a one-way street. He would confide to friends that Bella had caused him "much suffering" when he was preoccupied with building his career in the thirties. As one old friend of theirs delicately puts it, "They were not so very happy together in those days. She was a beautiful woman, and naturally many men courted her. And she was easily fascinated by the people she met. I believe he suffered a great deal because of that." There were whispers in later years about Bella's affairs; certainly, for someone who spent so much time apart from her husband, such adventures were not beyond the realm of possibility. But, this friend adds with a vocal flourish, "André loved her, eh? He loved her a great deal. He loved her despite all."

Whether he pursued other women to get back at Bella's own indiscretions or, as is more likely, because of his evergreen interest in the opposite sex, Meyer displayed the same impeccable taste in women that he showed in his selection of artwork. The women he surrounded himself with, on both the intimate and platonic levels, were invariably beautiful, talented, cultured, and for the most part strong-willed. Dumb blondes were not his style—much as he might appreciate their architecture.

Meyer's extramarital exploits began not long after he arrived in the United States, determined to carve out a new career for himself. During the war years he became intimate with Claude Alphand, the vivacious, ever so slightly bohemian wife of a rising young French diplomat, Hervé Alphand. Alphand had been financial attaché to the French embassy in Washington at the time of France's fall to the Nazis, and he promptly resigned to take a high position with the Free French in London, leaving his wife and mother-in-law behind in New York to fend for themselves. To make ends meet, Claude—who struck some as a Marlene Dietrich look-alike—began singing at the

Blue Angel and other New York nightclubs. Accompanying herself on a white guitar, crooning old, sad French songs, she was an accomplished *chanteuse* when she met André Meyer.

Their relationship soon became, in one New York socialite's words, *"very* common knowledge." Even after the war, when Madame Alphand rejoined her husband in Paris, their liaison apparently continued. Yet somehow during that period Hervé Alphand and Meyer became fast friends, with Alphand becoming part of the circle of French diplomats whom Meyer cultivated after the war. Meyer's relationship with Madame Alphand—which Hervé almost certainly was aware of—was never allowed to become an obstacle.

Nonetheless, strains began to arise in the Alphands' marriage, and in the late fifties they were divorced. Hervé, who by then was France's ambassador to Washington, remarried shortly afterward, and he and his new wife Nicole went on to become leading social figures of Kennedy-era Washington. Claude, meanwhile, resettled for a time in New York, began a decorating business, and became a fixture at the Carlyle. A thin woman with very long hair and very long legs, dressed in a black skirt, black tights, and boots, she seemed to have stepped straight out of a Toulouse-Lautrec painting. Amid the stuffy surroundings, she was a welcome—if unexpected—bit of French *insouciance.* Funny, sarcastic, zipping from one subject to the next, she would drape one long leg over a chair arm while munching on raspberries and wonder aloud, "How can I make a whole meal out of just berries?" She had never learned English, even during her brief stint as ambassadress to Washington, and would proclaim that the only way she could pick up the language would be to drive across the country in an ambulance with a driver who would speak nothing but English to her. Needless to say, she was a fountain of decorating tips; she would stride into the living room and tell Meyer what he *must* have was a couch here and a certain color there and another color someplace else.

And Meyer lapped it up. "She would get away with it because he adored her. Absolutely adored her," says his granddaughter, Marianne Gerschel. "She was just bohemian enough to appeal to his own sense of creativity. He enjoyed that in a woman." To those who were treated to this spectacle, it was not hard to draw the conclusion, as one friend did, that "Claude was the great love of André's life."

Not that there weren't others in the running. One very close relationship was with another French émigré, Henriette Bloch, who first met Meyer in the thirties when they belonged to the same Reform temple in Paris. A blond woman with pipestem legs and a birdlike voice, she was physically similar to Claude Alphand, though she lacked Claude's helter-skelter radiance. Like Claude, she was married when her relationship with Meyer first blossomed, to a quiet, pipe-puffing man named Maurice. And like Hervé Alphand before him, Maurice docilely accepted his wife's attachment to Meyer. "I think my grandfather was the one true man in her life," says Marianne Gerschel. "As far as she was concerned, he could do no wrong." This relationship, however, didn't prevent Mme. Bloch from becoming close to Bella as well; in fact, in later years she was one of Bella's closest friends. That was the way life was in the Meyer household.

The Meyers were once having dinner with Fred and Andrea Wilson when the subject of one of Ned Herzog's ex-wives came up. Bella said, "You know, we were *so* shocked when she wrote to André in Paris that she and Ned were getting divorced. She couldn't stay with him. There was no particular fight, but he *crushed* her personality." And André repeated, "Yes, he *crushed* her personality." Andrea Wilson stared hard at him and said, "And you've *never* done that." Several seconds of silence followed, and then, Wilson remembers, "he looked at me and laughed. Because if anyone ever crushed other people's personalities, it was André."

Few individuals felt this force as acutely as Meyer's own children. "For me, it was a great struggle," confesses Philippe Meyer, "because obviously he was a brilliant man, with great personality and force. And either you are completely crushed by him, or you fight to retain your own identity. Certainly my personality was forged in large part by my resisting being imposed upon by him. I could say that some of the best things I am I owe to this struggle against being crushed."

Where Meyer most tried to dominate Philippe was in his choice of a career. Like many a traditional European banker before him, Meyer nurtured dreams of creating a dynasty—which, by the very act of self-perpetuation, would uphold the worthiness of its founder's life. His whole career, it could be said, was played out in the shadow of such dynasties: the Rothschilds, the Lehmans, and most notably the David-Weills. To build a generational chain that would rival them—nothing he could do would matter as much.

But the first link in that chain, Philippe, would have no part of it. Philippe wanted to make a career in physics, not in banking, and nothing his father did could persuade him otherwise. "He made it clear to me," recalls Philippe, "that it was a disappointment to him, and he made it clear that it would give him great joy if I followed him into banking." Only after his son graduated from Harvard with a degree in physics in 1947 did Meyer begin to reconcile himself to the situation. Occasionally he would try to nudge Philippe, but his son says, "I never gave him the impression that I hesitated. And I think my very firm choice didn't leave him with any illusions that the subject was worth pursuing."

As Philippe rose in his chosen field, becoming a professor at France's prestigious École Normale et Supérieure, Meyer's earlier chagrin was displaced by a certain parental pride. "At first André had a bad reaction," comments French industrialist Francis Fabre, "but afterward he came to admire his son. He was very much impressed by the choice the boy had made *not* to be a banker, not to be interested in money, and he was fascinated by his cleverness in science. For him, his son was a terrific fellow."

Over time, in fact, Philippe became something of a confidant of his father. "He talked to me a lot about what he was doing, his business," the son says. "He liked me to be present when important people came to visit him." He even entrusted his son with the greatest secret of all: the sources, the nature, and the extent of his wealth. True, there were times when Meyer's underlying sadness about the course of events would come to the surface—such as his references to Felix Rohatyn as an "adopted son," leaving no doubt in the listener's mind that Rohatyn was fulfilling the role Meyer had once envisioned for Philippe. And the great balancing act—maintaining his independence, while avoiding an acrimonious rift with his volatile parent—remained a full-time struggle for Philippe. "Very few people have succeeded in resisting him and yet keeping with him a very good and very fond relationship," the son says. "It is very hard for an outsider to understand how difficult it was to keep these two things together."

In many ways, Philippe fared far better in that respect than his sister Francine. A year older than her brother, Francine seemed, at least temperamentally, to have much more in common with her father. Whereas Philippe is professorial in demeanor, with an air of inner calm and a reticence to speak in tones louder than a whisper, Francine is nervous, bellicose, and given to open, overwhelming displays of emotion.

Francine's emotional ties to her father were, if anything, even stronger than her brother's. According to her daughter Marianne, "The one true love of my mother's life was her father." But in her search for his approval and affection, Francine found herself competing not only with her brother—who early on, in a fit of sibling pique, she concluded was the favored one in the family—but with Bella as well. "Quite frankly, I think my grandmother was jealous of my mother," says Marianne, "jealous of the love my grandfather had for her. So my grandmother tried to get her way by being beautiful, and my grandmother was so terribly beautiful that she always held one's attention. My mother responded by taking the other tack: 'OK, I'll be showy and I'll like jewelry and I'll laugh loudly, and I'll get attention that way.' "

During her wartime stint in the WACs with Bella, Francine found another way to catch her father's eye: she brought home a young Frenchman she intended to marry. The man, Marc Gerschel, was a resistance fighter who had been captured by the Germans, escaped, and then made his way to London to join the Free French. He was wandering around Marks and Spencer one day, totally confused, when he bumped into Francine, who offered to translate for the befuddled soldier.

Gerschel had grown up in the seaport town of Calais, and when his relationship with Francine developed, he was still very much a small-town boy. He hadn't the slightest idea of the family he was marrying into until, one day, he, Francine, and Bella revisited the Meyers' old Paris apartment, just after the city was liberated by the Allies. While they were inspecting the place, someone rang the doorbell; when Gerschel opened it, he found himself face to face with a man asking, "Is this the Banque Lazard?" Gerschel told him no, but then Francine came to the door and began talking to the gentleman. Bewildered, Gerschel turned to her afterward and asked, "What do you have to do with the Banque Lazard?" When she told him, he was flabbergasted.

Still, the full scope of the world he was entering didn't dawn on Marc Gerschel until their return to the United States on a troopship, when a private boat suddenly pulled alongside in Boston harbor to take him, Francine, and Bella into port. The boat, Francine gently explained, had been dispatched by her father. Then there was their arrival in New York. While other soldiers were coming home to their old family walk-up apartments, Gerschel settled into the Carlyle Hotel, partaking of the sumptuous bed and board of the head of Lazard, who told the dazed young man he should consider entering Harvard Business School.

It was all too much for Gerschel. He and Francine were married and had three children, Patrick, Laurent, and Marianne, but by the time the third arrived in 1950, the marriage was over. Meyer was furious; he had checked the young man out, was told he was a war hero, and assumed from that the marriage would be all right. Now he had on his hands a husbandless daughter with three small children and an ex-son-in-law who was constantly pestering Francine for visitation rights. Francine didn't want Gerschel around, and so Meyer, ever the deal-maker, devised a solution. He would find Gerschel a position in a perfume factory—in Brazil. Gerschel, who needed the job, went, but after two years or so he was back in France, unemployed and destitute. For the father of André Meyer's grandchildren, this wouldn't do at all, and so Meyer arranged a low-level job for Gerschel at a Lazard subsidiary in Paris. Gerschel worked the rest of his career there, meanwhile settling down with a new wife in a tiny apartment financed by his ex-father-in-law. Once he had been caught in the Meyer family web, Gerschel could never quite make his way out.

Francine, meanwhile, also remarried, to a French diplomat, Michel de Camaret. Once again, her father went to great lengths to check the suitor out, calling up his many French government contacts to find out more about him. And once again, despite these precautions, the marriage broke up. After the breakup, Francine clung more than ever to her father for support. Yet as helpful as Meyer was, he never took his daughter seriously; his world, after all, was largely a man's world, and in that world, as Marianne Gerschel puts it, "You don't exist unless you're showy or unless you have money, because the money—it gets confused with the power."

Meyer still treated Francine like a wayward teenager, and Francine rebelled with a teenager's petulance. They would frequently have embarrassingly loud arguments in public, and those who spent time with the two were often shocked at the sheer nastiness of their relationship. At dinner parties, within earshot of her father, Francine would tell her companions, "That father of mine is no good. He has no love or affection. He's a crook, a thief, and a terrible father." Meyer would then tell her to shut up.

"Obviously to outsiders sitting in a restaurant or even friends who came and went, this looked rather peculiar," admits Marianne. "But it's really very understandable. You know, all my mother was asking for was attention. I mean, that's all it was. Her anger was that of somebody desperately trying to be her own person, trying desperately to grow up with a very strong father and a mother who didn't have much patience for her."

Unlike her brother, Francine did not have the inner fiber to break away from her father and yet remain on good terms with him. For her, the dependence was total, and so was the anger.

CHAPTER NINE

The Avis Saga

In 1955, a Memphis, Tennessee, homebuilder named Kemmons Wilson was searching for seed money to finance a small chain of motels he was planning to open. He made his way to a convention of young company presidents in Georgia and there bumped into Roger Kyes, the head of General Motors' Frigidaire division. Kyes greeted him warmly, as well he might; Wilson had bought plenty of refrigerators from Frigidaire over the years. "How are you doing?" Kyes asked. "I'm doing great," Wilson answered, "But I need money." Kyes thought for a second and then said, "I'm going up to New York tomorrow morning to meet with André Meyer. Why don't you come along?"

So the next morning Wilson and his wife boarded Kyes's corporate DC-3 for the flight to New York. A few hours later the young man from Memphis found himself in the Carlyle Hotel, telling his story to an owlish, bespectacled Frenchman. Meyer was interested in what Wilson had to say, and he suggested that Wilson come back the next day (Sunday morning) to meet with some of his associates. Wilson did so and told his story once more. Finally, Meyer asked, "How much money do you need?" Oh, about $2.5 million, Wilson replied. "You've got it," said Meyer. As Wilson recalls the scene, "He stuck his hand out. I stuck out mine. It was a deal."

What Meyer then did was sell $2.5 million worth of convertible debentures in Wilson's new motel company to the U.S. Steel pension fund. As his fee for the deal, Meyer kept $250,000 worth of those convertible debentures, for which he paid nothing. After a short while he converted the debentures into common stock of the company, and around 1960, when the company was just starting to prosper, he sold the stock for a modest sum. Explains one of his Lazard colleagues: "He thought the hotel business had peaked."

The company was Holiday Inns.

Two conclusions can be drawn from this episode. First, that

André Meyer played a vital role in launching the world's biggest lodging chain, one of the greatest corporate success stories of the postwar period. As Kemmons Wilson points out, "He got me the first real money I ever had. It got the company on the road." And second, that Meyer once again cashed in his chips too soon, missing out on most of the company's spectacular growth. In 1962 there were 275 Holiday Inns, all in the United States and Canada; today there are 1,750 on every continent except Antarctica. Once more, as was the case with Warner-Lambert, Meyer's bird-in-the-hand instincts prevailed. "You know the story in the Bible, where if you look back over your shoulder, you turn into a pillar of salt?" reflects a former Lazard partner. "That's the way André saw it."

Meyer's quick disposal of the shares would have been more understandable if he had simply been a silent, passive investor. But the fact was that Lazard paid considerable attention to Holiday Inns, helping with its early financial planning and coming up with various financing schemes. According to an ex-Lazard partner, "Wilson would come in and tell André, 'I'm just a poor country boy. I don't understand what you're doing. And, oh, by the way, we do hope to have these inns throughout Europe.' "

Nowhere were these conflicting traits of Meyer's—the unique insight into opportunities, and the wariness about seeing them through—more apparent than in the saga of the Avis Rent-a-Car Company.

Warren Avis was a Ford dealer in Detroit at the end of the Second World War, which was a very good time to be a car dealer. Automobiles, after all, were in short supply in an economy that was geared to wartime production; cars were so scarce that some dealers were even bootlegging them at substantially more than suggested list prices. But Avis had a better idea: he would use his coveted fleet of Fords to set up a rent-a-car company. In 1947, Warren Avis opened a rent-a-car counter at the old Willow Run Airport in Detroit; it was believed to be the first time anyone had ever rented automobiles at an airport (Hertz didn't start airport car rental until 1952, at Chicago's Midway Field).

With the Willow Run business booming, Avis began scouting other locations across the country and in short order had exclusive airport franchises in Miami, San Francisco, and Los Angeles. Soon he was blanketing the country with Avis franchises, at a time when

Hertz, which was then owned by General Motors, was dead on its feet. But by this time the business was getting too big for Warren Avis. When an eager buyer named Richard Robie came calling in 1954, Avis snapped up his offer and left the car-rental field.

The years that followed were not kind to the Avis Rent-a-Car Company. General Motors finally unloaded Hertz, selling it to the Omnibus Company, a bus-fleet owner, in 1953, and Hertz responded with a burst of energy that saw it totally outdistance its rivals in size and in revenues. The president of Hertz loftily dismissed the competition as "crabgrass; it dies out in one place, and springs up in another. It doesn't bother you." The auto-rental business was changing, with the old jerrybuilt franchise operations supplanted by huge networks of offices owned by the car-rental companies themselves. By 1960, when an antitrust decree finally slowed its expansion, Hertz had acquired most of the high-traffic offices and garages in major markets.

In this superheated environment, Avis posted one losing year after another; in fact, the only profitable year it had since 1949 was because of a change in accounting rules. The ownership shifted again in 1956, and Avis became the property of former New Haven Railroad president Frederic C. "Buck" Dumaine, Jr., who promptly appointed his son-in-law president. Dumaine didn't have any better ideas about how to save the foundering company than his predecessors had had, and the red ink flowed on, with annual losses reaching $1.2 million by 1961. The gap between number-one Hertz and number-two Avis yawned wider and wider, with Hertz bringing in revenues of $138 million in 1961 against a mere $24 million for struggling Avis.

In the New York offices of the Kinney System, Inc., meanwhile, Kinney boss Edward Rosenthal was mounting his own small challenge to Hertz. Kinney had gone into car rentals in the mid-fifties, as a bizarre sideline to its basic business, which was the Riverside Memorial Chapel chain of funeral homes. After all, Rosenthal already had a fleet of limousines—why not rent some of them out? Later, the enterprising Rosenthal began dovetailing the car-rental operation with the network of parking lots he had also built up in Manhattan. He offered free parking for Kinney rental cars in Kinney parking lots, a promotion that was far less generous than it seemed, since most people who rent cars in Manhattan use them to get out of town immediately. But, illusory as it was, the offer did bring the customers in.

The business did so well that by mid-1961 Rosenthal found himself in desperate need of more cars. He approached Hertz about buying some of its fleet, and when Hertz turned him down, he approached Avis. Avis was considerably more openhanded; Rosenthal was told by Avis executive vice-president Winston "Bud" Morrow that not only could he buy cars, he could buy the whole company.

Intrigued, Rosenthal talked the matter over with his son-in-law and business associate, Steven Ross. They had never acquired anything bigger than funeral homes and parking lots before and concluded they needed an investment banker. Rosenthal and Ross approached David Sarnoff, whose nephew worked for them at Kinney. "Get in the car," snapped Sarnoff. "I will take you down to see André Meyer."

Meyer heard them out and agreed to represent Kinney. But after several months of negotiations and study, Ross backed off. He felt Avis was too big, and the risk too great, for Kinney to swallow. Meyer and Felix Rohatyn (who by then had been brought into the talks) discussed the situation and, late in 1961, called Ross back. If you're not interested in it, they told him, do you mind if we buy Avis ourselves? Ross said he didn't.

(A postscript is in order here. The same Steven Ross who was so nervous about acquiring little Avis later went on to buy Warner Brothers and numerous other companies. Today the company isn't called Kinney Services; it's Warner Communications. And Steve Ross is one of America's most prominent corporate jet-setters. He also is no longer Eddie Rosenthal's son-in-law.)

Both Rohatyn and Meyer knew they were going out on a limb in buying the car-rental company. For Meyer, there was more than money at stake. For the first time, he was getting himself involved in a consumer product or service whose success or failure would be a matter of public scrutiny. Up to then he had only invested in companies that were obscure (even Holiday Inns was when he first moved into it) or else relatively uninteresting to the general public. But Avis—in the words of one Lazard partner, "It's different to buy a mine somewhere, and if it doesn't work out you sell it, and nobody knows the difference. But when you are renting automobiles at airports, I mean, some friend of André's is going to rent a car next week and she's going to come back and tell him what she thinks. And if the service is lousy, boy, he's going to hear about it."

(Not that the Avis experience changed Meyer's basic attitude toward highly publicized businesses. When, for example, he was approached about buying the Long Island newspaper *Newsday* in the 1960s, he turned it down flat. Being in the newspapers was bad enough, but *owning* one . . .)

Rohatyn's risk, if anything, was even greater than Meyer's. Though he was already in his early thirties, Rohatyn was still regarded as one of Meyer's flunkies, a bright young man the boss took along to meetings because, as Meyer put it, "he knows how to use a slide rule." Yet here was Rohatyn stepping out of his yes-man role and enthusiastically urging Meyer to buy the company. "Felix," notes one Lazard partner, "stuck his neck way out on this one."

Before he would go that far, however, Rohatyn wanted to be sure he and Meyer knew what they were doing. What they needed was someone with broad experience in the car-rental business, someone who could help them evaluate the dangers as well as the potential rewards. It didn't take Rohatyn long to conclude that the man he was looking for was Donald Petrie. Petrie, a fast-talking attorney with a hard New York edge to his voice, had all the right credentials: he was executive vice-president and chief operating officer of Hertz until 1960, when he became president of the joint international car-rental venture of Hertz and American Express. What's more, he was available, having left Hertz in January 1962 to go back to the practice of law in Mineola, Long Island.

"I got a call one day," relates Petrie. "It was from Felix Rohatyn. I had never heard of Felix Rohatyn. The firm is Lazard Frères. I never heard of Lazard Frères. He says, 'Mr. André Meyer would like to meet you.' Well, I never heard of André Meyer, either. So I said fine, how do I do that? 'You come to the Carlyle,' Felix says.

"So I go to the Carlyle. And since I'd never heard of him and I'd never heard of Lazard, I thought he was a guest, and I went and asked for his room number. And they said, 'No, no, no, you go up to the thirty-third floor.' So I went up and a man in a white coat took me into one room, sat me down, and I waited there for a while. And I looked on the wall, and there was a Manet and a Monet and a Corot and a Seurat. And I thought, 'Gee, this guy's a print nut. He's got beautiful prints.' Then they took me out and they put me in another room, and there was a Picasso and a Renoir. And so I went up and I felt one of them. I remember saying, 'Holy Christ, these things are real. Whoever this guy is, he's not kidding!' "

Meyer and Rohatyn then entered the room and explained their dilemma to Petrie. They had a ninety-day option to buy Avis, and after sixty days of studying it, moaned Meyer, "Nobody can explain to me how the business works." Would Petrie be willing to act as a consultant? Petrie said he would.

For the next thirty days Petrie gave Meyer and Rohatyn a crash course in the essentials of the car-rental business. And as Meyer turned those elements over in his mind, he deliberately veered away from a discussion of Avis's balance sheet, preferring to dwell instead on far more basic issues. Is there a real *need* for this kind of company, he asked Petrie over and over? How does it fit in with changing social and business patterns in the United States? What kind of people do you need to manage it? Recounts Petrie, "I don't think he ever asked me, 'How soon will it be before Avis is in the black?' "

Out of all this professorial probing came one hard conclusion: society did need rental cars, and the ability to fly into any airport in the United States and pick up a car there would be a permanent fixture of business travel. But then Petrie gently suggested to Meyer that he had to decide for himself whether there was going to be a travel recession; if he believed there would be a sharp downturn in air traffic, he better not invest in Avis. (At the time, Avis was almost totally dependent on airport rentals.) Meyer thought it over and decided there wouldn't be a downturn; even though the economy might be wobbly, businessmen, he reasoned, would still travel. Then there was the question of capital. Petrie told Meyer that aside from the $5 million or so that would be needed to buy control of the company, he would have to put in another $5 million, mainly to update the Avis fleet. Meyer didn't blink. If that's what was needed to turn the company around, then he would put up the money.

Meyer was plainly sold on Avis. The company, he was convinced, was a lot stronger than it looked. As he put it one day to a Lazard colleague, "Can you think of a company that badly run that hasn't sunk? It must have *some* internal strength." The company's mere survival spoke volumes for its potential.

Finally, Meyer had to grapple with the problem of who was going to run Avis. Meyer asked Petrie to do it, but Petrie, unwilling to return full-time to the car-rental business, declined. "But you know," Petrie told Meyer and Rohatyn, "nobody's asked me the next question." "What's that?" they said. "The next question is, do I know any-body who can run Avis?" "OK," said Rohatyn, "I'll ask you. Who should be president?" Petrie didn't hesitate. "Robert C. Townsend should be president," he said.

Townsend, at that point, was one of the top officers of the Ameri-can Express Company. Petrie had come to know him during the pe-riod he managed the Hertz-American Express joint venture, when Townsend functioned as a sort of Amex overseer of the operation. Petrie knew that Townsend was sprightly, energetic, and knowledge-able. He also knew he was disgruntled: Townsend had just lost out to Howard Clark in the battle for the American Express chairmanship.

The Avis job interested Townsend, especially since he would have the chance to become a substantial shareholder in the company. All that was left to discuss was his salary. Meyer offered him $50,000. Townsend turned it down. He wanted $36,000. "That is the top salary for a company that has never earned a nickel for its shareholders," he explained. *"D'accord,"* said André Meyer. It was his first glimpse of the way Townsend did business.

Townsend's involvement clinched the deal. On March 22, 1962, Lazard Frères and associates purchased a controlling interest in Avis—some 600,000 of the 1.3 million shares outstanding—for ap-proximately $5.5 million. And if there was any question about Meyer's high hopes for the enterprise, it was answered by the manner in which he structured the transaction. He formed a holding com-pany, Silver Gate Inc., to own the Avis shares, and invited many of his nearest and dearest friends to join him as shareholders. David Sarnoff was a Silver Gate shareholder. So were the Rockefellers. At-torney John Cahill was one. Even Anna Rosenberg Hoffman—for whom Meyer had refused deal participations in the past because he judged them too risky for her—was sold a piece. "Avis he felt was a sound investment," says Hoffman, who ended up owning close to 9,000 Avis shares. "If you looked at the company, you knew that with good management they'd be making money."

Meyer also invited, as reciprocation for past favors, his coven-turers: Lou Green, Arthur Ross, and, of course, Ferdinand Eberstadt. But Eberstadt declined; he had just had a falling-out with his key in-vestment-banking partners, and they were about to leave his firm to form their own banking outfit. Without anyone around to work on the Avis deal, and having made up his mind to get out of the invest-ment-banking business once and for all, he felt he had to say no.

Meyer's largesse didn't mean that he was trying to minimize his own involvement. In fact, he ended up owning, for himself or for family trusts, 266,000 Avis shares, well over a third of the total investment. What it did mean was that he was truly concerned about being accused later on of hogging a sure thing. For instance, he structured the deal so that Dumaine would remain a big shareholder, with Lazard holding options to purchase most of his shares over the next three years at ever-escalating prices. If Lazard exercised all those options, Dumaine would wind up making back all the money he had lost on Avis in previous years—although, to be sure, if Avis did really well, the stock would be worth far more than Lazard's option price. Meyer even went so far as to call Ed Rosenthal at the eleventh hour, offering him any part of the deal he wanted—even the whole thing. "We don't ever want to leave the impression of having taken it away from you," he told Rosenthal. But Rosenthal, once again, declined.

Of course, having effectively promised a sure thing, Meyer still had to deliver the goods. For that, he turned to Townsend and Petrie, who after much cajoling agreed to take on a part-time role at Avis, a role that increased considerably over the years.

Petrie remembers their first visit to Avis headquarters, which was then in Boston. "Buck Dumaine met us at the Eastern shuttle and drove us to the building, but didn't come in. I mean, these were his employees! And, at that point, the employees didn't even know the company had been sold. But I knew all these guys, Bud Morrow particularly, so I walked in with Townsend and met Bud, and he said, 'Hi, Don, what are you doing here?' And I said, 'Well, your company's just been sold, and here's your new president. Meet Mr. Bob Townsend.' "

That example of employee relations was typical of the way Avis had been run. "These people felt they were losers," says Petrie. "They were people who'd been consistently beaten every time they tried to get their heads above water. They were beaten by Hertz, and they needed a lot of attention." And if anyone was made to order for the task, it was Townsend.

By the time he arrived at Avis, Townsend had had his fill of the bureaucratic waste and organizational frou-frou that are the hallmarks of the modern American corporation. In Avis, he saw a chance to do things differently: to build a company where the term "delegation of authority" really meant something; where executives didn't hide behind their secretaries; where employees would be motivated not by brute force and stultifying rules but by the sheer enjoyment of their jobs and the chance to share in the profits they generated.

Years later, long after he had left Avis, Townsend expounded on these principles in his best seller *Up the Organization* (subtitled *How to Stop the Corporation from Stifling People and Strangling Profits*). The book, a freewheeling guerrilla guide for corporate managers, suggested such drastic measures as eliminating purchasing departments ("they cost ten dollars in zeal for every dollar they save in purchasing acumen") and getting rid of secretaries ("I got much closer to the people who reported to me when I didn't have a buffer state outside my office"). Much, but not all, of what Townsend proposed in his book was put into practice at Avis.

Townsend believed that by cutting back on memo writing, by delegating responsibilities to the lowest possible decision-making level, and by introducing a generous incentive-compensation system, based on the company's profits, he could turn Avis around. And he was right. As he comments in his book, "When I became head of Avis I was assured that no one at headquarters was any good, and that my first job was to start recruiting a whole new team. Three years later, Hal Geneen, the chairman of ITT (which had just acquired Avis), after meeting everybody and listening to them in action for a day, said, 'I've never seen such depth of management; why I've already spotted three chief executive officers!' You guessed it. Same people. I'd brought in only two new people, a lawyer and an accountant."

Even Townsend, though, had to admit that personnel motivation would take Avis only so far. If Avis was ever going to be anything but a poor also-ran in the car-rental business, it had to come up with an aggressive marketing strategy. On television and in print, Hertz was putting people "in the driver's seat"; what was Avis doing?

One Friday afternoon, Townsend, Petrie, and Rohatyn agreed that over the weekend each of them would come up with the names of three advertising agencies apiece. When they compared the lists on Monday, two names appeared on all three lists: Ogilvie & Mather and Doyle, Dane, Bernbach. To those agencies Townsend posed the following question: "How do we get five million dollars' worth of advertising for one million dollars?" (In other words, he wanted Avis's ad campaign to be as effective as that of Hertz, which had five times as much money to throw around.) William Bernbach, the head of DDB, had a ready answer: run our ads exactly as we write them, wherever we tell you to run them. "If you promise to run them just as we write them," said Bernbach, "you'll have every art director and copywriter in my shop moonlighting on your account." Townsend agreed.

As Townsend tells the story, "Ninety days later, Bill Bernbach came out to show Avis his recommended ads. He said he was sorry, but the only honest things they could say were that the company was second largest and that the people were trying harder. Bernbach said his own research department had advised against the ads, that he didn't like them very much himself—but it was all they had so he was recommending them. We didn't like them much at Avis, either, but we had agreed to run whatever Bill recommended.

"The rest," says Townsend, "is history."

America still had a passion for the underdog—1962 was also the year Casey Stengel's New York Mets began plucking the country's heartstrings. And when billboards, newspaper ads, and even buttons proclaimed, "We're Number Two. We Try Harder," people understood; after all, *they* were trying harder, too. Given the choice of renting from a smug corporate giant or a little, hip company that was clawing its way up the ladder, they increasingly chose the little guy.

But Townsend didn't stop there. One of the new ads pointed out that Townsend had no secretary and answered his own phone, and suggested that anyone with a complaint about Avis could call him directly at 516-CH. 8-9150. It was no joke. "Either Bob or I answered every one of those calls for sixty days," says Petrie. "The first day, it was mostly other ad agencies calling up to see who would answer the phone." Fire-engine-red blazers (Avis's official color) became required attire not only behind the counters, but in the company's executive offices, as were "We Try Harder" buttons—if you weren't wearing one, Townsend would throw one at you. An "Avis mystery man" would make the rounds of the car-rental locations, handing ten silver dollars to employees who were doing especially good jobs. And when the New York Society of Security Analysts, Wall Street analysts' staid professional association, invited Townsend and Petrie to make a presentation, the Avis executives agreed only on the condition that they could place an Avis charge-card application on every seat. The group agreed, and Townsend and Petrie appeared—dressed, naturally enough, in bright red jackets with "We Try Harder" buttons stuck in the lapels. "We talked to security analysts all across the country, and it was always the same," says Petrie. "Every security analyst had to take a charge-card application, or we wouldn't talk. I mean, we never stopped peddling, OK?"

Some of the eminent investors in Avis did not take kindly to this free-spirited approach. David Sarnoff, for one, was appalled. That ad campaign—who in his right mind would advertise that they are number two? And the way Townsend had structured the executive compensation, some lower-level people were actually earning more than the chief executive officer. In Sarnoff's world, *no one* was supposed to make more than the chief executive. During one board meeting, Sarnoff asked Townsend to leave the room. "I'd prefer not to," Townsend said. "Why not?" asked Sarnoff. "Because if I do, you'll raise my salary," Townsend answered.

But the man who really counted, André Meyer, took a far more benign attitude to the Townsend-Petrie sideshow. "He didn't know quite how flamboyant a thing he was getting into, but he enjoyed it," says Petrie. According to Bill Bernbach, "André expressed only admiration for our Avis campaign. But," adds Bernbach, "when you make money, people do tend to admire you for it." And make money they did. Indeed, any qualms Meyer might have had about Townsend and Petrie's high-octane methods were stifled by the results they produced. In 1963, Avis moved into the black for the first time, with net income of $1.2 million on total revenue of $34 million, up 15 percent over the year before. In 1964, net income was up to $2.9 million. True, Avis was reaping the benefits of an overall boom in the auto-rental business; from 1962 to 1964, the industry's revenues jumped from $250 million to $370 million. But all the same, there was no disputing the turnaround Townsend had effected.

Not that there weren't some touch-and-go moments. In 1962, Avis lost $3.2 million; and in the month of October 1962 alone, the losses totaled $400,000. When that happened, says Rohatyn, "I pushed the panic button. I went to see Mr. Meyer on a Saturday and told him I thought we ought to bring in outside consultants. He was relaxed about it all. He asked me what Townsend and Petrie thought, and I said they think it's coming along OK. He said, 'Let's wait, then.' And the next month we turned the corner."

In dealing with André Meyer, Townsend and Petrie soon learned a lesson many others, before and after them, have absorbed: that the easiest way to winnow your way into his heart was to keep him informed, constantly. Bad news he could take; what he couldn't take were people who held off telling him. Petrie once was informed at one o'clock in the morning that one of Avis's trucks had blown up. He promptly picked up the phone and called Meyer at the Carlyle. "One of our trucks just blew up," Petrie told him, "and I don't know whether it's killed anybody or not, but it could be in the paper tomorrow; and since it's an Avis truck, I don't want you to be surprised."

Far from fretting over the news, Meyer was exuberant—because Petrie had thought to call him at one o'clock in the morning. "You are wonderful to tell me this. Wonderful!" he gushed. "Please call me at any time."

As the months went by, Townsend and Petrie had very little bad news to tell Meyer. And that, paradoxical as it may seem, proved to be Townsend's undoing. Because as Avis became more and more successful, Townsend became more and more cocky. And if there was one thing Meyer liked less than a chief executive who didn't keep him informed, it was a chief executive who was arrogant.

According to a former Lazard partner, "Townsend would torture Meyer. André would carry on about something and Bob would say, 'OK, André, have it your way. I'll be out on Monday. You send somebody over to run the company.' And André would just go through the roof."

Then there was the matter of Townsend's hours. Townsend had always been an early riser, getting into the office at 6:00 or 6:30 A.M., which used to delight Meyer no end, since it meant he had someone to talk to during those early-morning hours when the rest of the American business world, to his utter frustration, was still asleep. But as Avis moved deeper and deeper into the black, Townsend began to *leave* the office at 10:00 or 10:30 A.M. Townsend explained it to Petrie this way: "I'm ahead of your plan, Donald. I'm ahead of my plan. I'm ahead of any plan André could possibly have had. I'm not only on budget, I'm ahead of budget. I'm ahead of our objectives for revenue, growth, return on assets, return on equity, and return on revenue. So what the hell do I need to be in the office for?"

Meyer, however, didn't see things that way. All he knew was that when he called Avis at 10:15 in the morning and asked for Townsend, he would be told that he was gone for the day. This did not please André Meyer.

"Townsend, frankly, was getting bored," explains Petrie. "I was also getting bored, but Townsend was getting *more* bored. At least I was working half-time on pay television and other things. He had to work full-time on Avis."

The last straw, for Meyer, came when Townsend decided to promote one of his subordinates at Avis to the company presidency. (Townsend by then had moved up to the chairmanship.) Meyer didn't think the man was right for the job, and he had nightmares about this man someday taking complete control of Avis. Meyer put his foot down; so did Townsend. Townsend won the battle; his candidate was named president. But Meyer won the war. "You insist on this?" he asked Petrie. Petrie said they did. "All right," says Meyer. "Now I sell the company."

But with the pixieish Townsend around, that proved easier said than done. Meyer lined up one likely buyer, the Mobil Oil Company, and summoned Petrie and Townsend to the Carlyle to meet Mobil's chairman, A. L. Nickerson, and president, Rawleigh Warner, Jr.

Townsend decided that he was going to kill the deal right then and there. He asked Nickerson and Warner, "Why in the world would you want to buy our company?" They were startled. "Oh," they said, "it's marvelous. You're doing such a terri—" Townsend cut them short. "Oh, God," he said, "the problems we have."

"Well," one of the Mobil executives said, "you have a lot of locations, and we have a lot of locations." Replied Townsend: "The kind of locations that you buy, you can't rent cars in; and the kind of locations we're interested in, you can't pump gas in. It takes a whole different order of scale, and none of our people could be of any use to you, and none of your people could help us at all."

"You have all these charge cards," the Mobil man remarked. "Oh my God," moaned Townsend, "our credit experience is terrible. Our credit losses, if you could see them . . ."

After about a half-hour of this, Nickerson and Warner stood up and said, "We *could* sell you gas."

"No, no," Townsend spluttered, "our people have to buy gas retail. The customer buys the gas. He's not going to go to any of your gas stations; he's going to buy it where it's most convenient for him. We're not going to louse up our business by telling people they have to buy Mobil. They're going to buy gas at whatever station they pass. Our people are very busy businessmen. They're not going to—"

Townsend went on and on, and the two men from Mobil slunk out of the room. "That," says Petrie, "was the last attempt Mr. Meyer made to have us participate in a sale."

On the Monday after New Year's weekend 1965, Petrie was summoned to the Carlyle again. This time Meyer's voice was icy. "Between Christmas and New Year's," he said, "I have met with Mr. Harold Geneen, and I have sold him your company." Petrie asked him what he had got for it, and Meyer told him. "You have been screwed," Petrie said. Meyer could barely contain his anger. "Do not tell me when to sell a business," he barked.

At least from one point of view—that of realizing the maximum capital gain in the shortest period of time—it was hard to fault Meyer. From an investment of a little over $5 million three years before, he and his partners would be getting ITT stock worth over $20 million. (About a third of that would go to Meyer himself.) But from a longer-term perspective, Meyer left himself wide open to second-guessing. Avis's greatest period of growth was clearly ahead of it. The company's own projections, upon which ITT based the acquisition, were for revenue growth of 25 percent per year from 1965 through 1967; earnings were expected to rise from an estimated $5 million in 1965 to $9 million in 1967, with pretax profit margins soaring from 6.7 percent in 1964 to 10 percent by 1967.

Once more, Meyer's urge to cash in overwhelmed his sense of the long-term prospects. To Felix Rohatyn, he would repeat his homily: "Nobody ever got poor taking a profit." And even Petrie, in retrospect, came to recognize a certain logic in Meyer's actions. In Petrie's words, "He put in five and a half million, and he got twenty million out, didn't he? If you do that in three years, that's not logical?"

And where did all this leave acid-tongued Robert Townsend? For one thing, considerably richer; in exchange for his Avis shares, he received some $1.5 million in ITT stock. And for another thing, out of a job; he resigned the day the deal was closed.

For the reasons why, it is not necessary to go any further than the chapter in *Up the Organization* titled "Mergers, Conglobulations, and Joint Failures." Wrote Townsend: "If you have a good company don't sell out to a conglomerate. Conglomerates will promise anything for your people but once in the fold your company goes through the homogenizer along with their other acquisitions of the week, and all the zeal and most of the good people leave. Two and two may seem to make five when a conglomerate is making its pitch, but from what I've seen they are just playing a numbers game and couldn't care less if they make zombies out of your people."

Then Townsend added this final, bitter note: "Don't expect lawyers or investment bankers to be objective about conglomerates. Visions of sugarplums dance through their heads at the mention of Gulf and Western."

To those who were witnesses to the direction in which Lazard was moving in those years, Townsend's words came to have a genuinely prophetic ring.

CHAPTER TEN

Sins of Pride

The Avis experience left a very sweet taste in the mouths of André Meyer and his associates at Lazard. They began to believe they could make a going business of rehabilitating broken-down companies. André Meyer said it often: "The art of investment banking consists of taking a button and making a suit out of it." How many more buttons might he out there?

It didn't take Meyer long to find one: a finance company, Allied Concord, that Lazard had acquired years before. But soon, certain differences between Allied Concord and Avis became apparent. First, Allied Concord was a company that had deteriorated under Lazard's stewardship, not someone else's. And second, Lazard stood to lose a good deal more in Allied Concord than just its investment. Indeed, by the time the dust settled, Allied Concord had come perilously close to wreaking real financial damage on Lazard and putting Meyer in the untenable position of choosing between Lazard's reputation and its capital base. "Allied Concord," sighs Felix Rohatyn, "destroyed a lot of people and a lot of reputations in the firm." It also showed that André Meyer, for all his meticulousness, was as capable of gross misjudgments and oversights as the next investor.

At first, Allied Concord was just another André Meyer venture-capital production; another company that would be bought now and sold later, when it was a lot bigger and could fetch a lot more money. Lazard had first become involved in the late 1950s when Transamerica Corporation decided to sell off a finance-company subsidiary called Allied Building Credits. Allied was in the prosaic business of facilitating home building and home improvement by buying up promissory notes from lumberyards. The way Allied worked, the lumberyard sold the homeowner or his builder $2,000 worth of lumber and building materials; the homeowner or builder signed a $2,000 note, which he gave to the lumberyard; and the lumberyard bundled up those notes and sent them to Allied Building Credits, which bought them at a discount.

The business was a familiar one to Meyer, being another variation of the consumer-finance business he had pioneered in France in the twenties through SOVAC. With one such success under his belt, he no doubt genuinely believed that lightning could strike twice. But, just to be sure, he merged Allied with the Concord Financial Corporation.

Concord was, ostensibly, in the same sort of business Allied was. But whereas Allied financed consumer lumber purchases, Concord specialized in commercial financing—inventories, receivables, and equipment. Meyer thought that the two companies would complement each other quite well. Furthermore, he felt that Concord's management was just what Allied needed. And when he talked about Concord management, he meant Harry Goldstein.

Goldstein, the former owner of Concord, was a hard-driving, charismatic businessman in his late forties who captivated André Meyer. Goldstein couldn't agree more with what Meyer had in mind for Allied Concord, which was to build it into a major factor in the finance-company business, like Walter Heller & Company or United Merchants & Manufacturers. Given his marching orders, Goldstein saluted and went off to the front.

But Harry Goldstein had a few handicaps. For one thing, he was, by all accounts, an ineffective administrator. For another, he had no understanding of the Allied end of the business. Not only did Goldstein not understand the consumer financing and factoring business, but he found himself overseeing a network of tiny, decentralized Allied offices in the Midwest run by people who were, by Goldstein's Boston-Philadelphia-New York standards, a bunch of cowboys.

Goldstein's worst failing was that he misunderstood (or chose to misunderstand) André Meyer. When Meyer talked about building Allied Concord, he meant upgrading it. "Even though the character of the company's loans was not great, the structure was, and André's thought was to get it into a better class of business," notes Arthur Bernstein, one of the people who was later brought in to unravel the mess. Goldstein, however, thought Meyer meant really *building*. As in heaping, accumulating, piling on. Says Bernstein: "Harry felt he had an infinite amount of financial support from André, and he proceeded to expand into marginal areas, almost shoveling money out."

The more money he shoveled out, the more bad debts and potential bad debts began to accumulate. Yet the possibility that something might have to be done to rein in Harry Goldstein never occurred to the two Lazard partners who were monitoring Allied Concord: ace technician Howard Kniffin and the boyish, enthusiastic Michel David-Weill, Pierre's son. "Harry Goldstein impressed all of us with his abilities," David-Weill says today. "We assumed that if there were problems, it was because he had gone from a business he knew to a business he did not know." But, ironically, it was the commercial factoring side—the business Harry Goldstein knew—that was the core of the problem. And there, they trusted Goldstein. Explains David-Weill: "You either take the management in your own hands, in a business you don't know much about, or you have a degree of confidence."

And André Meyer, normally the apotheosis of the jittery stockholder, trusted Goldstein, too. But when, as in early 1965, the United States finds itself in a credit crunch, the weak links in the economy usually are snipped off first. Sadly for Goldstein, his portfolio was full of weak links.

As the bad debts began to mount, Michel David-Weill suddenly left New York and took a position at Lazard Paris; inevitably, the conclusion drawn by his New York partners was that Meyer had exiled him because of his handling of Allied Concord. (David-Weill repeatedly denied that was the reason.) To fill the gap, Meyer tapped one of Lazard's brightest young stars, John Vogelstein. Vogelstein, son of the former chief financial officer of the giant American Metal Climax Company, had found a job at Lazard at the age of nineteen largely because Meyer wanted to curry favor with his father. But after the usual long, grinding apprenticeship, Vogelstein began to demonstrate a certain flair for investment banking. By the summer of 1965, he was mentioned more often than not in the same breath as Felix Rohatyn—whom Vogelstein, incidentally, had known since boyhood.

Vogelstein took a closer look at Allied Concord—and came away horrified. As he recounts it, "The company was overextended; it lacked sufficient credit to carry the business it had on its books; its loss ratios were out of line; its controls were appalling; and it was on its way to losing its bank credit, which would put it in the tank. It was clear that this thing had to be subject to drastic surgery."

Whether Vogelstein painted such a bleak picture when he talked to Meyer about the problem is unclear. Vogelstein says he did: "I went to see Meyer and said, 'You have a disaster on your hands.' He didn't know it then. And he said, 'You will fix the disaster.' " But others involved in Allied Concord insist that Vogelstein did not warn Meyer adequately. Like all too many partners of Lazard, he had become carried away with the firm's good fortune with Avis. Contends Arthur Bernstein, "Johnny did the best he could, but his efforts were hampered by the prior success of the firm. Nobody could foresee that Allied was anything more than another opportunity for a success *à la* Avis. Johnny, André, and Felix felt that all that was needed was a little expert Lazard Frères handling."

Meyer, in fact, turned for help to the architects of the Avis rehabilitation. Townsend wasn't available, but Petrie was. Petrie and Vogelstein talked about what had to be done. They agreed on one item immediately: Harry Goldstein had to be fired. But, as Vogelstein points out, "Selling it to Kniffin and then to Meyer was next to impossible. Kniffin was scared that if we fired Goldstein the banks would all pull out on us, because they had such great confidence in Goldstein. Finally, things got bad enough that we fired Goldstein, and the banks all said, 'Why'd you wait so long?' "

With Goldstein out of the picture, Petrie and Vogelstein finally were able to calculate exactly how much Allied Concord owed to banks and insurance companies. The figure they came up with was staggering: $150 million, $100 million of which was short-term debt. And as Petrie turned the number over in his head, he began to realize what it meant. As an investor, Lazard Frères was only legally liable up to the amount it had put into the company. But as Lazard Frères, it was morally liable for a lot more. "I don't care what the law says," Petrie told Vogelstein. "The fact is a firm like Lazard Frères can't afford to let the banks get stuck with a hundred-fifty million in bad loans. It can't afford to let them get stuck with even *half* that." Or, as Petrie later told Meyer, "The banks that are lending money to Allied Concord think they are lending money to *you.*"

Meyer was torn. If Lazard allowed Allied Concord to default on that debt, or even a major part of it, then the firm's reputation, the reputation he had guarded with almost manic zeal, would be irretrievably tarnished. But if Lazard itself was forced to honor that debt, the firm's capital base, as formidable as it was, could be wiped out. (At that point, the New York firm's reported capital was just $17.5 million, although it was always assumed that the true capital base of the firm was many times that figure.) Meyer phoned Pierre David-Weill in Paris. They agreed that they could not allow Allied Concord to go under—that if they had to repay the banks out of their own pockets, they would do it.

Vogelstein frantically went to work to salvage the company. "We cut overhead every place we could," he says. "We went through it office by office and closed down some, and tightened credit controls all over. Then we began to liquidate the commercial business as fast as we could. We took some enormous write-downs, to try to clean it up once and for all. We went out and estimated everything we wanted to write off on the most conservative possible basis. Each time we reacted exaggeratedly, over-writing off. And it *still* wasn't enough." Allied Concord was coming under growing pressure from the banks; a Midwest finance company, Pioneer Finance, had failed, and the banks responded by cutting back their commitments to medium-sized finance companies all across the country. "As fast as we liquidated receivables," says Vogelstein, "the bank lines kept dropping, so the company's access to credit to operate with kept going down." The vise was tightening very rapidly.

"I must say," says Vogelstein, "I was a bit young and naive at the time. I thought if I did the job as best I could, everybody would say thank you." But another top Lazard partner, Disque Deane, knew better. He told Vogelstein, "Keep saying it stinks, keep saying it's not fixable, or you're going to get caught with it." Vogelstein told Deane he couldn't do that. "You'll be sorry," Deane said.

Then, in the summer of 1966, another bombshell burst. Vogelstein found out that the man they had brought in to replace Goldstein had erred about one set of receivables. It turned out there was yet one more layer of bad debts Lazard hadn't been aware of.

Vogelstein phoned Meyer, who was in Switzerland. To the young man's surprise, Meyer took the news calmly, even consolingly. "My poor boy, it's not your fault," he told Vogelstein. Vogelstein said he knew it wasn't, but he felt badly anyway. Meyer was serene. "Well, we will get through this, too," he said.

Vogelstein went out to lunch, belted down a few drinks, and kept saying to himself, "My God, how unlike him." Later that afternoon, when Vogelstein returned to the office, his phone rang. It was André Meyer again, but this time a different André Meyer: a screaming man ranting about all the things Vogelstein could have done to find out about the elusive receivables. "Wait a minute," Vogelstein interrupted, "that's just entirely wrong." But Meyer continued his tirade.

"I suppose you think you've done a good job," he sneered.

"Well," said Vogelstein, "as a matter of fact, I think I have."

"Why?" demanded Meyer.

"Because if it hadn't been for me, you'd never have known you had a problem in the first place. At least now you know you have a problem, the size of which maybe you can begin to deal with. I'm the one who found it for you. I'm the one who's been cleaning it up for the last year."

"Then you and I disagree," shot back Meyer. "I don't think you've done a good job. I think you've done a *terrible* job." And with that, he hung up.

When Meyer returned in September, he continued to lash Vogelstein, often in front of groups of Lazard people the senior partner had summoned for the purpose. Then he put Vogelstein into the investment-banking equivalent of purgatory, removing him from the Allied Concord account and giving him nothing else to do. Vogelstein spent most of his time reading books. After three weeks or so of this treatment, Vogelstein said to his wife, "The next thing that will happen to me is that the increase in my partnership percentage that was promised to me two months ago will be rescinded, and he will never say a word. And when that happens, I quit." Sure enough, when the new partnership agreement came around, the promised increase had been rescinded, and no one said a word to Vogelstein about it.

Vogelstein asked to see Meyer. Meyer refused to see him. Vogelstein then wrote Meyer a letter, telling him he was quitting. Meyer called him into his office. He told Vogelstein he didn't want him to quit. Vogelstein replied that it was a little late for *that.*

But Meyer kept at him, and the young partner felt his resolve beginning to weaken. Then Meyer blundered. He looked Vogelstein in the eye and said, "What are you going to do when you go for a job to Loeb Rhoades or Goldman, Sachs or Lehman Brothers and they say how come after two years as a partner of Lazard Frères you left?"

To Vogelstein, the import of Meyer's remark was crystal clear. He was saying, in effect, "After I talk to the heads of those firms, they won't touch you with a ten-foot pole." Vogelstein felt himself wrenched back to reality. He stiffened. "Well, that's just a risk I'm going to have to take, Mr. Meyer," he replied.

As Vogelstein tells the story, "That's when I said, 'Enough. I'm thirty-one years old. I don't need this. If I'm any good, I can make a living. If not, I'm overpaid here.' I finally decided I wasn't going to live like *that* for the rest of my life." So Vogelstein quit.

But his resignation didn't solve the problem of Allied Concord. The company needed a new chairman, and Meyer tapped Arthur Bernstein, who had just joined Lazard from Ryder Systems. "I thought I was coming in to Lazard to do new investment-banking business," recalls Bernstein. "The next thing I knew, Felix told me, 'We have one particular problem we want you to look at.'" But Meyer also wanted a senior person working with Bernstein, and he turned once more to Petrie.

This time, though, Meyer had more than consulting work in mind. He summoned Petrie to his office and told him flatly, "You should come to Lazard and be a partner of my firm." Petrie, however, wasn't interested; he was living quite well off the money he had made from Avis and was looking forward to a nice, long sabbatical. Meyer was undeterred. "You should work," he told Petrie. Answered Petrie: "Why do I have to work, Mr. Meyer? Mr. Townsend doesn't work." Meyer just leaned back and replied, "Yes, Mr. Petrie, but Mr. Townsend is an aristocrat. You and I are *bourgeois*. And for a bourgeois, it is essential to work." Petrie signed on with Lazard.

(Petrie insisted, however, on taking a few months off before starting. Meyer agreed, and then a week or so later sent an announcement to the *New York Times* of Petrie's imminent arrival. He phoned Petrie: "You have been in the paper; everyone calls and wants to talk to you—you must come immediately." So Petrie came. What's more, since Petrie's partnership didn't start till the New Year, Meyer was able to get four months' work out of him for nothing.)

"You're not going to bring me in here to work on Allied Concord, are you?" Petrie asked Meyer after agreeing to join the firm. Of course not, Meyer replied; Petrie would be a member of Allied Concord's executive committee, but he would have no responsibility beyond that. The first executive committee meeting Petrie attended consisted of Meyer, Deane, Rohatyn, Kniffin, and himself. At the second meeting it was Kniffin, Meyer, and Petrie. The third meeting was just Meyer and Petrie. By the fourth committee meeting, Petrie was sitting there by himself. Like it or not, he was responsible for Allied Concord.

In the meantime, Bernstein had reached the conclusion that there was no way the company could be nursed back to health; it would have to be liquidated, hopefully as quickly as possible. Notes Bernstein: "If there was a rule at Lazard that should have been painted on the door, it was 'No Surprises.' And with Allied Concord, there was a surprise every day." Meyer, though, continued arguing that *something* could be done; perhaps they could turn Allied Concord into a leasing company. But Bernstein made it clear to him that "the patient is just too weak to survive long enough to bring that about." Reluctantly, Meyer agreed that the company would either have to be sold or liquidated.

Lazard partners scurried far and wide looking for someone who might be interested in acquiring Allied Concord's remaining receivables and other assets. But even though most of the doubtful loans had already been written off, there were no takers. Then, in late 1967, Meyer and Petrie stumbled upon the solution. They realized they had been focusing on the wrong side of the balance sheet; it wasn't Allied Concord's assets that were attractive, but Allied Concord's *liabilities*. The company, despite all it had been through, still had a fairly strong equity structure on the liability side. If they could use the equity as a lure, they might be able to find a buyer—such as a large finance company eager to grow but in need of a stronger equity base to do it. The catch, of course, was getting Allied Concord's lenders to agree to the plan; the only way they would was if the buyer was big and strong enough to reassure them that their loans would be repaid.

The buyer they hit upon (oddly enough, in retrospect) was Chrysler Financial, the finance-company arm of the big automaker. In those days, Chrysler was still in the blue chip league; what's more, the finance company was eager to expand. As soon as Petrie began uttering the name of its chief financial officer, Meyer cut him off. "Oh, Tom Killifer," he said, "oh, yes, of course, I know him well. I will get him on the phone." And within twenty minutes they were on their way to concluding a deal in which Chrysler acquired most of the assets, and the liabilities, of Allied Concord.

Exactly how well, or badly, Lazard and its coinvestors fared in all this is still a bit murky. Arthur Bernstein, who should know, says he never saw the final accounting. "My guess is they didn't lose a heck of a lot," he adds. Petrie, who should also know, maintains, "We didn't lose money on that. We made money on that." But he is similarly vague on details. "If you find out we lost money, tell me, will you? Because I've always gone through life thinking I got the firm out whole." A slightly less rosy assessment is offered by a former Lazard associate, Herbert Engelhardt, who worked closely with Bernstein on Allied Concord. "My guess is they lost a couple of million dollars on it," says Engelhardt. "But again, it's only a guess."

In any event, what was probably far more significant than the dollars-and-cents impact was the way the Allied Concord affair stripped away the thin layer of *hubris* in which Meyer and Lazard had been cloaked after Avis. Their ministrations did not always bring new life to troubled companies; in fact, the Lazard doctors were perfectly capable of leaving the patient in worse shape than when they arrived. André Meyer and Lazard showed that they were mortal. They almost died proving it.

Of course, André Meyer was never one to readily admit his mistakes. That was evident over a decade later, when John Vogelstein visited New York's posh 21 restaurant. Vogelstein had done quite well for himself since leaving Lazard, becoming a top partner at E. M. Warburg, Pincus, a small but highly profitable New York financial-services firm. And as he stood at the 21 bar, waiting for his wife to arrive, he spied his former boss, holding forth at one of the better tables. Vogelstein, who had not seen Meyer since his bitter parting years before, ambled over and exchanged pleasantries with Meyer and the rest of his party, which included Bella and Francine. After a few minutes of gentle banter, Vogelstein excused himself and returned to the bar.

But back at the Meyer table, the old man had suddenly turned very morose. His daughter could see that a volcanic rage was starting to build. She asked him what was wrong.

"That man," he sputtered. "I told that man if he ever left me he would not succeed. And he *has.*"

CHAPTER ELEVEN

Zeckendorf

At six-thirty or sometimes seven in the morning, all through the 1950s, a gray Cadillac limousine with license plates reading "WZ" would pull up in front of the Carlyle Hotel, and André Meyer would get in. There in the backseat, waiting for him, would be a big burly man in a gray pinstripe suit and a pearl-gray homburg. They would talk all the way down the East River Drive, and when the limousine arrived at Meyer's office at 44 Wall Street, they would stay inside the car, talking, for fifteen minutes, a half-hour, or more. Then Meyer would get out, and the gray Cadillac would return uptown, with the big burly man chattering nonstop into one of the two telephones he kept in the back.

George Ames dreaded those mornings. A square-jawed, tidy man with the hard-nosed, matter-of-fact bearing of a savvy old New York detective, Ames had prospered since joining Lazard in 1939; one Lazard wag once dubbed him "the world's richest Fordham graduate." He was an ace deals man who, ever since the Matador Ranch days, had helped steer Lazard through the most complicated transactions. Yet Ames always cringed whenever he arrived at 8:00 A.M. to find a message from Meyer waiting for him on his desk. He knew it could only mean one thing: André had been talking to Bill Zeckendorf.

Zeckendorf, at the time, was New York's, America's, and most probably the world's greatest real estate developer. In less than two decades he had pyramided a tiny Manhattan office-building manager named Webb & Knabb into a $500 million personal fiefdom. It was Zeckendorf who transformed some East Side Manhattan slaughterhouses into the site on which the United Nations was built. It was Zeckendorf who pioneered urban redevelopment in New York, Washington, and Philadelphia, and who became the biggest exponent of the modern shopping mall. It was Zeckendorf who viewed the whole of America as a giant Monopoly board, in which mammoth office towers such as the Chrysler Building were bought and sold almost at whim. A *New Yorker* cartoon of the late 1950s said it best: a father and his young son are surveying the Manhattan skyline from a penthouse terrace. "Someday, my boy," says the father, "all this will belong to Mr. William Zeckendorf."

But to George Ames, Bill Zeckendorf was also something else—a pain in the neck.

As soon as Ames saw the message from Meyer, he would walk over to the senior partner's corner office. There, Meyer would lay out the wondrous scheme he and Zeckendorf had cooked up in the car. Suddenly, in the midst of the presentation, Meyer would stop as if stricken with something. "I do not understand," he would say. "He said he would do so-and-so. But how can he do that?"

"Well, he can't do that," Ames would shoot right back. "It's impossible, because somebody else already has a mortgage on it."

Dazed, Meyer would say, "Well, you better call up and find out what he is doing."

So Ames would dutifully return to his office and phone Zeckendorf's right-hand man, Arthur Phelan. "Arthur," Ames would say, "the two of them had a meeting this morning, and Bill is talking about doing this deal. What's it all about?"

"I haven't any idea," Phelan would reply. "He hasn't told me yet. I'll have to go ask him."

After conferring with Zeckendorf, Phelan would call Ames back. "This is what Bill says," he would say and proceed to describe the scheme.

"No," Ames would say, "that isn't what André said Bill said. He said Bill said so-and-so."

"No, no, no," Phelan would protest. "That isn't what Bill means. He said he told André . . ."

Ames would hear him out and shake his head. "Well, that isn't what he told André. André said he said something else than what he says he said."

And so it would go.

Invariably, Phelan and Ames would sort it all out. And more often than not, the transaction would go forward, no matter how wild and implausible it might have seemed at first. As Zeckendorf's son-in-law and business associate, Ronald Nicholson, says today, "Almost every deal in those days that he would call Meyer about, they would do." In Nicholson's words, "Andre made a decision that Bill was a guy who was going to make a lot of money, and he was going to back this horse."

And back him he did. Zeckendorf had plenty of other financial sponsors. Notes Ames, "Bill was a genius at raising money. He had most of the banks in town under his thumb. Somehow or other he could always get money out of these guys, and they shouldn't have lent it to him." When one of Zeckendorf's banker creditors told him, "Bill, you look like a million dollars," Zeckendorf shot back, "I'd better. I owe you three million."

But in a crunch, when even Zeckendorf's seemingly inexhaustible sources of funds began to run dry, he knew he could always turn to Meyer for that extra few million dollars. "We went to him when we had to," says Arthur Phelan. "When all the other avenues were closed. He was sort of the court of last resort." The money came at a high price, and with so many strings attached that Phelan could joke that "their loans were very secure. They were *over*secure." But the funds were there.

The exchange seemed fair enough. Without André Meyer's backing, many of Bill Zeckendorf's most ambitious schemes would never have seen the light of day. And without Bill Zeckendorf, Meyer would have been considerably less wealthy. Meyer and Lazard, Zeckendorf would later maintain, had made more than $70 million from his real estate ventures; George Ames puts the figure at closer to $30 million.

Yet they were never friends. At best, they could be considered wary allies. "There was no sentiment, no auld lang syne at all," remarks Phelan. "It was strictly a business relationship. Meyer would say that all of his relationships were that way. He was kind of a cold entrepreneur of money."

And Bill Zeckendorf saw the best and the worst of that cold world.

William Zeckendorf, a New York University dropout, got his start in the real estate business in the 1920s, as a renting agent for the real estate firm of his uncle, Sam Borchard. Borchard had just bought a building, 32 Broadway, that was only half rented; on the eve of a trip to Europe, he told his nephew that his future would be assured if he managed to rent the rest of his offices in his absence. Young Zeckendorf went to work, canvassing every office in every building in the Wall Street area to make his pitch. By the time Borchard had returned, all but two small offices were rented. Beaming with pride, the young man eagerly waited for his uncle's ship to pull into New York harbor. At the dock, Bill broke the news to him, but instead of offering congratulations, all Borchard said was: "William, about those two offices—how long before you can get them rented?" Zeckendorf quit the next day. If he was going to make any real money in real estate, he decided, he would have to do it on his own.

After a few quick coups making the most of deflated real estate values during the Depression, Zeckendorf joined forces with a small New York building manager and broker named Webb & Knapp. The way the story was told on Wall Street, Zeckendorf walked into the Webb & Knapp offices one day to use the phone; when the partners came home from the war four years later, they found that they were millionaires, and that Zeckendorf was in charge. (Actually, Zeckendorf said, the story was not *precisely* true; when the Webb & Knapp partners returned, they were only worth between $500,000 and $800,000 apiece.) Wheeling and dealing in the wartime New York market, Zeckendorf drooled over the bargains he was uncovering.

One of these was a large parcel of land bordering the East River in Manhattan that was the site of two huge and odoriferous slaughterhouses. While prime midtown land was running then between $100 and $150 a square foot, prices in the area near the slaughterhouses were a mere $2 to $5 a square foot, with few buyers in sight. Late in 1945, Zeckendorf got a call from a broker who told him the Swift and Wilson meat-packing companies would be willing to sell him the slaughterhouse land for $17 a square foot and relocate elsewhere. Zeckendorf jumped at the offer, and then arranged to keep the deal secret until he had a chance to buy up as much cheap land as he could around the slaughterhouses.

Within a year, Webb & Knapp had acquired eight acres between Forty-second and Forty-ninth streets on the East Side of Manhattan at an average price of $9 a square foot, including the cost of the slaughterhouse property. Zeckendorf then came up with the first of his grand designs—a plan for building something he dubbed "X City" on the land. X City would stand on a massive platform, seven blocks long and two blocks wide, raised above the city streets, and would consist of four huge office buildings, a hotel, a series of apartment towers, and even possibly a new home for the Metropolitan Opera.

While he was in the midst of planning this development, Zeckendorf read of the debates going on in the newly organized United Nations over a permanent site for the world body. San Francisco and Philadelphia were in the running, but New York wasn't. Suddenly,

Zeckendorf realized that he had the ideal UN site—the place where X City was supposed to be. Putting down the paper, he turned to his wife and said, "I'm going to put those bastards on the platform!"

Zeckendorf contacted New York mayor William O'Dwyer and offered the site to the UN "for any price they wish to pay." The UN offered $8.5 million (donated by John D. Rockefeller, Jr.), and Zeckendorf accepted it. He had just made a fast $2 million profit. But more importantly, as he told his wife, "We have just moved the capital of the world."

What for most people would have been the capstone of a career was, for Bill Zeckendorf, only the beginning. In his mind's eye he could see big buildings, big shopping centers, big urban-development projects, all sprouting from the fertile loam of postwar America. Fortunately for Zeckendorf, the country's glistening promise was also evident to other people, people who had the wherewithal to help him transform his wild fantasies into reality. One of these people was André Meyer.

Ever since he had arrived in the United States, Meyer had been quick to grasp the opportunities in real estate. But aside from the Matador deal, he had been unable to cash in on them. "André always loved real estate," points out Fred Wilson, "and he always wanted to find opportunities to get into the real estate business. But maybe it was too early; the real estate market didn't really exist at that time. There were values, but never a market. So he wasn't able to push that as much as he would have liked to." Now, in the person of Bill Zeckendorf, Meyer had his market.

Yet Meyer couldn't refrain from driving a hard bargain, even at the outset. Zeckendorf had decided in 1948 to buy out his Webb & Knapp partners. The asking price was steep—$5 million—and Zeckendorf raced about frantically trying to raise the needed cash. Finally, he approached André Meyer (just how the two of them met, and why he went to Meyer, has never been clear). Meyer told him he would be glad to work out an arrangement whereby Lazard would advance $3 million for two-thirds of the Webb & Knapp stock—and then sell the shares back to Zeckendorf six months later for $4 million. The annual interest rate on the "loan," in other words, was an awesome 66 percent.

Under the gun from his partners, Zeckendorf actually was tempted to accept these exorbitant terms, until he looked up an old friend, New York Trust Company vice-president Charles Stewart.

Stewart was aghast at Meyer's offer. "I can't let him do that to you, Bill," he said. Applying all the ingenuity he could muster, Stewart arranged a series of sales, leasebacks, and loans that provided Zeckendorf with what he needed, *sans* any assistance from Lazard. (Ironically, Stewart later became a partner of Lazard.)

This sobering incident notwithstanding, Zeckendorf thought of Meyer when his next big venture was getting off the ground. The developer had come upon a decrepit old airport in the middle of Long Island called Roosevelt Field, and he immediately sensed its possibilities. Not only was the airstrip adjacent to such burgeoning suburban communities as Mineola, Garden City, and Westbury, but a planned highway extension, connecting the northern and southern sides of the island, would run right past the field. At that time (1953), there was not a single major shopping mall serving the island's growing suburban markets. What better place for one than Roosevelt Field?

Raising the $35 million he needed to buy and develop the property, though, would not be easy. But as he was casting for fish on a Hawaiian beach that year, Zeckendorf came up with an idea that he would later claim represented "a quantum jump in the financing of real estate." He dubbed it, appropriately enough, "the Hawaiian technique," though others in the real estate business soon found a far more fitting name for it—the "salami technique."

Basically, the "salami technique" involves slicing a given property up into a seemingly endless number of individual financing arrangements. Any major piece of urban property can be broken naturally into two parts: the land; and a lease which allows ownership of a building on the land. But suppose, as Zeckendorf did on that Oahu beach, the lease was split into two parts: an inner (or sandwich) lease, which would represent ownership of the building; and an outer (or operating) lease. The holder of the outer lease, who would actually run the building, pays rent to the inner leaseholder and collects rents from the building's tenants. Then suppose the land and each of the leases were mortgaged, and second mortgages were overlaid on top of those, and each lease was broken into subleases and subsubleases— with different groups of investors coming in at each level. The possibilities were mind-boggling.

"The Hawaiian technique," said Zeckendorf, "can become as complex as some of the long molecule chains chemists work with and link together to concoct new products." Indeed, in Zeckendorf's hands, it could, and did. But what the "salami technique" actually amounted to, as Zeckendorf himself readily acknowledged, was an adaptation to the real estate market of the conventional ways industrial corporations finance themselves. In industrial companies, there is common stock, and different types of preferred stock, and bonds, and convertible bonds, ad infinitum. All Zeckendorf was doing was treating a particular piece of real estate the same way, carving it up to meet the needs of different types of investors.

The "salami technique" gave Zeckendorf the mechanism he needed to close the Roosevelt Field deal. A new Webb & Knapp affiliate, Roosevelt Field, Inc., bought the land, financing it with a mortgage from the Prudential Insurance Company. The U.S. Steel pension fund leased the land, and Roosevelt Field, Inc., held the operating lease, giving it the right to actually run Roosevelt Field. And somewhere in the middle of this, Lazard invested $3.5 million and obtained an intermediate lease, which allowed it to obtain the depreciation tax benefits on the Roosevelt Field buildings and collect rents from Roosevelt Field, Inc.

"Our transaction was essentially a financial transaction," says George Ames, "and we felt reasonably comfortable with it." The real risks were all borne by Zeckendorf and his Roosevelt Field, Inc. If the new shopping mall didn't attract enough tenants, it was Roosevelt Field, Inc., that would suffer, not Lazard, which would collect its rent from Zeckendorf regardless. Thus, Meyer was once again able to realize his goal of taking the maximum return on the minimum risk. And Zeckendorf's "salami technique" helped make it possible.

Not that Meyer didn't take any risks in his collaboration with Zeckendorf over the years. Lazard, for example, was an equity partner in one of Zeckendorf's greatest coups: the purchase of two of Manhattan's landmark skyscrapers, the Chrysler and Graybar buildings. "It was one of the world's most complicated closings," remembers Ames. "It took us two days, practically around the clock." Lazard's investment went through various permutations: first it was a 25 percent equity interest; then Zeckendorf repurchased the interest; then he came back to Lazard offering a sandwich lease position. Eventually, Zeckendorf made out well, and so, presumably, did Lazard; he sold the buildings in 1958 for $66 million, giving him a $10 million profit. It was, at the time, the largest real estate transaction in New York City history.

Zeckendorf could never be accused of thinking small, and in those days he often tried to interest André Meyer in his grand visions. He would invite the banker over to his office in the old Hotel Marguery on Park Avenue, and the two would peer down from Zeckendorf's window at the solid blocks of residential buildings that then lined the midtown part of the avenue. "Ten or fifteen years from now," Zeckendorf would say, "this will be all office buildings, André, every bit of it. There's money to be made here." Zeckendorf ultimately was proven right, but he was never able to get Meyer to share his enthusiasm. Says Ames: "André was not keen on financing that kind of vision. He didn't mind a lockup deal, but he didn't want it to go on for twenty years. His theory was that he wanted to be able to see the way out, as well as the way in. He didn't want to just sit there and wait for something to happen."

The clash between Zeckendorf's grand designs and Meyer's stern parsimony came to a head during the development of Lincoln Towers, a major urban-renewal project on Manhattan's West Side. During the late 1950s, Webb & Knapp emerged as New York's biggest redeveloper, putting up such sprawling apartment complexes as Park West Village on the Upper West Side and Kips Bay Plaza on the East Side just south of midtown. But Zeckendorf viewed Lincoln Towers as potentially his crowning achievement, and he assigned to the task of designing it a young architect who was just beginning to gain renown—Ieoh Ming Pei. It was Zeckendorf who had plucked Pei out of academia in the late 1940s and put him to work on his buildings. One of Pei's first projects, in fact, was designing Zeckendorf's new office at 383 Madison Avenue. Displaying the flair he would later employ on a much wider scale, Pei enclosed Zeckendorf himself in a twenty-foot-diameter wood-paneled vertical cylinder which confronted visitors as soon as they came off the elevator. In this case, form definitely did follow function: explained Pei, "It would be ridiculous to create any environment for him other than one consisting exclusively of himself."

Pei had designed Kips Bay for Zeckendorf, and the buildings—with their stark concrete grid facades—were immediately hailed as a major breakthrough in apartment-block architecture. What Pei had in mind for Lincoln Towers was even more of a departure: a cluster of structures of varying sizes, laid out in a way that would avoid the monolithic overtones that had plagued so many other apartment developments (including Kips Bay). When Zeckendorf saw Pei's designs, he was ecstatic; Lincoln Towers, he declared, would be "one of the wonders of Manhattan." Unfortunately, Bill Zeckendorf had not reckoned on André Meyer's reaction.

Lazard had come into the deal as an equity investor, putting in some $5 million. Webb & Knapp, in fact, might have blown the whole transaction if Lazard had not come up with a check for $2.5 million for the closing. Now the Lazard partners wanted to see what they were putting their money into. I. M. Pei loaded his model of Lincoln Towers into a station wagon and drove down to 44 Wall Street.

As Ames tells the story, "Ieoh Ming arrived, with a smile as usual from ear to ear—he's a very amusing and wonderful guy. He takes the model and puts it on our conference table, and André comes in. And Zeckendorf and Ieoh Ming are smiling all over the place, and waiting for André to drool over this model. André looks at Ieoh Ming, and he says, 'Mr. Pei, I want you to bear one thing firmly in mind. Think of us as greedy Wall Street bankers. *Now* tell me what you have in mind.' "

According to Ames, "Ieoh Ming's face fell all the way down to the floor, and his prepared speech had to be hastily revised to emphasize how *little* it was going to cost to build this monster. Eventually, after a couple of passes at it, Ieoh Ming decided it was impossible, he couldn't do it. And he left."

Knowing he was beaten, Pei quit the project. To take his place, Meyer prevailed upon Zeckendorf to hire a man Ames himself describes as one of the leading cookie-cutter architects in town, "a guy who had built about a jillion apartments." What Meyer wanted was architecture on the cheap, and he got it. The result, predictably, was exactly the kind of dull, anonymous towers that Zeckendorf was so ardently trying to avoid.

"André knew good from bad," notes Ames, "and it didn't take him long to figure out that these apartment buildings were no triumphs of architecture. On the other hand, they worked, and that was what they were designed to do." By "worked," Ames means that they housed people reasonably comfortably and came in on budget.

Zeckendorf, meanwhile, was crestfallen. Once he had been hailed by no less a figure than Le Corbusier as having "done more than anybody else for architecture in America." Now he was putting up just another box. He regretted it to his dying day. "I'm not proud of the final product; I am ashamed of it," he wrote in his autobiography, published in 1970. "When these towers are torn down, no one will mourn their passing."

The irony of it all is that not long after Meyer ousted I. M. Pei, Lazard bailed out of the investment completely. Even with bargain-basement architecture, the costs, for Meyer, were escalating alarmingly. Zeckendorf was constantly trying to extract more federal and state subsidies. The project, from start to finish, was touch and go. "André complained and complained and complained," says Ames, "and eventually got Bill to find a way to take him out."

Zeckendorf was able to line up a new partner, the Aluminum Corporation of America. But the cost of buying Meyer out, by at least one account, wasn't cheap. According to William Zeckendorf, Jr., who worked with his father at Webb & Knapp, Lazard by prior agreement was able to sell its $5 million investment back to Zeckendorf for *$10 million*. Ames, however, insists that figure is exaggerated. "We made a small amount of money on it," he says, "but it wasn't much."

Lincoln Towers wasn't the only Zeckendorf deal Meyer bailed out of at the eleventh hour. Lazard also engineered a quick escape from Century City, one of Zeckendorf's biggest land plays. Century City was the site of the old Twentieth Century-Fox movie lots, 260 acres that were just south of Beverly Hills. Fox's boss, a volatile Greek named Spyros Skouras, realized that the huge tract was worth a lot more as real estate than as a movie studio. So he offered it to Zeckendorf. Once again, the developer dreamed big dreams: he saw office towers and high-rise hotels sprouting on the doorstep of the most desirable community in America. Certainly, it would be a lot for Webb & Knapp to swallow, financially. But as Zeckendorf confidently remarked, "If the Hawaiian technique could work for fractional parts of a building, why not a super-Hawaiian technique for Century City?"

After some haggling, he and Skouras settled on a purchase price of $56 million, with a down payment of $2.5 million. (Skouras, typically, complained to the end that he was being robbed: "Here is a Jew, Zeckendorf. He comes out here and out-trades me, a Greek. He steals the finest piece of real estate in all America.") Zeckendorf asked André Meyer for help, and Lazard agreed in early 1959 to lend him the $2.5 million. Other Webb & Knapp properties would be used to secure the loan, and Lazard retained the right to put the loan back to Zeckendorf—in other words, it could demand its money back at any time. "We toyed with the idea of becoming long-term investors," says Ames. "But we decided not to do it because we felt the pay-out was too long, the property was too big, and it was going to cost too much to carry it until it came to fruition."

Overextended as usual, Zeckendorf was unable to come up with the $3.8 million he needed for the second payment to Fox. Twice he asked for, and received, postponements. Then, just as he was scrambling for the additional money he needed to keep the deal alive, Lazard dropped the other shoe: it wanted its $2.5 million back.

Ames is hazy about just why Lazard decided to pull the plug at that moment. "Sometimes we did these things to make Bill get up and go," he says. "Bill was always so wound up that if you didn't raise enough hell, he'd just let you sit there for God knows how long." But in prodding Zeckendorf into action, Lazard plunged him into a crisis: he didn't have the $2.5 million. In desperation, Zeckendorf turned once more to Alcoa. The company's chairman, Frank McGee, was reluctant; based on the terms Zeckendorf proposed (two-thirds ownership for Alcoa, one-third to Webb & Knapp), it would be an unprecedented commitment to the real estate business by an aluminum company. But when Zeckendorf suggested that he could make a profit of as much as $50 a square foot on the land, McGee gave in.

"We needed the money on a Monday," recalls Nicholson, "and Bill was able to get a check for two and a half million that day with just a note. I mean, no security, no nothing!" Triumphantly, Zeckendorf headed for the nearest phone booth to tell his son and Nicholson the news. "Fellas, we just got a great deal," he announced. "We are out from under Lazard."

Considering the note of exultation in Zeckendorf's voice, it may seem strange that after all this he went on dealing with André Meyer. It was Meyer who quashed his grand vision for Lincoln Towers, and Meyer who almost pulled the rug out from under one of the greatest deals of his career. Yet the big gray limousine still made its early-morning stop at the Carlyle.

To those who worked with Zeckendorf, though, the reason was painfully obvious: he needed the money.

Says Nicholson, "You had to have money to close these deals, so you needed a money partner. No one said we had to go down there and borrow the money. We always felt it was worth what we were paying." Zeckendorf himself summed up this attitude best: "I'd rather be alive at eighteen percent than dead at the prime," he quipped. (Prime in those days, it should be added, was around 3 or 4 percent.)

For someone constantly closing new transactions and patching up old ones, there were other reasons for visiting Meyer. "We always got a fast answer from Meyer," points out Phelan. "He was very quick to pick up the financial facts, and you'd get an immediate yes or no. When you got the yes, you got his terms."

Those terms were onerous indeed. Meyer demanded security over and above the security of the project he was lending to; merely to accept the project itself as collateral, he felt, was tantamount to taking an equity participation in it, since he would be unable to get his money back if the deal went awry. Consequently, Meyer's loans to Zeckendorf were invariably secured by *other* Zeckendorf projects that were already producing revenues. What's more, the loans were usually very short-term, often no more than three or four months in maturity. And then there were the rates. In an era of a 3 percent prime, Meyer was charging Zeckendorf a staggering 18 to 24 percent.

"Bill knew he was not going to go down to Meyer and get a pie à la mode," remarks Phelan. "He was going to get tough terms. And he got 'em. Very tough. Meyer was cold, calculating, and at most times unbending. Unbending," he repeats.

On the other hand, Meyer appreciated Zeckendorf's genius for improvisation and knew how to squeeze the most out of it. Soon after Lazard took over Avis, for example, Avis decided to relocate its corporate headquarters from Boston. Petrie reviewed the possibilities and settled on a huge, empty warehouse in Roosevelt Field. The location, near New York's two major airports, was ideal; furthermore, Petrie knew the warehouse rental would be cheap, perhaps as little as a dollar per square foot.

Petrie asked Meyer to call Zeckendorf about it and listened in on Meyer's end of the conversation.

"Bill? This is André Meyer. We have an interest in a little company that's looking for a very cheap office space. No, they don't want to be in the city. They want to be out somewhere, maybe New Jersey or Connecticut or something like that.

"Roosevelt Field?" Meyer played dumb. "Bill, that's a shopping center. Oh, oh, oh, you—over in the industrial park is something that might—? Well, well, they can't pay very much, you know. I mean, I'm not sure that a shopping-center space would not be too expensive, you know."

In a few minutes Meyer had established a price of a dollar a square foot.

Two weeks later Petrie was all ready to sign the lease when he got a call from a Zeckendorf aide. "I'm sorry, Don, we won't be able to close this," the aide said. Thinking they were trying to renegotiate the deal, Petrie began hollering. The Zeckendorf man cut him short. "No, no, it's a different kind of problem," he advised Petrie. "Mr. Zeckendorf doesn't *own* that building."

When Zeckendorf was blithely renting the space to Meyer, he had completely forgotten he had earlier sold the building to someone else. But the Zeckendorf aide told Petrie he had nothing to worry about: "We have to go buy it first, but if you give us till Tuesday, we'll have it by then." The man was as good as his word: when Petrie showed up for the closing the following week, the Webb & Knapp executive proudly handed him a twenty-year lease. No sooner did Petrie sign the lease, however, than another man stepped forward—the man who arranged to buy the building from Zeckendorf as soon as Petrie put his name on the dotted line.

It was vintage business brinksmanship, Zeckendorf style. But while André Meyer could chuckle at such bravado, it also made him jittery. How long, he wondered, could Bill keep this up?

"André always warned Bill he was overextended," says Ames. "And Bill always told him he was crazy." Zeckendorf's typical response was to chide Meyer: "The problem with you bankers is that you never want to have any fun." Comments Nicholson: "The people at Lazard were always worried, always asking, 'What if you go bankrupt?' I must have been hearing that from the very first deal we did with them."

Zeckendorf was perennially on the verge of economic strangulation, yet somehow he had always been able to borrow his way out of trouble—at progressively higher rates of interest. By early 1963, though, the noose was tightening. Webb & Knapp was faced with $67 million in short-term debt coming due in the next twelve months, and it was already in arrears on another $10 million in rent, mortgage, and debt payments. Its supply of cash had dwindled to just $1.2 million. Zeckendorf had managed to arrange $43 million of refinancing a year earlier with a group of British investors. But when they urged him to sell off property to pay off the short-term debt, he opted instead to buy even more Manhattan real estate in the hopes that he would be able to resell it at a quick profit. The perverse explanation of a Webb & Knapp official was, "Sometimes you go further into debt to get out of debt." Zeckendorf got further into debt—but with the New York real estate market softening, he couldn't get out.

Zeckendorf was a veritable real estate junkie; he found it impossible to still what one competitor called "his compulsion to acquire." When he was putting a package of properties up for public auction, the reaction of one Webb & Knapp official was: "That's great, but how do we keep Bill from bidding?" In the midst of his troubles, for instance, he bought Freedomland, a low-budget Disneyland knockoff in the Baychester area of the Bronx. Freedomland was a disaster, and by the time it was shut it had siphoned off some $20 million from Webb & Knapp.

As his creditors closed in, Zeckendorf resorted to some unusual measures to keep them at bay. He had been one of the first to see the potential of Manhattan's Sixth Avenue as the city's next great office-building boulevard and had made great plans for a prestigious Hotel Zeckendorf on Sixth and Fifty-first Street, just west of Rockefeller Center. Short of cash to build and in need of some means of paying the hefty taxes on the property, he operated a parking lot on the site. But somehow he had to convince his lenders that he really *was* going to build something there, so he hired an old steam shovel to take a bite out of the ground every now and then. The problem was, every time the steam shovel dug another hole, he lost a parking place. It was, says Ames, "sort of a race to extinction."

Inevitably, the ruses and stopgaps fell short. Zeckendorf had no alternative but to liquidate his properties, one by one. Some of the properties were seized by creditors in satisfaction of debts; others were voluntarily disposed of by Zeckendorf.

Lazard bought, and Lazard seized. In 1960 it acquired Mountain Park, a 12,000-acre tract of land in the Santa Monica mountains that was the largest piece of undeveloped land in the Los Angeles city limits. The price: $8.5 million. Lazard purchased air rights over the Penn Central railroad yards on Manhattan's West Side; once, Zeckendorf had dreamed of erecting a spectacular Palace of Progress on the site, a "permanent world's fair," as he put it, where governments and private producers from every corner of the globe could exhibit and sell their countries' goods. He had even hired showman Billy Rose to find tenants for it.

In June 1963, Lazard took title to the Roosevelt Field shopping-center buildings when Zeckendorf was unable to repay some of his loans. Zeckendorf still retained the operating lease, but not for long. A year and a half later, with Zeckendorf lagging badly in his lease payments, Lazard terminated the lease. André Meyer was now in the shopping-center business, thanks to Bill Zeckendorf's salami technique.

Then, in late 1964, when Zeckendorf's back was foursquare against the wall, Meyer joined with David Rockefeller and other investors to buy Zeckendorf's *chef-d'oeuvre* of urban development, L'Enfant Plaza in southwest Washington. Stalled by political complications as well as by his own shortage of funds, Zeckendorf had never gotten around to actually building anything on the site. But the plans—which envisioned four office buildings, a thousand-room hotel, stores, restaurants, and four levels of parking underneath the plaza—were all his. When ground was finally broken for the project in 1966, Zeckendorf, attending the ceremony as a bemused, wistful bystander, joked with a reporter, "I'm the guy who got the girl pregnant. Those fellows you see around here are merely the obstetricians."

Yet even these sales, extensive as they were, were not enough to save Zeckendorf. The end finally came on May 7, 1965, when Marine Midland Bank called in an old $8.5 million Webb & Knapp note. Unable to pay it off, Webb & Knapp was forced into bankruptcy. Two months later, Zeckendorf resigned as the company's chairman.

Bill Zeckendorf spent the next five years watching his world fall apart. In May 1967, the Webb & Knapp bankruptcy trustee, former Internal Revenue Service commissioner Mortimer Caplin, filed a $50 million suit against Zeckendorf, charging waste and mismanagement. Ten months later, Zeckendorf's wife, Marion, was killed in an air crash in Guadaloupe. And in August 1968, he filed for personal bankruptcy. His assets were $1.8 million; his liabilities, $79 million.

Yet somehow, through all this, Zeckendorf seemed as buoyant, as indefatigable as ever. He even managed to rationalize Webb & Knapp's bankruptcy as a presage of things to come in the real estate business. "We're avant garde," he boasted to friends. What kept him going was his work; instead of bemoaning his fate, he simply formed a new real estate venture, General Property Corporation, with his son and Nicholson. He even was able to keep his old office at 383 Madison Avenue. Seated in his I. M. Pei-designed teakwood igloo, his bald pate bathed with alternating red, white, and blue lights from overhead, Bill Zeckendorf was back in business.

Of course, he still needed some capital, about $250,000, to start. And who was going to give him any money *now?* Zeckendorf thought it over and concluded there was someone who might. So, homburg in hand, he ventured over to the Carlyle.

Zeckendorf had reason to believe that Meyer would respond favorably. After all, Lazard had made a fortune from his projects over the years—not to mention what they stood to gain from all the choice properties they had picked up during Webb & Knapp's death throes. And all he was asking for was $250,000; they could chalk it up to goodwill, or gratitude.

Meyer listened to Zeckendorf's proposal and came back immediately with an answer: yes, he would be willing to put up the money. But there was one small condition: Lazard would have to have the right of first refusal on all General Property Corporation projects.

Zeckendorf was shattered. "Such an arrangement," he wrote in his autobiography, "would in effect make us lifelong vassals of Lazard." Rather than accept those terms, he determined, in his words, "to set up the new company on a more modest scale with our own financing."

Why had Meyer insisted on setting such an impossible condition? The answer Meyer's associates give is unequivocal. He didn't want to help Zeckendorf. So he made him an offer that Zeckendorf *had to* refuse. "We just decided there was no substance there," explains Ames. "If you were going to build a real estate company, you wouldn't build one where the principal architect is in bankruptcy."

In the end, Zeckendorf was able to scrape up enough cash to get General Property Corporation off the ground. But his "second career," as he bravely called it, was short-lived. In 1970, he suffered the first of a series of strokes; after that, says Nicholson, "he was not really himself at all." Six years later, Bill Zeckendorf died.

"I wouldn't say Bill was bitter about the way André treated him," Nicholson remarks. "But in private—and I was with him a lot in private—I think there was some feeling of being let down. You know, the idea that you've made a lot of money for people, and when you're in trouble they ought to help you out. But you know how Bill was— he would shrug it off."

Meyer, for his part, felt sorry for Zeckendorf. But he never allowed that sentiment to get in the way of his banking judgment. "André was very fond of him," relates Ames, "and he regarded Bill as well ahead of his time—but absolutely incapable of taking advantage of the brilliant ideas he had. And he had brilliant ideas. Much of what Bill foresaw has happened. He was right about Park Avenue, and he was right in saying, 'Sixth Avenue is going to be the next one. You wait and see.' But the poor guy was psychologically unable to stand still long enough to reap the benefit of anything he did.

"André's instincts about these investments were not the same as Bill's. He could not have foreseen what was going to happen to Park Avenue or Sixth Avenue. But he had the investor's ability of knowing how to do it, and of knowing when you are getting yourself overextended and when you are going too fast or too slow."

If Zeckendorf had had that ability, and if he had lived long enough, his real estate empire could have been truly awesome. "We thought real estate was a great game in the fifties and early sixties because of inflation, and inflation was running one percent a year at that time!" reflects Nicholson. "Can you imagine the difference in that game with inflation running at twelve percent? If Bill Zeckendorf were alive today, he would have been worth a billion dollars, without any question."

But for Zeckendorf, that day never came. As for Meyer, his initial investment in Roosevelt Field had been $3.5 million, and after he took it over, Lazard spent another $4 million to $5 million turning it into an indoor mall. When it was merged—tax-free—into a Lazard-sponsored real estate investment trust, Corporate Property Investors, in the early 1970s, Roosevelt Field was valued at $21 million to $23 million.

Today, Roosevelt Field is one of CPI's most prized assets, worth $120 million.

Bill Zeckendorf was right about Roosevelt Field. And André Meyer was right about Bill Zeckendorf.

CHAPTER TWELVE

The Incomparable Investor

The shadow of the tax man had long haunted André Meyer. A banker who knew him since the late 1920s remembers that "André always became terribly angry when he found he had to pay tax. He *hated* paying tax." And as Meyer became wealthier and wealthier, and older and older, that hatred coalesced into a determination to apply his ingenuity and that of his partners to the high art of tax avoidance. He turned increasingly to the one type of investment that not only offered the promise of a big killing, but the possibility of substantial tax write-offs along the way: oil and gas drilling.

Meyer was extremely secretive about these investments in drilling programs on the Gulf Coast, in Louisiana, and in western Oklahoma, usually engineering them through shell companies he had set up with such nondescript names as Nassau Oil & Gas. He was also extremely clever in how he deployed these assets. Leveraging his oil properties to the hilt, he would frequently use them as collateral for bank loans, which were *then* used to invest in real estate. Meyer would thus get tax write-offs on the drilling and depletion of the properties, tax deductions on the bank loan, and tax write-offs on the real estate investment.

The oil investments, to Meyer, were more then just columns of figures on his tax forms. He hired his own petroleum engineers and often, on Sunday mornings, would summon them to the Carlyle to be briefed on how the wells were doing. "He wanted to know everything that was going on, in minuscule detail," recalls one of those engineers, Edward Baker. "When we were active in western Oklahoma, I would call him daily, even if he was in Europe." Meyer's hunger for information could take absurd forms; he would, for example, ask for daily reports on oil-drilling activity. So each morning the bulletin would arrive on his desk: "The well is drilling at 12,501." "The well is drilling at 12,522." "The well is drilling at 12,544."

"What does that mean?" he would demand of his engineers. "Is that good or bad?" Rarely did the engineers have the nerve to tell him that the figures were neither good nor bad—that in the context of the oil business, they were meaningless.

And as beneficial as the drilling was for his tax status, Meyer could never stop yearning for more. "In oil, he really wasn't interested in the mundane twenty-thousand-dollar well that can make forty-thousand-dollars," says one of his Lazard subordinates. "He wanted the three-hundred-thousand-dollar well that made a hundred million dollars, even though the odds are a thousand to one against it. He was always looking for the hundred-million-dollar, big, big thing."

Even in the early 1970s, with his net worth in the hundreds of millions, André Meyer lusted for it. "He always thought that we were on the verge of *finally* making a fortune," says Michel David-Weill. "We had a well in Oklahoma that we had been drilling for years; it was the deepest well in the world. And he was convinced on the strength of the reports that it would be extraordinary." So convinced was he that the last cable he sent to the dying Pierre David-Weill in early 1975 reported that the well was finally going to come in. "He thought that that was the thing that would please my father the most," says Michel. "Which was absolutely untrue. It left my father completely cold—especially since he didn't believe a word of it." Pierre David-Weill's skepticism was well founded; the well never did produce. But Meyer never stopped hoping that it would.

Meyer also tried his hand at mineral exploration. He and his old partner George Murnane engineered a lucrative investment in the Magma Copper Company in the southwest United States. They did so well, in fact, that they promptly put more money into another southwest property that Meyer had been assured was rich in lead and zinc. Murnane's son, George Murnane, Jr., was sent to investigate it. "We took some test bores," he recalls, "and found it was very rich. We only had to put in a couple of hundred thousand, but we figured we'd make a million out of it. So we went to work—and we found that we had without fail put our test holes down into the pillars of an old mine that had already been completely tapped out." Meyer should have known he was in trouble when he bought the property. Its name was Sucker Flats.

Just about the only mineral Meyer was not interested in—or, at least, professed not to be interested in—was gold. He refused to share his native countrymen's almost mystical attachment to the yellow metal, and he lost no chance to pontificate, with a certain bemused detachment, about the strange hold that gold had on people. In the early 1950s, when Europe was struggling to get back on its feet, he suggested to friends that the continent's economic problems would disappear overnight if only people would stop their gold hoarding. Once, when some of Agnelli's people complained about the lack of cash flow from a land investment Meyer had made for them in California's San Joaquin Valley, Meyer shrugged. "You buy gold, don't you?" he asked the Agnelli man. The man said yes. "Well," André Meyer said, "I'd rather have land in California than gold. What do you think of that?"

Meyer scorned gold not only because of his belief that much of its value was based on foolish superstition, but because he was an American citizen. And American citizens, at the time, weren't allowed to own gold. Meyer may have condoned stretching the law to its fullest extent—he did it all the time in his tax shelters—but breaking the law was another matter. He valued his reputation, and that of his firm, too highly to allow it. Of course, there were some anomalies in his code of ethics, most notably his attitude toward trading on inside information not available to the public. In the United States this was illegal, but in Europe it wasn't, and Meyer could never grasp why he couldn't do it. "André always wanted to know when something was going to happen in advance of everybody else," relates a former Lazard colleague. "He felt that trading was a business that should not only be rooted in the disciplines of the trader but in the loose lips of the people he was dealing with."

But gold was another matter entirely. A British Lazard partner once mused out loud on whether there might be some way for Americans to purchase the metal surreptitiously. Meyer, in a sudden fury, cut him off. "I will not have this discussed in the firm," he bellowed.

Gold was not the only investment vehicle Meyer was prejudiced against. He also took a dim view of investing anywhere outside the United States. Agnelli, who was often the recipient of such advice, remembers that Meyer's opinion was, "If one wanted to be very, very risky, one *could* go to Canada. But South America he considered a complete snake pit. He would have nothing to do with it. Australia he thought might have a future, but it was a land of a lot of adventurous people."

As strange as these views may seem for a self-avowed international banker, they were perfectly consistent with the global outlook he adopted upon his arrival in the United States. There are so many opportunities in America, he would tell his Paris partners; why would any sane person extend his interests elsewhere? Besides, he would say, dealing in most countries was a no-win proposition: "The opportunities that are good the local people take, and the rest, the ones that aren't good enough, are the only ones that are peddled around."

Over time, Meyer's conviction softened at the edges, and he allowed himself to be talked into investing in office buildings and forestland in his native France. Yet whenever he ventured into riskier territory, he invariably was burned and would come away with a vow never to be so foolish again. On one occasion, he and other Lazard partners invested in a copper mine in Chile and found themselves the victims of a classic developing-country squeeze: Lazard received the official dollar-peso rate for its copper but had to pay black market prices at several times the official rates for supplies. Fortunately, Meyer was able to pull out of the deal quickly, with a minimum of damage.

Against Meyer's better judgment, the Paris firm became heavily involved in Sahara oil drilling in the 1950s. And, sure enough, not long after Algerian independence, the fields were nationalized. Thanks to protracted negotiations by the French government, Lazard was able to come out whole. "We have been lucky enough to get our money back," Meyer counseled his Paris partners. "No more wildcat operations." Yet when an enticing opportunity presented itself in Indonesia, Lazard plunged ahead once more.

Even though the Indonesian field proved successful, Meyer could never be convinced the investment was anything but a mistake. When it came to oil exploration outside the United States, he would tell his associates, only one rule applied: "You find it, they take it away."

A direct line connected André Meyer's phone to Lazard's trading desk, and he used it—to buy and sell stocks for his own portfolio, to check on how the market was doing—as many as sixty times a day. Yet he always displayed a certain ambivalence about the market. In the words of one former subordinate of his, "Mr. Meyer didn't like the stock market. He liked a sure thing. The idea of finding a good company, with a good price-earnings ratio, as a straight investment—he was not interested in that at all." While this description is a bit exaggerated, it contains a kernel of truth. Meyer wasn't crazy about the idea of watching a stock inch its way up, year after year—he wanted lots of movement, and he wanted it quickly. But always, there was the having-your-cake-and-eating-it-too syndrome. He didn't want anything too risky.

High-technology stocks, to give but one example, were strictly off-limits. Not that he didn't understand them; he understood them well enough to know that if a company had a gadget that was going to make it tens of millions of dollars, then it was perfectly possible that the day after tomorrow someone else would come up with a gadget that would take the business away from it. "I think he was more comfortable with businesses that weren't as susceptible to that kind of shock," says Lazard partner Peter Corcoran.

Hence, Meyer's emphasis on natural-resource stocks and heavy industry. After all, who was going to invent a new form of copper? Furthermore, they were investments in things of substance and of intrinsic value which did not rely for their success on the vagaries of human beings, whom he inherently distrusted.

These convictions notwithstanding, Meyer's attitude about his stock market investments was roughly akin to Groucho Marx's view of clubs that accepted him—if he bought a stock, there had to be something wrong with it. "You might say that once he bought something, it depreciated in his value scale," says one of his longtime Lazard aides, Peter Lewis. "The way André looked at it, if you don't own something, it must be good. When you do, it must be bad, because what are you doing with something that's good?"

Meyer was constantly questioning his own and his colleagues' judgments, endlessly reassessing and reevaluating. Michel David-Weill remembers that Meyer would "tell you to buy the stock of X corporation, and you did, and then you saw him two days later and you would say, 'I bought the stock of X corporation.' 'Ah, you did?' he would say. 'Oh, I don't know if I like it.' And you say, 'Well, you told me you liked it two days ago.' And he says, 'Well, that was two days ago. You know something happened—Sadat was killed.' I mean, I am positive that the morning Sadat died, Mr. André Meyer would have held a meeting to review *everything.*"

To some extent, this attitude was simply Meyer's old trading mentality coming to the fore, a mentality ingrained in him ever since he was a runner on the Paris Bourse. As David-Weill points out, "Most professional traders are never sure, because it's a business where you are proved wrong fifteen times a day. So your only safety is in changing your mind." But with Meyer, there was always something deeper at work, a well of insecurity that went beyond the bounds of mere financial prudence.

Yet, when it came to his investments, Meyer did trust one person implicitly: Albert J. Hettinger, Jr., the lanky, pipe-puffing ex-Harvard professor whom Meyer hired shortly after taking over Lazard. In fact, Meyer's support of Hettinger was probably the shrewdest investment decision Meyer ever made.

What Cézanne was to painting, what Rodin was to sculpture, Al Hettinger was to undervalued stocks. No one, not even Meyer, could match Hettinger's artistry at ferreting them out. Partly, his skill was rooted in native shrewdness, but mostly, it was the product of sheer doggedness—Hettinger probably read more annual reports than any other investor in America—and a devotion to business fundamentals. Hettinger had never forgotten what he had learned from his first investment in 1921: two shares of the National Biscuit Company. Hettinger sold the stock when he thought it had reached its peak, but he had neglected one very important point—that Nabisco, with the help of the rather informal accounting standards of those pre-SEC days, was deducting its plants as expenses rather than charging them as a capital investment. The stock, thanks to those write-offs, zoomed upwards. Hettinger resolved never again to overlook the fundamentals.

Having steered Meyer and Lazard into their first real postwar bonanza, the undervalued utility stock investments, Hettinger began to study the insurance industry. The more annual reports he read, the more he became convinced that insurance companies were the stock market's equivalent to King Solomon's Mines. Peering through the underbrush of the insurers' mundane underwriting business, Hettinger was one of the first to get a glimpse of the glittering unrealized values in the companies' investment portfolios. His first big plunge was in Connecticut General, around 1948, and in the succeeding years he began loading up on the stock of other insurers. By the late 1950s, thanks largely to his insurance holdings, Hettinger was a multimillionaire—and André Meyer, who tagged along on most of those investments, was a lot wealthier, too.

That was only the beginning. Hettinger's attention was drawn to the Japanese insurance industry. Once again, he saw investment portfolios ripe with unrealized values; and once again, he and Meyer moved into the market in a big way. Soon their personal accounts were bulging with shares of Tokyo Marine, Taisho Marine, Sumitomo Marine, and Yasuda Fire & Marine, to name just a few. Patiently, Hettinger and Meyer waited for the buds to blossom—and with the inevitability of tulips in the spring, they all did. An investment in Tokyo Marine, which cost Hettinger in the neighborhood of $3 million when he first bought it in the early 1960s, was worth at least $35 million a decade later. And, with gritty persistence, Hettinger kept accumulating more and more stock as the price went up. According to a former aide, Hettinger maintained accounts at the Chase Manhattan Bank that automatically invested $10,000, $20,000, and more *a week* in a selected list of Japanese issues. "The way he worked it," says this aide, "if the market went down, he simply bought more shares."

By the 1970s, this former professor, once scorned by his Wall Street peers as a hopelessly weird, head-in-the-clouds old drone, was said to have been worth in excess of $100 million. And, perhaps most astounding of all, he had done it all after the age of fifty-seven.

And as Hettinger prospered, so, too, did Meyer. Hettinger's buy-and-hold philosophy may not have been in keeping with Meyer's quick-profit inclinations. But André Meyer believed in Albert Hettinger. And, to Meyer's credit, he willingly adjusted his own investment style to fit Hettinger's, rather than the other way around.

The two were kindred souls in ways that weren't immediately apparent. As demonic a workhorse as Meyer was, Hettinger was even more so. In his seventies and eighties, he could still be found in his little office poring over his annual reports, long after men thirty and forty years his junior had gone for the day. Once, tiring from his labors, he stretched out on the floor of his office to take a nap. The cleaning woman came by, spotted the old man sprawled on the floor, and promptly called for an ambulance. Even the 1977 New York blackout couldn't stop Het, as he was affectionately known around Lazard; with the elevators out of commission, he climbed thirty-two floors to his office. He was eighty-six years old at the time.

Hettinger also shared Meyer's aversion to unnecessary expenditures, often making Meyer seem like the Aga Khan by comparison. Het would customarily bring home sandwiches he had filched from the Lazard dining room to eat for dinner. He never traveled around town in anything more expensive than the subway. One time, in the midst of a subway fire, a young Lazard hand exiting the station encountered Hettinger walking down the stairs. The young man begged

Hettinger to turn around. "Dr. Hettinger," he pleaded, "there's a fire down there." Hettinger was unfazed. "Well, son," he said, "this is still the best way to get around."

While there was never any doubt as to why Meyer stuck with Hettinger, it was never quite so evident why Hettinger, once he had made his initial fortune, continued to hang his hat at Lazard. One reason, no doubt, was sheer gratitude to Meyer for the base of operations he had been given and for the faith Meyer had shown in him. Then there were the contacts that Meyer and other well-connected Lazard partners like George Murnane generated; Hettinger was shrewd enough to realize that there was more to ferreting out investment opportunities than just reading thousands of annual reports.

Finally, there was the aura of André Meyer: like so many others, Hettinger was at once spellbound and unnerved by the Frenchman. In Meyer's presence, this supremely self-confident investor would become completely unwound, his fingers nervously working the fabric of his pockets. Sometimes Hettinger would say something, and Meyer would immediately dismiss it out of hand, snapping, "That is too cavalier." (This was one of Meyer's favorite expressions.) Hettinger would promptly apologize. "He never seemed able to separate himself from a fierce, unbending abnegation to André Meyer," says a man who worked for them both.

Indeed, as late as 1979, in a conversation with the author, the then-eighty-seven-year-old Hettinger still seemed almost embarrassingly awestruck by Meyer. "There is no living man I revere as much as André," Hettinger said then. "No one is infallible, but André came as close to being infallible as anyone I can conceive of. I can't emphasize too strongly that he was Lazard and the rest of us were miles behind him. Anything he wanted me to do, I was his to command."

Hettinger willingly gave Meyer the benefits of his research. But he was not nearly as accommodating with others at Lazard. "The things he initiated," says one man who worked for him, "he didn't share." Asked once if Hettinger had come up with any great ideas, Ned Herzog shot back, "Oh, sure. For himself." (There never was much love lost between Herzog and Hettinger. Herzog would take a certain glee in telling people how Hettinger's first wife ran off with one of his students. "That's what happens if you're a Harvard professor," Herzog would say.)

Time and again, colleagues would level the same accusation at Hettinger—that his advice to other people usually differed markedly from his own actions. "When you talked to Het," says an ex-Lazard executive, "he always told you to buy only the biggest and safest stocks. Meanwhile, he was loading up on three-cents-a-share Japanese insurance companies."

In that respect, Hettinger and André Meyer had a lot in common.

They were called "AM" accounts—accounts of wealthy private investors at Lazard in which André Meyer took a personal interest. Even though he shunned retail business and closed Lazard's branches, Meyer still allowed a small money-management operation to function that would cater to the needs of a select clientele. The most select of these were the AMs: the accounts of the David Sarnoffs, the Kay Grahams, the Jackie Kennedys, the Charlie and Jane Engelhards.

Meyer did not manage these accounts personally; instead, he assigned the portfolios to a professional in Lazard's investment-management department. But if the professional wanted to make any major changes in the account, he first had to check with Meyer. And Meyer did from time to time review the portfolio, putting a stock in here, eliminating another there—in much the same way that a master chef in a great restaurant oversees his *sous-chefs'* creations.

Something, however, was always missing from these accounts: the Meyer flair. It was as though he only allowed these clients to see one side of his investing personality—the finicky, conservative side— while deliberately concealing his risk-taking character. Rarely, with the exception of a sure thing like Avis, did these accounts share in the venture-capital deals, the oil plays, the mining ventures. With his money, he could take these chances; with his friends' money, he never did.

"André treated these accounts in an extended-family manner, rather than in a professional sense," relates a former head of Lazard's research department. "The key was preservation of capital. Most of the stocks were solid inflation hedges, raw-material stocks. And we were all afraid of taking a risk for a client and then having to explain to André why the stock went down. You just couldn't strike out. And he didn't want you to deal with things on an average or composite basis. If you put one stock in the portfolio that was a disaster, heaven help you."

In fact, Meyer was as nervous about the winners as he was about the losers. "Once we found an attractive stock and tried to put it in the portfolios," this man says. "But he didn't want that, he said, because if it went up, what would he do for an encore?"

This conservatism, of course, had its benefits. In down markets, the Lazard accounts generally held their own. On the other hand, when the market rallied, they rarely reaped big gains. The result, invariably was the chorus of complaints from Sarnoff and others about Meyer's supposed "wizardry" and how infrequently it ever rubbed off on them. But Meyer figured that while missed opportunities would merely make his friends angry, big portfolio losses would make them bitter. Anger never lost friends, but bitterness did.

Meyer and Hettinger may have thought their schizoid investment approach—one way for themselves, another for everyone else—was a wise and prudent course. Yet, ironically, it produced one of the greatest debacles of their careers: the abysmal results of the Lazard Fund.

The Lazard Fund was born in 1958, when open-end mutual funds were the hottest new game on Wall Street. These funds—unlike those rickety old investment vehicles, the closed-end funds—could issue an unlimited number of shares. The investor could redeem open-end fund shares at any time at their net asset value, whereas with a closed-end fund, the investor had to sell at an open-market price that would often be at a discount from net asset value. Eager for a cheap, convenient way to play a soaring stock market, the public snapped up shares of such open-end funds as the Dreyfus Fund in record amounts.

As much as André Meyer liked to keep himself and Lazard aloof from the public, the notion of starting a Lazard-managed open-end fund was extraordinarily tempting. There were certainly some sound financial reasons for climbing on the bandwagon: mutual-fund management fees were quite lucrative and would go a long way toward easing Meyer's ever-present worries about paying the Lazard overhead. Intramural rivalry also entered into his decision. Lehman Brothers had formed the One William Street Fund, and whatever Bobbie Lehman did, Meyer usually liked to do one better. And while he never admitted as much, the formation of the Lazard Fund may also have been the product of the tug-of-war that was constantly raging in Meyer's soul over the matter of his public image. He wanted the world to recognize his brilliance; he didn't want publicity; perhaps a mutual fund, whose results would show everyone how shrewd Lazard was, was the answer.

Certainly the investing public thought so. In the initial 1958 offering, they bought $125 million worth of Lazard Fund shares. Leonard Howard, a former Lazard partner who helped organize the fund, recalls, "The great excitement seemed to be that if a person put his money in the Lazard Fund, the magic, the mystique of Lazard Frères would give him something extra. He would be participating in Lazard's achievements."

In selling the fund, Lazard did little to disabuse investors of that notion. Even though Hettinger, who was chairman of the fund, cautioned at the time of the offering that "anyone expecting us to pull rabbits out of a hat and to follow unorthodox investment procedures better look elsewhere," he nonetheless indicated that "we hope to add ten percent to thirty percent to the income of our subscribing shareholders."

While Lazard Fund investors were sitting back waiting for Hettinger to work his wonders, they were unaware that someone else had the final word on the fund's portfolio. That someone else was André Meyer. Here, once more, Het's obsequiousness came into play. "I remember once we were discussing some paper stock," says Howard, "and Het gave a treatise on why it shouldn't be in the fund's portfolio. Well, André simply said, 'I think we should buy some of that for the fund.' And so Het turned right around and gave a learned treatise on why we *should* own the stock."

Lazard Fund shareholders may have thought that in buying the fund, they were buying a piece of Lazard's investment genius. But they really weren't, and never would. Meyer and Hettinger had no intention of putting them into venture-capital deals or Japanese insurance stocks or anything else that smacked of high risk. So when the Lazard Fund strategists decided to move 100 percent into equities, Hettinger came up with a bright idea: "Let's buy AT and T." The stock soon afterward split three-for-one, and, says Howard, "We looked brilliant. But it was just luck. AT and T was a parking stock. You don't know what to do, so you park the fund in Telephone."

Meyer would blow hot and cold on the question of the Lazard Fund's investment philosophy. Early in 1961, for example, Fred Wilson, who also worked on the fund, came to the conclusion that General Motors stock was undervalued. "It's the cheapest thing I ever heard of," he told another partner. "I think we should buy some for the fund." A short while later, the partner asked Wilson what happened. "Well," he said, "I took the idea to André, and he said he couldn't use it, because the Lazard Fund was supposed to be a highly

imaginative sort of thing, and how could we buy General Motors?"
General Motors then went on to one of its biggest run-ups ever.

Yet the fatal flaw of the Lazard Fund wasn't so much its fuzzy investment strategy as its sales approach. Unlike other open-end fund managers, Lazard refused to hire a retail sales force to sell fund shares to the public. The very thought of a retail sales arm still made Meyer's blood run cold; he feared it would damage the exclusive, high-quality image he had labored so hard to create for the firm. He had gotten rid of the salesmen when he took over Lazard, and he had no intention of bringing them back now.

But without anyone to sell the fund, investor withdrawals, when they came, could deal the fund a crippling blow. And come they did, thanks to the fund's indifferent performance. From 1958 to 1962, years when other open-end funds were rapidly expanding, the net asset value of the Lazard Fund actually *shrank* from $125 million to $91 million.What's more, withdrawals exposed the peculiar Achilles' heel of the open-end fund concept: the more money that is pulled out of a fund, the less leeway its managers have, and the poorer their performance is likely to be—which in turn will prompt even *more* withdrawals, until the fund disappears into the investing business's equivalent of a black hole, from which no dividends or capital gains ever emerge.

That was precisely what happened to the Lazard Fund. An investor who plunked down $14.45 a share when the fund opened for business on September 30, 1958, would have seen his stake climb to a mere $15.17 a share eight years later, an increase of less than 5 percent. He would have been better off buying U.S. Savings Bonds.

In May 1967, Meyer finally gave up on the Lazard Fund and sold it to Dun & Bradstreet. Typically, Meyer managed to turn the fiasco to Lazard's financial advantage, receiving as compensation 75,000 Dun & Bradstreet shares valued at around $2.5 million (although he later had to give $1 million of this back to the fund shareholders after they sued, charging that Lazard had illegally profited from its fiduciary role). But the gain did little to assuage the blow to his pride. The geniuses of Lazard, as far as the investing public was concerned, weren't so smart after all.

In private, of course—in dealing with his own portfolio—André Meyer was still very smart. And one of the things he was most intelligent about was real estate.

As Meyer became more familiar with the real estate business, he began to realize that real estate offered a veritable cornucopia of possibilities for tax deferrals and write-offs. This insight into real estate as a tax shelter was shared by few other investors in the late fifties and early sixties. The prime objective of developers like Bill Zeckendorf was to realize as much income as they could from the property; the tax benefits of depreciation, mortgage interest, and the like were useful, but they weren't the point of the exercise. For an André Meyer, though, struggling to protect his burgeoning wealth from the IRS, the tax benefits largely *were* the point.

Increasingly, Meyer cast about for projects that would yield these benefits. And once again, he brought someone into his orbit who could help him achieve these designs: an energetic young investment banker named Disque Deane.

"I'll never forget the first time I went to see André Meyer," Deane says. "He looked at me and I looked at him, and the first thing he said to me was, 'What do you think about overhead?' I said I hate it, and he said, 'You and I agree on the first principle of my business. And what about publicity?' And I said I hate it, I never cared about publicity. We kind of fell in love with each other."

Imaginative, feisty, and thoroughly in love with the creation of wealth, Deane seemed to have been born for the real estate business. And no sooner did he join Lazard as a partner in 1963 than he set to work proving it. Deane sold Meyer on the idea of buying supermarkets and then leasing them to chains like Safeway; the tax advantages, he assured Meyer, would be enormous. Deane was even more enthusiastic about the enormous potential of federally and state-subsidized housing. The bulk of the financing, Deane and Meyer realized, would come from the government, yet the bulk of the tax benefits would go to private investors. So, beginning in the mid-1960s, Meyer, Deane, other Lazard partners, and a few close friends like Charlie Engelhard took major stakes in such new housing developments as Capital Park in Washington; El Monte in San Juan, Puerto Rico; The Farm in Brookline, Massachusetts; Lambert House in the Bronx; and Bellevue South in Manhattan. "At one time," says Deane, "we owned in a very quiet way just short of thirty-thousand subsidized middle-income housing units."

For all the tax write-offs they generated, these projects were not without their difficulties. The Brookline development ran into serious construction problems, including wobbly foundations. The Washington project was neither well marketed nor well maintained. And in San Juan, Meyer and his partners completely misjudged the Puerto Rican housing market; they set up El Monte as a rental development even though the sort of apartments they were building were nearly always sold as condominiums. "We never did get El Monte fully rented," remembers George Ames. "We would get it up to eighty percent rented, which in an apartment project is catastrophic. Most of them break even at ninety percent. And if these projects didn't break even, you were in trouble, because then you had to start feeding the kitty to keep them alive." All told, the additional sums Meyer and his partners had to put in to keep these projects going negated much of the tax-benefit advantage. The investors still came out ahead, but not by as much as they had hoped.

"The people at Lazard always viewed real estate as a numbers game," points out a leading developer who dealt extensively with the firm. "Everything came from the numbers. And I was unimpressed. They were just Wall Street bankers trying to act as developers, and the two don't mix."

Deane, meanwhile, was proving to be something less than the most popular man in real estate. "Let me tell you what it's like to deal with Disque Dean," this developer says. "Deane is the kind of guy who would sell someone a field. A few months later the guy comes to Deane and says, 'You told me I could grow nuts on it. I can't.' And Deane would answer, 'Oh, my goodness. I never said that. I said you could *go* nuts in this field.' "

Still, Meyer couldn't care less, as long as Deane helped him cut his tax bill. And that much Deane accomplished; at one point, he estimated he helped Meyer shelter at least $5 million a year through real estate transactions. Deane's masterwork in that regard—the deal he calls "the most unique I have ever been in"—was Starrett City. A 6,000-apartment, 150-acre, middle-income housing development in the Spring Creek section of Brooklyn, just west of Kennedy Airport, Starrett City had been foundering, uncompleted, because of the financial problems of its developers, the Starrett Housing Corporation. During Christmas 1972, Deane and Meyer came to the rescue, putting up $37 million in cash as an equity investment. (The New York State Housing Finance Agency had already agreed to a $307 million mortgage, and additional federal subsidies were forthcoming.)

By November 1974, Starrett City was nearly finished and ready to accommodate the first of its 25,000 residents. But for Meyer, Deane, and the other investors they had brought into the deal, the tax write-offs were only beginning. "We made the equity payment over a four-year period," recollects Deane, "and we *expensed* it. We expensed it *all*. And we have gotten out of that project so far very close to two hundred million dollars of tax losses." It was, Deane claimed, the biggest tax-shelter deal ever.

For all the clinical detachment Meyer usually brought to his property investments, real estate was never *completely* a numbers game to him. He loved to visit construction sites; when he was working on Lincoln Towers with Zeckendorf, for instance, he became inexplicably obsessed by the type of brick that was used. He and Ames would go off on brickwork-inspection tours on weekends. Relates Ames, "One day he went up to some building in Harlem, because there was some kind of brick there he was thinking of using. And André was a little naive about those things. He didn't realize what the security was like in a brand-new apartment building in Harlem. So he goes marching in there on Sunday morning, and Christ, the bells go off, and the guards come running out, trying to find out what the hell is this guy with the homburg and the glasses and the fur-lined coat doing there? But he was very good at that kind of stuff. He walks in and he says, 'Ah, you know I am an architect, a builder, and I have come to look at this beautiful building.' So they let him in."

Sometimes Meyer even seemed to fancy himself as a real estate developer. His better judgment invariably overruled such fantasies. But not always. After he and a group of coinvestors purchased the West Side Manhattan parcel behind Penn Station that Zeckendorf envisioned as the site for his Palace of Progress, they began mapping out plans for a sprawling commercial and residential development. It was an ambitious scheme for an otherwise desolate, warehouse-clogged area, and to the utter astonishment of those accustomed to Meyer's frugality, he chose as its designer one of the most distinguished architects in America, Philip Johnson.

But Meyer hadn't totally abandoned his tightfisted ways. He would frequently summon Johnson to his Wall Street office and lecture the architect about keeping the cost per square foot down; Johnson would in turn give Meyer a lecture about the amenities. To keep Johnson honest, the investment banker brought into the project the same sort of penny-pinching architects he forced Zeckendorf to employ in Lincoln Towers. Somehow, Johnson took it all in stride.

"I think Johnson accepted this as kind of a challenge," relates

Ames. "He got kind of fond of these other guys after a while. They would all sit around the table, and these birds would say, 'You can't do that. Why, you wasted four feet there! Who needs a twenty-four-foot living room? Who needs a twelve-foot terrace? Give 'em eight!' And Johnson would say, 'I see your point. But we can't make it look like a closet, goddamnit.'"

In September 1967, the fruit of their labors was finally unveiled at a city hall press conference. The plan for the project, which would be known as Chelsea Walk, called for a four-tower, 1600-family apartment complex aimed at middle- and upper-middle-income families, as well as a fourteen-story office building and distribution center. And the design that Johnson came up with would have done Bill Zeckendorf proud: huge, rough-concrete structures whose flat roofs and broad, sloping sides gave them a distinct resemblance to Mayan temples. With Disque Deane looking on as New York mayor John Lindsay lauded the project, it seemed that Lazard and André Meyer were finally going to make their mark on the landscape of midtown Manhattan.

But after the hoopla had died down, one slight complication began to present itself: to make Johnson's master plan work, Meyer and his coinvestors had to control the entire 350,000-square-foot site. And what everyone overlooked was that while they owned most of it, they didn't own it all. The exception was an old loft building housing some printers. Lazard tried to buy the building. The owner wouldn't sell. Lazard tried to get the New York City Board of Estimate to condemn the property. The Board of Estimate wouldn't do it. "It was a disaster," says Ames. "The city wouldn't condemn it, there was no way we could get at it, so we just finally abandoned the chase and said to hell with it." They did manage to build the office tower; but without the plot that the loft building stood on, the apartment complex was impossible. So Lazard, in disgust, sold part of the land to Sears Roebuck, which promptly announced plans to erect a new headquarters building on the site. In time, that plan, too, was dropped, after Sears was persuaded it would be better off renting space on Broadway and Fifty-first Street than building a whole new structure.

That was how the matter stood—and still stands, to this day. Sears owns part of the property, and Lazard partners own the rest. There is some hope that the planned New York convention center will reawaken interest in the site. In the meantime, all that remains of Chelsea Walk is the office and warehouse building: a lone, foreboding Mayan temple in the midst of a vast plain of railroad tracks.

Meyer's grand design went unfulfilled. But he had the satisfaction of knowing that for every disappointment like Chelsea Walk, there was a Starrett City, yielding tax write-offs galore. The numbers still added up.

CHAPTER THIRTEEN

Money Hungry

Accumulation. Preservation. More accumulation. It was the pattern of Meyer's postwar career, a constant, unvarying rhythm. Never did Meyer give any thought to sitting on his hoard, clipping his coupons, and confining himself to the role of an investment-banking elder statesman. Through all the venture-capital coups, all the real estate triumphs, all the winning stock plays, the appetite for more still burned.

To some, Meyer's unchecked avarice seemed perverse; didn't Meyer already have enough to buy almost anything that caught his eye, from a Ming vase at Sotheby's to a château on the Loire? But for Meyer, mere purchasing power had never been the source of money's allure. Money, for Meyer, was first and foremost a way of keeping score. As Fred Wilson points out, "In the financial business, the measure of success is how much money you make. That was the game he was playing, and whatever he played he played for all it was worth. He had to win. He just had to."

Nothing aroused Meyer's competitive instincts as much as comments about someone else's wealth. He would constantly moan about all the fuss people made about the Rothschilds: "Everyone believes the myth they have created of how much money they are worth," he would say. "So many times people come to me and say they are interested in a transaction because the Rothschilds are interested in it, the Rothschilds who have unlimited money. But, you know, there are so many Rothschilds, and they spend so much that most of them don't have a lot. They have a lot of paintings, but no liquidity."

Money to Meyer also meant freedom. The freedom to act or not to act, to take risks or hold back—in short, the freedom to follow his instincts. Plus the freedom to ignore and dismiss the fools from his presence.

Money also was power. The power not only to buy and sell companies, to shape deals as he saw fit, but to influence other movers and shakers. The mystique of wealth was the ultimate magnet—and Meyer knew that the greater the fortune, the more unimaginable and mythical its dimensions, the more compelling its attraction.

And money, finally, was a psychological bulwark—a critical prop for Meyer's ever-fragile self-esteem. "I always had the feeling that he sought money to overcome his feelings of inferiority," says a Paris friend. Other Meyer intimates had the same impression: that his wealth was a source of reassurance, a confirmation that he really did matter. It was a wellspring of psychic income from which he was constantly drawing.

Conserving his fortune, for these same reasons, became as much of a passion as obtaining it. "He didn't live rich," comments his friend Anna Rosenberg Hoffman. "Not that he lived like a pauper, but his life-style was never quite in keeping with the wealth he had amassed. He did what he had to, to maintain appearances, but that was all. Besides, the trappings of wealth barely interested him. All that he was truly interested in was his work."

Despite the persistent entreaties of friends, for instance, he adamantly refused to buy himself a New York country house after he gave up his rented one in Ossining. When pressed, he could produce a dozen reasons why: it took too much time to go out there, too much time to come back; he worked on Saturdays; he had to be in town on Saturdays. "I'm not the kind of man who has to have a country house," he would declare with finality.

Just as stubbornly, he refused to buy himself a limousine. A rented car was perfectly adequate, Meyer would say, and you never had to bother about the repairs. Besides, he would add, "I go two months a year to Europe, and I don't have to pay for it then."

Still, like any self-respecting *bourgeois,* Meyer would occasionally fantasize about luxuries. But, in the end, he shuddered at the thought of actually indulging in them. "He wanted so badly to drive around New York in a Rolls-Royce," says former Lazard partner Robert Ellsworth. "Ned Herzog always had a Rolls-Royce, and André felt it was so awful that he couldn't have one, too. Yet he knew that he *couldn't* drive around in a Rolls-Royce. Maybe it was all right for Herzog, but not for André Meyer."

Indeed, if Meyer luxuriated in anything, it was in his own stinginess. He loved to boast, for example, that he bought his shoes at Macy's. Not that he actually went to Macy's—he would send someone there with his shoe size—but he *did* buy them there.

A former Lehman Brothers partner remembers an evening when, as a young executive at the firm, he took a client to dinner at 21. "When the check came, I barely glanced at it and signed it with a huge scrawl. Then, out of the corner of my eye, I spotted André at another table with his gold pencil out, going over *his* bill item by item. That was the evening I discovered why I would never be rich."

He wasn't the only person to be intimidated by Meyer's tightness. An elegant lady friend would visit Meyer at the Carlyle and be told, "That's a lovely dress. Where did you buy it?" Frightened to tell him that it was from the House of Dior, she would mumble, "Ohrbach's." "Ah, Ohrbach's," Meyer would say, nodding his head approvingly. "And how much did you pay for it?" Afraid to admit the price was $1,500, she would say, "Thirty-nine ninety-five." "Ah, thirty-nine ninety-five," Meyer would repeat, nodding his head again. "That is a very good price."

In some respects, of course—in his passion for collecting great art and in the sumptuousness of his surroundings at the Carlyle—Meyer did live rich. First-time visitors to the Carlyle were invariably taken aback; how could a man with such a reputation as a tightwad live like *this*?

In the entrance hall was a Louis XV commode faced with Japanese lacquer hunting scenes. The living room featured a collection of small Louis XV and Louis XVI writing tables, a pair of Meissen porcelain vases mounted in gilt bronze, and a Louis XV clock of tortoiseshell and gilt bronze inlaid with engraved brass flowers. The library included more Louis XIV and Louis XV writing tables, along with a Louis XVI mahogany cabinet with white marble top. In one of the two bedrooms stood a Louis XVI mahogany and marble commode, along with a pair of Louis XV gilt bronze candelabra. In the other was a small Louis XVI reading table, inset with a panel of gold-decorated black lacquer; a Louis XVI gilt bronze inkstand, decorated with the arms of the kings of Savoy; an eighteenth-century gilded silver toilet brush; and a small eighteenth-century gold dog, a pug with red stone eyes whose collar was inscribed *"Toujours Fidèle"* ("Always Faithful").

Also in Meyer's possession, though not so prominently displayed, were such novelties as a George II gold-and-agate musical scent flacon; a Louis XV gold-mounted mother-of-pearl box; a blue enameled pencil, set with very small rubies and an amethyst; and numerous eighteenth-century snuff boxes, including a Russian box decorated with scenes commemorating the reign of Empress Elizabeth of Russia and a Louis XVI box with a diamond thumbpiece.

Then there were the paintings and sculpture. On the wall behind Meyer's library desk was Manet's *Woman with a Fur Coat;* on the desk itself was a figure by Maillol; and sharing one living room wall were Rembrandt's *Portrait of Petronella Buys* and Picasso's *Boy with a White Collar.* Some of the other masterworks he owned included Renoir's *The Little Gypsy Girl,* Cézanne's *The Jas de Bouffan,* Degas's *Portrait of Mary Cassatt,* Bonnard's *Three Bouquets,* and Van Gogh's *The Bridge at Trinquetaille.* His collection was rounded out by sculptures by Picasso, Rodin, Moore, and others; Roman and Greco-Roman bronzes; ancient Chinese wine vessels from the Ku Dynasty; and six Sino-Tibetan gilt bronze Buddhas.

In his more expansive moments, Meyer would tell friends that he had once cherished the idea of becoming the curator of a great museum. While few of his listeners really believed that, Meyer did evince an interest in art as far back as his first flush of prosperity in the 1930s; the respectable collection he amassed then was confiscated by the Germans in the 1940 invasion. Rebuilding from scratch after the war, he became a familiar figure in New York galleries and auction houses. As with any other banker *cum* collector, there were suspicions that artistic considerations were secondary. "The difference between Bobbie Lehman and André," maintains former Lehman partner Frank Manheim, "was that Bobbie was truly interested in art. For André, it was like hunters hanging antlers on the walls."

But other intimates insist his love of art was genuine. His granddaughter, Marianne Gerschel, saw it as a natural outgrowth of his inherent creativity. "His collection became very cubist," she points out, "and if you looked at one of his paintings, you would notice that that's how he put a deal together: the pieces would fit in such a way as to turn into something completely different that no one would have thought of.

"There were very few people who would think of putting Louis XVI furniture under a Picasso," she adds, "but for him it worked. It worked because of the color, because of the shape, because of the browns and the reds with a light coming in the window that brought out an auburn color. But you had to watch. You had to be sensitive to it."

All of which isn't to say that Meyer didn't know a bargain when he saw one. "He used to beg me to buy surrealists," says Ned Herzog. "I'd say no, and he'd say, 'But that's what's going up twenty times.' "

Herzog and Meyer were once at an auction at Parke-Bernet where Meyer purchased a Seurat. He leaned over toward Herzog and said, "That picture is *cheap*. I want you to buy it." "But you just bought it," Herzog protested. "I'll transfer it to you," Meyer replied. "You buy it. I *promise* you you're going to make ten times your money."

"I didn't do it," Herzog says today. "And of course it did go up."

In the fall of 1968, Meyer took part in one of the greatest art acquisitions of the twentieth century—the purchase, for some $6.5 million, of Gertrude Stein's monumental collection of Picassos and Juan Gris. The syndicate he joined to buy the works was a cross section of New York power and wealth, consisting, besides Meyer, of David and Nelson Rockefeller, John Hay Whitney, and William Paley. "The estate wanted the whole thing sold," recalls Paley, "and none of us could swing it—I couldn't, at least. Maybe the Rockefellers could, but they thought it would be better to get five or six people to share the costs and then have the joy of picking out what we wanted." At David Rockefeller's request, the group agreed to donate at a later date five of the paintings to New York's Museum of Modern Art, of which Rockefeller was chairman.

So, in early 1969, the five men gathered at the museum to inspect and divide up their cache. The method they chose was disarmingly simple: they tossed five slips of paper in an old hat and drew lots to determine who would get the first choice. They then went round in turn, choosing their paintings, in the closest thing the art world has seen to the pro-football draft. Meyer ended up with several treasures, including an early Picasso cubist masterpiece, *Homme à la Guitare,* that he agreed to later donate to the museum. "We thought we paid an awful lot of money for that collection," says Paley. "But looking back at it now, it was sort of a steal." *Homme à la Guitare* alone was later valued at $1.9 million.

Such coups, as satisfying as they were, didn't fully explain why Meyer collected so avidly and was so ready to put up vast sums if the right piece came along. Certainly, his love of the work had something to do with it. But equally important, in the view of some who knew him, was the cumulative impact this array of priceless canvases had on visitors. In his journals, David Lilienthal wrote, "I am always so overwhelmed with delight with André's fabulous paintings that I hardly notice anything else, such as the exquisite French furniture or food." Lilienthal wasn't the only visitor to feel that way; the overall reaction of people stopping by the Carlyle often was one of awe. In a living room crammed with Picassos and Manets and Van Goghs, how could one feel otherwise? Along with all that heavy, gilded Louis XIV and Louis XV furniture, they provided a magnificent stage set in which André Meyer could deliver some of his best lines.

But, at heart, André Meyer was still a *bourgeois*. And nowhere were his true tastes more in evidence than in his other home, in the Swiss mountain village of Crans-sur-Sierre.

While Crans's location conjures up images of lederhosen and quaint little chalets, Crans actually seems more like a bustling resort town on the Côte d'Azur than a bucolic Alpine hamlet. The center of the village is chockablock full of Yves Saint Laurent boutiques, Les Must de Cartier shops, and Tissot-Omega stores; and the town's major landmark is the Club Sporting, with its lush golfing greens and its honeycomb of tennis courts. Remote, Crans is—to get there, a visitor must either drive up a long, winding mountain road from Sierre, or take two dizzying funiculars and then a bus, or, if he is particularly wealthy, a helicopter. But a pristine Swiss hideaway, it isn't.

Meyer's house was at the end of a lane of rambling, mock-rustic homes. In this part of the world, houses are given names (one along the way is sweetly dubbed Veronica), and Meyer's was known as Les Romanettes. A stylish four-story structure of dark brown wood and (on the lower floor) white stucco, it was guarded by two foreboding signs: "Les Romanettes—Private Property" and "Entry Forbidden—Mad Dog." (A dog was in residence, but he was quite sane.)

Very little about Les Romanettes suggested great wealth. The place did have a lot of rooms—fifteen in all—and a large, sun-drenched terrace in the back looking out on a well-manicured expanse of lawn. But the rooms were small and Spartanly furnished; no Louis XIV here. The choicest antiques in sight were some rugged chests crafted by local Valais carpenters. There were some paintings, but in nowhere near the awesome abundance of the New York apartment. The living room, study, and salons were dominated by heavy, inelegant black leather sofas and plain cloth armchairs.

The overall atmosphere was one of relaxed, old-fashioned simplicity and, in the sitting rooms, of businesslike sobriety. Telephones were everywhere; the author, during one visit there, counted seven. The phones were ubiquitous at the Carlyle, too, but somehow, amidst the mahogany commodes and gilt bronze inkstands, no one noticed them as much. To summon the servants, an old annunciator box was used; when Meyer pushed a button, a slip of paper dropped into a slot in the box bearing the name of the room he was in.

Les Romanettes was a place where Meyer felt very much at home—which meant it was a place where he could go about his business all day long during the summer months he spent there. Arising as usual in the early-morning hours, he would phone and phone and phone. The phone would be alongside his place at the dinner table. The phone (with the aid of a monstrous extension cord) would be with him in the garden; he would sit there, chatting away furiously, his secretary Miss Rosen at his side, while watching the golfers at the Club Sporting next door teeing off. (One of the incongruities of Meyer's life there was that he had chosen as a summer retreat a house next door to a golf course, even though he himself never played.) Sometimes, in the early afternoon after lunch, he would nod off in one of the armchairs, his head sagging, and then suddenly spring back to life: "I must phone Agnelli," he would mumble to no one in particular.

Meyer's world was never very far away. Often, to the great consternation of the golfers next door, the tranquility was shattered by the deafening drone of a helicopter touching down on Meyer's lawn. The helicopter door would slide open—and out would step David Rockefeller or Gianni Agnelli or Chuck Percy or some other notable, come to sip tea and chat with an old man on his terrace.

For André Meyer, a villa in a Swiss mountain resort with helicopters landing on the lawn, golfers teeing up next door, and telephones ringing all day long was the ideal vacation hideaway.

In one sense, Meyer was an extravagant man: in his gifts to charity. His tax bracket, needless to say, did much to hone his charitable bent. But even allowing for his obsessive distaste for the Internal Revenue Service, Meyer was an especially generous and unstinting donor. "One thing I know for sure," says George Ames, "is that he tended to be *overcontributed* much of the time. His charitable contributions were relatively large." Lazard partner Robert Price once asked Meyer for a $5,000 contribution for an Israeli hospital, and Meyer dismissed it out of hand. "André Meyer does not give five thousand dollars," he told Price. "If we believe in it, we give a lot of money." And he did.

When André Meyer gave, he gave whole laboratories and complete hospital wings. One of the greatest beneficiaries of his largesse was New York's Mount Sinai Hospital. When Mount Sinai was about to found a medical school, it turned for help to David Sarnoff. While he couldn't contribute much himself, Sarnoff told the hospital fund raisers, "I think I know someone who might be generous to you." He put them in touch with Meyer, who promptly agreed to contribute $3 million for the medical school. In his lifetime, he gave at least $2 million more to Mount Sinai. Earlier, he had given a physiology laboratory to the Sloan-Kettering Institute of Memorial Hospital in New York, the donation reportedly coming about after Bella was treated there. Another $1 million went to the Institut Pasteur in Paris, to found a laboratory in molecular biology. Five million dollars was donated to Israel's Technion Institute for a Bella Meyer Laboratory. And in 1965, he contributed $2.5 million for a new physics building at New York University, to be named the André and Bella Meyer Hall of Physics.

Meyer rarely made a great to-do about his charitable gifts, with the notable exception of the big donation to NYU. That contribution prompted a "Man in the News" profile in the *New York Times*, the first full-length article on Meyer ever to appear in the general press. Meyer made it plain to the reporter that he had originally requested anonymity but had yielded to the insistence of university authorities that his name be made public. "Maybe it's an excess of humility," he said. "I'm terribly allergic to any kind of article about me." Aside from containing a certain amount of misinformation furnished by Meyer about his reading habits—"I read history, science, all kinds of things, and study contemporary history," he said, when in fact all he ever read were newspapers—the profile allowed him to extol the special role of philanthropy in America. "I believe," he said, "that people are very generous altogether, and that marvelous results have been obtained here like in no other part of the world. It's a great credit to the American people."

Often, Meyer's charitable contributions cut two ways: not only were they instruments of largesse *per se,* but also tokens of friendship. Out of consideration for Sarnoff, he gave to Mount Sinai and NYU; to help David Rockefeller, he gave to Rockefeller University; out of his devotion to the Kennedys, he gave large sums to the John F. Kennedy Library; to help Lyndon Johnson, he gave to the LBJ Library; and partly because Metropolitan Museum of Art chairman

Douglas Dillon was a good friend (and partly because of his own love of art), he was a major donor to the museum.

Once, in the early 1970s, RCA general counsel Robert Werner was having problems obtaining round-the-clock nurse service for his wife at New York Hospital. Remembering vaguely that Meyer had some association with the hospital, Werner called him up and explained his dilemma. "I've got some friends over there," the financier said. "Let me see what I can do." Within five hours, the nurses came, and came, and came: "We had nurses coming out of our ears," says Werner.

After all, what good was charity if you couldn't help your friends?

CHAPTER FOURTEEN

Madeleine Malraux

In the early 1960s, yet another woman entered the Carlyle scene. Like the other women in André Meyer's life, she was very French and very beautiful, and she was married. But her resemblance to Alphand and Bloch ended there. Serious and quiet, she had as much affinity for the shadows as Claude Alphand had for the spotlight. This was Madeleine Malraux, the wife of André Malraux.

A certain air of gravity came naturally to Madeleine Malraux; much of her life, after all, had been tempered by tragedy. A promising young pianist from Toulouse, she had been married originally to Malraux's half-brother Roland. Roland, a resistance fighter, died in 1945, after being deported by the Nazis, and shortly afterward Madeleine began a relationship with André Malraux that culminated in their marriage a few years later. Raising Malraux's two young sons, Pierre-Gauthier and Vincent, alongside her own by Roland, Madeleine was content to remain in the background, ever the loyal wife and mother, as her husband moved to center stage in the postwar French literary world.

Then, in 1961, Pierre-Gauthier and Vincent were killed in a car crash. Their father, already prone to bouts of depression, plunged into a deep melancholia that Madeleine was helpless to alleviate. Other strains were arising in the marriage, as André became increasingly preoccupied with his role as one of French president Charles de Gaulle's closest advisers. Madeleine wanted to resume her career as a concert pianist, but her husband wouldn't hear of it. Neglected and adrift, she journeyed to New York in 1966. There she turned for solace and comfort to André Meyer.

They had first met in the early sixties, when André and Madeleine Malraux came to the United States as official guests of President and Mrs. Kennedy. The Malraux had heard of this émigré financier, with his spectacular collection of paintings, and decided to pay him a visit during a stop in New York. Like so many others before them, they came away entranced—so much so that on the Malraux' next trip to the States, accompanying the *Mona Lisa* on its once-in-a-lifetime exhibition tour of the country, Madeleine took pains to ask about Meyer's health (he had fallen ill on the eve of the tour). Nothing cemented Meyer's friendship as much as inquiries about his health; by the time Madeleine returned to New York to begin rebuilding her life, she was a warmly welcomed guest at the Carlyle.

"I counted for much to him," she would later recall, "just as he counted for much to me, because I could confide in him completely all my problems. That created links between us that were very affectionate, and truly profound."

She could talk to him of affairs of the heart, and affairs of the pocketbook. "He loved to intervene for you in business affairs," she remarks, "but if you asked him for advice, he expected you to follow it." Only once did she defy him—when he urged her after André Malraux's death to sell their art collection, she refused. He also encouraged her musical aspirations, and after twenty years on the sidelines Madeleine made her recital comeback at a Berlin music festival. Not that Meyer himself ever was an avid music-goer; dragging him to concerts, Madeleine found, was like tugging at the leash of a reluctant terrier. "At concerts," she explains, "it is necessary to concentrate, not to budge; and with him, if he couldn't budge, he fell asleep."

It was evident that Meyer, too, derived much from the relationship. Partly it was a matter of companionship; his longing to have his friends around him always, his ever-present fear of being abandoned. "I need your presence," he would tell her. And during Bella's long sojourns in Paris, the need became particularly acute. As Madeleine remarks, "He didn't like to be out in the world, but he could not live with solitude. It was necessary for him to have *someone.*"

She would later describe their liaison as "a very profound platonic relationship. We did not have what one would call a love affair, in the common sense of the term." Yes, she stayed with Meyer at the Carlyle, and yes, she stayed there even when Bella was away—but, she would laugh, "That's not the same as saying I put myself in his bed." Nevertheless, she did concede that, physical relationships aside, Meyer figured as something of a substitute husband for her—and that she, along with other women, could be described as "wife-mistress" to him in the closeness of their emotional bonds.

In the late 1960s and early 1970s, Madeleine Malraux was a fixture at the Carlyle. In the end, it really didn't matter if Bella was there or not; as was the case with other women before her, Madeleine became fast friends with Bella, too. She was thoroughly absorbed into the extended family Meyer surrounded himself with, in which the distinction between wife, lover, confidante, and friend inevitably became a hopeless jumble.

On a given Sunday afternoon in the late sixties, a visitor to the Carlyle might encounter them all at the same table: Claude Alphand draping her arm languidly behind her chair and talking of berries; Henriette Bloch chirping, "Really, André? Ah, André, really?" over and over; Madeleine Malraux silently taking it all in; and Meyer himself at the head of the table, presiding over the scene like a Gallic Mad Hatter. "You'd sit there and look at this," says Marianne Gerschel, "and you'd say to yourself, 'I don't believe this. This isn't for real. Is this really happening?' "

But these sideshows didn't blind Gerschel to the fact that these women all were important to her grandfather. And perhaps none more so than Madeleine Malraux: "Madeleine in her own way, I think, tried terribly hard to act as a buffer between my grandmother and grandfather. She was always trying to say, 'Now, you know, wait a minute. Let's calm down.' "

"I always tried to straighten out their complications, as much as I could," Madeleine relates. "Sometimes a little psychology was necessary. Sometimes it sufficed to speak to one and then the other, to take the first step. But I wouldn't say it was easy."

The Meyer household was often badly in need of a calming influence. There were fights between André and Bella, fights between André and the children, fights between Bella and the children, fights between the children and *their* children. "André always said he did not understand his family," Madeleine says. "He would always remark, 'Oh, my family, there is nothing to say.' It was the side of his life that was very somber."

Despite Madeleine's diligent ministrations, Meyer would turn more and more for solace to the one mistress in his life who truly understood him: his work. "A person's personal life," he once told Disque Deane, "is so fragile that you cannot depend upon it for happiness. But if you have created a firm the way I have, and it is successful, and it will tolerate you, it is a wonderful insurance policy against the failures that people have in their personal life.

"Regardless of how old you are," he would say, "if you have cared for the firm, it will be *tender* to you all the time."

CHAPTER FIFTEEN

Life at Lazard

The offices of Lazard Frères, investment bankers, located on the twelfth and thirteenth floors of 44 Wall Street since the late 1940s, were remarkable in only one respect—as eyesores. Often, they were compared to a Dickensian countinghouse, or something out of Victor Hugo's *Les Misérables*. The working spaces were cramped, the rugs were threadbare, and the furniture had all seen better days. Someone once asked Meyer why he didn't replace the reception-area sofa, which was full of holes. His reply: "Show me one client we lost because the sofa was full of holes."

Exposed pipes were everywhere. If a partner decided his office needed painting, someone would come around to check which of the walls looked the worst and would only paint that one, ignoring the other three. The bathrooms were dingy and dark, with the men's room sporting a window that couldn't be closed, turning the lavatory in the dead of winter into an icebox.

The story goes that in the 1950s the partners became so upset about their working conditions that one of them actually suggested to Meyer that they move. Meyer said fine, let's take a vote on it, and just to avoid anyone feeling pressured, we'll have secret ballots. The vote was unanimous—to stay. (The tale says more about their fear of Meyer than it does about 44 Wall.) Even Meyer's closest friends couldn't convince him to move. When Chase Manhattan Plaza was under construction in lower Manhattan, David Rockefeller invited Meyer to inspect the building, in the hopes the investment banker would relocate his office there. Meyer dutifully trekked over on a cold winter day, listened to Rockefeller's enthusiastic pitch as frigid winds whipped through the construction site, caught a terrible head cold, and told the Chase boss thanks, but no thanks.

(Later, in 1969, the senior partner finally gave in and moved the firm into General Dynamics Company's old offices uptown at One Rockefeller Plaza. The move, however, was accomplished with the utmost frugality. Lazard made no effort to refurbish the space; the wood paneling, the office layouts, even the carpeting were holdovers from General Dynamics, and the office furniture was simply transported from downtown. Meyer took special pride in the bargain-basement rent he had wangled. "We shall pay no more than seven seventy-five per square foot so long as I am alive," he solemnly declared.)

While the notion of a firm as prosperous as Lazard inhabiting such run-down quarters may have startled some visitors, the fact was that the office conditions were perfectly consistent with Meyer's business philosophy. After all, if the only essentials, as he saw them, were a pad and a pen, who needed fancy desks and plush carpeting? Furthermore, far from alienating clients, Meyer was sure the dingy atmosphere reassured them. As Michel David-Weill points out, "People come to a lavish place, and they say, 'My money is paying for *this?*' Luxury helps at home, not in the office."

Aside from the dreary surroundings, the most distinctive aspect of 44 Wall Street was the omnipresence of André Meyer. Not only was the whole place suffused with his spirit, but *physically* he was everywhere as well. "He would prowl the halls like Captain Ahab prowling the deck of his ship," one old Lazard hand recalls. "Everyone knew he was coming, because there were swinging doors in the corridor, and he would hit the doors with his body, with a *whamm.* He would stand in the doorway and say in his high-pitched voice, 'Where is Mr. Troubh? Where is Mr. Troubh?' " (Processed through his French accent, it came out "Twoubh.")

Even when he confined himself to his office, Meyer was a bundle of nervous energy. Says Partner Frank Pizzitola, "One time I saw him pick up the phone, ask a guy a question, put the phone down, pick up the second phone and ask him if he had the answer yet." When he had to summon someone, he would sometimes forego the telephone altogether and simply scream at the top of his lungs. Pizzitola remembers standing outside Meyer's office once and hearing the old man bellowing, "Mool-larkey! Mool-larkey!" Even Meyer's secretary, Simone Rosen, couldn't figure out to whom he was referring. *"Vous-voulez qui?"* she asked him. "Mool-larkey! Mool-larkey!" he answered. Finally, Pizzitola was able to translate. "He wants Tom," he whispered to Rosen, referring to Lazard's in-house counsel, Thomas Mullarkey.

Simone Rosen, for her part, had become used to such displays.

Her own relationship with Meyer had come to resemble that of a battling husband and wife in a French farce. He would yell at her, and she would yell right back at him, calling him, in French, "pig" and other such epithets. He would crumple a piece of paper, toss it on the floor, and tell her, "Pick it up." "*You* pick it up," she would snap. Despite such treatment, she was totally devoted to him, and he to her; she never dreamed of working for anyone else.

One of her many jobs was to amass and relay the piles of memorandums that came to Meyer every day. No executive ever received so many memos and sent out so few himself. His hunger for information was insatiable; consequently, even the most nonsensical material (such as the level at which his oil wells were drilling) made its way into memorandums. Whatever didn't get to him during the day had to be on Miss Rosen's desk by 5:15 in the evening, so she could send it up to the Carlyle. And, almost invariably, those memos would be returned to the sender by eight o'clock the next morning. If Meyer didn't like something, he would scribble notes all over the margins. If he approved, he would just scrawl a big, bold "A." "If you got the 'A,'" says one man, "it was legal tender. You could go with it."

While some at the firm couldn't believe Meyer plowed through the dozens of memos he got every day—they figured he put an "A" on many of them just to let people know he was watching them—others insisted that he did, and that it added immeasurably to the *espirit de corps* at the firm. "Lazard benefited from the fact that it had a brilliant, aggressive leader who could give you an answer immediately," says former partner Ray Troubh. "You don't know how important it is to write a memo at five P.M. and have an answer on your desk at eight A.M."

Indeed, there was considerable method to Meyer's madness. Even his most bizarre practices were outgrowths of his basic business tenets. His obsession with having his partners available at a moment's notice was part and parcel of his views that corporate doctors should be on call as much as medical doctors. His taste for minutiae sprang out of his beliefs that fortunes can often be won or lost for want of a nail. His basic attitude was that the only way to succeed in a treacherous world was to have total control of your environment, and of yourself.

The trouble was that Meyer always went overboard. Sound business practices were grotesquely exaggerated and distorted by the twists and turns of his psyche—particularly his overpowering need to dominate the affairs of those around him. During the summer, he would convene partners meetings at 8:30 on Monday mornings— knowing, as he must have, that many of the partners had summer homes in the Hamptons or in Connecticut, and that there was no way they could get to the office from their weekend retreats on time. The partners consequently had to trek back to the city on Sunday night.

He would subject his partners to violent tongue-lashings; all too often, the eruptions were designed to put the poor victim in his place—in full view of his peers. One man who was summoned to witness a Meyer dressing down is still slightly shaken by the experience. "André just made an ass of this guy," he recalls. "I was so damn uncomfortable, and I remember saying to myself, 'Boy, I've heard a lot about this, but this is the first time I've actually seen it. Once is enough.' " (A few Lazard partners, it should be noted, were able to take these spectacles in stride. One man once looked on as Meyer flayed one of his colleagues, then said to the old man afterwards, "You know, Mr. Meyer, it's Saturday afternoon. I should be paying for this matinee performance." Meyer looked at him quizzically: "Was it too much?" he asked.)

"After a while," says a former partner, "your reactions became a bit Pavlovian." People who under other circumstances were strong, independent businessmen underwent a form of spinal erosion after prolonged exposure to André Meyer. One such case involved Charles Stewart, who joined Lazard after a distinguished banking career at the U.S. Trust Company. Upon being invited to a golf tournament by U.S. Steel, Stewart felt compelled to ask Ned Herzog, "Do you think André will let me go?" Replied Herzog: "I don't know." In Peter Lewis's words, "Here was a man who was the head of U.S. Trust, talking to the number-two partner at Lazard about whether it was OK to go for a weekend of golf with the head of U.S. Steel. And *they don't know.*"

To someone looking in on the firm from the outside, the whole scene had elements of comic opera. One leading investment banker who was an occasional visitor remembers, "When you sat in André's office you'd see this steady stream of people coming in, almost clicking their heels as they told him some little bit of picayune information that he wanted to know about." But to a new recruit to the firm, this cavalcade of obsequiousness was a chilling sight. One man who joined Lazard in the late 1960s comments, "What struck me was that these competent, professionally accomplished people had so little control of their own self-respect. They were emotionally dependent on André Meyer in an absolute way, and they were treated like infants."

"André used to complain all the time about the anarchy around here," Fred Wilson remembers. "He complained, but he didn't really mean it. It was only anarchy when guys got out from under *his* control—then it became anarchy. As long as he still had the reins, it was not anarchy."

In truth, Lazard under Meyer was a hopelessly disorganized place. There were no committees to speak of, no chains of command, no systematized ways of coping with problems. Lazard wasn't the only Wall Street firm to operate that way: nearly all the old-line partnerships suffered from amorphous management structures. The difference was, at other firms, partners were partners; at Lazard, partners were employees.

Meyer's attitude on the subject was summed up by his oft-repeated admonition to his colleagues: "I do not pay you to think." One "partner" found that out the hard way when he was once told by Meyer, who was in Europe at the time, to send a telegram to the president of a major American bank. "Some part of me," the man recalls, "said we shouldn't send this. So the next morning I went to see another partner about it, and he said if it was *his* decision, he wouldn't send it. So I didn't." When Meyer called that day and was informed the cable hadn't been sent, he erupted with white-hot fury. He screamed at the man, "When I tell one of my *clerks* to do something, I do not expect him to think. I expect him to do what a clerk is supposed to do."

No one who was subjected to this treatment should have been surprised; the relationship between Meyer and the other Lazard partners was clearly spelled out in the partnership agreement. "It was basically an autocratic document," says one ex-Lazard executive. "It said the senior partner had the power to hire; fire; allocate income, assets, and losses; and do so without limit." The lone exception to this was Pierre David-Weill, who owned the same percentage of the firm (25 percent) as Meyer. As far as Meyer was concerned, David-Weill was the only partner he really had—a fact that was underscored in Don Petrie's mind when he went to see Meyer about a problem. "I must discuss this with my partner," Meyer told him. "But Mr.

Meyer," Petrie protested, "I *am* your partner." "Oh, of course," Meyer mumbled. But Petrie got the message.

In the system Meyer constructed, all the partners, and many of the associates, reported to him directly; for one partner to tell another about something, without simultaneously informing Meyer, was virtually an act of treason. The flow of information had to be constant, particularly if there was a piece of bad news. "If I had known that as soon as you had known it," he would tell people, "we could have figured out how to do something about it. But if you don't tell me, how can I help?" On the other hand, a lot of the information he sought, even in this area, could be of no real use to him; he just wanted it anyway. According to Peter Lewis, "I would go someplace like Radnor, Pennsylvania, and he would call me up there and say, 'Why didn't you tell me you were in Radnor, Pennsylvania?' "

Meyer was forever seething at the possibility that someone at Lazard, somewhere, was holding back. One time a Lazard Paris partner was asked by Meyer to contact a company on behalf of RCA. As soon as he walked out of the meeting with the company, he rang Meyer. "Ah," said Meyer, his voice dripping with weary irony. "You have finally decided to call me."

Peter Lewis tells of the time he was sent some material by someone at another leading investment bank, First Boston. The First Boston executive explained that the bank's chairman, George Woods, would be talking to Meyer about it at some point, but he didn't know when. "I'm not authorized to send it to you," the man told Lewis, "but I may be away. Put it in your file, and if it comes up, you've got the material."

"The material came," relates Lewis. "I was busy on something else, and I did exactly what he said: I took it and put it in the drawer. About two days later, Mr. Meyer came up to me and said, 'Ah, Mr. Woods called me about a prospect for a deal, and you'll be getting some papers from First Boston.' I thought to myself, 'Those must be the papers. I don't know; I haven't looked at them. I don't know what the hell they are.' So I decided to keep my mouth shut and didn't say anything.

"Mr. Meyer said, 'When you get them, look at them, look at the papers.' So I went back to the desk and I started to look for where I'd put the goddamn papers. I didn't remember in what file or where I had put it in the drawer or anything. Three minutes later, I'm looking for the goddamn papers, and Mr. Meyer comes running down. 'You

lied to me,' he said. 'I talked to George. He said you have the papers.'
I said, 'But, but, but . . .' 'Where are the papers?' I started to explain the thing to him but couldn't. 'You got the papers,' he said, 'and you didn't even read the papers.' And this was New Year's Eve, by the way.

"I remember standing there while a whole bunch of people were watching André scream. 'It is disgusting. How can I have trust in you? First of all, you lied to me. You didn't have the papers.' 'Mr. Meyer,' I said, 'I didn't know that those were the papers. I knew there was a—' 'Ah, you didn't know they were the papers! Why didn't you read the papers? You are here and you're a responsible person and I think you have some brains. I am disgusted with you; I have lost my confidence in you. Where are the papers?'

"At that point, I didn't know where the hell the papers were, so I go looking for the papers and I come back, and he's stormed off. And the guy who was sitting next to me said, 'When you went in the other room, he winked at me.' Well, did he wink at him because he was embarrassed for screaming? Did he wink at him because he was putting on an act? Who the hell knows? But it was very effective."

To facilitate communications, Meyer had a special direct "hot line" installed between his office and those of the partners. In the days before that technological breakthrough, he would summon people through the switchboard, which was under orders to hold the ring button down until someone picked up. "Did you ever hear a phone ring for ten seconds?" cracks an ex-partner. "You'd go out of your mind."

On the other hand, Meyer was not a great believer in two-way communication. Everything going on in the firm was on a "need to know" basis; if you didn't have to know, you didn't. Deals would be broken up so that each partner and associate would be working only on a small piece. The only person at the firm who could fit the whole jigsaw puzzle together was Meyer himself. He delighted in getting on an elevator with six partners and asking them each the most minute questions on the way down—knowing that each of them hadn't the slightest idea what the others were talking about.

To be sure, some of the partners occasionally rebelled against this fragmentation. Frank Pizzitola remembers complaining once to Meyer about an investment the firm had made which Pizzitola described as "garbage" and being told by the old man, "You are a garbageman. You are supposed to deal with garbage." (Meyer often liked to refer to himself as a "garbageman," cleaning up after other people's mistakes.) To which Pizzitola replied, "I don't mind garbage, Mr. Meyer, but the least you can do is open the bag and let me smell it. Don't just hand me the bag."

Perhaps it was because of such complaints that Meyer in the late 1960s did an abrupt about-face and decided to hold regular meetings with his partners. More likely, it was because, as Peter Lewis puts it, "David Rockefeller or somebody said you have to have meetings." In any event, he made a series of attempts at encouraging a free flow of information. Predictably, they were absolute busts.

He would hold "executive committee" meetings of key partners, but anytime someone brought up something he was interested in, or didn't want the others to hear, Meyer would cut the man off with "We'll talk about that later." Notes one attendee: "They were a joke, because everyone was afraid to bring something up with him they hadn't brought up privately with him before. Anytime you did it, you would have to preface it with something like, 'Mr. Meyer, on my way in I got a phone call, and I heard . . .' Of course, he knew you were lying, so it didn't make any difference." He would invite groups of partners to lunch, but as one points out, "You know how it is when you're in school, and your only prayer is that the teacher won't call on you? That's what those lunch meetings were like. Everyone was afraid of slipping up and telling him something that they hadn't told him before."

On the rare occasions when some juicy new piece of information was forthcoming, it would be couched in a verbal shorthand that only the speaker and Meyer could decipher. Relates one partner, "He would say to Howard Kniffin, 'How about that?' and Howard would say, 'Well, it looks pretty good, Mr. Meyer, but Jack thinks that we'll hear in two days.' Then sometimes André would say, 'Why don't we have any discussion?' What the hell—you didn't know who Jack was, you didn't know what the deal was, you just didn't know. He always wondered, how come we didn't have these great brainstorming discussions he'd heard about? But most of us would keep quiet because we didn't know what the hell he was talking about."

Eventually, Meyer gave up on the idea of big meetings (although he still flirted with the notion of organization charts; before Lazard entered one real estate venture, he insisted on such a chart, even though only three executives were assigned to the deal.) Which, given his temperament, was just as well. Notes Felix Rohatyn: "Nobody who was as autocratic as André could feel comfortable with a system that isn't autocratic." And nobody who *wasn't* as autocratic as Meyer could feel comfortable with the system he had created for himself. Once, before Meyer went off on a trip, he told people, "If there is anything you want to check on, clear it with Felix." One partner proceeded to call Rohatyn with the sort of information he customarily furnished Meyer. "Why," Rohatyn asked, "should I give a shit about *that*?"

The routine rarely varied: asleep by ten, up by four. Such was the daily cycle of André Meyer's life ever since he had been a young trader on the Paris Bourse. Even in old age, he seldom veered from it. Upon awakening, he would fix himself a pot of coffee, read the newspapers (he once got into a major row with the Carlyle over the hotel's failure to have the papers outside his door at four), and then begin dialing the telephone. By the time he was finished dialing, two or three hours later, he would be fully informed on the state of the European market and completely briefed on the coming day's business at Lazard Paris. Even with the six-hour time difference, he sometimes called before his Parisian partners arrived in the office.

Then, at around six-thirty or seven, he would dress and be driven downtown to Lazard's Wall Street office. Arriving before anyone else, he would pace the empty corridors, aching for the day to begin. A young Lazard partner encountered Meyer early one morning as the old man was prowling the halls. "Is there anything I can do for you, Mr. Meyer?" he asked. "Yes," Meyer snapped. "You can get people to sit at all of these desks."

Meyer always had difficulty grasping the fact that other people couldn't and wouldn't work the same staggering hours that he did. He worked twelve hours a day; he worked weekends; he worked on his supposed vacations in Crans-sur-Sierre. "Life is a discipline," he would say over and over. Why the rest of the world didn't have such discipline, he didn't understand.

While he couldn't do anything about the rest of the world, he could do something about the people at Lazard.

Early one Monday morning, he phoned a partner to find out what six-month Eurodollar interest rates were. The man gave Meyer the quote from the close of business on Friday. No, no, Meyer said, what are today's rates? "I don't know, Mr. Meyer," the partner confessed. "I just got in. It's only eight-ten." To which Meyer replied, "Well,

I've been up since four o'clock; why don't you do the same?" So after that, the partner dutifully awakened three or four times a week in the wee morning hours to phone Europe; he even had to install a separate telephone line in his home so the ringing wouldn't disturb his wife.

Not everyone was compelled to go to these extremes. But many partners did find themselves summoned to 7:30 A.M. breakfasts at the Carlyle, which for those living in the more distant suburbs meant rising at 4:00 A.M. Coming down in the elevator from one such session, George Ames was heard to remark, "I didn't know you could get heartburn from corn flakes." And there was an ironclad rule at Lazard that if any meetings between partners were to be held, they had to begin no later than 8:30. "André thought all the meetings ought to be over with by eight forty-five so you could do a day's work," explains partner Peter Corcoran. "He didn't consider the meeting as part of the day's work. A meeting was just communications." Lateness was inexcusable. One partner who arrived late for an 8:30 meeting thought he had a perfect alibi. "My train caught fire," he told Meyer. The senior partner was not impressed. "You should have taken an earlier train," he grumbled.

"Weekends," Meyer would say, "are for thinking." But by "thinking," he didn't mean several hours of quiet contemplation at the seashore. Meyer would customarily haul partners up to the Carlyle on Saturdays and Sundays, to discuss deals; to interview job candidates; and, infuriatingly for those subjected to it, to engage in seemingly idle chatter. Those who were spared such treatment nevertheless had to report to Meyer (and the other partners) exactly where they could be reached that weekend. Without exception, they had to always be on call.

Meyer's doctrine of availability meant that the partners were virtually enslaved by the telephone; they couldn't go anywhere where one wasn't within reach. Meyer would fly into a near-frenzy when someone, for some reason, couldn't be contacted. He once bawled Corcoran out for not answering his phone for eight hours in a row. Corcoran had to gently explain the reason: he was in an airplane flying from London to New York during those eight hours. Another partner one time was told by Meyer that the old man would be calling him about something on Sunday evening. The phone rang that Sunday, and the partner was greeted by an irate Meyer: "Your line has been busy for over an hour. You should have known I was trying to call." The man explained that his wife had been using the phone. "You should have told her to get off," fumed Meyer.

It was the same for vacations. When Meyer left the office for his summer sojourn in Europe and someone wished him a pleasant stay, he would protest, "Oh, but I am working. I am working"—and rattle his briefcase for emphasis. A vacation for vacation's sake was beyond the realm of comprehension. He granted them grudgingly to his partners, and he reserved the right to revoke them at a moment's notice.

So George Ames learned one summer when he decided to take his family to Honolulu. Ames was in California, all set to embark, when he got the call from Meyer in Switzerland. "You should go back to New York," Meyer said. "There are all sorts of things to deal with." As Ames tells the story, "I said no, I'm taking my family to Honolulu. And he got himself all upset and said, 'I'm going to call you tomorrow at the same time, and you're going to tell me you have arranged to go back to New York.' So he did call me the next day at the same time, and he said, 'Are you going back?' And I said, 'No, I'm going to Honolulu tomorrow morning.' He said, 'You're fired!' and hung up.

"So I figured shit, if I'm fired, I might as well go to Honolulu. There's no point in going back to New York. So I went. I came back to New York a couple of weeks later, and he was still in Europe. I went back to my desk and did what I was supposed to be doing, in the usual way. He came back from Europe a few weeks later, and as usual he chewed me out for various things I hadn't done. But he never mentioned he fired me, and I never paid any attention to it."

Two Lazard people were once chatting in an elevator about the imminent departure of a colleague.

"Are you going to say good-bye?" one asked the other.

"Nope."

"Why not?"

"Didn't say hello."

For someone whose evaluations of people were prized by tycoons the world over, Meyer's judgment of the personnel with whom he chose to man his own shop was notoriously erratic. He loved to stockpile people; at one point, it seemed that almost everyone he came in contact with, in business, in government, or at dinner parties, was offered a Lazard partnership. The way he figured it, he would give them a desk and a phone and *then* decide what to do with them. "He took them on, gave them big titles, and then didn't use them," says an ex-Lazard partner who observed the process for years. "In his opinion, it was easy and cheap to discard them and get new ones if they didn't work out."

Meyer's hiring procedure also embodied some bizarre and contradictory elements. On the one hand, he insisted on subjecting potential recruits to the scrutiny of a private detective agency. The recruits were never informed of the investigation; a potential partner was greatly taken aback one day when one of Meyer's close aides whispered to him, "Your neighbors in Manhasset love you."

On the other hand, he would bring people into the firm for no other reason than their connection to some friend of his. "If Gianni Agnelli wanted a young Italian in there," relates a former Lazard executive, "he got him in there.

"In general," says this man, "their people were attractive, socially acceptable, and undereducated. They just didn't bring anything to the pie. André would customarily recruit aggressive individuals and intersperse them with people who would fit right into the movie *La Dolce Vita.*"

Among Meyer's stylish recruits were Serge Reynaud, the son of the former French prime minister; Guy de Brantes, Valéry Giscard d'Estaing's brother-in-law; and Egon von Furstenberg. While generally harmless, they were the object of some bewilderment to the more plebeian Lazard types. As one man put it, "What do you say to someone who tells you, 'I'm *so* excited. In three weeks I'm going to be coming into my money'? Once," this man adds, "I tried to explain the Bronx to Egon von Furstenberg." They could often get away with astounding feats of impudence, such as the time one young aristocrat called Meyer—to his face—an "idiot and a fool" when the old man suggested he get a haircut.

"Their attitude was, 'I'm with André now, and soon I'll be merging ITT with Mobil,'" says someone who worked with them. But they soon learned otherwise. Meyer may have had a weakness for the well-coiffed and well-heeled, but he never kidded himself about their place in the firm. They were decoration, frou-frou, a convenient means of repaying past favors and laying the groundwork for future ones. Most were unwilling and unable to do the hard work and numbers crunching necessary to get ahead at Lazard; they simply drifted off to sunnier climes and occupations more conducive to their skills.

Meyer was similarly susceptible to people with government backgrounds. Government had always had the allure of the exotic to Meyer; even though he was on intimate terms with countless politicians, it remained a mysterious realm. He once confided to a friend that his great dream was to be driven in a police motorcade, sirens screaming and lights flashing, from the Paris airport to the center of the city. He knew, he said, that it would never happen, but that didn't stop him from wanting it. The very inaccessibility of that world, it seemed, led him to hold a rather exalted view of those who populated it. If they could succeed in government, he felt, they could succeed anywhere.

Over the years, he wooed numerous government officials, dangling before them offers of million-dollar partnerships at Lazard. Some, such as future Secretary of State Cyrus Vance, rejected Meyer's entreaties out of hand; but others, like David Lilienthal, succumbed. The fact that these men knew nothing about the investment-banking business was irrelevant to Meyer. All you needed, he would repeat over and over, was a yellow pad and a pencil.

So the former public servants would arrive at Lazard and sit there, pencil in hand, yellow pad at the ready, waiting for something to happen. And often, nothing did.

The experience of Robert Ellsworth was typical. Ellsworth, a former Illinois congressman and NATO ambassador in the Nixon administration, came to Lazard through the good offices of then-Attorney General John Mitchell, who suggested to Rohatyn that Ellsworth might make a solid addition to the firm. Meyer was enthusiastic, even though his reasons were somewhat vague. "He just thought I was close to the White House and close to Nixon and close to Congress and close to the international scene, all of which was true," says Ellsworth.

Meyer's first assignment for Ellsworth was to head up something called Lazard International, which was supposed to be a cooperative venture among the three Lazards in New York, London, and Paris. But as Ellsworth recalls, "André didn't know what it really did, and I didn't know, either. I mean, it was actually ridiculous—the concept of having something called Lazard International. What would it do? Lazard *was* international."

After that scheme fell through, Meyer gave Ellsworth various odd jobs. He sent him to the annual International Monetary Fund meeting in Washington to "gather intelligence," which mainly involved reporting back to Meyer on what the delegates were saying about interest rates and the world economy. He arranged Ellsworth's appointment to some corporate boards, including those of Fiat and General Dynamics, and generally spent hours agonizing over what role in Lazard Ellsworth would play. "I'd go over to his apartment on Sunday afternoon, and we'd talk about that," relates Ellsworth. "Then he'd say, 'Now we're going to get organized. Next Sunday we'll have Felix over.' so Felix would come over and enter into the conversation, but nothing ever happened."

After a while, it became clear to Ellsworth that what Meyer mostly wanted out of him was, in Ellsworth's words, "trivial political gossip." He would summon Ellsworth to Crans—a rare honor for a partner—and, says Ellsworth, "We would discuss politics all day long. He would tell me how stupid James Callaghan was when he was chancellor of the exchequer, and how he could never understand how a guy that dumb could be chancellor. We'd talk about Israel, and how intransigent Mrs. Meir was, and what a self-defeating policy that was. And in the United States who were these people in the White House, and what kind of advice were they giving Nixon? He'd call me sometimes when he was in Switzerland after Nixon had given a speech, and he'd talk about the speech, and what it meant."

Yet, strangely enough, Ellsworth came away from all this with an almost boundless respect, and even awe, of André Meyer, "I don't think I've ever dealt with anyone anywhere under any circumstances with the brilliance and scope and sensitivity and insight of André," he says. "In negotiating with someone, he seemed to have some kind of a secret radio with which he could listen to the other fellow's innermost thoughts." But his appreciation for Meyer's genius didn't quite offset the frustration of a pointless, directionless job. After four years as probably the world's highest-paid political sounding board, Ellsworth resigned from Lazard. Shortly afterward, he became deputy secretary of defense under President Gerald R. Ford.

It was never hard to understand why Ellsworth accepted such a nebulous position, or why so many otherwise intelligent people put up with Meyer's eccentricities. They knew that if they hung around long enough, Lazard would make them rich. And, in most cases, it did.

In 1965, for example, Lazard's profits were $7.5 million, and a partner of middling seniority could count on 2 or 3 percent of that, or $150,000 to $225,000. (Those were, it should be remembered, pre-Vietnam-inflation dollars.) By 1968, with the firm's merger-and-acquisition business in full gear, that partner was probably pulling in between $500,000 and $600,000.

Aside from their share of Lazard's profits, partners were also offered a chance to participate in the various venture-capital, real estate, and tax-shelter deals that Meyer was engineering. Each partner was given the option of investing in a deal in proportion to his partnership percentage. If he declined, his share of the deal was split among the other partners. Rarely did partners have to put up any actual cash for their investments; the amounts were simply debited from their partnership accounts, which held their accrued earnings from the firm. In many cases, if a partner didn't have enough in his account to cover the investment, Meyer lent him the money.

The mechanism worked beautifully. The partnership accounts gave Meyer a ready source of capital for his deals, which in turn would hopefully generate substantial capital gains for the partners. And the richer they became, the more money Meyer would have available for his next deal.

On top of that, there were all sorts of other *sub rosa* arrangements with individual partners, in which they were given percentages of deals they brought to the firm or business they created. Justin Colin, for instance, was given a share of his arbitrage profits. "André was a sucker for making special deals," notes Colin. "His firm was one mass of special deals. Almost every partner had his own deal with André." As Colin saw it, "You weren't automatically going to get rich because you were a partner. What you got when you went to Lazard was a hunting license. You had to figure out a way to make it work."

After ten years or so of venture and tax-shelter investments, special arrangements, and escalating partnership profits (Lazard never had a losing year under Meyer's reign), a man could pile up quite a sizable nest egg. And no one was more aware of that than André Meyer himself. "For the money you are making," he would tell his partners, "you should be working twenty-four hours a day."

During a visit to the Carlyle, Lehman partner Frank Manheim watched in amazement as Meyer pulled from his pocket a slip of paper on which he had written exactly what each Lazard partner was worth. "He wanted to show me how rich he had made all these guys," says Manheim. "I think he kept it daily. And it killed him to look at it. He would speak of his partners so contemptuously. 'So-and-so is a dope,' he would say, 'and look at *him.*' " This display wasn't reserved only for guests. Once, after George Ames said something Meyer thought was stupid, Meyer turned to another Lazard executive and groaned, "Can you imagine? I made that man millions."

Nevertheless, even in his most acerbic moments, Meyer recognized that these people had their uses. "Money is a tool," he would say. And in the case of the Lazard partners, money was a lever with which he could pry out of them marathon hours, intense dedication, and a willingness to subordinate their professional and personal lives—and their personalities—to his whims. "It was a paternalistic society," says Colin. "He took care of you, and therefore he expected you to care for him like a son cares for a father." Disque Deane refers to the relationship as "a blood bondage. André was a very possessive lover. He didn't think you had a personal life or a life that was separate from the firm."

Meyer loved playing the paterfamilias; if someone at the firm was getting married or divorced or expecting a child, he had to know about it. No one minded this very much, although occasionally Meyer would take his fatherliness a step too far—such as at Christmastime, when he would roam the firm bestowing benign pats on the derrières of secretaries. One Christmas, thinking holiday bonuses weren't enough, he walked around Lazard handing out boxes of Brooks Brothers ties and shirts.

Meyer dealt with his partners' paychecks like a father doling out his child's allowance. Under the Lazard partnership agreements, the partners were only wealthy on paper; Meyer had absolute control over how much they could draw out of their accounts. They were usually given enough to pay their taxes, and provided with a decent but unspectacular wage. (Associates who became partners were astonished to find that their exalted status meant a cut in pay.) If a partner planned a major expenditure—such as the purchase of a cooperative apartment—the money was available, but first he had to go through the indignity of approaching Meyer and explaining to him why he needed the money, which meant explaining to him just why he needed a cooperative apartment. "You were put in a frame of mind where you apologized before you took money out," remarks Tom Mullarkey. "Anything that went beyond your living expenses, you literally apologized for. You were both embarrassed and afraid."

As onerous as these strictures were, many in the firm felt they made sense. In Mullarkey's words, "André felt that this business runs on money, and everybody should have a stake in it. You shouldn't be carried as a drain." On the other hand, Meyer's iron grip on their purse strings meant that Lazard's twenty-odd partners were often hard pressed to maintain the sort of life-styles that Lazard partners, in the opinion of the outside world, were supposed to have.

One partner who apparently felt the strain most acutely was an affable, well-connected man named Edward T. Shean. A protégé of Ned Herzog, Shean had a taste for the finer things—as the opulent Sutton Place apartment he shared with his second wife, Elizabeth Meehan (the granddaughter of a prominent New York Stock Exchange specialist), clearly showed. A Lazard colleague remembers a visit to the Sheans: "I looked at the decor, and I knew what Shean's percentage of the firm was, and I said to my wife afterwards, 'I don't know how he's doing that.'"

Then, in April 1967, headlines blared forth in the New York papers: "Wall Street Broker Mysteriously Missing." A seventeen-state missing-person alarm was sent out for Shean, who had disappeared while en route to Columbia Presbyterian Medical Center for a checkup. The police could not find any evidence of foul play, and soon the real reason for Shean's disappearance emerged: he had fled to escape an Internal Revenue Service investigation into his tax returns. Eventually, Shean surfaced and in April 1970 was indicted by a federal grand jury for failing to file returns from 1963 to 1965. Four years later, he disappeared again, and has not been heard from since.

How could Shean have gotten himself into such a mess? No one at Lazard claims to know for sure, but the guessing is that it had something to do with his lavish life-style and Meyer's tight control of his partnership account. Comments one of Shean's old Lazard cohorts, "My suspicion is that he needed the money to live on, but he didn't have the guts to go to the firm and say he wanted to take the capital out. I guarantee you dollars to doughnuts that he could have paid the taxes out of his interest in the partnership."

This timidity was not unique to Shean. Most partners quivered at the thought of requesting an increase in their partnership percentages. Those who summoned up the courage were dismissed with a curt take-it-or-leave-it. And if it was insolent to ask for a raise, it was a special act of temerity for a partner to request details of Lazard's financial condition. Nothing illustrated their partner-in-name-only status better than the fact that the only financial statement they ever saw was the little slip of paper they received at the end of the year—the size of a W-2 withholding form—telling them how much the firm had made that year, and what their share of it was. The size of the firm's capital base was a complete mystery; while it was officially reported as $17.5 million, that figure had not changed since the end of the Second World War, and everyone knew that the true sum had to be many times that. But not a single partner, with the exception of Meyer and Pierre David-Weill, had any idea of the exact figure. If a partner pushed hard enough, he could obtain more information. But usually Walter Fried, the firm's administrative partner, would try to discourage him. "Don't you trust Mr. Meyer?" Fried would ask.

"One time," recalls Frank Pizzitola, "André wanted me to put capital in the firm. I said fine, but I'd like to see the books. 'Don't you trust me?' he asked. 'Of course,' I said. 'Don't *you* trust *me?*' He really got upset. Nobody had ever asked to see the books before. He turned blue; I thought he was going to have a heart attack." Did Pizzitola invest in the firm? "Yes." Did he see the books? "To a degree."

Yet, by and large, the partners were perfectly happy to live with such restrictions. After all, most of them had brought little or no capital into the firm, yet within a few years they were able to lay claim to substantial chunks of the firm's profits. What's more, most were indemnified against the standard risk of a partnership: the risk of sharing in Lazard's losses, if any.

The bargain seemed a fair one: a child's security for a child's treatment. But for some, the cost was steeper than it first appeared.

André Meyer often referred to Ned Herzog as "the best syndicate man on Wall Street." While few on the Street would second that opinion, there was no question Herzog was the *richest* syndicate man on Wall Street. Herzog could always be counted on to put his money into every investment opportunity Meyer offered him. "In the main, I took all the deals that came along," says Herzog. "I had the greatest respect for Pierre and André. If they went in, I would go in."

If his approach to the acquisition of money paralleled Meyer's, his attitude toward the disposition of it couldn't have been more different. "Herzog enjoyed every *sou* of his money," says one of his old colleagues. "He caressed it; he ate it; he drank it." Not only did Herzog own a Rolls-Royce, but the Rolls and chauffeur would customarily be waiting for him outside 44 Wall. Not only did Herzog collect antique furniture, but "just for fun" he opened an exclusive antiques shop in London's Claridges Hotel.

Herzog's wealth, however, did nothing for his self-confidence, particularly during the latter part of his career in the 1960s. Perhaps fearful that he was being frozen out of the mainstream of the firm, he would sometimes take younger people there out to lunch in the hopes that *they* could tell him what was going on. He began drinking heavily. "He would come to the office late, order a steak, and close the door," recalls a former Lazard associate. Yet he remained steadfastly loyal to Meyer. "If you hear anybody saying mean things about Meyer, you call me up and ask me if it's true," he once told the author. "I'll defend him, even if I have to lie."

Overweaning loyalty was also a trademark of two other veteran Lazard partners, Howard Kniffin and Walter Fried. Each in his own way was indispensable to Meyer. Kniffin was a master technician. "He didn't know values or stocks," says one of his former partners, "but he knew the technical aspects of how to put a deal together as well as anybody I ever saw. It was Howard who taught Felix the deals business." Fried, meanwhile, was the top administrative partner, the man who did the dirty work of hiring and firing and breaking the news about partnership percentages. But he was more than just a hatchet man. Fried was that rare administrator with a flair for *understanding* what he was administering: he could comprehend the most complex deals and, better yet, serve as a buffer between Meyer and the younger partners who were working on them.

As important as they were to the firm—or perhaps precisely because they were important—Kniffin and Fried were not spared Meyer's daily regimen of tongue-lashings and browbeating. And after twenty years, the brutalization began to take its toll. "Howard Kniffin was a psychological wreck," says a man who worked closely with him. "He shook whenever André walked in the room." Another co-worker recalls, "Howard was completely nonfunctional when André was around." Despite a terrible case of emphysema, Kniffin would nervously drag on cigarettes all day long. A drained, sad old man, he died in December 1980 at the age of seventy-two.

Fried was similarly beleaguered; says his successor, Tom Mullarkey, "Someone would scream on the phone to him, 'How's that Dubai deal coming?' And he would ask himself, '*What* Dubai deal?' " Peter Lewis remembers Fried as "the chief worrier. He worried all the time. 'Is the contract going to be right? Are the people working on the contract doing it right?' And then, after the signing, 'Was the contract right? Did they make a mistake? Did they forget anything?' "

In this capacity, Fried served Meyer well. But he served himself less well. He ended up suffering a nervous breakdown, left the firm in the early seventies, and died shortly afterwards. Like Kniffin, he never had either the time or the energy to get much satisfaction out of the millions he made at Lazard. In both their cases, the bondage to André Meyer was truly one of blood.

Younger partners who watched what happened to Herzog and Kniffin and Fried did so with a sense of foreboding. That, they reasoned, could be *them* in five or ten years. But few of the key people felt strongly enough about it to break away. Some, to be sure, were held in place by the electric atmosphere of Lazard, and by the stimulation of working with one of the greatest investment-banking minds of the century. But for others, the lure of Lazard boiled down to a matter of dollars and cents. At Lazard, they could be millionaires; at any other firm, they would simply be partners.

Nevertheless, there were those who got up the courage to sever the tie. One was Rainer Gut, a native Swiss who came to Lazard after a stint as New York representative for the Union Bank of Switzerland. Gut never quite acclimated himself to Meyer's stifling control. He would look on in amazement as people like Disque Deane and Herzog spoke out in favor of deals in Meyer's presence that only minutes before, in private, they had been staunchly against. When Gut held fast and voiced his objections to the deal, Meyer would cut him off with, "What do you know?" Gut and Meyer would have shouting matches at least once a week, which usually ended with Meyer berating him as "a stupid, stubborn German Swiss" and hurling a rolled-up wad of paper at him.

The last straw for Gut came one summer when he was off on a fishing trip in Canada's Laurentian Mountains with his son and George Murnane, Jr. As the three watched in amazement, a seaplane landed on the lake and the pilot shouted out, "Is there a Mr. Gut here? I have a message for you to call your office." Since there were no phones around, Gut had to hop in and fly to the nearest one—some sixty miles away. When he was finally connected to Meyer—after a wait of over an hour for Meyer to call him back from Paris—the old man asked him, "When are you coming back?" Gut was dumbfounded; Meyer could easily have gotten that information from his secretary. Why did he have to fetch him in a seaplane to find that out? "I have something important to discuss with you on Tuesday," said Meyer. Gut said he would be back a few days earlier. "Fine," Meyer said. "Good-bye."

Gut was still shaking his head over the conversation when he boarded the plane for his return to the lake. But heavy, ominous clouds began blowing in, and no sooner did he take off than he was forced to turn back. An hour later, he tried again, and almost crashed. With a plane flight out of the question, Gut decided to rent a car, but the nearest rental agency was forty-five miles away. He didn't return to camp until 5:00 P.M. the next day.

When he got back to New York, Gut managed to stifle his fury long enough to figure out what Meyer was up to. Gut suspected that what happened was that Meyer had called his office, had asked for Gut, had been connected to Gut's assistant, and had been told that Gut could only be reached in emergencies. It was like waving a red flag at a bull. "I'll show that Gut," Meyer must have seethed, "who can only be reached in emergencies."

Understanding why Meyer had pulled the stunt, however, didn't make it any easier for Gut to swallow. One of the big three Swiss banks, Crédit Suisse, had been dangling an attractive offer at him for over a year, but Gut had always fended them off. Now, he told them, he would be willing to talk. After nailing the position down, Gut went to see Meyer, but the old man, apparently, already knew. "Do you want to quit?" he asked his younger colleague. "Not exactly, Mr. Meyer," Gut replied. "I want to leave the firm."

Meyer pulled out all the stops to try to lure Gut back, offering to increase his partnership percentage and put him in charge of Lazard's foreign department. But Gut stood firm. As he once put it, "I had to decide between becoming extremely rich and losing my identity, or being my own self."

At Crédit Suisse, Gut moved rapidly up the hierarchy, eventually becoming chairman. In 1977, he spearheaded the bank's recovery from the effects of the worst scandal in its history, and Meyer beamed with fatherly pride. "It's so nice to see our former partners do well," he would tell people. Gut reciprocated with kindly gestures of his own. On Meyer's seventy-fifth birthday, he sent the old man flowers, prompting Meyer to remark to Mullarkey, "You know, this fellow Gut, he knows how to behave."

From his vantage point atop Crédit Suisse, Gut could certainly afford to wax sentimental. But he had no illusions about the life he had left behind. "It's almost like hay fever," he told a friend. "The moment it's over, you can hardly imagine how bad it was."

CHAPTER SIXTEEN

Pierre the Duke

In the incendiary atmosphere fostered by André Meyer, one soothing influence could always be counted upon: Pierre David-Weill. Where Meyer was irrational and arbitrary, David-Weill was calm and logical. Where Meyer was a human caldron, forever sputtering and fuming, David-Weill was perennially detached and disinterested. Meyer would stride through the office like a man possessed; David-Weill would casually saunter around as though he were out for a stroll on the Left Bank.

The son of David David-Weill and grandson of Alexandre Weill, he carried the Lazard heritage in his veins. He had spent his whole life working for the firm and was devoted to it; in his quiet way, he took as much parental pride in Lazard as Meyer did. But while Meyer had virtually given up on France after the war, preferring to keep nearly all his eggs in his New York basket, David-Weill's commitment to his native land was unshaken. He installed himself as senior partner in residence of Lazard Paris and set out to rebuild the firm from the war's ashes.

Despite the head start of David-Weill's inherited wealth and position, he and Meyer were equal partners by the early fifties. Their equality was symbolized by their office arrangements: each had a desk in the other's office, so that when Meyer called someone on the carpet, David-Weill would often be looking on, quietly taking it all in. He and Meyer were the only ones who knew the true financial condition of the firm, and they would jointly decide on such matters as hiring and firing, and changes in partnership percentages. "They talked everything over together," says Ned Herzog. "Lots of times André would say to Pierre, 'What do you think? Pierre, what do you really think?'" Their investments—in real estate, in venture-capital deals, in oil wells—were almost always identical.

Nevertheless, those who were close to both men sensed a certain tension between them. "They got on each other's nerves a lot," comments Pierre's son Michel. "It was a strange combination."

Partly, the strangeness was due to the divergent natures of their personalities. David-Weill disliked open manifestations of affection and emotional outbursts, and he especially disliked shouting and slamming. Their relationship to worldly goods also differed dramatically. While Pierre would sometimes complain that his huge tax bills were forcing him to pinch pennies, his life-style showed not the slightest crimp. Among his residences were a house in Paris; a house in the south of France; and a four-story Fifth Avenue townhouse in New York, almost directly opposite the Metropolitan Museum. "He lived like a duke," says Judge Simon Rifkind, the influential Manhattan lawyer who was a friend of both David-Weill and Meyer.

Then there was Pierre's approach to his job. "Pierre was an aristocrat," Fred Wilson remarks. "He was extremely able and extremely smart, with a remarkable memory, but he wasn't driven the way André was. Pierre didn't like to work. There were other things in life he cared more about." Furthermore, the crisp decision making that Meyer fancied was not exactly David-Weill's style. A Lazard Paris partner would suggest a deal between Royal Dutch Shell and Anaconda Copper, and David-Weill would ramble on and on about just to whom at Shell he could talk about it. "I could call up Loudon," he would say, "but maybe he's not the right person. I could call up Wagner, but he's quite ill." A half-hour would go by, and David-Weill would still be musing on whom he might approach.

In a world Meyer saw divided into the serious and the nonserious, David-Weill often, in Meyer's eyes, fell into the latter category. Behind his partner's back, Meyer would refer to him as *"un playboy de la finance"*: "He lives so well, you know, and he doesn't work very much." Meyer would constantly complain about David-Weill's extravagance: *"La grandeur, l'élégance*—look what goes on there," he would murmur to friends. Meyer would boast that if David-Weill was on such-and-such a board, it was because he, André Meyer, had put him there. The general drift was that Lazard was a one-way street: he gave, and Pierre took.

Yet as Michel David-Weill saw it, these complaints revealed something far more profound about the relationship between his father and Meyer: "André Meyer, with all of his tremendous achievements, had never stopped having an inferiority complex vis-à-vis my father. My father was in many ways what André Meyer was not, and wished to be. It was very difficult to ruffle my father; he was at ease with the world. He was known and liked by enormous numbers of people, both here and in Europe. All that made André Meyer very uneasy." Try as he might, Meyer knew that such aristocratic style and grace would always be beyond him. He could never be at ease with the world.

Yet even as he moaned about David-Weill's laziness and excesses, Meyer never ceased to rely upon him for advice and support. He appreciated David-Weill's extraordinary memory, indispensable in a world where who said what to whom at what dinner party was always a crucial element. And, more importantly, he valued David-Weill's dispassionate judgment, the cool, utterly objective way in which his partner would dissect a problem or a dispute. Whenever Meyer criticized Pierre David-Weill in front of Michel, he would always preface his comments with: "Look, I admire his judgment, and I think his judgment is always the best. But . . . but . . . but . . ."

Those who came into contact with David-Weill also learned to appreciate his shrewdness. As a former Lazard partner once put it, "Pierre was the smartest person in the firm. He had André Meyer working for *him.*"

If Lazard in New York was the unmistakable handiwork of André Meyer, its sister firm in Paris had a far more ambiguous parentage. Part of it was pure Meyer, but part of it was very much Pierre David-Weill. As in New York, the offices on Rue Pictet-Will in the ninth arrondissement were dingy and rundown. It is said that when François Michelin, the tire magnate, was offered a chair there one time, it almost collapsed under him. As was the case in New York, there was an obsession with remaining small—280 people in Paris, compared to 250 in New York—and with understating the true capitalization of the firm. Lazard Paris's reported capital was a meager 17 million francs.

But unlike New York, Lazard Paris was a real bank, making loans and accepting deposits, albeit on a relatively tiny, refined scale. And banking was more Pierre David-Weill's métier than it was Meyer's. True, under U.S. law, Lazard New York was not permitted to enter into normal commercial banking—but even if it were legal, Meyer would abstain. "It's a completely stupid business," he would tell people. "You risk a hundred dollars, and your margin is one. So you have to be right ninety-nine times out of the hundred in order not to lose money." David-Weill, on the other hand, had an affinity for banking—it was secure and it was permanent, qualities that his counterpart in New York was often prone to disparage. Nothing, as far as André Meyer was concerned, was secure and permanent. David-Weill also was self-assured enough to tolerate the idea that Lazard, by dint of its size, would always be an also-ran in the commercial-banking league, while Meyer regarded such status as shocking. With his ever-present sense of institutional snobbism, he pronounced it "not dignified."

Still, in other ways, Lazard Paris was a firm very much after Meyer's own heart. It became a powerhouse on the French merger scene, putting together the giant French metals combine Pechiney-Ugine-Kuhlmann, merging the Peugeot and Citroën automobile firms, and spearheading BSN-Gervais Danone's unsuccessful bid for industrial giant Saint Gobain. And, acting for its own account, the Paris firm was often just as venturesome as its New York cousin. It sponsored several successful oil ventures in the North Sea and Indonesia; invested heavily in real estate in Paris, Lyons, and Marseilles; and had major holdings in French and foreign insurance companies. Through SOVAC, the finance company that Meyer organized in the late twenties, Lazard was an important force in consumer credit, automobile financing, and equipment leasing. It even controlled 80 percent of the French television-rental market through a company called Locatel.

But the French partners always emphasized that in these developments it was they, not Meyer, who were the driving forces. "André Meyer was not the motor in France," insists Antoine Bernheim, one of Lazard Paris's top partners. "We are the ones who pushed. He was always telling us that a catastrophe would happen to us." To be sure, Meyer was skeptical about many of the French bank's moves, such as its involvement in foreign oil exploration and in the insurance business; he wanted to sell the major French insurers Lazard controlled to ITT. And, at least until Charles de Gaulle came to power in 1958, he remained thoroughly skeptical about France's economic prospects.

Meyer's lack of physical proximity—at best, he would visit the Paris firm once every three months for two weeks or so—also helped diminish his influence on his French colleagues. "The fact that he was here so little," points out Paris partner Jean Guyot, "did not make for the same kind of relationship you have with a man who is every day on the spot."

André Meyer: The deal-maker in his prime, striking a characteristic pose. (RICHARD KNAPP)

Little André already at work?   (PHILIPPE MEYER)

Young André leading his sister through the streets of Paris. It isn't clear why she was dressed in white; possibly it was for her confirmation.

(PHILIPPE MEYER)

The young man on the move at around the time he was breaking into banking at Baur & Sons. (PHILIPPE MEYER)

André and Bella soon after their marriage. Not yet thirty, he already exuded self-assurance. (PHILIPPE MEYER)

The family on a seashore holiday. Note the formality of dress. From the left: daughter Francine, André, Bella, son Philippe, and nephew Michel Weill.   (PHILIPPE MEYER)

Meyer in the late 1930s, at the peak of his Paris success. A recipient of the Legion of Honor, a confidant of ministers and trusted adviser to tycoons, he seemed destined to play a preeminent role in French finance. Then the Germans came.   (PHILIPPE MEYER)

An office party at Lazard, New York, sometime in the mid-1950s. By Meyer's edict, nothing stronger than champagne was served. From the left: Meyer's secretary, Simone Rosen; his urbane Paris partner, Pierre David-Weill; and Meyer. (PHILIPPE MEYER)

Bella in her forties. She tolerated André's affairs; there were whispers about hers. (PHILIPPE MEYER)

A casual dinner in a Crans-sur-Sierre restaurant with Common Market founder Jean Monnet (*foreground*). Bella is on Monnet's left; on André's left is his son Philippe. (PHILIPPE MEYER)

Fiat boss Giovanni Agnelli with the Meyers at Crans. Agnelli came to rely on the financier totally. "André was always the main architect, the last judge, and the last word." (PHILIPPE MEYER)

Meyer and LBJ. The two had a lot in common. (WHITE HOUSE PHOTO)

With Jackie at *Hair*. "His name constantly came up in conversations with her," recalls one close friend. "It was always, 'I'm going to talk to André about this, see André about that.' " (RON GALELLA)

André and Bella in Crans, drawn together once more after the long years of estrangement. She was constantly by his side, ministering to his every need. "Bella's an angel," André would say to a friend, and the friend would reply, "I've told you that for thirty years." (PHILIPPE MEYER)

Nevertheless, no one denies that Meyer maintained a strong veto power over the affairs of the Paris firm. "Nothing would be done, or could be done, without his agreement," says a former Paris partner. Every weekday morning, without fail, the Paris partners would ring Meyer at the Carlyle at 5:30 New York time to inform him of their day's activities. One young partner who had just clinched a major financing for a big industrial client was immediately accosted by one of his colleagues. "Did you tell Mr. Meyer?" the man asked. No, the young partner confessed, he didn't. "Well," the other man barked, "do it before something happens." Upon being apprised of a deal by someone in Paris, Meyer would typically preface his remarks with the disclaimer, "As a principle, I never interfere with the decisions in Paris," and then say something like, "First, you must ask whether Agnelli has any objections."

As he did in New York, Meyer would concern himself with seemingly trivial accounting matters. Paris partners who had just arrived for their day's work would find themselves greeted by a phone call from Meyer in New York berating them on some aspect of the balance sheet. He once phoned partner Jean-Claude Haas and said, "You have thirty-five thousand dollars listed to be delivered in September. What is it?" Haas, befuddled, replied, "I'm terribly sorry, but I don't know. It probably comes from Manufacturers Hanover or Chase, or somebody who probably sold francs against dollars." "Tsk, tsk, tsk," Meyer answered. "Have a look at it."

Paris executives were also no more immune to flashes of the Meyer temper than their New York colleagues. He once exploded at a French partner who had not risen to say hello to him at a Paris restaurant in which they were dining. Notes Haas: "On the telephone, if he thought you were wasting his time, he'd just hang up. You'd say, 'Sir, I've now got something very important to tell you.' And bang!"

On one occasion, Meyer began spreading the word that something Haas had done was crazy. Haas phoned him about the accusation, and Meyer tried to pooh-pooh it. "It's all right, it's finished, let's talk about something else. I bury it," Meyer said.

"I'm very sorry you told me that," Haas replied. "Because I've been told a number of times that when you say, 'It's finished, let's get over it,' you don't really mean it."

"Do you mean to say," snarled Meyer, "that not only do you do crazy things, but on top of that you call me a liar?"

But for all that, what always struck the Paris partners was that from the moment Meyer arrived at his desk in New York, Paris did not exist for him until the following morning. He shut it out completely. The early-morning hours may have belonged to Meyer, but the rest of the day in Paris was Pierre David-Weill's.

Nothing pointed up the contrasts between Pierre David-Weill and André Meyer better than their respective attitudes towards the third side of the Lazard triangle—Lazard Brothers in London.

Lazard Brothers was a far different animal from its sister firms. It was a traditional British merchant bank, offering such traditional merchant-banking services as acceptances (the purchase and resale of short-term paper to the Bank of England) and export credits. Its banking orientation and slow, careful cultivation of corporate clients struck a responsive chord in David-Weill. Meyer, however, had different feelings. He thought the British were lazy, unambitious, and dim-witted.

"We should never have allowed them to use our name," Meyer would tell friends. Indeed, while there was a common ownership pattern in Lazard New York and Paris, through Meyer and the David-Weills, Lazard London remained a franchise operation. Since the First World War it had been in the hands of the Cowdray family, whose $200 million empire also included ownership of London's *Financial Times* and a 50 percent interest in the *Economist*.

The Cowdrays delegated the running of Lazard Brothers to a hard-nosed, influential stockbroker named Robert Kindersley, who not only sat on the board of the Bank of England but was also a governor of the Hudson's Bay Company. It was Kindersley (who would later become Lord Kindersley) who set the style of the firm: very subdued, very traditional, and very English. At one time no fewer than five British peers were on its board. And it was Kindersley who stoked Meyer's formidable ire.

According to someone who knew both men, "Kindersley was quite a forceful man, but he did not have a very subtle intellect. He did not appeal too much to André. They had enormous rows." Not only did Meyer fight with Kindersley, but as the years rolled by he fought with Kindersley's son and grandson, too, both of whom were also with Lazard Brothers. Only the intercession of the second Lord Kindersley's wife—for whom Meyer had developed a fondness—saved matters from becoming worse.

"It wasn't a question of personal animosity," insists Hugo Kindersley, Robert's grandson. "It was André Meyer's failure to understand anybody who did not immediately fall under his spell. He didn't appreciate the fact that we were a different animal, a merchant-banking organization, while his firm was one of deals and financial engineering.

"What my father and grandfather felt was of first importance was that the name of Lazard be above reproach. André Meyer felt that way, too, but he also felt that if there was a deal that could make money for Lazard Frères, he should do it."

Not only would Meyer excoriate the Kindersleys, but he would maintain that had it not been for him and the other French partners, the British house would have gone bankrupt in the early 1930s. (This assertion turned out to be considerably exaggerated. Lazard Brothers was indeed almost forced to close in July 1931 because of fraudulent dealings by its Brussels foreign-exchange trader. But out of the £5 million bail-out package, £4 million came from the Bank of England, and just £500,000 from Lazard Paris. A larger contribution, the British Treasury was told, might unduly weaken the Paris firm.)

Meyer refused to attend Lazard Brothers board meetings, and strictly forbade any contacts between Lazard Frères people and the London firm unless they had been cleared by him in advance. "A lot of New York partners caught hell for talking separately to me or someone else here," says the present Lazard Brothers chairman, Ian Fraser. "They'd say when they called, 'Don't tell the old man about this.' "

The tension eased for a while when Oliver Poole took over the stewardship of Lazard Brothers in 1965. Poole, a longtime business adviser to the Cowdrays, was no less British than the Kindersleys—he had, in fact, been a member of Parliament and chairman of the Conservative Party. But, unlike the Kindersleys, he was openly admiring of Meyer—Poole once called him "the most remarkable man I've ever met"—and insightful as to what it took to get along with him. "I came to the conclusion that André is a difficult man and likes to have his way," Poole told a friend. "So I said I will try not to fight with him and try to agree with him. I agreed with him ninety-five percent of the time. But it didn't work. I agreed with him ninety-six percent of the time. It didn't work. Finally, I decided to agree with him one hundred percent of the time. And *then* it worked."

Under Poole's leadership, Lazard Brothers became as much of a mirror image of its New York sister firm as it was ever likely to be.

Notes a London Lazard executive, "Poole was much more akin to a Rockefeller Center mentality, a person whose mind-set is, 'Let's buy half of Venezuela and part of Uganda and take five percent along the way.' It was more of an unorthodox, wheeler-dealer approach than our clients were used to." Poole not only steered the firm into Lazard New York investments but began prodding it into the unfriendly merger business. Unfortunately, he took the wheeling and dealing a bit too far. An attempted takeover of the giant P&O Shipping Company by Bovis that Lazard choreographed fell flat on its face. Then, in the early 1970s, Poole decided to merge Lazard with the high-flying British securities firm of Slater-Walker. *That* was too much for even André Meyer; he personally stepped in and helped kill the deal. It was a fortuitous move, in view of the fact that not long afterward, in 1975, the overextended Slater-Walker empire collapsed. "Poole very nearly put us back to 1931," says a Lazard Brothers executive. "It was André who saved us from that fate."

The Poole era at Lazard Brothers ended in 1973, when a stroke left him permanently incapacitated—and with it any chance, it seemed, of a further rapprochement between the London firm and André Meyer. The London house returned to what Meyer felt were its sleepy ways (though Hugo Kindersley takes issue with the term "sleepy." "Let's just say we're conventional," he says.) Poole's successors made an effort to reason with Meyer, to no avail. "I tried to explain our business to him two or three times," says Fraser, "but he just got bored."

CHAPTER SEVENTEEN

The Sage of the Carlyle

Bobbie Lehman was always the first to admit that he was no great genius at the technical aspect of investment banking. But he knew how to give advice. Hosting a dinner one evening at his opulent, art-filled apartment for the top executives of a major U.S. company, Lehman was asked by one of the guests, "Mr. Lehman, do you think the capitalization of our company is too large? Some people say it is."

Lehman looked his interrogator over, as though simultaneously taking the measure of the man and his company all at once. Then he responded. "Do you know," Lehman said, "what the capitalization of General Motors is?" The table fell into silence as those assembled deciphered the import of Lehman's words. A young Lehman Brothers partner in attendance smiled as he thought to himself, "That's the most preposterous thing I've ever heard. What does *that* have to do with the price of eggs?"

In truth, it was a typical Lehmanesque banality, the sort of non sequitur he customarily uttered when he was at a loss for anything else to say. ("The secret of sound investment banking," Lehman once intoned, "is to put your money in the right place at the right time.") But the remark was taken with utmost seriousness by Lehman's guests. The executives went back home, looked up the capitalization of General Motors, and quoted it to all and sundry—citing it as divine guidance from the lips of Robert Lehman.

André Meyer's pronouncements had much the same mystique. The difference was that for Bobbie Lehman, the mystique usually was the message, while for Meyer it was merely the gift wrapping for something rare and valuable. Meyer had never lost sight of the importance of giving good advice; it was still, after all, at the core of what investment banking was all about. And despite his many triumphs as an investor, Meyer considered himself, first and foremost, an investment banker. The main business of Lazard, as far as he was concerned, was advice to corporations: on acquisitions and mergers and divestitures, and above all on financings. He called it "financial engineering."

Through a shrewd combination of personal relationships—his own and those of colleagues like Murnane and Hettinger—word of mouth, and the leverage his investments gave him, Meyer had built an impressive clientele for Lazard's wisdom. RCA, Fiat, the Chase Manhattan Bank, General Dynamics, Allied Chemical, Owens-Illinois, Engelhard Minerals & Chemicals, Newmont Mining, United Artists were all among the companies in Meyer's orbit. Multinational bodies like the European Economic Community consulted with him on their financing plans. Even the developing world—the same developing world that Meyer was so loath to invest in—was the beneficiary of Lazard's advice. This counsel first came through Development & Resources Corporation, an organization founded, with Lazard's backing, by David Lilienthal in 1955 to help needy countries realize their human and natural resources. Then, in 1959, Lazard and Chase helped found the Iranian Development Bank to act as a source of capital for a country in dire need of investments. Not long afterward, Lazard and Chase collaborated on another development bank in the Ivory Coast.

Meyer's reputation even caught the attention of reclusive billionaire Howard Hughes. In the late 1950s, as his business empire tottered because of the hopeless condition of his pride and joy, Trans World Airlines, Hughes began seeking the help of Meyer and Bobbie Lehman. The two were summoned by Hughes to a face-to-face meeting at the Beverly Hills Hotel, where Hughes lived in a bungalow. As unaccustomed as Meyer and Lehman were to being summoned anywhere for anything, they went.

They were told to rent bungalows at the hotel and wait for a call. They waited and waited, and finally were instructed to show up at a banquet room at the hotel at a certain time. But when they entered the room, Hughes was nowhere to be found. They waited, and waited, and still no Hughes. After hanging around the hotel awhile longer, Meyer and Lehman gave up and returned to New York.

But no sooner had Meyer written the whole experience off than he began getting phone calls—from Hughes himself. Hughes pleaded with him: wasn't there something Meyer could do to help him stave off TWA's creditors? Hughes phoned him incessantly; an unnerved Meyer complained to an aide, "You know, he is crazy. He calls me at three o'clock in the morning and tells me this complicated story. What does he think I can do?"

On December 15, 1960, as part of a TWA refinancing, Hughes was forced to sign a voting trust agreement that effectively ended his control of TWA. But right to the end he was convinced that the one investment banker in the world who could come up with a way out of his dilemma was André Meyer.

Meyer owed his success as an advice-giver to the same two qualities that made him such a unique investor: an ability to cold-bloodedly dissect opportunities, problems, and personalities; and the iron determination to follow through and get what he and his client wanted.

Rather than dwell on technical details and jargon, Meyer preferred to boil a discussion down to the essential human elements. He would classify people in three categories—*"première, deuxième, troisième"*—and would suggest to clients that they have nothing to do with the *troisième* and barely tolerate the *deuxième*. When a visitor would voice astonishment about how a bright executive had botched a situation, Meyer would simply comment, "He is intelligent, but he has no judgment." With clinical precision, he could pick apart an executive's strengths and weaknesses. "He was the most ruthless judge of people I've ever seen," says Felix Rohatyn. "He was absolutely without illusions."

Meyer thoroughly distrusted the American corporate mentality. Too many executives, he complained, thought and acted like civil servants. He was forever suspicious of management's projections about the future of their business; his attitude towards such forecasts was, "So what else is new?" And, unlike other bankers, he assiduously avoided being seduced by the physical grandeur of American industry. "He never wanted me to go on plant tours," recalls Lazard partner Frank Pizzitola. " 'You do not learn anything in plants,' he would tell me. He was always afraid that you'd fall in love with the machinery, and it would warp your thinking."

Instead, Meyer preferred to focus on personalities. And in that area, by the testimony of his former partners, his influence was positively Svengali-like. Relates one: "He had an uncanny ability to make people do what he wanted, even though they had no reason to want to do it. Sometimes he bullied them; sometimes he flattered them; sometimes he seduced them; sometimes he bribed them."

Often, Meyer's steamroller style of reasoning was enough. During lunches with clients, he would sometimes grab the menu and begin scribbling on it. After a few minutes, he would hand the menu to the client. "Here is your scheme," Meyer would tell him, adding, "You may keep this."

Simon Rifkind once arranged a meeting between Meyer and a corporate executive they both knew. The executive had a project he wanted to discuss with Meyer. It took the man a half-hour to outline the idea; after another half-hour, says Rifkind, "I knew that the project was as dead as if it had never been mentioned, because André overwhelmingly established that it would be a great mistake. When we left the Carlyle, the man said to me, 'Well, I guess we won't do it.' And that was that."

Sometimes, Meyer resorted to sheer persistence to persuade clients. He would constantly preach to Newmont Mining president Plato Malozemoff the gospel of sticking to the United States. "If you must go overseas," Meyer would tell him, "then counteract it with something here in the United States as well." Not content with that word to the wise, Meyer devised a grand strategy for increasing Newmont's North American earnings stream. It involved a takeover of the Magma Copper Company, a sister company of Newmont's (both had been founded by the same man, Colonel William Boyce Thompson) in which Lazard had long been active. Newmont already owned 22 percent of Magma. Why not, Meyer asked Malozemoff, buy it all?

But Malozemoff, whom Meyer had once dismissed as a "fresh upstart" for not following his advice, didn't want it all. He was reluctant to force all of Magma's old shareholders, many of whom he knew personally, to sell out. What's more, he figured that an 80 percent holding in Magma would give Newmont the same advantages that 100 percent would. This time, Malozemoff had his way. In April 1962, he and Meyer structured an offer that would give Newmont 80 percent of Magma.

In the long run, however, Meyer was not to be denied. He went on badgering Malozemoff about buying the whole thing. Finally, in 1968, he called the Newmont boss and told him flatly, "Now is the time." For once, Malozemoff yielded to Meyer's better judgment and went ahead with the purchase of the rest of the stock. And in retrospect, he realized, "Mr. Meyer's sense of timing turned out to be uncannily correct. If we had waited four or five more months, the market would have changed, and we could not have done that deal."

Meyer was also not above throwing a tantrum or two to get his way. When Meyer served on the Allied Chemical board, he chaired the board's auditing committee and quickly came to the conclusion that the company's accountants were careless and should be fired. Allied's chief financial officer, Walter Sykes, balked; a change now, he thought, would cause operational difficulties. He suggested they wait a year. "Out of the question," Meyer loudly replied. "And if you don't change now, I will resign from the board." Sykes fired the accountants.

The Meyer temper often flared in underwritings. Lazard was once doing a new stock issue for the Alexander's department-store chain. The Alexander's people were holding out for a higher price for the stock, while Lazard partners were trying to make the case that the higher price would mean the issue would be impossible to market. They were at an impasse until Meyer stormed into the conference room. "We are your investment bankers," he bellowed. "You hired us to rely on our judgment. Why do you use us if you do not want to rely on us?" Meyer's whole body quivered; one partner thought the old man was about to have a heart attack on the spot. Meyer excused himself, walked out of the room, and stopped at a secretary's desk. "Isn't it fun?" he whispered to her with a wink. Then he turned right around, went back into the room, threw another fit, and convinced Alexander's to accept Lazard's offer.

Meyer employed his theatrics with good effect on behalf of his clients, too. In 1970, for example, Meyer represented Henry Crown, a millionaire Chicago investor who had just taken a major position in General Dynamics. Meyer sought to clarify Crown's relationship with General Dynamics' management; on the other side of the bargaining table, representing chairman and president Roger Lewis and the rest of management, was attorney Roswell Gilpatric, the former deputy secretary of defense in the Kennedy administration.

"My task was to prevent an open breach between Crown and the management," recalls Gilpatric. "But Mr. Meyer used to go into a rage with me, blaming not me but my principals at General Dynamics. I had some stormy sessions with him. He'd lash out with all sorts of expletives about Lewis and his people.

"It wasn't really a negotiation," Gilpatric concludes. "Mr. Meyer made up his mind in advance and told you exactly what he wanted." What Meyer wanted was six seats on the fourteen-member board and the ouster of Roger Lewis. Eventually, he got it.

Occasionally, as in so many other aspects of his life, Meyer's anger took on a darker, more savage dimension. He would lash out indiscriminately and brutally at any obstacles that lay in his path. No corporate chief executive experienced this side of Meyer more graphically than did Dannie N. Heineman.

Heineman was head of Sofina, a Brussels-based multinational public-utility investment company which controlled power and light companies in Lisbon, Buenos Aires, Mexico City, Barcelona, and other cities around the globe. He had been one of Meyer's earliest sponsors, appointing the then-unknown young banker to the Sofina board in 1929. When Meyer emigrated to America, it was Heineman who helped him negotiate with the U.S. government the release of the assets Meyer had taken out of France.

Meyer, in turn, helped Heineman when the Sofina empire began to be torn apart by expropriations in the years after World War II. He worked with Heineman during the frustrating, futile struggle to maintain control of one of Sofina's flagship companies, Barcelona Traction. At one point, Meyer even brought David Rockefeller into the battle; together, Meyer and Rockefeller persuaded one of America's most eminent attorneys, Arthur Dean, to represent Sofina.

But as the fight went on, year after agonizing year, Meyer began to tire of it. He thought that Sofina should cut its losses, regroup, and strike out in new directions. Heineman, though, could not be moved. "Those companies were like his children," remembers his former aide, Nathaniel Samuels. "He built them up. The idea of abandoning them was totally foreign to him."

Then, out of the blue, came an opportunity to force a change. The Belgian government decided to sell its sizable block of Sofina shares, and two groups soon emerged as the chief bidders. One was the prominent Lambert family of Belgium, headed by the hungry young Baron Léon Lambert. The other was the Boëls, the industrial aristocrats who were Meyer's devoted friends and clients. After some hemming and hawing, the Belgian central bank made its decision. The block would be sold to the Lamberts.

Meyer, in a fury, blamed Heineman for tipping the scales against the Boël group. True, it was a central bank decision, but he was convinced that Heineman, in a backhand move to thwart Meyer's desire for change, had communicated his preference to the authorities.

Not long afterward, Heineman—badly shaken by the uproar—retired, ending a forty-eight-year association with Sofina. Despite a close relationship that spanned more than a quarter of a century, the rupture between him and Meyer was complete.

* * *

If Meyer never forgave a slight, he also never forgot past favors—his as well as other people's. Once, Meyer was overheard talking on the phone to a corporate chief executive. Lazard was managing an underwriting for the company, and the executive expressed some interest in bringing in a comanager to help Lazard out. The suggestion, which would have meant sharing fees with the other firm, incensed Meyer. Suddenly, he began yelling, "We're not cattle, Fred. Do you understand? We're not *cattle*, Fred." No one at Lazard could figure out why Meyer kept repeating that cattle line, over and over again. Then someone remembered: Meyer had once given Fred a piece of a tax-shelter cattle deal.

This side of Meyer, however—the ruthless, bludgeoning side—always coexisted with that other André Meyer, the genial old sage of the Carlyle, the André Meyer who would wrap an understanding arm around the shoulder of a troubled corporate client, who would discourse pithily but with appropriate world-weariness on politics and the state of the economy. This gentle, avuncular André Meyer, in fact, was sometimes the only André Meyer corporate executives ever saw.

For such clients, Meyer would often be knowing, but cryptic. In late 1972, for example, Georges Plescoff, the head of France's second biggest insurance company, Assurances Générale, asked Meyer about a U.S. insurer with which he was thinking of undertaking a joint venture. "I never heard of these people," Meyer replied. Plescoff, thinking the old man might have misunderstood him, mentioned the name again. "Yes, I understood," said Meyer. "I never heard of them." Plescoff left the meeting stunned: how could Meyer not have heard of one of the biggest insurance companies in America? But as he tossed the answer around in his mind, Plescoff suddenly realized, "When a clever banker—and Meyer is clever—wants to tell you somebody is a crook, he tells you, 'I don't know them.'"

Plescoff proceeded to cut off the negotiations. And, sure enough, six months later the company, Equity Funding Corporation, was exposed as the biggest fraud in the history of the American insurance industry. On his next visit to New York, Plescoff thanked Meyer for telling him he didn't know the company. "Ah, you understood," said Meyer—in a tone of voice that indicated not everyone did.

Such conversations not only imparted wisdom, but reinforced the Meyer mystique—the seductive aura of a man who knew all but said little, who had, as one of his partners once put it, "mysterious forces at his command." For much the same reason, Meyer delighted in pulling strings: phoning the French Finance Ministry, for instance, if a corporate client was having trouble arranging government-guaranteed loans there. Or "paving the way" for Jean Monnet to extract a lower interest rate from Washington on an EEC loan. These exercises—exercises that hinted at his power—were, for Meyer, the best form of advertising.

In impressing corporate clients, Meyer had another card to play: his reputation, and Lazard's, as "financial engineers," skilled strategists who could steer companies through the most complex financial problems. Meyer savored complicated problems, since they called for equally complicated solutions. "With André," said a Lazard partner, "the more byzantine, the better."

For Newmont's buy-out of the Magma shareholders, Meyer devised a package that would not only lure the shareholders into accepting the offer, but would eventually bring them in on terms that were most desirable to Newmont. The Magma shareholders could exchange their shares for Newmont convertible preferred stock, but Meyer gave Newmont the right to redeem the preferred at steadily decreasing prices over a period of years. In effect, there was a heavy inducement for the new preferred shareholders to convert to common as soon as possible—which, in the end, was what Newmont really wanted.

Meyer was equally clever in the service of Allied Chemical. Allied, at the time, had stockholdings in a number of other industrial companies, and the management decided the moment had come to sell its interest in Owens-Illinois. The sale, however, would have generated a huge capital gain, and a huge capital-gains tax. So Meyer and chief financial officer Sykes came up with a better idea: why not swap the shares for Allied Chemical stock that Owens-Illinois held in *its* portfolio? Stock swaps weren't taxable, and Allied could then sell the shares to raise cash or use them for mergers and acquisitions—again, without paying a penny in tax.

The only difficulty was that the Owens-Illinois people did not want to go along with the deal. Thus stymied, Meyer took off his financial engineer's hat and became the other André Meyer, badgering and cajoling the chairman of Owens-Illinois, another longtime Lazard client. "André got quite exercised about it," remembers Walter Sykes. "He would be on the telephone to them, and suddenly look at me and say, 'These men do not understand,' and slam down the receiver." Eventually, after throwing a few more fits, Meyer persuaded the Owens-Illinois boss to cooperate.

Indeed, the histrionic side of Meyer was never far from the surface. During his tenure as an Allied Chemical director in the 1960s, Meyer would regularly doze off during board meetings. His eyes would close; his head would droop; he would start to snore. His fellow director and friend, Richard Perkins of Citibank, would occasionally nudge his arm. "André, André," Perkins would say under his breath.

Then an Allied executive would raise some sticky issue, and the great, well-tonsured head would rise with a start. "Pardon me, sir," Meyer would blurt out . . . and before the startled executive knew what hit him, he would be assaulted with one penetrating question after another—from an old man who just a minute before had seemed to be peacefully snoozing away.

In the words of Sykes, "It was all part of the act." And in the new business environment of the mid-sixties, the act's time had come.

CHAPTER EIGHTEEN

Merger Making

In January 1961, the son of a one-time stock market speculator took the oath of office as president of the United States. While his ascension to power was hardly greeted with universal hosannas on Wall Street—he was, after all, a Democrat—even the most diehard GOP boosters in the financial community couldn't help but be caught up in the fervor the new administration was generating. They, too, wanted to see the country "get moving again," especially after over two years of the Eisenhower recession. In fact, it might be said that at the very moment John F. Kennedy was letting the word go forth, to friend and foe alike, that the torch had been passed, businessmen and investors across the nation were already laying the foundations of a new frontier of their own.

Their new frontier would not be defined by liberal social policies, swank cultural extravaganzas, and touch football. Rather, it would be highlighted by exaggerated stock price-to-earnings ratios, go-go money managers, and ravenous conglomerates. But the spirit would be much the same: the sweeping away of encrusted old attitudes in favor of a new era of vigor, vitality, and enterprise.

It would be several years before this new frontier of American business and finance would fully manifest itself. But already in 1961, the first signs of things to come were starting to appear. The stock market was embarking on a sustained boom that, except for a few fits and starts, would not be sidetracked until Kennedy's old adversary Richard Nixon took office eight years later. Larger and larger blocks of securities were being traded, and more and more institutions were reappraising their shopworn buy-and-hold investment strategies.

Most significantly, a smattering of venturesome entrepreneurs such as James Ling and Charles Bluhdorn were coming to the conclusion that the easiest way to expand their companies was not to sell more of whatever it was they were making, or to bet on a one-in-a-thousand technical breakthrough. The easiest way to expand was to buy other companies. They also reached a corollary conclusion: the more they bought, the more they could buy.

Twice before in this century did corporate entrepreneurs move en masse in this direction. The first time was in the early 1900s, when the Rockefellers and the Carnegies were building the great trusts. These were what is known as horizontal industrial combinations, in which many companies in the same industry are merged, to put effective control of the industry in the hands of one or two men. They were classic monopolies.

Then, in the 1920s, came another great merger wave. This time, so-called vertical combinations were in vogue, in which avaricious industrial enterprises took control of their suppliers. General Motors was one of a number of corporate behemoths spawned by this acquisition boom.

By the time the 1960s rolled around, most textbook horizontal and vertical combinations were either illegal or passé. In their place was a new concept: that many different smaller companies, not necessarily in the same industry, could be strung together in such a way that the whole would be far stronger than the sum of its parts. This was called synergy. Underlying this notion was the curious self-fulfilling logic of an increasingly hyped-up stock market. To wit, the companies most likely to acquire other companies, and thus achieve synergy, were those with higher stock prices. And the companies most likely to have higher stock prices were those that achieved synergy.

Eventually, would-be conglomerateurs realized that if the numbers were right, they could pull together companies that had absolutely *nothing* to do with each other (say, an aircraft manufacturer and a meat packer) and still get synergistic effects. Suppose, for example, an aircraft company with $10 million in earnings and a price-earnings ratio of 40 decided to acquire a meat packer whose earnings were also $10 million but whose price-earnings ratio was just 20. The aircraft maker would swap one of its shares for every two of the meat packer's shares. The new company that resulted from this merger could now report double the earnings it posted previously, while its number of shares outstanding increased only by 50 percent. Consequently, its earnings per share—the key figure the stock market looks at—would rise by 33 percent as a result of the amalgamation. Such an earnings-per-share increase, needless to say, would not go unnoticed by the stock market; it would mark up the price of the shares accordingly. Which, in turn, would put the company in a better position to make even *more* such acquisitions.

Thus, Ling's tiny Ling Electronics Company, with sales in 1958 of $7 million and earnings of just $227,000, could emerge, one decade and twenty-seven acquisitions later, as the mighty Ling-Temco-Vought, boasting revenues of $2.8 billion and net income of $36 million. And Charles Bluhdorn's Gulf & Western, which entered the 1960s as a minuscule manufacturer of auto bumpers, could be raking in sales of $1.3 billion and net income of $69 million by the end of the decade—thanks to some eighty acquisitions along the way.

The age of the conglomerate had truly begun.

As André Meyer sat in his dingy office on 44 Wall Street and surveyed this marketplace of the early sixties, he came to certain conclusions of his own.

To start with, he knew what he *didn't* want to do. He didn't want to join his friendly competitors on the Street in chasing after the booming stock-trading business of the big financial institutions.

This business was turning into a huge profit center for many firms, especially since in those days commission rates were fixed at abnormally high levels by the New York Stock Exchange. But Meyer didn't want any part of it. For one thing, he would have to hire salesmen. For another, he would need to build up his research department, which at that time was a small, ramshackle operation servicing the Lazard Fund and the firm's exclusive clientele. Not only would he have to add research analysts, but these analysts would have to publish research reports, since that was the only way their institutional clients would know they existed. But the idea of *public* reports was anathema to Meyer. "He was hypersensitive about being wrong," explains John Vogelstein, who suggested just such a research buildup when he was at Lazard. "He was deathly afraid we would recommend something that wouldn't work out, and that would hurt his reputation."

At the same time, Meyer also realized that the days when he could range far and wide in the venture-capital business were fast coming to an end. The simple, sobering fact was he could not compete with the avaricious new conglomerates, awash in overpriced stock, that were buying up everything in sight. "I made my money in the fifties," he would tell his friends. "I've never made any money since." As blatantly false as that assertion was—Avis, after all, had not come about until 1962—no one would deny that the opportunities had dwindled since Meyer and Ferd Eberstadt had first turned their attention to the postwar scene.

But Meyer was not one to sulk over lost opportunities. His old business associate David Lilienthal once told him, "What attracted me to you is that you see the job as one of adapting finance and banking to the facts as they are, rather than complaining because the world has changed." If Lazard couldn't go the venture-capital route, and wouldn't go the institutional brokerage route, there was another road it *could* take: playing the adviser to the swarm of acquisition-hungry corporations. The "financial engineering" expertise, the bevy of corporate contacts, the reputation Meyer and his partners had as sounding boards could all be put to work to carve a unique role for the firm in this new environment. Meyer was also well practiced at corporate mergers, having employed them with good effect in his venture-capital investments. If the master deal-maker couldn't do deals for himself, he would do them for other people.

This approach also had a certain side benefit: it would help him minimize that dreaded item on the budget called overhead. Let other people build their fancy trading desks and acquire high-priced analysts; Lazard would live on wits and save the expense. Let others try to insinuate themselves with corporate clients by taking on risky underwriting positions; Lazard would win friends and influence people by being, quite simply, the best and the brightest.

There was one other aspect of the corporate matchmaking role that appealed to Meyer: the secrecy of it. In the words of one old hand at the firm, "The secret of Lazard is keeping secrets." Putting together a big merger required the utmost discretion and confidentiality. And these were attributes that Meyer and Lazard had in profusion and relished having.

But Meyer, who by then was in his late sixties, knew that he could not do it alone. He needed a younger man who could spearhead the hard, slogging negotiations, who could maintain the contacts and massage the corporate egos—while Meyer himself played the role of overall mastermind and *éminence grise*. Fortunately, there was someone in the firm who fit the bill perfectly. His name was Felix Rohatyn.

Felix Rohatyn was born in Vienna in 1928 into a prosperous Polish-Jewish family. His grandfather was a member of the Vienna Stock

Exchange and proprietor of a small bank, Rohatyn & Company. "He was a speculator, really," Felix Rohatyn once remarked. Felix's father, Alexander, ran various breweries that grandfather Rohatyn controlled in Vienna, Rumania, and Yugoslavia. In 1933, the Rohatyns moved to the French city of Orléans, where Felix's father set up another brewery business. The Nazi invasion changed all that, just as it changed the life of André Meyer in Paris. In June 1940, at the same time the Meyers were fleeing across the Spanish border, the Rohatyns were plotting a similar escape, via Biarritz.

Rohatyn remembers well their last night in a Biarritz hotel. "We had a few gold coins with us," he once recalled. "That was our fortune. And I spent that night opening the back ends of toothpaste tubes and stuffing these few gold coins into the tubes. It created in me a notion of wealth that is not exactly supply-side economics, in terms of what is real. What is real to me is what I can put in the back of a toothpaste tube, or what I carry around in my head." It was a notion that André Meyer could well understand.

The Rohatyns ended up journeying to America, via what their son refers to as "the traditional route of Casablanca and Rio de Janeiro." Arriving in New York in 1942, Felix was enrolled in a Manhattan high school (where he learned English) and entered Middlebury College in Vermont "because I liked to ski." He studied physics there with notable lack of success. As he puts it, "The physics faculty and I both reached the conclusion that I did not have a future in the sciences."

During his summers home from Middlebury, Rohatyn picked up spending money working as a clerk at Lazard. He got the job through his stepfather, Henry Plessner (Rohatyn's parents had been divorced). Plessner was a precious-metals dealer whom Meyer had worked with since the late 1940s; according to one man who knew him then, Plessner had more in common with Meyer than just a feel for the commodities markets. "Henry Plessner was a very, very rough guy," says this man. "He screamed as much as anyone I ever knew." Some Lazard partners, in fact, always suspected that one reason Rohatyn was able to put up with Meyer's temper tantrums over the years was the basic training he received from Henry Plessner.

One evening, when everyone else at the firm had gone, Meyer was walking through the office and stumbled upon young Felix Rohatyn. Impressed by the dedication of a $37.50-a-week clerk, Meyer marked the young man as a comer; what he didn't know was that the only reason Rohatyn was there was because he had a late date that evening. In any event, upon Rohatyn's graduation from Middlebury in 1949, Meyer offered him a job at Lazard. Not seeing much future for himself in the world of physics, Rohatyn accepted.

For his apprenticeship, he was dispatched to London, Paris, and Switzerland. But when he came back to Lazard after a two-year stint in the army during the Korean War, Rohatyn found himself assigned to a routine job in the foreign-exchange area. "It was extremely dreary work," he recalls. It was at that point that he had a conversation with whiskey magnate Samuel Bronfman that, in retrospect, changed his life. "André Meyer is interested only in mergers and corporate finance," Bronfman told him. "And if you want to get anywhere, I'd advise you to get into that end of the business." When Rohatyn approached Meyer about a switch, the senior partner grumbled—"You don't know anything about it," he told Rohatyn—but agreed to the transfer.

At first, Rohatyn was assigned to the same mind-numbing sorts of assignments that he thought he was escaping when he left foreign exchange. On numerous late 1950s deals he was nothing more than a glorified numbers cruncher, someone Meyer would bring along to meetings because "he knows how to use a slide rule." Nevertheless, it was apparent to anyone who worked with Rohatyn in those years that he was a fast learner. And it was also evident that he was beginning to develop a special kind of relationship with André Meyer.

"Rohatyn would always be talking French to André in our presence," relates a 1950s Lazard partner. "He was always at André's elbow, even though he wasn't a partner. André would turn and ask him, *'Qu' est-ce que vous-voulez faire?'* It was hard to catch on; they talked in a patois that even those of us who knew some French had trouble understanding." Sometimes Meyer would even come to dinner at Rohatyn's little apartment in the East Nineties; it was rare that partners were so honored, let alone a young, untried associate. On those occasions, Meyer would let down his jaded banker facade, roll up his sleeves, and help Rohatyn's wife in the kitchen.

Looking back on those days, Rohatyn recalls, "I genuinely liked André. I could talk to him. And I think I understood him. I think we looked at the world in many similar ways; I mean, André used to say, 'Well, if I weren't so rich, I'd be a socialist,' and I suppose I feel that way. We both always felt like outsiders in that respect; we were both refugees, we were both Jewish, and we both felt outside the American Establishment and power structure. I don't think either one of us ever had any illusions about it."

Still, Rohatyn knew that, as he puts it, "one had to be careful about André. It was like the moth and the flame: if you got too close, it was a very dangerous exercise." No matter how intimate their relationship was, Rohatyn was careful never to address Meyer in anything but the formal *"vous"* style. Despite such precautions, Rohatyn was singed more than once. He and Meyer may have had a special rapport, but that didn't spare Rohatyn from the same tongue-lashings his Lazard compatriots were regularly subjected to. Says one of Rohatyn's contemporaries at the firm, "Face to face Felix couldn't deal with the old man, in the sense that if Meyer went after him, Felix cringed just like the next person."

"I almost quit a couple of times," Rohatyn would confess many years later. "I just thought life was too short, you know—who needs this?"

Nevertheless, Rohatyn hung in there, displaying the same coolness under pressure that, two decades later, would help pull New York City out of its worst fiscal crisis. "I think either it's bred into you or it isn't," comments a former Lazard partner. "You can either deal with the kind of brutalization Meyer dished out, or you can't. I suspect it probably comes from Felix's upbringing. Whatever the reason for it was, there was some part of Felix that had a thick enough skin that when he went home in the evening it didn't bother him anymore."

A thick skin partly accounted for Rohatyn's ability to endure and succeed with Meyer. Equally important, from the viewpoint of those who worked with both men, were Rohatyn's masterful political instincts. Cracks one ex-Lazard colleague, "They don't call him Felix the Cat for nothing." Rohatyn had a remarkable talent for reading Meyer's personality, for sensing what would and wouldn't impress the old man, and for knowing exactly which levers in that complex psyche to pull.

One of the best appraisals of how Rohatyn did it is provided by Felix Rohatyn himself. "There were a couple of people I began to work with and who sort of took a shine to me," he says. "One was Chuck Percy at Bell and Howell when we started doing their business, another was Harold Geneen at ITT, and a third was

David Sarnoff. It's a classic story: I began to rise in André's eyes not because of what he saw in me, but because there were some people whom he admired and respected who seemed to like working with me.

"So that was one thing. The other thing was that I lived a fairly modest life, not because I consider it a virtue, but because it just never interested me to spend a lot of money. I think André liked that, especially since we had partners here who lived very very lavishly. At the same time, living so modestly made me a little bit less accessible. It was something that I always felt: the only way you could really cope with André was to be rather independent of him. And the only way to be independent of him was to contribute more to the firm than you took out, because then he wasn't doing you a favor. He couldn't feel that he owned me."

All that, of course, isn't to say that there wasn't one other reason why Rohatyn succeeded so well with Meyer: pure native ability. In Rohatyn's own words, "I survived rather well because I did a lot of things rather well, things that he admired." While others at Lazard could be lumped into two broad categories—the deal-making negotiators, and the technicians—Rohatyn demonstrated he had both sets of skills, in abundance. What's more, during his tenure as Meyer's watchdog over Avis, he displayed a dedication and attention to detail that was bound to impress his obsessively thorough boss. Once a month Rohatyn would visit Avis headquarters to debrief the company's executives; he would accompany Townsend to Avis sales meetings; and one time, after he and Townsend made a decision without checking with the Avis board that wound up costing the company some $15,000, the two reimbursed Avis out of their own pockets.

In short, Meyer came to see in Rohatyn the closest thing he would ever find to an alter ego. And the senior partner was astute enough to appreciate something else: that Rohatyn could offset Meyer's own very evident shortcomings. Instead of frightening or overpowering corporate chief executives, Rohatyn would soothe them, dealing with their problems in a sympathetic but matter-of-fact way. Rohatyn's age also made a difference; as he puts it, "I was a lot younger, and therefore it was a lot easier for a Chuck Percy or a Harold Geneen to talk to me than to talk to André. And André could feel that, because he was very sensitive to these things."

So Meyer had in place someone who could do great things for him in the merger-and-acquisition game. Now all he needed were some suitably acquisition-hungry clients.

And that was where Hal Geneen came in.

Harold Sydney Geneen had spent most of his business life champing at the bit. A native of Bournemouth, England, he came to the United States with his parents at the age of one, and by the time he was sixteen he had decided it was time to strike out on his own. He got a job as a page at the New York Stock Exchange, took evening accounting courses at New York University, and within a few years found a position at Lybrand Ross Brothers and Montgomery. But the mundane life of an accountant soon began to pall on the impatient Geneen, and he moved into a succession of jobs in industry. First he was at Bell & Howell with Chuck Percy; then at Jones & Laughlin, the Pittsburgh steel company; and finally he became an executive vice-president at Raytheon, the giant Boston-based electronics manufacturer. Yet as successful as he was at these companies, he tired of each of them in short order; none offered the absolute control for which Geneen so desperately yearned.

Then, in 1959, he got a call from the International Telephone & Telegraph Company. ITT was a multinational telecommunications company that had been rudderless since the retirement of its flamboyant founder, Colonel Sosthenes Behn, in 1956. Hearing of Geneen's reputation as a master manager, the ITT board approached him about taking over—and Geneen, with barely concealed excitement, accepted.

The ITT that Geneen inherited was a sprawling, disorganized agglomeration of largely non-U.S. communications companies. Determined to tame it, the new boss began to set up a system of management controls that, in its byzantine complexity, probably had no rival in the annals of international industry. There were divisional reports, corporate reports, corporate cross-check reports, five-year plans, monthly management letters, weekly meetings, monthly meetings, international management meetings. It was all summed up by Geneen's steely admonition to his underlings: "I want no surprises."

But managerial tightening was only part of what Geneen had in mind for ITT. Alarmed by Fidel Castro's nationalization of ITT's Cuban phone company in 1969, he decided that ITT had to be insulated once and for all from such foreign shocks. A mere 18 percent of ITT's earnings came from its U.S. subsidiaries, and as far as Geneen was concerned, nothing less than 55 percent would do. So he embarked on the only possible way he saw to achieve this—the outright acquisition of American companies.

When Geneen in early 1961 settled on his first acquisition—a little $20 million California electronics company called Jennings Radio—he turned immediately to Lazard for help. This was not because Lazard was a big factor in the merger business (at that point there wasn't any merger business to speak of), or because he knew Meyer and Rohatyn (he didn't). Rather, it was because of his friendship with one of the old Jones & Laughlin directors, the ubiquitous Albert Hettinger. In fact, had it not been for Hettinger, the great ITT acquisition program might never have gotten off the ground.

The ITT board had balked at the Jennings purchase, and the newly arrived Geneen was wary of pressing the issue. Hettinger invited Geneen over to Lazard and, after closing his office door, asked him, "Harold, do you want to make a lot of acquisitions as ITT chairman?" Geneen told Hettinger he did. "Well," Hettinger said, "if you don't get this one through, they'll never let you do another one." So Geneen went back to his board, pressed the directors on the issue, and squeezed out their approval. After that, whatever Geneen wanted, Geneen got.

The Jennings deal was also the first Geneen did with Felix Rohatyn, and here again Hettinger was the key. Hettinger was going out to lunch one day when he bumped into Rohatyn. As he waited for the elevator, Rohatyn asked the older man where he was going. Hettinger replied that he was having lunch with Harold Geneen. Rohatyn didn't miss a beat. "Can I come along?" he asked. Sure, Hettinger answered, why not?

Still, it would be several years before the Lazard-ITT relationship would fully jell. The company's regular investment banker then was Kuhn Loeb, and at the outset Geneen saw no reason to change things. In time, though, he began itching for a second opinion and set up a lunch with André Meyer. Former ITT chief financial officer Hart Perry remembers that first encounter well.

"It was a fascinating meeting," he says. "Lazard was still downtown then, and André had his telephone on the lunch table, and during lunch he'd call Europe. We thought it was more a matter of show than anything else, but since he spoke French we didn't know what he was talking about. Anyway, we were enormously impressed by his broad knowledge of U.S. industry and people."

Then along came Avis. "We heard that it might be for sale, and that is why we were interested in it," Geneen said some years later. "It seemed to have possibilities for growth." While outsiders always assumed that it was the Avis deal which cemented ITT's link with Lazard, the fact is that Avis almost was the relationship's undoing. According to Perry, "After the Avis merger, André demanded a seat on the ITT board, and he went about it in a way that really offended Geneen. I don't know why, because I didn't sit in on the meeting. But I do know that afterwards Geneen called me in and said that André had demanded a seat, almost as a right. And you don't push Harold Geneen that way. So we flatly turned him down."

Fortunately for Lazard, Meyer's outburst wasn't the only by-product of the Avis transaction. In the course of the negotiations, Geneen had dealt extensively with Rohatyn. And in their quiet, methodical ways, the two men had begun to hit it off.

"Geneen is a very difficult person," comments Rohatyn. "A *very* difficult person. But I always knew where Geneen was going." And where he was going, of course, just happened to be where Lazard was also heading: the seemingly boundless, fertile field of corporate mergers and acquisitions.

Together, they took that field by storm. Over the next three years after the Avis deal, ITT acquired forty-eight companies, and while many of those were smaller operations ITT purchased unassisted, Lazard was almost always in the picture whenever anything major had to be done. In 1968 alone, the ITT-Lazard team absorbed such giants as William Levitt & Sons, the home builders; Pennsylvania Glass & Sand, the country's biggest producer of silica and clay for glass and ceramics; the $300 million Rayonier Corporation, which owned over a million acres of forests in the United States and Canada; and Continental Baking, the largest bakery company in America. By 1971, ITT was the ninth largest industrial corporation in the United States, with $8.8 billion in revenues—and 75 percent of that total came from acquired companies.

In a business world ruled by great corporate piranha, ITT was clearly the hungriest and most fearsome fish in the sea. No company, large or small, seemed immune to Geneen's grasp—be it the Nancy Taylor secretarial schools or the Sheraton hotel chain. And no matter how many acquisitions he feasted upon, Geneen's appetite never slackened. He would carry with him the ponderous Moody's manual of industrial companies and casually leaf through it on airplanes as though it were the latest Agatha Christie thriller. During meetings with his staff about possible purchases, his acquisitions people would wheel in a shopping cart full of annual reports for Geneen to peruse. Geneen's technique for sorting through these reports never varied: he would start with the financial statements in the back and then work his way to the front, where he found out what it was the company actually did. Yet as hard-boiled as Geneen usually was, his judgments sometimes had their quirky side. Once, he was given the annual report of a key-maker to look at. He seemed intensely interested for a few minutes, but then suddenly tossed the report aside and said to his aides, "What's next?" "You don't like it?" a staffer asked him. "No, I don't," Geneen replied. "Did you happen to look at the chairman's picture? I don't like his eyes."

According to a former Lazard merger-and-acquisition man, "If we had a deal set for company A, and company A didn't want it, we'd bring it to Geneen. Geneen never quibbled. We never had an engagement letter from him," he said, referring to a letter authorizing an investment banker to seek out merger opportunities. "We never needed one."

It was perfectly obvious why Lazard didn't need one: Felix Rohatyn was practically an employee of the company. "Felix would be in virtually every day," remembers Hart Perry. "Generally, he'd come by the office around six or six-thirty in the evening and stay for an hour or two with Geneen. Just the two of them." Often, Geneen would hold executive brainstorming sessions over dinner at ITT's suite at the Waldorf (conveniently right across the street from ITT's world headquarters), and Rohatyn would be a fixture at those, too.

Rohatyn by then was an ITT director—but the services he provided went above and beyond the call of any director's duty. "Felix might come in with an idea for a sector or an industry, and then we would go out and do our own research," says Perry. "But where Felix was really helpful was in giving us a good fix as to whether something was doable or not. We might come up with an idea that looked good, and he would say, 'It's a good idea, but . . .' And most of the decisions got down to whether the deal was doable. Usually, you came up with a story about *why* you wanted to do it after the fact." Since Geneen hated hostile takeovers—he was usually ready to pay whatever was necessary to keep the target company's management and shareholders fat and happy—doability was always a paramount consideration.

Rohatyn was a master at figuring out what inducements—stock, cash, or otherwise—would be needed to turn a reluctant acquiree around. In the Continental Baking deal, for example, he scanned a list of Continental's directors and found that Fred Klingenstein, the head of the Wall Street firm of Wertheim & Company, was a director. So he approached Klingenstein about doing the merger jointly and sharing the fees. "From that point on," says an ITT insider, "it was a shoo-in."

Geneen even came to rely on Rohatyn's advice on things that had nothing to do with mergers and acquisitions. "I remember once I was invited to become a director of the European American Bank," relates Perry. "I thought it made sense because the owners of European American were our principal bankers in Europe. But Geneen said, 'Let me check it out with Felix,' and the word came back no, it wasn't a good idea because it might be a discordant element in our relationships with U.S. banks."

To some ITT executives, such advice seemed to have someone else's stamp on it—that of André Meyer. The senior partner was never the omnipresent force at the company that Felix Rohatyn was, yet the impression persisted that the old man was lurking, like Polonius, somewhere behind the curtains. Notes Perry, "I always went on the assumption that anything Felix did, he cleared in advance with André. I don't mean to take anything away from Felix, but that's the kind of operation that André ran. Felix was the agent, but it was hard to separate Felix's contribution from André's." Asserts another former ITT insider, "Geneen would talk to André first, and then Felix would do the deals."

Rohatyn, though, always insisted that exactly the opposite was true. "You have to differentiate between clearing something with André and getting his judgment on it," he says. "You mustn't forget that when I started working with ITT I was thirty-two years old; and it's clear that while we were negotiating something, if I said, 'Listen, this is what we think,' Geneen wanted to know that the 'we' included André's views. But when I then went off and negotiated something, I didn't have to check with André. I mean, I knew the numbers better than he did."

Still, that often wasn't the impression that those on the other side of the bargaining table had. One investment banker recalls a negotiating session that broke up, inconclusively, at six in the evening. While this man packed up his briefcase and went home, Rohatyn made it known that he had to tramp up to the Carlyle to give a full report—even though nothing had really happened.

Wherever the advice originated, it reaped handsome rewards for Lazard. Between 1966 and 1969, ITT paid the firm $2.1 million in fees for its merger work. That may not sound like a princely sum by today's standards, when a single deal can reap a lucky investment banker as much as $20 million, but by the norms of the 1960s it was considered enormous. In fact, when a House antitrust panel investigated the conglomerate movement in 1969, Rohatyn was pointedly asked how he could justify such huge fees. His reply was that he could justify them on the basis of the deals he talked Geneen *out* of doing, such as buying Pan American World Airways. As Rohatyn remembers it, "I took the annual report out and I called Geneen and I said, 'Listen, I read the footnotes. I've seen deals that could hurt us, but this is the first one that can bankrupt us.' "

What the House panel only dimly perceived was that Lazard was also compensated in other ways by ITT: namely, in its new role as co-lead underwriter for ITT, a role the firm won solely by dint of its merger-and-acquisition work. This was a serious loss of face for ITT's traditional lead underwriter, Kuhn Loeb, but Geneen insisted on it.

To Kuhn Loeb's distress, it soon became apparent that Meyer and Lazard were out to squeeze every nickel they could from their new position. Meyer continually railed against Kuhn Loeb's tight pricing of ITT bond issues; the generous pricing Lazard wanted clearly would guarantee a sellout of the issue, but would also come at the expense of ITT. The reason why Meyer took this route, to Perry at least, was obvious: "He didn't want to be stuck with any merchandise."

Meyer was paranoid about the possibility that Kuhn Loeb was doing him out of underwriting fees. In one particular deal, he became so incensed that he took the matter straight to Geneen—and not via Rohatyn, either. "He went into Geneen's office, and his voice went up and up and up," says Perry, who was at the meeting. "He was just livid, just furious." To mollify Meyer, Geneen told Perry to investigate the situation and lay the facts before ITT board member and former World Bank president Eugene Black, an old Meyer friend, who would be the judge. Black ruled in favor of Kuhn Loeb.

Another time, Kuhn Loeb arranged a syndicated bank loan for ITT in Europe, and Lazard insisted on being paid half the fee, a sum Lazard felt entitled to as ITT's co-lead underwriter. Kuhn Loeb balked—its partners didn't see why a bank loan should be treated the same as a securities underwriting—and Lazard promptly threatened to resign as an ITT underwriter. Desperate to keep peace in the family, Geneen was all set to pay Lazard a separate fee, for a deal which the firm had had nothing to do with, when Kuhn Loeb's quiet, patrician senior partner, John Schiff, stepped in. Kuhn Loeb, Schiff told Geneen, would pay Lazard the fee after all, out of its own pocket. Perhaps the most illuminating aspect of this story is the amount of money involved: all of $40,000.

But Meyer felt Lazard deserved every penny. And as he looks back on those days, Hart Perry agrees. "When it came to the nitty-gritty of sitting down and finally negotiating the terms," he says, "I think our in-house people were much better than they were. But the key to any merger is finding the thing that's going to unlock the door—the approach—and that's where Lazard was always very, very creative. In terms of the strategic thinking that went into the mergers and how you pulled them off, Lazard was simply outstanding."

Many other companies were coming to the same conclusion.

By 1968, it seemed that whenever you opened the financial pages, another Lazard deal was coming to fruition. The honor roll of Lazard-arranged mergers and acquisitions was truly a daunting one: Loews. Theaters' takeover of Lorillard; RCA's acquisition of Hertz and of Random House; Atlantic Richfield's purchase of Sinclair Oil; Kinney National Service's acquisition of Warner Brothers-Seven Arts; McDonnell Company's takeover of Douglas Aircraft; Transamerica's tender for United Artists; R. J. Reynolds' acquisition of McLean Industries; AMK Corporation's takeover of United Fruit.

To complete all these transactions, of course, Lazard needed a good deal more than just Meyer and Rohatyn. Accordingly, a large proportion of the firm's partners and associates were pressed into merger-and-acquisition duty; even old-timers like Hettinger became involved.

The muscle that a firm of Lazard's relatively small size could throw into a deal was surprisingly awesome. In the McDonnell Douglas deal, for instance, no fewer than six partners were involved. When Lazard was retained by Douglas Aircraft in late 1966, the company was on the verge of bankruptcy; it had, at best, six weeks before it ran out of money. Realizing that the only solution was a merger, the Lazard team solicited bids, sorted them out ("and," says Stanley Osborne, who headed the team, "this was in the early days of the computer, so you couldn't just throw them into the computer and have them analyzed"), and came up with the winning bidder, McDonnell—all between Thanksgiving and mid-January. For its panzer-division effort, Lazard asked for, and got, the first million-dollar fee ever in the merger business. "Actually," says Osborne, "we were entitled to *twice* that, under the terms of the contract. But we thought a million dollars was enough. Even so," he adds, "Mr. McDonnell wasn't particularly pleased."

But for every McDonnell Douglas deal, there were many more whose success mainly depended on the brainpower of Meyer and Rohatyn. "I worked very hard on those deals," comments one of Rohatyn's former subordinates, "but I realized that what Felix scratched on an envelope while riding to work in the morning with Harold Geneen was the five percent that made the deal."

Indeed, the actual mechanics of putting a big merger together are usually only the barest fraction of the battle. "No matter what anyone on Wall Street tells you today," says an ex-Lazard partner, "a third-grade competence in arithmetic is about the level of sophistication that is needed. You get more complicated than that, and you're gold-plating the crowbar." Meyer and Rohatyn's genius actually had very little to do with mathematics and complicated tender-offer formulas, and everything to do with human beings. "The merger business," Meyer once opined, "is ten percent financial analysis and ninety percent psychoanalysis." And Meyer and Rohatyn, if they were anything, were psychiatrists in residence to the corporate world.

As a case in point, there is this February 1, 1966, memo from Rohatyn to Meyer on the subject of William Levitt, the Levittown mastermind whose home-building business ITT wanted to acquire: "Mr. Levitt is apparently a rather mercurial individual, with a highly developed sense of his own importance and requiring a somewhat highly personalized approach. He knows you by reputation, and Carr [the Levitt general counsel] believes that at the appropriate point a meeting between you and Levitt should be arranged.

"The problem will undoubtedly be Mr. Levitt's personal ambitions and requirements for continued unquestioned control over the operation once the company is owned by somebody else, and possibly an overly inflated idea of value." Rohatyn's assessment was right on the mark: Levitt required a good deal of "highly personalized" reassurance before he agreed to sell out to ITT for $92 million.

Sometimes the mergers turned into exercises in group handholding. That was what happened during the Kinney-Warner Brothers talks, when a last-minute tender offer from a rival bidder threatened to upset the whole deal. The transaction turned into an old-fashioned shoot-out, with each Kinney bid met by a higher offer from the opposition.

"The meetings with the Kinney people seemed endless," Rohatyn once recalled, "sometimes two and three a day, on weekends and at night. We'd meet until two in the morning, and the lawyers would keep going 'til five preparing statements. We'd hold meetings when, half the time, there was no need for one. But you draw close to the people involved, and the tendency is, when anything happens, to call another meeting. Someone would call and say the opposition was coming out with an eighty-dollar cash bid, so we'd get in a cab and dash uptown and have coffee and feel warmer and on the right track just being together, talking about what kind of securities we could manufacture to fight back—when actually the bid was never made." Kinney's persistence, and Rohatyn's, finally paid off; the other side eventually threw in the towel, and Warner Brothers belonged to Kinney.

When it came to psychological tactics, even Rohatyn was no match for André Meyer. More than ever before, Meyer was the wise old man, advising, consoling, and ever so subtly planting merger ideas in the minds of the corporate executives who paid him homage. Among the deals that Meyer nurtured in this low-key way was the purchase of Bantam Books by IFI, the Angelli-controlled holding company. Gianluigi Gabetti, the head of IFI's international arm, had known Meyer ever since Gabetti had masterminded Olivetti's takeover of the Underwood typewriter company in the early sixties, and he truly worshipped the investment banker. "When we were working on a deal," Gabetti would say of Meyer, "he had all the energy of a young man, and all the wisdom of a senator." When Gabetti would visit Meyer at his chalet in Crans, Gabetti was more than slightly inclined to heed what Meyer had to say, and it was on one such visit that Meyer brought up Bantam. "I remember we were sitting on his sun deck," says Gabetti, "and he mentioned this name. He immediately said there are many strong points and there are these weaknesses. 'On balance,' he said, 'I think I would do it.' " And Gabetti did, in November 1974. The deal didn't quite turn out as planned—Meyer proved to be as perceptive about the weaknesses as he was about the strengths—but Gabetti had no cause to complain. When IFI sold Bantam to the German Bertelsmann group in 1979, it made a $20 million capital gain on the deal.

Alongside the benevolent banker, of course, coexisted the bullying banker—and Meyer was able to take full advantage of that aspect of his personality as well. Suspicions arose at RCA that it was Meyer's hectoring, as much as anything else, that pushed Robert Sarnoff into making so many acquisitions for RCA in the late sixties, after the younger Sarnoff took over as chief executive. Aside from Hertz and Random House, Sarnoff picked up such seemingly unrelated companies as Banquet Foods, Cushman & Wakefield (the big real estate operation), and Coronet Industries (a South Carolina carpet manufacturer). Sarnoff seemed to be taking not just a page but several chapters out of the Harold Geneen textbook on corporate expansion. And some RCA insiders concluded that the ghostwriter, in both cases, was André Meyer.

"There is no question in my mind that Meyer's influence was the reason RCA went the way it did," asserts a longtime top executive there. "Meyer was the principal instigator. And let's face it, André Meyer and Lazard Frères made millions on those deals. They had the Lazard imprint." Not everyone in the upper reaches at RCA felt that way; former general counsel Robert Werner, for one, insists, "It was Bob Sarnoff who really pushed for diversification. I think André was a factor in the diversification of RCA. Had he recommended against it, it wouldn't have taken place. But I distinguish that from beating the drums for acquisitions for acquisitions' sake."

Nevertheless, there is very little doubt that Meyer did bully Bob Sarnoff. Not in an overt, screaming fashion, but with a sort of polite, albeit thinly camouflaged, condescension. "André always treated him as David Sarnoff's son," notes Rohatyn. "Even when he was chief executive, I don't think André ever really took him seriously."

It was also true that in the sixties Meyer was extremely active in promoting RCA acquisitions. At the time United Artists was talking merger with Transamerica, for instance, UA was also discussing the sale of its film library to RCA's National Broadcasting Company. Sensing an opportunity, Meyer swooped in and suggested that RCA buy out UA completely. "Don't just buy the movies," he told the RCA board, "buy the whole thing." Relates former UA boss Arthur

Krim: "The next voice I heard was that of Bernie Siegel of Philadelphia, RCA's counsel. We talked it over and came to the conclusion that the Justice Department would not permit that kind of acquisition." NBC went ahead with the film deal, paying $125 million for the network rights to the UA film library. But as Meyer had astutely perceived, it could have owned the whole United Artists Company for just $50 million more, since that's what Transamerica ended up paying.

Then there was Hertz. The deal had originally been structured by Lehman Brothers, not as an RCA acquisition but as a CBS one. At least, that was where the matter stood until Meyer got wind of it during the autumn of 1966. True, Bill Paley was a good friend, but David Sarnoff was a better one, and a client to boot. And so Meyer and Paul Mazur, the Lehman Brothers senior partner on the RCA board, began to pressure Bobbie Lehman to change horses in midstream. Remarks one Lehman Brothers executive who worked on the deal, "The idea that Paley was going to get this jewel, that we hadn't given it to RCA—this was the worst thing that could possibly happen."

One morning, Lehman partner Frank Manheim was summoned to Bobbie Lehman's office. Manheim had been one of the prime architects of Hertz's rehabilitation in the late fifties and early sixties, and now he was handling the sale of the company to CBS. When he entered Lehman's cubbyhole of an office, he noticed that someone else was there, too—André Meyer. As Manheim recalls the scene, "Bobbie asked me about the Hertz deal, whereupon Bobbie and André said what a terrible thing I was doing, and that I really shouldn't take it to CBS. Well, I wasn't one to fight city hall, so I said OK, but who's going to tell Paley? So they said, 'You will.' "

Manheim was too scared to break the news to Paley in person, so he wrote him a note. Manheim never heard anything from Paley on it, "but I'm sure he must have thought I was a lousy bastard, and Lehman Brothers were a bunch of stinkers." RCA, meanwhile, walked off with probably the most successful acquisition it ever made.

No one would suggest that Meyer railroaded these deals through over RCA executives' objections. As Rohatyn points out, "There was no way to do a deal with RCA unless there was internal sponsorship in the company. It was a highly staff-dominated company." And certainly the Sarnoffs were, at the very least, willing accomplices. Says Rohatyn: "Bobby was clearly in favor of diversifying, and so was the General."

But as the acquisitions piled up, the conviction grew internally that RCA's spree would not have been as wild, or as unchecked, if Meyer hadn't been on the scene.

CHAPTER NINETEEN

Cashing In

By the late 1960s, André Meyer's Lazard Frères was known throughout the business world as "the merger house." No other investment-banking firm did as many mergers, nor was paid as royally for them; between 1964 and 1968 Lazard pulled in some $10 million in merger-and-acquisition fees. To give some idea of how fast the business was growing, Lazard's total income during that period increased 256 percent, but its merger income grew by 584 percent. While ITT was the biggest single contributor, it by no means dominated the firm's revenue stream. Even in the banner year of 1968, ITT fees accounted for no more than 28 percent of Lazard's merger-and-acquisition income.

Having broken the $1 million barrier by billing that much for the McDonnell Douglas merger, Lazard had established the principle that an investment banker's fee for such deals was whatever he felt like charging. This was no doubt reinforced by the informality of Lazard's invoices; no matter how complicated the transaction, all that was sent to the client was a single sheet of paper on which was typed something like "BILL: $750,000."

"André and Felix really were able to build in the client's mind the value of being their banker and solving their financial problems," says a rival Wall Street executive. "They made the client feel that he was so fortunate having them do this for him that whatever the bill was, it was totally secondary." Meyer and Rohatyn, in short, were helping to transform investment banking from a sales-oriented business—in which firms earned their livelihood from commissions on underwritings and stock trades—to a professional, fee-oriented business, much like medicine or law. It was exactly the position toward which Meyer had been striving ever since he took over Lazard.

Not that the firm didn't make money in other ways, too. During the sixties merger mania, huge profits were reaped from risk arbitrage—the trading of securities of possible merger partners, in the hopes that when the deal went through, the securities would skyrocket. Lazard had moved into risk arbitrage earlier in the decade under the brilliant but temperamental Justin Colin, son-in-law of Meyer's old coventurer Lou Green. And as the merger movement swelled, so did Colin's profits—in one year alone, he made as much as $10 million for the firm. A fair chunk of these profits, as it happened, came from mergers in which Lazard was also acting as an adviser to one side or the other. (In the ITT-Rayonier deal, for example, Colin made $286,000 by buying Rayonier stock and short-selling ITT.) While some outsiders questioned the propriety of this double-dipping, such misgivings did not appear to be shared by the denizens of 44 Wall Street. "The rule was that any deal in which Lazard was involved as an adviser, I was expected to use my common sense," notes Colin. "The rule was, simply, don't get Lazard in trouble."

Meanwhile, the firm had broken new ground, and made huge profits, in yet another area. Lazard had made an acquisition of its own. But this wasn't just any acquisition. It was a *hostile* one.

As commonplace as hostile takeovers (in which the company being sought doesn't want to be taken over) are today, they were still regarded as exotic and vaguely reprehensible in the mid-1960s. Harold Geneen, as was noted before, avoided such maneuvers like the plague, paying huge premiums to forestall any nasty confrontations with the target company's management.

But some time in 1963, Lazard uncovered a company that was worth the aggravation. Its name was Franco Wyoming.

Franco Wyoming was, as the name implies, a French-owned company with diverse interests in oil and gas fields and ranches in the western United States. Somewhat listlessly managed, it had its headquarters in Paris and had long been regarded as a sitting duck by Wall Street analysts. Its oil and gas properties alone were worth far more than the $40 to $50 a share at which the company's stock was usually traded. Yet until Lazard came along, no one had had the nerve to mount an outright takeover effort—principally because it was known that Franco Wyoming's management would staunchly oppose such a move.

But André Meyer, with his taste for the sure thing, was interested, and told Michel David-Weill to study the company and report back to him. Meyer's instructions were precise: "If you don't see us getting back two hundred percent of what we put in, then forget it." When the young man returned with his report, he was enthusiastic—but confessed that he could only come up with a return of 197 percent. As David-Weill recalls, "I had to persuade him the other three percent."

Persuaded, Meyer brought into the deal as partners Lazard Paris and the Cowdrays, owners of Lazard Brothers. (It was a rare instance, under the Meyer regime, of all three Lazard houses working together.) Plans were laid for a public tender offer in which Lazard would seek up to two-thirds of Franco Wyoming's shares at a price of $55 a share, $6.50 higher than what it was currently trading at. Yet even though he had been assured that he would at least double his money, Meyer wavered. On the eve of the tender offer, he was on the phone in Paris to Raymond Troubh at Lazard in New York, who was working on the deal. Says Troubh: "All night long it was should we, shouldn't we, should we, shouldn't we. Finally he said, 'OK, we go.' "

And so, on the morning of April 8, 1964, large ads appeared in the *New York Times, Wall Street Journal,* and other papers announcing the Lazard bid. And, just as expected, the Franco Wyoming management fought back—but with a ferocity that few thought its stodgy old management was capable of. To counter Lazard's ads, Franco Wyoming placed even bigger ones, headlined, "Do not be misled by this tender offer." The company's ads insisted that Franco Wyoming's assets were worth a lot more than what Lazard was willing to pay; the securities in its portfolio alone were valued at over $40 a share.

Fighting fire with fire, Lazard came back the next day with another ad of its own: "It was not the intention of the purchasers to provoke a controversy with the management of the company, nor do they intend to engage in such a controversy. We do, however, suggest that the isolated figures used in the company's statement of yesterday be analyzed against the figures contained in the annual reports which have been issued by the company over the years."

But if Lazard thought its rebuttal would finally shut the rebellious management up, it had another think coming. Franco Wyoming promptly filed suit to block the bid and asked for $20.4 million in damages for the "moral and material prejudice" caused by the offer. Four days later, it sent a letter to stockholders advising them that its own physical valuation of assets—on a conservative basis—topped $80 a share, and that even more could be obtained through negotiation.

This war of words did not exactly stir André Meyer's competitive juices. On the contrary, each blast from the other side seemed to send him more and more into a funk. Remarks Michel David-Weill, "I am pretty sure he thought to himself, 'Why do I go through all this? Is it really worth it?' "

But his aides knew it was and knew they could win. "Everyone sort of assumed that the management of Franco Wyoming, the chairman and his friends, all owned the shares," says Peter Lewis. "But, as it turned out, they owned very few shares." Adds Troubh: "We knew the company was owned by Belgians and Frenchmen, and that their stock was held by banks in Europe. So what do you do? You run ads, and in Europe you alert the banks by mail."

Lazard's message, in the end, came through loud and clear. On May 7, a month after the operation started, the firm announced it had received "substantially more than a majority" of the Franco Wyoming shares. The cost: $45 million. A short while later, at Franco Wyoming's annual meeting, the change of ownership became official. A multinational delegation of Lazard people arrived in Wilmington, Delaware, and walked into the meeting room. Says David-Weill: "We voted our shares. The president stepped down. And one of us walked up to the podium. It was the only *physical* takeover I've ever seen." And choreographing it, via telephone from New York, was André Meyer. Lazard Paris partner Jean Guyot, who was in Wilmington, remembers, "He had two people from his office in New York with us, and they were constantly going to the telephone to give him every detail. But constantly. Every time there was a new motion, someone ran to the phone."

Now that Lazard had the prize, the firm still had to figure out what to do with it. The Lazard partner who stepped up to the podium and took the helm, Stanley Osborne, concluded, as he puts it, "Franco Wyoming was a pretty dead company, a royalty company in effect. They had these wells, they had these lands, and they were living off that. André saw the possibilities of Franco Wyoming being a much bigger operation than the management was making of it, but it would have to be divided up. Because the overhead of running that company in so many different places would be too much."

So rather than try to run Franco Wyoming itself, Lazard merely liquidated it—which, many observers suspected, was what Lazard had had in mind all along. The firm and its partners auctioned off the oil and ranch properties; sold the securities; and, after deducting the cost of severance pay to Franco Wyoming's employees, walked off with a fortune. In fact, the outcome even exceeded David-Weill's "197 percent" expectations. "I know we made quite a lot of money, clearly more than twice what we put in," he says. "It was probably closer to three times the amount."

But the real significance of the Franco Wyoming deal wasn't the huge capital gain Lazard reaped. It was that an eminent group of investors, led by one of the world's most prestigious investment banks, had mounted a tender offer against the target company's wishes, had weathered the storm, and had won. The hostile takeover had, in a sense, finally come out of the closet. And the ramifications of that, for the business world, would be profound.

If André Meyer was at all disturbed by what he had wrought, he certainly didn't show it.

"I guess he came out where I came out," says Felix Rohatyn, "which is that if your client was a reputable company and if you were offering cash and not funny money, there was no reason not to do a hostile takeover. Now, what he didn't like were the lawsuits and the publicity. But the moment the clients who were making the hostile bids became respectable, the whole exercise became respectable."

The litmus test of Meyer's attitude was in a case that hit very close to home. In the late 1960s, Boussois Souchon Neuvesel (BSN), an aggressive French conglomerate run by the energetic young Antoine Riboud, made a bid for one of the pillars of France's industrial establishment, Saint Gobain. The move was regarded among the French business elite as a shocking bit of effrontery, a reaction that André Meyer would have been expected to share. But instead, his firm represented BSN. And Meyer was actively involved in the decision to stand by Riboud.

Guyot, who played a large part in the battle himself, notes, "André Meyer was quite sympathetic with someone of this dynamism, a kind of a new entrepreneur." Meyer expressed his feelings about this takeover attempt, and others like it, succinctly: "This is the kind of thing you have a right to do—if you succeed." (Actually, even though Riboud didn't succeed, Meyer remained one of his staunchest supporters.)

Nevertheless, side by side with this pragmatism existed a growing distaste for some of the personalities the new era was spawning. Meyer loved to boast about how snobbish he was in his business dealings. The comment he came to use, when someone particularly offended his sensibilities, was, "We decline to do business with this man." His standards, though, could be wildly inconsistent, as his flirtations with such high rollers as Eddie Gilbert and Bill Zeckendorf clearly showed. At times, Meyer would be snootily standoffish with perfectly respectable clients. Once, for example, a Lazard executive sent him a memo indicating that the internationally renowned Harry Winston jewelers was for sale and suggesting that Lazard ought to aggressively pursue this with Winston. The memo came back with a huffy note from Meyer scrawled on the bottom: "If Mr. Winston wants to see us, we will be glad to do it."

As the decades wore on, Meyer "declined to do business" with several very prominent conglomerateurs. One was Charlie Bluhdorn, the enigmatic mastermind of Gulf & Western. "I can't give you a matter of degree," says Justin Colin, "but certainly Bluhdorn was not looked upon with favor. Any deal involving him was such that André just threw up his hands." No one was ever quite sure why Meyer felt that way. Another "new entrepreneur" declared persona non grata for a time was Laurence Tisch, the dynamo responsible for Loews Corporation's expansion. "André and Larry Tisch didn't hit it off at all," relates Felix Rohatyn. "I think Larry disliked André fairly intensely, and André felt these things. The chemistry was just all wrong. They're both very strong-minded, intelligent, hard-driving men, and Larry probably didn't treat André with the reverence that he was accustomed to, and André reacted in a way that Larry didn't like."

Tisch, however, denies that there was any such acrimony in their relationship. "We had our disagreements," he says, "but when I disagreed, it was respectfully, not as an enemy." In any event, Meyer eventually softened his attitude, and Tisch became a Lazard client; Lazard, through Rohatyn, ended up handling the Lorillard takeover for Loews.

Victor Posner, though, was another story. A gruff, reclusive Miami Beach wheeler-dealer, Posner virtually made a career out of hostile takeovers, mainly through his personal holding company, NVF Corporation. Posner had long been skating on thin ice; in a prospectus accompanying NVF's successful offer for the Sharon Steel Company, he admitted that the earnings of the combined companies might not be enough to cover the interest payments on the securities he issued to finance the deal. Perhaps it was Meyer's concern about the flimsy foundation of Posner's empire that turned him off, or perhaps it was Posner's less-than-blue-chip reputation. In any case, Meyer determined early on that he would not do business with Victor Posner.

This judgment, unfortunately, did not sit well with Justin Colin, who wanted to invest for the firm's arbitrage account in the same stocks Posner was buying. "The fact is, a great deal of money could have been and was made playing Victor Posner deals," gripes Colin. "The question is, who makes the judgment? André doesn't trust the man but doesn't know him. I know the man, because it's my job to know him as well as I can, and I feel that he is reliable." By all accounts, the arguments between Colin and Meyer on this subject and others become quite heated. According to one man who worked with Colin, "Justin and André would have huge fights, yelling and screaming at each other. André would be florid, and Justin would be on the verge of tears. 'But Mr. Meyer,' he would say, 'you're being unfair. You *promised* me.' "

To Colin, Meyer's reluctance to deal with the likes of Victor Posner betrayed a fundamental unwillingness to take big risks, in a market where big risks were bound to pay off. Unlike the old-line arbitrage Meyer was used to, in which the arbitrageur's risk could be completely hedged, the arbitrage Colin was doing had far fewer safeguards. "You would get into a situation where André would look at the long side and the short side, and they wouldn't balance," relates Colin. "And that automatically upset him."

Meyer was so upset that he told Disque Deane to keep an eye on Colin. The problem with that, says Colin, was, "Disque fell in love with what he was supposed to supervise. He became as much involved as I was, and he wanted to take bigger risks than I did." Meyer then turned to Peter Lewis, who had just come back from a tour of duty with the U.S. Budget Bureau. "André said to me, 'I have no patience anymore. *You* find out what he's doing,' " remembers Lewis. "And what Justin was doing was plunging into situations which were low-grade stocks, where when a deal broke, he got badly hurt. If they were deals involving AT&T or Du Pont, André Meyer could accept that, because he understood fundamentally that something was probably going to happen. But with two companies he never heard of, and Justin spending a million dollars here and a half-million dollars there, that's where the issue came to a head."

The headstrong arbitrageur annoyed Meyer in other ways. Colin was a bit of a free spirit. Notes one coworker, "If André drew a line on the floor and told him that under no circumstances was he to cross it, Justin within two minutes would be inching his way over it." One morning, Meyer wanted to talk to Colin about something, but the arbitrageur was nowhere to be found. He called him at home: "Mr. Justin Colin, please." He waited for Colin to be fetched. "Oh, Mr. Colin is in the shower." Meyer put the phone down, glanced at the clock—it was eleven in the morning—and turned to Peter Lewis. "Mr. Justin Colin," Meyer announced, "is in the shower!" As Lewis recalls, "Mr. Meyer wasn't amused."

More seriously, Colin's arbitrage activities were starting to become a thorn in Felix Rohatyn's side. The fact that Colin was avidly buying and selling the stock of companies involved in a merger, while Rohatyn was negotiating that very same merger, made for some awkward moments at the bargaining table. Rohatyn became convinced, in his own words, "Risk arbitrage is a business that really doesn't belong within a firm that is really active in mergers. We were too small a place to be absolutely sure there is a Chinese wall between the arbitrage department and the merger department, and unless you're sure there is a Chinese wall, from where I sit I couldn't sleep at night." (The term Chinese wall is banker's parlance for restrictions on members of one department communicating with members of another.)

Colin, for his part, felt there was a certain hypocrisy in Rohatyn's position. While railing about the conflicts of interest, Rohatyn nonetheless often turned to Colin for help in gauging the market's reaction to the terms of a potential deal. "Felix, I'm sure, spent as much time with me as he did with any other partner in the firm," says Colin. "Maybe more. He sucked information out, like a pump.

"But," Colin goes on, "that doesn't mean I was an asset, necessarily. Because against that was a threat that I could get Felix into trouble. And that would destroy *everything.*"

Still, if Colin had continued to bring in $10 million and more of annual profit to the firm, he could have withstood even Rohatyn's pressure. But as the decade drew to a close, Colin's big bets started to boomerang. Comments one former Lazard executive, "The two things you couldn't do with André Meyer were lose money or get involved in bad-quality deals. And Justin managed to do both." With Meyer constantly screaming at him and imposing new restraints on his operation, and Rohatyn complaining that arbitrage was a menace to Lazard's merger business, Colin knew the handwriting was on the wall. He left the firm in 1970.

Yet Colin, who a little more than a decade later would declare personal bankruptcy after a commuter airline he was backing went out of business, always insisted that it wasn't his arbitrage losses that did him in at Lazard. Rather, it was Meyer's inherent discomfort and nervousness about the go-go stock era, an era in which in many ways Lazard had reaped handsome profits. "The market of the 1960s was one he no longer understood," maintains Colin. "It had run away from him. Kids were making millions of dollars without laying a foundation for it, in his opinion. He thought it was all sheer unadulterated madness. And the fact that I made so much money from arbitrage *proved* it."

Yet Meyer's skepticism about the go-go years—which proved, in retrospect, well founded—never extended to the great engines of those years, the conglomerates. While he complained about the insanely inflated price-earnings multiples of the period, he never questioned the mergers that were at once the products of, and the driving forces behind, those multiples. It would be easy to dismiss this as simply a matter of greed; but as his reluctance to move into institutional stock brokerage shows, avarice wasn't everything. What seems more likely is that Meyer was so caught up in the sheer joy of performing the elite "financial engineering" role that its consequences never occurred to him. True, he had certain scruples about dealing with the Victor Posners—but, to repeat Rohatyn's point, "If your client was a reputable company and if you were offering cash and not funny money, there was no reason not to do it." That there might be something vaguely contradictory about singing the praises of low overhead and small, streamlined organizations, and then going out and building huge companies for other people, never seemed to have crossed Meyer's mind. That there might be something inherently *wrong* about the conglomerate movement was a totally alien notion to him.

Nevertheless, if André Meyer didn't see the danger of conglomeratization, much of the public did. In January 1969, a new administration took office whose attorney general, John Mitchell, warned, "The danger that super-concentration poses to our economic, political and social structure cannot be overestimated." In July 1969, the U.S. Congress got into the act. A House antitrust subcommittee, chaired by crusty old Emanuel Celler, launched a major investigation of conglomerate corporations. Coming under its scrutiny were the workings of such new industrial titans as Litton, ITT, and Gulf & Western—and the "merger house," Lazard Frères.

Never before, in its one-hundred-odd years of existence, had the august investment-banking firm been subjected to such an inquiry.

Celler's panel wanted to know how much Lazard was making from the merger business (the firm, for the first time, was forced to disclose all its fees) and how many companies for whom Lazard was negotiating mergers also had Lazard partners as directors. The panel learned that ITT was hardly the only such case; of sixty-eight mergers that Lazard negotiated between 1965 and September 1969, twenty-seven were deals in which a Lazard partner was a director of one of the companies involved. Rohatyn, in fact, could only recall one instance where Lazard missed out on a merger-and-acquisition deal for a company in which it had a director.

But the most revealing moment in the investigation came when Celler tried to come to grips with Lazard's exact role in sparking the merger movement. Rohatyn, who testified on behalf of the firm, had quibbled with the committee counsel's description of Lazard as "marriage brokers." "We don't view ourselves as marriage brokers," he said. "But in terms of what we render, it is a very personal service." Then he went on:

> ROHATYN: I think we are much more an effect than we are a cause ... I don't believe we provide the initial impetus except in the cases where we do originate a transaction from time to time. The majority of these transactions are not transactions that would not have seen the light of day without us.
> CELLER: Profit is a great motive, isn't it?
> ROHATYN: Yes, Mr. Chairman.
> CELLER: It is a motivation of most of these transactions, isn't it, one way or another?
> ROHATYN: Certainly, Mr. Chairman. We run our business to make a profit.
> CELLER: Wouldn't that be a part of your motive to bring about mergers?
> ROHATYN: Certainly, Mr. Chairman, we certainly like to be involved in these transactions because, as you say, they are profitable for us, they are prestigious. We feel we are doing something professionally that we are supposed to do for our clients. But I was trying to differentiate our power to actually be a factor in these transactions taking place as opposed to the service that we render, and which we are very happy to render.
> CELLER: If there were no Lazard Frères, would there be less mergers?
> ROHATYN: I think there may have been a few less, Mr. Chairman.

* * *

By the time Rohatyn uttered these words, the sixties merger-and-acquisition boom had already begun to run its course. Largely to blame was the stock market, which by mid-1970 could best be described as "gone-gone." The dazzling price-earnings multiples that had sent these companies into orbit were no more; bereft of them, the conglomerates sank to earth like expended satellites. Many of them quickly lost a third or more of their market value, and the more heavily leveraged ones were soon tottering on the brink of bankruptcy. Ling-Temco-Vought, whose stock had soared as high as 169 in 1967, was down to 27 by January 1970.

Only one conglomerate seemed immune to the oncoming recession. All through 1969 and 1970, while other high fliers fell by the wayside, ITT went on reporting steadily increasing earnings, quarter by quarter. What's more, ITT and Lazard were on the verge of closing their biggest deal ever: the acquisition of the $2 billion Hartford Insurance Group.

But for ITT, other sorts of storm clouds were developing. The Justice Department, under its tough new antitrust chief, Richard McLaren, was making good on its promise to crack down on the conglomerates. And it was clear that as far as McLaren was concerned, public enemy number one was ITT.

In August 1969, McLaren filed suit to block the Hartford merger—the first of a string of legal actions that would take the better part of a decade to run their course. And before it was all over, the effect on Geneen, on Rohatyn, and especially on the Frenchman behind the scenes would be shattering.

CHAPTER TWENTY

Jackie O.

André Meyer's preoccupation with the affairs of great corporations did not slacken his interest in the affairs of his wealthy and powerful friends. Often, as in the case of the Agnellis and the Engelhards, the twin threads were so tightly intertwined that for all intents and purposes they were one. Agnelli was a client; Agnelli was a friend; which came first was a chicken-and-egg question whose answer eluded even Meyer's closest disciples. His was the ultimate investment-banking achievement: the drawing together of one's business and personal lives into a single great continuum.

The decade of the 1960s, consequently, was as much a time for building and reinforcing Meyer's personal relationships as it was for forging corporate colossi. And it was also a period when Meyer's penchant for secrecy began colliding head-on with a growing desire for recognition by the world at large. True, he continued to make a fuss about his "allergy" to newspaper articles. But, as his friend and partner Fred Wilson points out, "André began to change over the years with regard to publicity. As his success grew and he became more comfortable, he began to actually like publicity. He would have reporters in for interviews, which he *never* would have done in the earlier days." A young partner who contritely and nervously confessed to Meyer that he was about to be quoted in the *Wall Street Journal* was shocked by the senior partner's equanimity: "You know," the old man told him, "it is not so bad to be quoted in the paper with regard to Lazard."

For these reasons, Meyer did not flinch when a new family of advice-seekers came calling on him, a family whose very presence at the Carlyle threatened to engulf him in celebrity. He was ready—quite, quite ready—for the Kennedys.

A Kennedy in-law, Eunice's husband Sargent Shriver, was the first of the clan to make contact with the émigré financier. Shriver's father was an investment banker—he was, in fact, a friend of Frank Alt-schul, Meyer's predecessor at the Lazard helm—and it was through his father that Shriver came to know Meyer, on a casual basis, during the fifties. But Meyer meant little to the Kennedys until their move to the White House, and then only because of the intervention of an-other in-law, Jean's husband Stephen Smith.

As the family fanned out early in the administration into positions of power, Smith was given responsibility for a government program called the Redevelopment Loan Fund, which raised capital for devel-oping countries. "There was a question about an African project we were working on," recalls Smith, "and I made an effort to talk to some investment bankers about it, and among them was Mr. Meyer. And I remember telling the president afterwards how impressed I was."

That was in the spring of 1961. President Kennedy may have had some reason to recognize Meyer's name, since they were neighbors at the Carlyle, with Kennedy living one floor above Meyer. (Meyer would sometimes complain that there were so many leaks in his apartment ceiling that one day he expected Jack Kennedy to tumble into his bathtub.) But the financier could hardly have been counted among the new president's staunchest supporters in the banking com-munity. In January 1962, a year after Kennedy took office, Meyer grumbled to a friend, "Kennedy is intelligent, very intelligent. He is popular in the country. But nothing happens. We are not making progress. In Europe, he means nothing, nothing at all; he has no standing at all." Then he added, "This is not par-*ti*-zan, I hope. That is the way it is."

Meyer and the president, in all likelihood, did not actually meet until May of that year. The occasion was a fund-raiser at the Four Seasons restaurant hosted by United Artists chairman Arthur Krim. Krim brought Kennedy over to Meyer's table, and the three men sat down for a brief but pleasant chat. The conversation led to a modest campaign contribution by Meyer, but it also stamped a firmer impres-sion in Kennedy's mind of the Franco-American investment banker. In October 1963, he named Meyer to a blue-ribbon panel that was looking into ways of cutting the country's balance-of-payments defi-cit. It was far from the usual arm's-length presidential appointment dictated by aides for the chief executive's signature. The committee's chairman, then-Treasury Undersecretary (and later Treasury Secre-tary) Henry Fowler, recalls, "President Kennedy suggested that

André would be a good person from Wall Street to have, that he'd been friendly, and that he'd welcome his advice. And the word came *directly* from Kennedy."

Still, there is no evidence that Meyer and JFK were ever especially close. Not once during Kennedy's presidency, for example, did Meyer visit the Oval Office, though Smith says, "I think he was at the White House for a couple of state dinners." Meyer, however, did come around to admitting, after the assassination, that his initial assessment of the president had been mistaken. As he told David Lilienthal, "You said he was very good, long before the convention, and I said you were completely wrong. Do you remember? Well, I was a thousand percent wrong. Such intelligence, such sensitivity, such understanding of the world!"

The feeling seemed to be mutual, at least as far as other members of the Kennedy family were concerned. Because in early 1964, when the family was looking for new trustees for the vast trust funds established by patriarch Joseph Kennedy, Robert Kennedy approached André Meyer. "I don't think it was a difficult choice for us," says Stephen Smith, who by then was overseeing the family's business affairs. "We all knew him; he was very much respected; his strengths were obvious. We said, 'If André would do it, that would be great.' I think it was that simple."

Sargent Shriver, who claims to have been the original proponent of Meyer's selection in family councils, details the reasons why the Kennedys turned to the investment banker: "We needed trustees who would be beyond doubt or beyond criticism, men of superlative judgment, experience, and prudence. After all, there were six living members of my wife's generation, some of whom were very conspicuously involved in politics, which meant to me that the trustee ought to be somebody whose judgment was beyond question and whose reputation was so high that nothing could hurt any of them politically." He and other family members believed they had found such a man in André Meyer. No scandal had ever tarnished his name; his judgment and prudence were praised by his ever-expanding circle of acquaintances, in the United States and overseas; his worldliness, in the best sense of the word, was beyond question.

When Bobby Kennedy approached him with the offer, Meyer was plainly flattered. The Kennedys, after all, represented the ultimate connection. The Meyer mystique—which had opened so many business doors to himself and to Lazard—couldn't help but be enhanced by such a relationship. "He was a name-dropper, no question about it," says a rival investment banker who occasionally lunched with Meyer. "He wanted to be sure you knew how extremely important he was. He'd always mention, 'I'm very close to the Kennedy family,' to give you the impression that it was typical of the influence that he commanded."

Oddly enough, despite Meyer's money-spinning reputation, the Kennedys did not ask him to vastly enhance their fortunes. This was largely because of the conservative way in which the trusts had traditionally been run. Joe Kennedy may have built his fortune through swashbuckling speculation, but he clearly wanted his descendants to take a different tack entirely. Totaling some $100 million, the trusts were designed to provide taxable income of about $500,000 a year for his widow Rose and each of his surviving children. The securities portfolio, consequently, was impeccably blue-chip. Furthermore, the family-owned enterprises—overseen by a Kennedy company with the innocuous name of Park Agency, Inc., run by Smith—were managed with a similar bent toward preservation of capital. The main revenue source was Chicago's Merchandise Mart, a giant office and showroom building that was bought by Joseph Kennedy in 1945 for a mere $1 million. By the late seventies, it was said to be worth in excess of $150 million, and its 1,000 or so tenants netted the family about $7 million a year in pretax profits.

What was asked of Meyer, then, wasn't the hot stock of the week, or an early crack at his venture-capital investments. Mainly, recalls Shriver, "He looked over the portfolio to see if it was reasonably well organized and managed. His contribution was more in the strategic evaluation of what was being done, rather than in the day-to-day tactics of making money." On the strategic side, he *did* play an important role—particularly when the Merchandise Mart was threatened by a plan by Chicago real estate interests to lure its apparel-company tenants into a new building. The Kennedys, under Meyer's prodding, countered with a new structure of their own to house the clothing companies. The proposed Apparel Center would be a costly undertaking for the family—the price tag, according to Shriver, was in the neighborhood of $45 million—and would tie the family fortune even more closely to the Chicago real estate market. But Meyer insisted that the move "is not only prudent, but necessary." As Shriver recounts Meyer's rationale, "He felt it was necessary to protect the existing investment, and therefore it was very prudent, despite the fact that it required more investment in the same place, in the same business, in the same city." Meyer made no bones about his distaste for the clothing business—it was another one of those retail endeavors that he scorned—but since the Kennedys were already committed to it, he felt they shouldn't hesitate to protect themselves. They followed his advice, built the Apparel Center, and the family bulwark was once again secure.

To the extent that the family made speculative investments, mainly in oil and real estate, Meyer was usually relied upon as the ultimate clearinghouse. At one point, he had Disque Deane reviewing the Kennedys' real estate holdings, and Peter Lewis their oil interests, and for a while there was even talk of Lazard-Kennedy joint ventures in these areas. "We discussed a couple of them," says Smith, "but they didn't materialize."

In the meantime, the links between the secretive financier and the country's most celebrated family grew more and more intimate. Meyer became a member of the board of the John F. Kennedy Library and, along with former Treasury Secretary Douglas Dillon and IBM chairman Thomas Watson, served as a key fund-raiser, soliciting contributions from such diverse acquaintances as Félix Houphouët-Boigny, the president of the Ivory Coast Republic, and Gianni Agnelli, whose companies gave $100,000. And when construction of the library was delayed by the heated debate over where to locate it, Meyer stepped in to help manage the $60 million building fund that had accumulated. All the fund's portfolio transactions, during that interim period, were handled by Lazard.

Meyer rapidly graduated from investment adviser to personal adviser. "Our conversations with him would be on three levels: business, personal, and family matters," says Smith, "the whole range of concerns that all of us were involved with then. It's a big family, it's close, and this place"—referring to the family office where he works—"acts as a sort of a stockholder for the family, so we're involved in most aspects of their lives. So, in the course of that, it would be natural that you'd talk to a friend about this problem or that problem."

The discussions ran the gamut from soul-searching over the family's political future to minor money matters. Often, they took the form of private conferences—at the Carlyle, at the Kennedy offices, in restaurants—between Meyer and Robert Kennedy. Meyer had a special affection and respect for Bobby. Gianni Agnelli remembers, "André liked Teddy, too, because he thought Teddy was much more intelligent than most people thought he was. But Bobby was the one he *really* liked."

For Bobby Kennedy, the friendship with André Meyer filled a deeply felt need. Kennedy intimate Roswell Gilpatric notes, "Robert Kennedy was always trying to find someone in the business and financial community, someone he could come to for help. I think it was because neither he nor his brother Jack understood what made the business and financial community tick. And there was no one for whose financial acumen he had greater respect." But Meyer was more than just a businessman-sounding board for Bobby Kennedy; he was also a father confessor, someone to whom Kennedy could easily and confidently turn for counsel as he rebuilt his life and career after his brother's death. One of Kennedy's top aides in those years, Thomas Johnston, says, "André was one of the relatively small group of people whose judgment Robert Kennedy would trust, not only in things related to the buisness world but things in general. It was a very close relationship."

Kennedy always was secretive about his *tête-à-têtes* with Meyer. Johnston recalls, "He never spoke to me about the content of those meetings. They could have been about family finances, but I never knew for sure." But his aides concluded that some of those sessions were pivotal ones for Kennedy. According to Stephen Smith, Meyer was one of the small group of people Kennedy turned to for advice during his period of soul-searching over a presidential run in 1968.

In his journals, David Lilienthal recalls a meeting with Meyer in late June 1966 that was interrupted by two phone calls. "Both of the calls," Lilienthal relates, "had to do with 'Jackie' and 'Bobby.' " After he put down the phone the second time, Meyer shook his head and sighed: "These Kennedys," he told Lilienthal, "are difficult people to do things for. Bobby has such energy, is moving about constantly. The other evening we had dinner together on Third Avenue in a small restauant. During the meal he had to go to put in an appearance at *three* dinner meetings; three times."

Concludes Lilienthal, "Well, with help from André, they are in good hands, and I am sure they know it."

No one knew it better than Jackie.

They were seen *everywhere* together—at dinner parties, at the theater, at the Caravelle restaurant. Often, they were followed by that inveterate *paparazzo*, Ron Galella, who once even photographed a radiant Jackie, dressed in black evening cape and fall, and an equally radiant André, at the hit musical *Hair*. Read the magazine caption: "André Meyer, an old friend and frequent escort, was enjoying a remark by Jackie at the intermission of *Hair* when Galella, who had naturally followed them into the theater, shot this picture."

Meyer was hardly Jackie's only escort during those mid-sixties years. Her other distinguished squires included Defense Secretary Robert McNamara, former British ambassador to the United States Lord Harlech, and Truman Capote. One caustic socialite summed up the lot this way: "Jackie's dates are all very married, or very old, or very queer." Whatever they were, all seemed abashed by her presence on their arm. About McNamara, *Time* wrote, "When Jackie's around, the Computer turns into a puppydog."

The hard-bitten old French deal-maker was no more immune to the charms of the president's widow than anyone else. When Jackie was with him, he would dote on her in a half-fatherly, half-amorous way; when she wasn't, he would talk about her constantly. "He got a certain kick out of the relationship," says Gilpatric, who also squired Jackie from time to time. Adds Gianni Agnelli, "Jackie opened up his life. She was a part of those aspects of life that he really didn't know. And he absolutely *adored* being with someone that important."

And if André was preoccupied with Jackie, Jackie seemed similarly taken with André. "His name constantly came up in conversations with her," says one close friend. "It was always, 'I'm going to talk to André about this, see André about that.' But she never actually talked about the relationship. You just sort of knew it was there."

Her family and friends could see clearly that Meyer was more than just a safe date, and that he played a central role in her life in the years after the assassination. In many ways, it was similar to the role he played for Bobby: that of sounding board, confidant, father confessor. But in Jackie's case, the vitality and intensity of the relationship transcended those classifications. In the first, uncertain years of her widowhood, and even after her marriage to Aristotle Onassis, Meyer was one of the few truly steadying influences in her life. "She greatly appreciated the father figure that he was," says Meyer's old friend Andrea Wilson. "She *needed* that."

It was not hard to understand why Jackie turned to Meyer when she resettled in New York in 1964. First, they had many friends in common, people like Gianni Agnelli and Hervé Alphand, who praised Meyer's wisdom and his value as a counselor. Then there was Meyer's Frenchness; of French descent herself, Jackie always had a weakness for things Gallic. And, of course, Meyer's celebrated financial genius also played a part. Former World Bank president Eugene Black, who was another of Jackie's elderly advisers, puts it this way: "Jackie had money and Jackie liked money, and she felt André would be a pretty damn good fellow to handle the money for her. It's that simple."

While her business affairs, like those of the other Kennedy heirs and dependents, were initially handled by the family office under Stephen Smith, Jackie began bridling very early on at the family's all-encompassing control of her life. Turning to an independent adviser—albeit one who was closely tied to the family as a trustee—was one way she could declare her independence from the clan. (Marrying Onassis, it was later obvious, was another.) "I don't recall her ever talking about going to Steve Smith for advice," says a friend. "It was always André."

A good deal of his counsel, naturally enough, had to do with her investment portfolio. She became one of those AM accounts at Lazard, in which the assets were run by one of Lazard's investment managers under Meyer's watchful eye. He also advised her on such sundry matters as the purchase of a cooperative apartment in Manhattan. Upon finding just the right place at 1040 Fifth Avenue, she went immediately to Meyer. "It's perfect," she gushed, "and if you think it's a good investment, I'll buy it." He looked it over, pronounced the $200,000 price a fair one, and Jackie closed the deal.

But Meyer's guidance, her friends insist, extended far beyond the financial realm. Says McNamara: "He was a very respected and admired close friend and personal adviser, on both financial matters and more broadly on other matters. She had the most immense admiration and respect for him." Just what those "other matters" were, neither McNamara nor her other friends will say; Jackie herself steadfastly refuses (through a spokeswoman) to talk about the relationship. But undoubtedly one frequent subject of their discussions was the upbringing of her two children, Caroline and John, Jr. Meyer plainly took an adoring, grandfatherly interest in the Kennedy kids; one frequent visitor to the Carlyle says, "I'd often see the three of them there. They all seemed on a very familiar, close personal basis."

Meyer could sometimes be found telling the children stories or helping them with their math homework.

"He had a very protective feeling about Jackie Kennedy," comments Meyer's old friend Anna Rosenberg Hoffman. "He felt sorry for her. And she clung to him; it was a very paternal relationship." The problem was, the closer she clung, the greater the shock waves sent through the Meyer household. In a little apartment already crammed with women vying for the old man's attention, she was more than just another celebrity coming to call; she was an intruder and a competitor.

Bella, it was obvious, felt this keenly. Says Marianne Gerschel: "My grandmother realized that this, after all, was an elegant, dark-haired woman who was younger than she. Before Jackie would arrive, my grandmother would go around asking everyone, 'Do I look all right? Do I look all right?' "

What drove the women around André Meyer to distraction, even more than Jackie's presence, was her manner, particularly the breathless, little-girl-lost way in which she would implore Meyer, "André, what should I do? I don't know what to *do*." As Gerschel remembers the scene, "This little-girl voice coming across the room would be enough to drive you absolutely out of your mind. I suppose I was fourteen at the time, and I remember thinking, 'My God, you know, he can't be taken in by this garbage.' But it was something my grandfather just couldn't see."

Another member of the Carlyle retinue who was cynically watching the interplay, in her own quiet way, was Madeleine Malraux. Jackie, she decided, was a very intelligent woman, but also very superficial—and Malraux was certain that Meyer agreed with this assessment. But, she says, "He did not want it pointed out to him." Searching for a word to describe Jackie, Malraux came up with the term *allumeuse.* "It's someone who gives you hope, someone *qui craque l'allumette*—who lights the match, you know?

"Jacqueline Kennedy," Malraux concluded, "is a coquette."

Furthermore, Malraux had little doubt that Jackie, quite literally and quite deliberately, lit André Meyer's *allumette.* "He must surely have been in love with her," Malraux would say many years later. "And why not? She is very charming, and he was very sensitive to feminine beauty. He thought she was *extraordinary.*"

Meyer, in the manner of a love-struck swain, refused to hear anything that smacked of criticism of Jackie or her motives. Once, during her run-ins with Galella (she eventually sued the photographer), Meyer groaned to his family, "Oh, this poor woman. We have to leave her alone. She doesn't like publicity, you know." To which his granddaughter shot back, "Grandfather, what are you talking about? This woman *adores* publicity. She lives for it. And I guarantee you that within two years she'll be married to someone who gets just as much publicity as she."

Meyer was enraged. "How dare you say something like that?" he barked. "Out! Get out!"

Gerschel proved to be a little off on her timing, but not by much. In October 1968, just four months after the death of Robert Kennedy, Jackie announced her engagement to Aristotle Onassis. "I remember getting a call in boarding school," says Gerschel. "It was from another member of the family. 'Well, Marianne,' they said, 'you were right. But for God's sake, don't tell your grandfather, "See, I told you so." ' "

Meyer did not take the news with equanimity. "He was furious!" says Malraux. Partly, he was upset about her choice for a marriage partner. He had had some business dealings with the Greek shipping tycoon and viewed him as a most unsuitable spouse for the former First Lady. "He did not feel it was a good merger," cracks one of Meyer's Paris friends. When asked why, Anna Rosenberg Hoffman responds, "Did you know Onassis? I did. I knew him well. He had great charm and great intelligence. *Great* intelligence. But he was rough, yacht or no yacht. And there was his reputation—with Callas and all that." (Referring to his stormy, long-running liaison with opera star Maria Callas.) "I don't think André or the Kennedy family felt that it was right to the memory of Jack Kennedy for her to be married to a man like Onassis."

Still, Meyer's intimates felt there was something else that sparked his rancor over the impending marriage. Comments Marianne Gerschel: "I think he was probably upset because she had really played the little girl to the hilt, OK? And, you know, no man wants his little girl to get married—it's that sort of feeling. If you're going to play the little girl, you will always be the little girl, and therefore you're not allowed to get married. You're *not* allowed.

"And there's also this feeling, 'If she's going to marry somebody, why can't she marry me?' I mean it's totally illogical, but it's totally the way fathers behave."

After the initial explosion, Meyer managed to swallow his pride and settle into the role that came most naturally to him: that of the merger broker. Onassis came to call on him, just as though the banker really were the father of the bride. "You know, she's in love with me," he reportedly told Meyer. "What do you think?" How Meyer responded went unrecorded, but shortly afterwards he met with Jackie. According to later accounts by one of Jackie's many unauthorized biographers, Meyer spent two weeks trying to change her mind, telling her she was making a monumental mistake. But Stephen Smith, who was said to have been equally upset about the marriage, doubts that Meyer was one of the dissuaders. "I have some idea who was," Smith says, "but I don't think he was among them."

What Meyer *is* known to have done was plead with Jackie that if she was going to go through with this marriage, she should make the best of it for herself, financially. At least, he told her, let me work out a financial arrangement for you.

Out of these conversations, according to several of Jackie's biographers, came the idea of a detailed premarital agreement between Jackie and her spouse-to-be; in effect, a marriage contract. This contract, said to have been thrashed out between Meyer and Onassis's lawyers and signed by the couple just three days before their wedding on the Greek island of Skorpios, was reported to have contained no less than 170 clauses. Among them: a guarantee of at least $600,000 a year for Jackie's travel, pleasure, safety, and children. Furthermore, the contract was said to have provided for all sorts of contingency payments in case the marriage fell apart. If Onassis left Jackie, he would have to pay her a sum amounting to $9.6 million for every year of the marriage. If she left him before their fifth anniversary, she would be paid a lump sum of $18 million; if she stuck it out longer and then left him, he would also pay her alimony of $180,000 a year. And if Onassis died while they were still married, she would be bequeathed $100 million.

Aside from these financial arrangements, the contract was also reported to have spelled out some of the most intimate aspects of their married life. It was said to have stipulated, for example, that they have separate bedrooms and even specified the times of the year that they would spend together. This, it was said, explained why Jackie had her own house in Skorpios after they were married, and why in New York she always stayed in her 1040 Fifth Avenue apartment while her husband rented a suite at the Pierre Hotel, less than a mile and a half away.

Neither Kennedy nor Onassis aides ever confirmed the existence of this "contract." In fact, the primary source of information on it, in all cases, appears to be Christian Karafakis, the former chief steward of Onassis's yacht *Christina*. Karafakis disclosed the details of the contract in a newspaper interview in October 1971, three years after the marriage, but did not explain how he became privy to them. When Nancy Tuckerman, Jackie's spokeswoman, was asked by reporters about Karafakis's revelations, she described them as "ridiculous. It's really quite unfair and unkind," she said. "It's so fabricated. Mr. Onassis doesn't have an apartment at the Pierre. There is no contract."

The only recorded comment Jackie herself made on the matter come in a conversation she had with Truman Capote. The marriage-contract rumor was "a lie," she said. "I didn't make any premarital agreement with Ari. I know it's an old Greek custom, but I couldn't do it. I didn't want to barter myself."

A similar denial comes from Stephen Smith, although in a roundabout way. "It's not true, period," he says. "I don't know what contract there was. I'm not aware there was one. And if there was one, I don't know what was in it. And I don't believe there was one. I'm not aware of it, and I have no knowledge whatsoever that André Meyer was involved.

"There *was* a different story," Smith continues. "I don't know about a marriage contract, but there was a story that André had a conversation in which he made certain suggestions. But when you use the word contract—to my knowledge there was no such thing, nor did I ever hear at the time of the marriage any discussion of it. Whether or not André Meyer had any discussions prior to the marriage with Aristotle Onassis about the forthcoming marriage—it was quite possible he did. But I would hardly characterize whatever it was as an effort to draw up a contract."

Judge Simon Rifkind, who has represented both André Meyer and Jackie, told the author, "This is the first time I've ever heard it mentioned that André had anything to do with a contract. That he watched over her, and some of her affairs, I knew then. But I didn't know anything about it until you mentioned it yourself."

And Anna Rosenberg Hoffman, who was told by Meyer of his efforts to get Jackie to agree before the marriage to a financial arrangement with Onassis, says that, in fact, Meyer's entreaties were rejected by Jackie. "She would have none of it," Hoffman says. "She wouldn't let them have *any* arrangement. André was very upset about it. He told me about it; that's how I know."

The best evidence that there wasn't a contract—or, at least, a contract along the lines suggested by Karafakis—was what happened after Onassis died in March 1975. In his will, he left his widow a bequest of $100,000 a year from tax-free bonds, and an additional $100,000 for herself and $50,000 for her children—a far cry from the $100 million Karafakis claimed was stipulated in the contract. There was no reference in the will to a premarital agreement, though Onassis did claim in the will that Jackie had signed a document giving up all claims to his estate. The will's terms were unacceptable to Jackie; after apparently threatening to take the matter to court, she settled with Onassis's daughter, Christina, for $20 million. Again, as handsome as that sum was, it was nothing like what a supposedly ironclad agreement would have provided. The deal Meyer was said to have cut for Jackie either didn't stand up, or was voided by her renunciation of estate claims—or didn't exist in the first place. Most likely, in view of Jackie's ready acquiescence to the $20 million settlement, it was the latter.*

A year after the marriage, Roswell Gilpatric went to a party Jackie was throwing at 1040 Fifth. There, as much the object of the hostess's solicitude as he'd ever been, was André Meyer. From what Gilpatric could surmise, "The marriage really didn't rupture their relationship." Other close friends of hers reached the same conclusion. "It was still a very, very warm, affectionate friendship," says Robert McNamara. "And I saw enough of them both after the marriage to feel quite certain about that."

Meyer would still be seen escorting her to dinners and benefits, sharing whispered confidences at Caravelle and Côte Basque. And Jackie, along with John Jr., and Caroline, remained a fixture at the Carlyle, soaking up Meyer's wisdom in her meek, little-girlish way. "Jackie comes every week," he once berated Katharine Graham. "What about you?"

But those closest to Meyer could see that something had changed, that something was held back by him that hadn't been held back before. "It was the one thing about him," says Marianne Gerschel.

---

* After Onassis's death, there were reports that he had arranged a change in Greek law that, in effect, voided the marriage contract. Those reports, however, were never substantiated.

"When he knew he had been emotionally had, he would continue the relationship, but it would go on in a different way. Suddenly, the real emotional relationship is gone."

She was Jacqueline Kennedy Onassis now. The little girl had grown up quickly.

CHAPTER TWENTY-ONE

A Rendezvous with LBJ

On an early morning in April 1968, André Meyer awakened not in the French-provincial surroundings of his Carlyle Hotel apartment but in a plainly furnished ranch house somewhere in central Texas. As the first wave of consciousness broke upon him, he thought he saw something moving in his room. Slipping on his glasses, Meyer was startled to find someone there. Seated at the foot of the bed, eyeing Meyer with all the urgency of a child eager to play with his slumbering parent, was the ranch owner, who also happened to be president of the United States.

Lyndon Johnson, quite literally, couldn't wait to talk to his weekend houseguest, André Meyer.

Meyer, by then, was used to the chief executive's urgent questioning. During the previous four and a half years, while his relationship with those pretenders to the throne, the Kennedys, flourished, the investment banker had also taken care to build close ties to the crown. Between 1964 and 1968, Meyer visited the Johnson White House twenty-four times, including eleven private Oval Office chats. And that didn't count the innumerable occasions when Johnson would pick up the phone and call Meyer, or ask an intermediary to check with the financier. "At least five or six times a year, LBJ sought André's opinion on something," says former UA chairman Arthur Krim, who often served as a liaison between the two men.

Meyer's dealings with Johnson, though less personal than those he had with the Kennedys, sprang from mutual strivings. Johnson, like the Kennedys before him, was greatly in need of a window to the world financial community, someone who could give him honest, straightforward advice that wasn't colored by gross self-interest or expressed in impenetrable jargon. Moreover, he also needed someone who could counsel him about that perennial thorn in his side, French President Charles de Gaulle, particularly on economic issues, which were some of the main stumbling blocks for Franco-U.S. relations in those years. Few men, if any, in America were better suited to render such advice than André Meyer.

For Meyer, the opportunity for influence in the corridors of power was irresistible. To a man who still displayed a childlike awe of governments and the people who ran them, such unfettered access to the president of the United States was a unique thrill. Former Lazard partner Robert Ellsworth, himself an ex-government official, remembers, "André would talk *endlessly* about his contacts with Johnson. He always had a silver-framed photo of him and Johnson on the White House north portico prominently displayed. To me, it was ridiculous; to me, Johnson was just a politician. There was no mystery at all. But to André, it was all magic."

Despite the enormous differences in their backgrounds and vocations, the French banker and the Texas politician had a lot in common. Both, obviously, were self-made men who had struggled ferociously to get where they were. Both were shrewd negotiators who could alternately charm and bully their way to an objective. Both were workaholics with an insatiable hunger for facts, facts, and more facts. Both were obsessively thorough. Both sought to dominate, through sheer force of will. And both had a permanent sense of urgency about them.

Certainly Meyer wasted little time cozying up to LBJ. "Shortly after the assassination, Johnson asked me to carry on with the fundraising events we had had in mind for Kennedy," relates Krim. "And I soon found out that André was very enthusiastic about Johnson. He became an important contributor to the 1964 campaign." Meyer was hardly the only businessman-booster of LBJ in 1964; in those pre-supply-side days, nearly every man of substance in the United States cringed at the thought of "radical" Republican Barry Goldwater moving into the White House. But Meyer did manage to stand out from the crowd by making his active support known to White House insiders, including special presidential assistant Walter Jenkins. "I enjoyed seeing you this past weekend," Jenkins wrote Meyer three weeks before the election. "We are most appreciative of everything you are doing for us."

Meyer's first recorded meeting with Johnson was earlier that year, on April 27, when LBJ heard a report from the foreign-investment task force to which Kennedy had appointed Meyer in October 1963. But their relationship was still a distant one. Johnson, for example, responded to Meyer's congratulatory letter after the election with a stiff "Dear Mr. Meyer" salutation. And a White House staff memo in March 1965 suggesting that Meyer be invited to a dinner for the president of Pakistan identified him simply as "a rich New York banker."

But Meyer kept at it. He was one of the organizers of a lavish $1000-a-head fund-raising ball for the president in May 1965 at New York's Waldorf Astoria Hotel; this prompted a letter from another of Johnson's special assistants, Jack Valenti, telling Meyer, "From what I have learned about you from those friends of yours who are unstinting in their praise about you, I am greatly aware that the success [of the ball] was due largely to your efforts." Two weeks later—coincidentally or not—Meyer was named to yet another prestigious presidential study group: this one, chaired by former Treasury Secretary C. Douglas Dillon, would look into the question of international monetary reform. Henry Fowler, the new treasury secretary who organized the panel, had come to know Meyer during their service together on the balance-of-payments committee. He says he submitted Meyer's name for the new group, "and there was no question about it being accepted."

From that point on, Meyer became part of the coterie of business leaders who were regularly invited to the White House for state dinners, signing ceremonies, and special briefings. Meanwhile, he assiduously endeavored to put his relationship with LBJ on a personal footing. When Johnson underwent a gall-bladder operation in October 1965, Meyer sent this effusive cable to his wife Lady Bird: "Delighted to know that the President is well stop we were so deeply disturbed that he had to go through an operation and are so pleased with the wonderful results you know how much I love and admire the President with my warmest wishes to both of you and the expression of my respectful affection André Meyer."

Meyer's case was also helped by the appointment of former NBC president Robert Kintner, an old friend, as one of Johnson's new assistants. It was Kintner (with some behind-the-scenes help from Arthur Krim) who opened the Oval Office door for Meyer. The breakthrough came in May 1966, in the form of a memo from Kintner to another top LBJ aide, W. Marvin Watson. "André Meyer of Lazard Frères will be in my office at five P.M. today, for a short time," Kintner advised Watson. "I do not know the President's plans or his inclination, but if there is a chance he might want to say hello to Mr. Meyer who is a very large contributor to the Democratic Party and a staunch supporter of the President." Johnson agreed to say hello, but not much more—the meeting was all of two minutes long. Nevertheless, at the end of August, Meyer was invited back, and this time the banker and the president conferred for an hour and twenty minutes. Kintner was asked to sit in on that meeting, but when Meyer showed up again at the White House less than a month later, he and Johnson met alone.

It was not hard to see why Johnson increasingly sought the investment banker's counsel. Not only was the president wrestling with the financial consequences of the escalating war in Vietnam and his ambitious Great Society social programs—the great "guns and butter" debate—but he was faced with growing European unrest, particularly by the French, over mounting U.S. balance-of-payments deficits. To bring matters to a head, the French were threatening to exchange their dollar holdings for the gold that supposedly backed those holdings, a development that could lead to a worldwide run on the dollar and the collapse of the delicately balanced international monetary system.

With his knowledge of global high finance, and especially his familiarity with the French, Meyer was an ideal adviser during this period of economic saber rattling. All his wining and dining of French dignitaries and his careful cultivation of his reputation as a Gallic financial genius in residence at the Carlyle had not been for nought. Meyer knew the up-and-coming young French finance minister, Valéry Giscard d'Estaing; he was on intimate terms with de Gaulle's top economic adviser (and fomenter of much of the anti-American agitation), Jacques Rueff; he was even close to Prime Minister Georges Pompidou, whom Meyer had known since Pompidou was a top director at the Rothschild Bank in Paris. Consequently, Meyer was an invaluable resource for an American administration struggling to come to grips with French hostility. "In private talks," recalls Fowler, "André gave me a very sophisticated understanding of the French position. Sure, we had our battles with the French, but it could have been much worse if I had been completely unknowledgeable about the substance of the French position. He played the role of a friendly intelligence agent, so to speak, as to what their thinking was."

Yet in many ways Meyer was a double agent—since the French also relied on him to give *them* a better understanding of what U.S. officials were thinking. Georges Plescoff, France's financial attaché in Washington during that period, remembers often turning to Meyer for "a judgment on the balance payments, on the measures the U.S.

would take, and the success or failure of these measures." What's more, the French government trusted Meyer to relay its viewpoint (on an informal basis, of course) to high U.S. officials. As Plescoff points out, "He knew perfectly well what would be done from the French side—he could even say it in advance."

By the summer of 1967, the United States and France had come to see eye to eye on the need for a new international reserve asset that would supplement, and possibly supplant, gold and the dollar. (But not before the French had cashed in a fair chunk of their dollar holdings for gold.) This new asset, dubbed Special Drawing Rights (SDRs), would be a composite of a basket of currencies administered by the International Monetary Fund. The original idea for the SDR had come out of the Dillon committee, of which Meyer was a member. Here again, it was Meyer the pragmatist who came to the fore. According to Dillon, Meyer's contribution was "less on the conceptual thinking, and more on how to make it work so it would be accepted." The SDR officially came into being in September 1967 and was immediately hailed as a major step toward restoring order to the world's financial system.

Meyer's role in all this was not unappreciated by the man in the White House; more and more, the Texas president would turn to the Gallic banker for advice on the French political situation, the economy, taxes. "Johnson thought of André as a financier with ideas," suggests Douglas Dillon. "And as a Southwest populist, Johnson tended to be skeptical of big commercial bankers, so he talked to André Meyer because he wasn't the head of a big commercial bank. Talking to the head of Citibank was somewhat different; Johnson was more on guard with people like that. He felt more at ease with André."

Not that Meyer was any less gloomy than the next banker. From the outset, he warned Johnson that the country's economy could not pay for both guns and butter without inflationary consequences, and he was an early supporter of major tax increases to pay for the war. In a July 23, 1966, memo to the president, Kintner reported that Meyer's viewpoints "are somewhat pessimistic," and relayed the banker's concern about the volume and interest rates of U.S. government borrowings; Meyer also expressed some uncertainty "about what will happen to the economy if the Vietnamese operation would end very quickly." Kintner, however, saw fit to add this postscript: "André, as you know, is a strong supporter of the President's."

Much as he might have reservations about certain administration policies, Meyer's overall confidence in Johnson remained undiminished. "The president is better than he looks," he cryptically told one associate in October 1966. Throughout the Johnson years, there was a constant interchange between Meyer and the White House of congratulatory notes, autographed photos, and other testaments of mutual affection and respect. Even Meyer's growing reservations about the Vietnam War didn't seem to taint the relationship. Johnson continued to turn to Meyer for guidance in an economic crunch—such as when a run on gold got out of hand in early 1968, and Johnson asked Meyer to brief him on the workings of the gold market.

On April 1, 1968, a day after Johnson startled the nation by announcing he would not seek another term, Meyer sent the president a telegram: "In these important days I want to assure you of my admiration and of my deep and faithful affection." Johnson didn't forget the gesture; three weeks later, Meyer (along with Jane Engelhard) was his houseguest at the LBJ Ranch, and in the remaining months of the LBJ presidency, the banker lunched privately with Johnson twice. A week before the election, Meyer was one of a small group of Johnson intimates who feted the president and his family at a reception at the Arthur Krims' New York apartment.

The occasion prompted Johnson to write a "Dear André" letter. "Your friendship is one of our most cherished possessions," the president told Meyer. "It was so thoughtfully expressed by your warm telegram on the birth of Lucinda," daughter Lynda Bird Johnson's child. "I hope you are exactly right on the little girl's inheritance of beauty." Handwritten on the bottom was a note from Lady Bird: "And may I add Lynda's thanks for those exquisite white roses?"

In the fall of 1966, just as Meyer was beginning to establish an intimacy with the resident of the White House, Robert Kennedy and his aide Tom Johnston came over to the Carlyle for breakfast. What was on Kennedy's mind this time was not the family finances, nor his political future, but Bedford-Stuyvesant, the Brooklyn slum that epitomized the vicious circle of decay and destruction and despair in the nation's ghetto areas. A year earlier, bloody rioting had broken out in the Los Angeles slum of Watts, and now Americans were beginning to awaken to the powder-keg conditions in other urban areas throughout the country. Searching for something, anything, that would break the chain, dissatisfied with the conventional welfare-state solutions, the junior senator from New York had come up with a scheme that would combine strong community involvement with private business initiative. And now that he had his proposal mapped out, Kennedy wanted to show it to André Meyer.

"We put together a list of people who would be on a businessmen's committee," Tom Johnston recalls. "We wanted to structure it to get results, to get a real commitment from the white business people involved. And that's when Kennedy said, 'I think we should go see André.' He was not the obvious person to see about this, but Kennedy said that that's the point. 'He'll give us good advice, and if he takes charge of it, it'll be a signal to people that it's serious.' "

And so, on that fall day in 1966, Kennedy leaned over the breakfast table and asked Meyer if he would be willing to chair the Bedford-Stuyvesant business advisory group. Meyer demurred on taking on the chairmanship—"That's not something I like to do," he told Kennedy—but he agreed to serve on the panel and help in any way he could. He and Kennedy found another personage to head the committee—their mutual friend, Douglas Dillon—and lined up other heavyweights, including IBM chairman Thomas Watson, Jr., Bill Paley, and David Lilienthal.

The Kennedy plan for Bedford-Stuyvesant was formally unveiled on December 10, 1966. Aside from the corporation run by business leaders, to be known as the Development and Services Corporation, there would be a sister company, the Bedford-Stuyvesant Renewal and Rehabilitation Corporation, run by a board of community leaders. The two corporations would work together, Kennedy explained, so that the business group could help translate the "talent and energy" of the local community into the "power to act.

"The power to act," Kennedy went on, "is the power to command resources, of money and mind and skill." And Kennedy knew as well as anyone that when it came to commanding such resources, few could rival André Meyer.

From the outset, Meyer left no doubt in anyone's mind that he regarded this as more than just another advisory-committee assignment. Whether this was because of his loyalty to the Kennedys or because of a deep-seated interest in urban redevelopment, no one could say; certainly up to that time he had never evinced any overwhelming concern for the plight of ghetto-dwellers. Be that as it may, there was never any question that he took the Bedford-Stuyvesant group *very* seriously.

Setting aside his distaste for committee meetings, Meyer attended a number of the parleys between the business leaders and community groups—although, as was his habit at corporate board meetings, he often seemed to be nodding off. Franklin Thomas, who headed the Renewal and Rehabilitation Corporation and now is president of the Ford Foundation, remembers, "He would appear to be inattentive, even asleep, and yet he always asked the right question at the right time. If that was sleep, it was the strangest sleep I ever saw."

At those meetings, Meyer stressed that where he could be most helpful wasn't in determining what should be done, but in figuring out *how* it could be done. He was, in essence, offering to be the deal-maker for Bedford-Stuyvesant. "We were more than a little aware of his reputation for big operations and big deals," relates Thomas, "and we were flattered that he would devote the time and the effort to what, from his standpoint, were small deals. I guess what captivated his interest was that this was so damn hard to do."

One of the first tests of Meyer's ingenuity was the chronic unavailability of mortgage credit for the ghetto community. His solution was to spread the risk by setting up a mortgage pool to which various major banks and insurance companies would contribute. Along with another member of the business advisory group, Citibank chairman George Moore, Meyer put his contacts to work, arranging the necessary meetings with the big banks and insurers. The result: a $65 million mortgage pool for a previously untouchable area.

Then there was the plan for a badly needed Bedford-Stuyvesant shopping center. Here was something Meyer knew plenty about, and he dug into the venture with a zest that astonished even his closest associates. Mustering his Lazard subordinates Disque Deane and Felix Rohatyn into service, Meyer attacked the project as though it were another Roosevelt Field. One Saturday morning, he took Thomas and attorney John Doar, another old Kennedy associate who was working with the business panel, on a tour of possible sites. They walked up and down Fulton Street, the neighborhood's main thoroughfare, inspecting vacant lots and abandoned buildings. When they finally settled on a location—an old milk-bottling plant and the land surrounding it—Meyer's advice to Thomas and Doar was succinct: "You have to tie it up." When Meyer talked about "tying up" the property, he meant it in the classic real estate developers' sense of the term: buying the property by stealth, through anonymous nominee companies, so that the owners wouldn't know just who was buying and wouldn't have the chance to jack up the price accordingly.

Doar and Thomas did just what the old man advised, assembled the land parcels, and began the conversion of the milk-bottling plant into the Bedford-Stuyvesant Commercial Center.

The work on these and other projects wasn't very far along when the driving force behind them was felled by an assassin's bullet in June 1968. Robert Kennedy's death might have also meant the demise of his plans for Bedford-Stuyvesant. But, says Thomas, "There was a point at which each of us, including André, rededicated ourselves to the work following the assassination." Meyer continued to devote time to the group right up through the early seventies, offering financial advice, employing his contacts, suggesting ways this or that might be accomplished.

In 1978, Michael Harrington, the author of *The Other America*, a searching mid-sixties look at the country's poverty, revisited the Bedford-Stuyvesant project. He called it "a modest success—which in the context of so many failures, is to say a remarkable success." For André Meyer, too, it could be termed a modest success— but one which, in the context of his own life's work, loomed very large.

When Robert Kennedy first approached Meyer about joining the Bedford-Stuyvesant panel, the banker said fine, but under one condition. Kennedy and Johnston steeled themselves for what would come next—probably, Johnston thought, some sort of outrageous money-grubbing demand.

"I will come in," Meyer told them, "if you will stand up in the Senate and make an even stronger speech on Vietnam than you have. Bedford-Stuyvesant will have no meaning if we don't end that terrible war."

Kennedy and Johnston then listened in stunned silence as Meyer went on about the French experience in Indochina, and about what would happen to the country and its economy if the American involvement continued. When Kennedy interjected that he *had* spoken out against the war, Meyer snapped, "I know. But you must be more forceful." Kennedy promised that he would. Remembers Johnston: "Kennedy was very impressed. It was quite moving."

Meyer's pronouncement was all the more remarkable because of the paucity of opposition that existed at the time. The antiwar movement had not yet fully coalesced—and in American business, particularly, the war was still regarded as a bloody but necessary patriotic exercise. For an old Wall Street tycoon to utter such sentiments—especially one with a pipeline to Lyndon Johnson—was nothing short of extraordinary.

And Kennedy was hardly the first person to be exposed to Meyer's distress over Vietnam. Already, in numerous conversations with his family and close associates, the banker voiced his disgust and apprehension over the Southeast Asian quagmire. "He hated that war," says his granddaughter, Marianne Gerschel. "For him, Vietnam was a true tragedy." What was especially tragic about it, for Meyer, was that the war was being waged to save the South Vietnamese, whom he regarded as indolent, slovenly, and debauched, from the North Vietnamese, whom he regarded as hardworking, industrious, and patriotic. So many of the South Vietnamese, he warned David Lilienthal in late 1966, "are just crooks. I know Saigon's reputation; I have known that city for fifty years. It is a sordid place."

Undoubtedly, Meyer was also haunted by the fact that he had two American grandsons of draft age. Talking about his then-nineteen-year-old grandson Patrick Gerschel, Meyer muttered, "Why should I see him and others sent to the jungles of Vietnam? Young men like him, like the young Frenchmen who were lost in Algeria and Indochina. Particularly since the Vietnamese—I know about them—don't care whether we are there or not, don't care one bit."

As early as January 1966, Meyer was suggesting a complete U.S. withdrawal. Lilienthal, who wasn't convinced the United States could do that without great loss of prestige around the world, asked him if there were any precedents for this. "Algeria, Algeria," Meyer answered, his voice booming as he threw back his head. "Three generations of French life in that country. A far more difficult case. When you have hurt your finger, why should you go ahead and lose your hand, then your arm, perhaps your whole body?"

He told Lilienthal this. He told his family this. He told Bobby Kennedy this. But did he tell Lyndon Johnson?

Arthur Krim, the frequent go-between for the banker and the president, insists Meyer did. "He was one of the few people around Lyndon Johnson who thought Vietnam was a mistake and whose opinion Johnson accepted. Johnson didn't *like* it, but he accepted it." Krim says he knows this for certain because he was sometimes asked to relay Meyer's misgivings to Johnson. "André was very emphatic about it," Krim recalls. "He had a recollection of the Indochina experience of the French, and he knew the cost of that kind of involvement. And he disagreed with the president's idea that guns and butter would be doable at the same time."

But if Meyer was vocal about the war in his conversations with Krim, he was strangely silent on the subject when he chatted with two of Johnson's closest aides—Treasury Secretary Henry Fowler and Defense Secretary Robert McNamara. Fowler has no recollection of Meyer ever expressing such reservations, and neither does McNamara. "I don't recall talking about it with him," says McNamara, "and I could recall many other people talking to me about it. If he did talk to me about it, it wasn't with such force that I would have remembered it." McNamara does remember Meyer voicing strong opinions on the guns-and-butter issue; the banker was certain that inflation would result if the country tried to pay for both an ambitious social program and a costly war. But, according to McNamara, the solution Meyer proposed wasn't a Vietnam pullout but an increase in taxes.

And, judging from Meyer's warm relations with the president— the two drew closer together in the last two years of Johnson's term, when the chief executive was most embattled—it is doubtful that Meyer was very strident about Vietnam in his Oval Office sessions. He would bring up the mounting national debt and its inflationary consequences (Johnson prepared for one meeting with Meyer by studying a detailed breakdown of Treasury borrowings). But to go farther—to push the antiwar arguments so ardently that he risked alienating the supersensitive president—was definitely not his style. If it had to be done in public, then he would rather Bobby Kennedy do it.

To some friends, Meyer's hesitancy to push Johnson brought to mind the battles they would have with Meyer in the 1950s on the subject of U.S. Secretary of State John Foster Dulles. "He liked Dulles," recalls Andrea Wilson, "and I felt we should not support him. And he said, 'Well, I have to support him because he was so nice to me. He was very helpful to me.' And I said, 'If Ribbentrop had done you favors, would you support Ribbentrop?' He slammed down the phone, and we didn't talk for several hours. It was terrible."

As much as Meyer detested the war, Meyer could never bring himself to make a public break with its main architect. After all, Lyndon Johnson was his *friend.*

By early 1970, even Wall Street had become a battleground, with hawkish construction workers tangling with student protesters in the concrete canyons of the financial district. In the midst of one such confrontation that spring, a young Lazard associate spotted a familiar old figure leaning against a parking meter, transfixed by the angry scene. The young man approached him. "Hello, Mr. Meyer," he said.

But the old banker barely acknowledged him. He was completely caught up in the unfolding spectacle: the scruffy youths chanting anti-Vietnam slogans, the hard-hatted workers cursing and shaking their fists.

Meyer's influence and celebrity then were at their peak. He was the trusted adviser of the Kennedys and Lyndon Johnson and the Rockefellers. His firm dominated the merger-and-acquisition business that was changing the landscape of corporate America. Two years earlier, *Fortune* had published the first full-length look at Lazard, calling the firm's senior partner "the single most intriguing and influential figure now operating in the capital markets of the free world."

But none of that mattered very much now. What Meyer had most feared was coming to pass: the society in which he lived was once again drifting into chaos, once more disintegrating before his eyes. Thirty years later, it was happening again.

CHAPTER TWENTY-TWO

Tidying Up

On the surface, not much had changed as the new decade began.

Richard Bliss, a mid-thirtyish senior vice-president at Bankers Trust Company, was putting together a $75 million floating-rate note issue for Pepsico. When he assembled the underwriting group, he neglected to invite Lazard, one of the company's traditional investment bankers. One day Bliss's phone rang, and on the other end of the line was the legendary André Meyer. "I must come see you," Meyer said. Utterly astonished that this living monument would deign to visit a lowly senior vice-president, Bliss nervously prepared to receive his esteemed guest. When the appointed hour arrived, Meyer stormed into Bliss's office. "Never," began the old man, "have we been so insulted. . . ." As Bliss recalled years later, "In my entire business career I have never received such a tongue-lashing." Hesitantly, Bliss interrupted Meyer in mid-tirade, telling the Lazard chief that he didn't have his facts right. Meyer then went through a total transformation. He told Bliss what a clever young man he was. How he had been following his career closely. How he was an old man, but he could still bring Bliss some business. Remembers Bliss, "He just instantly switched from the angry, insulted bank head to a sweet, unctuous, dear old man. I knew it was an act, but he had me eating it up with a spoon." By the time Meyer walked out, he had Bliss—and the underwriting invitation—in his pocket.

One after another, Meyer's comrades in arms passed from the scene. In August 1969 Bobbie Lehman died; then, in November of that year, Ferd Eberstadt passed away; and in December 1971 David Sarnoff, bedridden for almost two years, died, too. But Meyer, for all his constant protestations to the contrary, seemed as vigorous as ever. Helped along by weekly vitamin shots, he still arose at four each morning, still called Paris at five, still prowled the halls of Lazard at seven. His countenance was untroubled by wrinkles, his black hair unsullied by gray. Older-looking than his years when he was in his mid-thirties, he now was an astonishingly youthful septuagenarian.

But if the physical package was still impressive, the inner man nonetheless was showing his age. Meyer had always been doleful about the state of the world. "He has the air of expecting the worst," David Lilienthal wrote in his diary in 1950, after vainly trying to reassure Meyer over dinner that the world was not about to plunge into a nuclear holocaust. "Whenever you asked André Meyer what was going to happen," says Michel David-Weill, "he'd always describe to you a catastrophe." But Meyer's fundamental pessimism had always been counterbalanced by his boundless energy and his conviction that while the world might end tomorrow, *today* there was plenty of money to be made. "Economically, he was always gloomy," recalls Richard Perkins, a Citibank executive who was a frequent Meyer luncheon guest. "But then he'd get to talking about a deal, and he'd light up like a Christmas tree."

Now, however, that was changing. When Frank Pizzitola joined the firm in 1973 he was told by Meyer, "I have all the bankers that I want. I am looking for an *indoostrialist.*" (Pizzitola's entire background was in private industry.) Pizzitola was told he would be spearheading a rejuvenation of Lazard's venture-capital activities, virtually dormant since the mid-sixties. The firm would search for an asset-rich company, buy 20 to 25 percent of it, and Pizzitola would then join the company's board to work with management. But when the new partner came up with just the right target after nine months of study, the old man waved him away. "Ah, I am getting old," Meyer told him. "I do not want to do this."

Rather than chance new ventures, Meyer was preoccupied with liquidating what he had. His favorite investment now was not oil wells or drug companies, but U.S. Treasury bills. Partly this was because he was beginning to get his estate in order, but mostly because he was weary and frightened. More than ever before, he seemed to be preparing himself to go downstairs, hand in his key to the Carlyle concierge, and take off.

There was, of course, much to be gloomy about. At the top of the list was Vietnam, spilling blood and shattering the country, living up to the worst of his forebodings. Then there was the vicious inflation the war had set into motion—the inflation Meyer had warned Lyndon Johnson about. With the onset of the Nixon years this became stagflation, an economic conundrum that was the worst of both worlds: recession *and* inflation, all at once. Meyer only saw the situation getting worse. "We will have a depression that will curl your hair," he warned a client in 1972. His cynicism was compounded by his detachment from the Nixon administration; while Meyer was, like most businessmen, a Nixon supporter in 1972 (he contributed $60,000 to the campaign), he never enjoyed any access to Nixon, except indirectly, through former administration officials like Bob Ellsworth.

The politics of oil was also on Meyer's mind. Long before the warnings of an energy crisis became commonplace, Meyer was already sounding the alarm. In March 1973, Meyer granted a rare interview to *Business Week* magazine in connection with a cover story the magazine was preparing on Felix Rohatyn. The comments were vintage Meyer: pessimistic ("I do not believe in the future of investment banking as we know it"), parsimonious ("We shall pay no more than seven seventy-five per square foot for space so long as I am alive"), gently self-deprecating ("I tell my colleagues that my function is to be a garbageman and a patrolman"). And among them was this:

"The problem of energy is far more important than a deficit in the balance of payments. It is a key to a lot of the economic problems here and abroad. It is of the greatest importance that, now that the producing countries have allied themselves into a common position, the consuming countries must band together and have a common policy."

Yet even though Meyer could see an oil crisis coming, he was unable or unwilling to capitalize on it. He did not load up on oil-company stocks, nor did he expand his oil-drilling investments. He didn't even take advantage of the vehicle he already had in place for tapping into the vast pool of new oil wealth: the Iranian Development Bank.

The brainchild of World Bank president Eugene Black and Iranian planning minister Abol Hassan Ebtehaj, the Iranian Development Bank was founded in 1959 to serve as a source of capital for a country that, before the big run-up in oil prices, was in desperate need of investments. Half of the bank was owned by Chase and Lazard, and half by Iranian private interests. Meyer had always regarded the institution as more of a prestige-builder than a profit center—and, indeed, over the years Lazard had stockpiled an ample hoard of Iranian goodwill as a result of the pioneering venture.

But Meyer, from the mid-sixties onward, had been growing disillusioned with the Iranians. In late 1966, David Lilienthal told Meyer that Iran was chronically slow in paying his Development and Resources Corporation for its services. The reason the country gave was "a shortage of foreign exchange." Meyer snorted: "Swiss accounts," he said. Then, after a pause, he related, "A few weeks ago the head of the Bank Melli"—a big Iranian bank—"was here visiting at Lazard, an excellent young man. Left to go to Paris. To buy more than a million dollars' worth of diamonds for the coronation—you know, they are going to have a coronation soon. Yes, I know that they already have royal jewels by the bushel, but they aren't just right; they have to spend a fortune on special diamonds."

But in the interest of good relations, not only with the Iranians but with David Rockefeller, Meyer kept his skepticism in check. Then, in early 1973, Iran invited a group of high-level Western businessmen to tour the country. No one from Lazard was on the guest list. Furious at the snub, Meyer promptly announced that he was terminating Lazard's involvement with the Iranian Development Bank. Oil crisis or no oil crisis, he would not allow Lazard to be treated in such a cavalier fashion. The timing of Meyer's outburst, it almost goes without saying, could not have been worse. As someone involved in the development venture for Lazard later groaned, "Just when we should have been making our big push in Iran, we were out of the picture."

The lost opportunities, however, did not appear to weigh heavily on Meyer's mind. He had too many other things to think about now, too many past deals whose loose ends still dangled. Among them was Mountain Park.

Mountain Park, George Ames remembers, "was too big, too difficult to build on, and everybody was against developing it. But apart from that, it was a great site."

Indeed it was. Sprawling over 12,000 acres in the Santa Monica Mountains, Mountain Park was the largest tract of undeveloped land within the Los Angeles city limits. It rose from sea level to a 1,900-foot elevation and extended from Sunset Boulevard to the San Fernando Valley, encompassing several major canyons along the way. Standing on its highest peak, a visitor could view a panorama of downtown Los Angeles in one direction; the San Fernando Valley in another; and, out to sea, Catalina Island.

Bill Zeckendorf had purchased Mountain Park for $2.4 million in 1947 but had never gotten around to doing anything with it. (At one point, he offered to swap the property for Howard Hughes's RKO Theater stock, but Hughes wasn't interested.) Desperate for cash to keep his overextended real estate empire afloat, Zeckendorf sold the tract to André Meyer in January 1960 for some $8 million. To join with him in the purchase, Meyer put together one of his typical assemblages of old, moneyed friends and Lazard partners. The Mountain Park syndicate included the Rockefellers, David Sarnoff, Ludwig Jesselson of Philipp Brothers, Pierre David-Weill and various others from Lazard, and successful urban-real-estate developer Roger Stevens, who was instrumental in convincing Meyer to buy the site.

George Ames did not see the property until after the deal was closed. And when he was finally sent out by Meyer to inspect it, he recalls, "I damn near died. It was too difficult to build on, it was so mountainous. The cost of the land bore almost no relationship to what you finally had to do with it. You could buy land out there for two thousand dollars an acre, but it would cost you fifty thousand dollars to make it developable. And there was no infrastructure at all. No paved roads, no nothing. The only roads on the place were dirt roads, fire roads, so the fire department could get around to put the forest fires out."

Meyer decided at the outset that *he* would not be the one to develop Mountain Park. Not only would the cost be staggering, but he had an ironclad rule about not involving himself directly in development (a rule that he later broke, to his ultimate regret, with Chelsea Walk). Instead, he and Ames went back to their old Matador Ranch formula. They would divide the land up into smaller pieces, each owned by a separate corporation, and resell each piece to individual developers. Their one concession to a unified scheme for Mountain Park was to come up with a master plan which would include not only residential but commercial uses. What they had in mind, however, was "clean" industry, such as research facilities, not heavy industrial development.

Nevertheless, from the outset the Lazard plan came under fire from environmentalists and local civil groups intent on leaving Mountain Park in its pristine state. "Every time we went to the City Planning Commission," says Ames, "we would be greeted by three busloads of women with white gloves, screaming and yelling." One developer who bought a tract dropped out of the deal when the opposition became too great. In an effort to mute the uproar, Meyer donated a portion of the land to the University of California at Los Angeles, but he still could not get any development concessions from the city.

Floundering for a way out, Meyer turned for ideas to the man who had brought him the vast problematic parcel in the first place. With his own empire by then in tatters, Zeckendorf was more than willing to help, and he came up with a typical Zeckendorfian solution: a huge fifty-story apartment tower set in the middle of the mountains. He reasoned that if the rest of the property was left undisturbed, Mountain Park's opponents would go along with the scheme. But when Zeckendorf presented his plan to Lazard, recalls his son-in-law Ronald Nicholson, "I thought Meyer was going to fall through the floor." The banker regarded it as just another harebrained Zeckendorf scheme, a monolith in the middle of nowhere.

So the decade passed with Mountain Park looming as André Meyer's great California white elephant. A few tracts were sold to developers, and some roads were permitted to be built. But, for the most part, the land remained vexingly virginal. Ames realized, too late, that he and Meyer had taken the wrong approach: had they rushed in to develop the land themselves at the beginning, says Ames, "we might have been able to outflank the opposition." By taking the more cautious, middleman tack, they had merely bought precious time for the opposition.

Finally, after ten years of frustration, André Meyer had had enough. If he couldn't sell Mountain Park, or develop it, then he would bite the bullet. He would give it away.

He dispatched attorney Benjamin Bartel to negotiate on his behalf with the state of California for the donation of much of what was left of the property to the state-park system. The gift, however, did not come without a few strings attached; Meyer wanted *something* for his trouble. His idea of giving Mountain Park away, it turned out, was not an outright donation, but a sale at below market value. "You're asking too much from them," a disgruntled Bartel told Meyer at one point. "I might as well not even go."

"No, no, you must go," Meyer protested. "You'll see, you'll get even more from them."

In the end, Bartel was able to extract $6.2 million from the state for the 5,500 acres Meyer was offering. At that price, Mountain Park was still a bargain. The state undoubtedly would have had to pay far more for the land if it had bought the tract in the open market, particularly considering how much land prices had skyrocketed in the sixties. On the other hand, the fact that Meyer had sold California property at well below market value enabled him to reap an extra bonus from the deal: a massive tax write-off. In all, Mcyer obtained write-offs of around $3,000 an acre for land that had cost him and his syndicate members less than $700 an acre. "The numbers were big," claims Disque Deane, "so big that for many years Mr. Meyer could not give more money away to charity because the Mountain Park contribution offset as much as twenty-five to fifty percent of his adjusted gross income." Yet Ames always felt those huge write-offs were justified by the *real* magnitude of Meyer's investment. "When you consider how much the seven hundred dollars an acre would have been worth ten years later," he says, "and the carrying cost of the property, and the money we spent on it—spending God knows how much designing highways we couldn't build, and being unable to write those expenses off because you had nothing to write them off against—we invested a lot of money. By any fair standard, we at least doubled the amount we initially put into Mountain Park, and probably more."

By 1973, the transfer of the land to the California state-park system was complete. And in September 1973, on the occasion of André Meyer's seventy-fifth birthday, the California State Assembly passed a resolution congratulating and thanking the banker "for his generosity and his efforts to [sic] the People of California."

Meyer, in turn, sent the following note to the resolution's author, Assemblyman Paul Priolo:

> I was deeply moved to learn that you took time out of your busy schedule to introduce a resolution in honor of my 75th birthday. It is a birthday gift I will long remember and treasure.
>
> Mr. Benjamin Bartel has advised me of your tremendous efforts in shepherding the Legislation for the State to acquire the park property. I hope that I will have the opportunity to some day meet you personally.
>
> In the meantime, it is gratifying to me that I was able in some small measure to enhance the beauty of the State of California.
>
> I trust that the citizens of California will enjoy the park for many years to come.

André Meyer came out of the battle of Mountain Park not only unbloodied, but positively triumphant. He had cash in his pocket. He had huge tax write-offs. And he had the gratitude of the state of California.

Would that his other affairs could be patched up so neatly.

CHAPTER TWENTY-THREE

Eddie Gilbert ... Again

In May 1970, almost eight years to the day after he fled to Brazil, and barely one year after his release from federal prison, Eddie Gilbert reentered André Meyer's life.

Gilbert made no bones about his intentions: he was out to settle old scores. And the instrument of his revenge would be the same court system that had dispatched him to the penitentiary. Seeking $25 million in damages, the one-time Wall Street wunderkind charged in New York State Supreme Court in Manhattan that Meyer had been his partner and co-conspirator in the events that brought about Gilbert's undoing.

The complaint tersely spelled out the links between the convicted embezzler and the world's most influential investment banker. Gilbert portrayed an André Meyer who was eager to help the young hotshot accomplish great things, offering him Lazard's services and even, in early 1961, lending $2 million to E. L. Bruce & Company, the big hardwood concern Gilbert had just taken over. The complaint described how Gilbert told Meyer of his plan to buy control of another big hardwood company, Celotex, and merge it into Bruce, and how Meyer had offered to provide him with "whatever financial backing was necessary." Then Gilbert outlined the arrangement he and Meyer allegedly worked out together: Lazard's agreement to purchase 250,000 of the 500,000 shares Gilbert needed to gain control of Celotex—to be exchanged later on, when the deal was done, for Bruce convertible debentures at a locked-in 50 percent profit for Lazard. Meyer, in essence, would help bankroll Gilbert's takeover of Celotex.

"It was understood that this agreement would never be reduced to writing," Gilbert charged in his complaint. "Where any disclosure of the plan was required by lawyers or other parties, its terms and structure would be misrepresented to create an outside impression of independent action, specifically that Gilbert was purchasing his Celotex shares by himself for his purpose and that defendants were purchasing their Celotex shares by themselves for their purpose."

Then Gilbert described the double cross. How, after he had started his Celotex buying campaign, Lazard demanded repayment of half the 1961 loan at twice its face value before the firm would buy any Celotex shares. How Gilbert's repayment of the loan, out of his own pocket, had allowed Lazard to acquire 87,000 Celotex shares "at no real cost to themselves." How Lazard assured him that it would buy more Celotex shares and encouraged his own continued acquisition of the shares. How, with Gilbert already badly overextended, Lazard had hammered the last nail in his coffin in May 1962 by demanding he repay the other half of the 1961 loan, again at twice its face value. And how, after he had fled to Brazil, Lazard and Meyer took the Celotex shares they had acquired—with money they had wrung out of Gilbert—and used them to bring about a merger of Celotex and the Jim Walter Corporation.

Gilbert did not implicate Meyer or Lazard in the actual crime: the embezzlement (or "borrowing," as Gilbert's complaint delicately puts it) of $2 million from the E. L. Bruce treasury to meet margin calls on his Celotex shares. But he made it clear that the whole chain of events that led to his disgrace would not have come about if Lazard had not pulled the rug out from under him financially. The Celotex undertaking, he insisted, had been a joint venture; he and André Meyer had plotted it together. But instead of supporting Gilbert, Meyer squeezed him dry.

"Loathsome! He is loathsome!" Meyer sneered when he was told of the suit. Eight years earlier, when the Gilbert affair first hit the headlines, Meyer confessed to friends that he was "worried sick" about the whole thing. But he had made a clean breast of it then; two weeks after Gilbert's flight, Lazard disclosed that it was the unnamed "investment banker" that had been repaid $4 million by Gilbert for loans with a face value of $2 million. The firm offered to refund the money to E. L. Bruce if it was shown that Gilbert had used Bruce funds to pay Lazard. "We are not concerned with any question of legal liability," the firm said then. "We have been advised by counsel that there can be none. But we have maintained a high tradition in our dealings for a century"—and "in that spirit" Lazard was willing to reverse the transaction. (In the end, Lazard was able to keep the $4 million, since the funds Gilbert embezzled were used to meet margin calls, not to repay Lazard.)

With his limited *mea culpa,* Meyer had good reason to believe that the scandal was behind him. But now, almost a decade later, his good name and Lazard's were being dragged in the mud again. The lawsuit unnerved him, and not simply because Eddie Gilbert was on the other side. Litigation—any litigation—had always been anathema to Meyer, even if *he* was the aggrieved party. Rather than pursue judicial remedies, Meyer always preferred to settle his disputes quietly, out of court. As Lazard partner David Supino, himself a lawyer, explains, "Mr. Meyer came from a background where litigation was not a gentlemanly way of doing things. And with litigation there is much more uncertainty, much less control than there is in negotiation. And control was an important element in Mr. Meyer's personality."

His efforts at avoiding the courts had always been successful; in almost half a century of wheeling and dealing, his life had been remarkably free of legal complications. Now he not only had a lawsuit on his hands, but one that involved one of the sleaziest operators in the business.

Gilbert would later say that Meyer had tried to reach an accommodation with him, offering Gilbert $250,000 if he would drop the suit. (Lazard officials denied that any such offer was made.) In any case, Meyer was soon turning for advice to one of the shrewdest legal minds in New York, Simon Rifkind of Paul, Weiss, Wharton, Rifkind & Garrison. And Rifkind was thoroughly simpatico with Meyer's view of Gilbert. "I just wanted to beat Gilbert into the ground," the attorney would recall.

But before he could do that, Gilbert drew first blood. In his depositions and documentation, the one-time boy wonder revealed in full, for the first time, the extent of his relationship with André Meyer, Michel David-Weill, and Lazard Frères. He had been introduced to Meyer, he said, by David-Weill (David-Weill later admitted as much, noting that *he* had first met Gilbert in the south of France). "From the beginning," Gilbert alleged, "I was in virtual daily contact with Lazard and/or Meyer. . . . In fact, Lazard and/or Meyer were advising on all financial decisions for myself and my companies, always, of course, after consultation with me."

That relationship, Gilbert showed, was put into writing in the agreements attached to Lazard's $2 million loan. They called for Gilbert to consult with Lazard "with respect to any material transactions" by E. L. Bruce. Furthermore, Gilbert produced another document, signed by Lazard, Lazard Paris, and himself, in which

Gilbert and the Lazard firms offered each other the right of first refusal on any E. L. Bruce securities they planned to sell.

But the ultimate confirmation, as far as Gilbert was concerned, of
how close he was to the Lazard partners was an October 1961 letter in
which Gilbert directed that David-Weill and Howard Kniffin be
named "trustees" of his estate. The designation had only minimal
legal value—"This letter," Gilbert wrote, "is not intended to become
a part of my Codicil nor Will"—and it merely requested his executors
to give careful consideration to David-Weill and Kniffin's advice on
the handling of Gilbert's E. L. Bruce stock. Nevertheless, Gilbert said
in his complaint, Lazard had "demanded" it.

Gilbert also sought to impugn Meyer and Lazard by recounting
their initial conversations about Celotex. In the first place, said Gilbert, Meyer demanded that Lazard and two other Wall Street firms,
Loeb Rhoades and Wertheim & Company, be Gilbert's only financial backers in the takeover effort. Gilbert described an early "explor-
atory" meeting at Loeb Rhoades's offices, attended by Loeb
Rhoades's two principal partners, John Loeb and Henry Loeb;
Meyer; David-Weill; and himself, and later meetings at Lazard's offices to finalize the "joint venture." In his deposition, Gilbert said this
about Meyer's role:

> Meyer was pushing for the deal. Meyer got them all together,
> brought them to his office. He was my spokesman in this thing, he
> was going to get this deal across. He would talk to Loeb, to Werth-
> eim. "Don't worry, I will get them to go along."

Gilbert then related how David-Weill called him one morning
and said, "It's a deal. Everything is agreed." Afterwards, according to
Gilbert's testimony, Meyer made it clear to him that whatever private
understanding they had about working together on the Celotex share
purchases, their story for public consumption would be something
else again:

> I remember one specific conversation that we had. In fact, he said to
> me, "Remember, Eddie, that the purposes of this meeting, and so
> on and so forth, are in friendly hands but that we have no agree-
> ments to sell you the stock or turn over or do this or that. What we
> do between ourselves is another story. But, for the public, for the
> Bruce Company, for everybody's benefit, each one owns his own

shares. We are at arm's length transaction here and this is the way it is going to have to be outwardly. It is going to have to appear this way."

Gilbert testified that Meyer then held another meeting to put their public position on the record. "There were at least ten or fifteen people at this meeting," Gilbert remembers, including "several lawyers" representing Lazard. As Gilbert recalled the session:

> This was to, sort of on the record, say that, "My shares couldn't be included with his shares and there was no acting in concert, collusion . . ." The meeting was called, obviously, for each one to go on the record saying at that time, in front of lawyers—this was my understanding of it, and I believe this is what transpired—"Mr. Gilbert, you own fifty thousand shares of Celotex stock. We own seventy-five thousand shares of Celotex stock or we may decide to buy"—I don't know if they owned it, or not, at that time—"Of course, you understand, we may not sell you these shares. We have no obligation to you, whatsoever, with these shares, other than the fact that they are in friendly hands."

The meeting, in short, was simply staged by Meyer for the benefit of lawyers. "The whole thing," Gilbert testified, "was a charade."

All along, Gilbert insisted, he and Meyer had had "an inward" understanding that they would work together on the Celotex takeover. But the vagueness of that understanding, if one existed, and the fact that it was never reduced to writing, gave Rifkind just the opening he was looking for. The lines of his defense were clear: he would maintain that the supposed "joint venture" was a figment of Eddie Gilbert's overripe imagination.

"Gilbert's testimony with respect to the alleged agreement brings into serious question whether an agreement ever existed," said Lazard in-house counsel Thomas F. X. Mullarkey in an affidavit. "Gilbert gave varying descriptions of the terms of the alleged agreement; he was almost totally incapable of specifying when and where the alleged agreement was reached; and he was often inconsistent and his testimony amorphous."

Aside from the fuzziness of Gilbert's recollections, Rifkind and Mullarkey asserted that the supposed arrangement between Meyer and Gilbert had none of the essential elements of a joint venture. In deposing Gilbert, Mullarkey was able to extract from Gilbert an admission that he and Lazard had had no agreement to share profits:

> Q.: Did you agree to share any profits you might make with Lazard?
>
> A.: No, I wasn't going to make any profits, so how could I share a profit?
>
> Q.: You were going to benefit as a stockholder in Bruce, were you not?
>
> A.: On the Celotex shares I was not going to make any profit. You mean, if my Bruce shares went up, was I going to give Lazard the profit?
>
> Q.: Right.
>
> A.: Of course not.

Nor, Mullarkey established, did Gilbert and Meyer have any agreement to share their losses, or hold their Celotex shares jointly. How, then, could the arrangement be a "joint venture"? What's more, said Mullarkey, "Gilbert testified that he did not remember the term 'joint venture' being used by any of the defendants."

A nebulous "inward understanding," Rifkind and Mullarkey argued, was hardly ironclad evidence of a partnership between André Meyer and Eddie Gilbert.

But just in case the judge felt otherwise, Rifkind had another arrow in his quiver: the statute of limitations. The state of New York had a six-year limitation on fraud actions, and certainly more than six years had elapsed since Lazard and Eddie Gilbert had parted company. On statute-of-limitations grounds alone, Rifkind contended, the court should dismiss the case.

Gilbert's response to *that* was to point out that his two-year-seventeen-day stint in prison should be excluded from the six-year count. Furthermore, he suggested that Meyer's frequent prolonged absences from the state of New York should also be deducted. Of course, Gilbert did allow as to how he did not have a precise fix on Meyer's out-of-state visits—and for that reason, he cheekily suggested, "I should be afforded the opportunity of examining Mr. Meyer so as to determine the exact dates of his absences from the state of New York."

Eddie Gilbert did not get his wish.

On January 26, 1971, the New York State Supreme court dismissed his suit against André Meyer and Lazard Frères. The judge ruled that the statute of limitations had run out; as for Gilbert's argument about his prison term, the judge noted that "the plaintiff had five years in which to sue before he was imprisoned." What's more, the judge agreed with Rifkind and Lazard that the essential elements of a joint venture had not been present. At best, the judge said, Gilbert *might* have a case of breach of contract—but that, too, was barred by the six-year statute of limitations.

André Meyer had won the battle. But Eddie Gilbert had stored too much venom inside him during those years in Sing Sing to concede the war. He asked the Supreme Court appellate division to reverse the decision. This time, to get around the six-year statute, he contended that Lazard, as his investment banker, had breached its fiduciary responsibilities; the statute of limitations on fiduciary violations was ten years. The appellate division, however, didn't agree that a fiduciary violation was involved; it let the supreme court ruling stand. Gilbert then took his case to the state's highest court, the court of appeals. Once again, he lost. The court of appeals upheld the earlier decisions, without issuing any opinion of its own.

Still unwilling to give in, Gilbert opened a second front, filing suit against Meyer in May 1972 in Manhattan Federal Court. Once again, Rifkind rose to Meyer's defense. "There isn't any merit whatsoever to the claim," he told the *Wall Street Journal*. "It is the purest fiction."

But Eddie Gilbert *wanted* André Meyer—and just how badly he wanted him was demonstrated by a maneuver attempted by Gilbert's lawyer, Peter Fleming, shortly after filing the federal suit. Charging that Meyer had not answered Gilbert's complaint within twenty days of receiving it, Fleming asked the court for a default judgment against Meyer—which would have meant paying the $25 million in damages. He told Meyer's lawyers he would drop the default request on one condition: that they produce Meyer for a deposition.

The tremors of outrage could be felt from One Rockefeller Plaza clear through to the Paul Weiss offices on Park Avenue. "The plaintiff has made it clear," responded Rifkind's partner Edward Costikyan, "that perhaps his chief interest here is to annoy and persecute Mr. Meyer." Costikyan charged that Gilbert was using the case "as a roving commission and license to harass defendant Meyer."

Indignantly refusing to give in to Fleming's demands, Costikyan was able to prove that the complaint had not been served on Meyer on the date Fleming had claimed it was. A default judgment, therefore, was out of the question. With that maneuver scotched, the case proceeded on by-now-familiar lines. Gilbert charged that Meyer had breached his responsibility as his investment banker: "The conduct of Lazard and Meyer," he asserted, "constituted a corruption and violation of our relationship of confidence and trust." Meyer's attorneys maintained the statute of limitations had run out. What with Gilbert filing yet another lawsuit in New York State Supreme Court within days of instituting the federal action, the federal suit, the Paul Weiss lawyers insisted, "is a transparent effort to get a third bite at the same apple."

The third bite went no deeper than the other two. The federal court ruled, as had all the other courts before it, that the statute of limitations rendered Gilbert's case moot.

With that, Eddie Gilbert gave up. He dropped his state-court action, paid his lawyers, and ended his pursuit of André Meyer.

The court victories, as decisive as they were, were hardly ringing votes of confidence in Meyer's behavior. True, the state court had found that Meyer and Gilbert were not involved in a joint venture. But by suggesting, at the same time, that there *might* have been breach of contract, the court left the impression with anyone following the case that some sort of arrangement, however vague, however ill defined, had existed between the two. Rifkind may have squashed Eddie Gilbert, but the stain still showed.

Meyer would continually try to expunge it, even at the cost of playing fast and loose with whatever facts were at hand. Eddie Gilbert had been *Felix*'s client, Meyer at one point told Lazard partner Robert Price; he, André Meyer, had warned against doing business with Gilbert, but Felix wouldn't listen. (Never, in any of Gilbert's complaints or his supporting documentation, was there any hint that Rohatyn had been involved.) Later, Meyer went even further. He insisted that he had never even known Eddie Gilbert.

Many years afterward, when the mention of Celotex and E. L. Bruce & Company would not prompt the barest glimmer of recognition in a Wall Streeter's eyes, Tom Mullarkey was asked about Eddie Gilbert. Throughout the court battles, the Lazard counsel had adamantly insisted that there was no joint venture between Gilbert and Meyer. Now, when the subject of Gilbert came up, Mullarkey began laughing uproariously.

"To his dying day," said Mullarkey, after he had calmed down, "André would repeat over and over, 'I never knew Eddie Gilbert.' "

Did he? Mullarkey was asked.

"Did he?" chuckled Mullarkey. "They were like two peas in a pod."

The Gilbert case, as much as it gnawed at Meyer, was but a pinprick compared to what was to come. Another past deal of his was emerging from the shadows to trouble his old age, to preoccupy his lawyers and threaten his reputation. This time, the issue would not be a murky transaction with a convicted embezzler. This time, the players in the drama would be blue-chip, and the deal one of Lazard's supreme achievements.

André Meyer, the financial engineer, was about to go on trial.

CHAPTER TWENTY-FOUR

A Deal Under Fire

If any banker could be said to cast no shadow, it was Enrico Cuccia.

Cuccia had run Italy's most successful merchant bank, Medio-banca, since the end of World War II. He was the prime mover in countless Italian mergers and corporate reorganizations, including the marriage of the Dunlop and Pirelli tire companies; the formation of the country's giant chemical combine, Montedison; and the Libyan government's purchase of 10 percent of Fiat. Yet all his dealings were conducted in utmost secrecy; André Meyer was a veritable publicity hound by comparison. Cuccia never gave interviews and rarely allowed himself to be photographed. "The standard shot of him," wrote London's *Financial Times*, "conveys a man in a homburg hat, coat tightly wrapped around him, giving a hasty backward glance down a foggy Milan street."

So elusive a figure was Cuccia that those who knew him couldn't even figure out his age. In his younger days, he would be taken for thirty-five one moment, fifty the next. About all that anyone remembered about Cuccia, after meeting him, was the jaunty way he wore his homburg: all the way back on his head, the brim turned up. "On his desk in Milan," related David Lilienthal, "there is only one object: a piece of statuary, quite small, a head of a young man, with a hat way back on his head!"

If Cuccia opened up to anyone, it was to André Meyer. They had known each other since the mid-fifties, when Cuccia, in search of foreign investors in his bank, talked Lazard and Lehman Brothers into taking a 10 percent stake in Mediobanca. From that point on, Cuccia and Meyer were close comrades in arms, working together on numerous international deals involving Fiat and other Italian companies. "Their relationship was exceptional," recalls Meyer's Paris partner Jean Guyot, who was close to both men. "There was a fundamental confidence between them, which was relatively astonishing, because the two were so different. But they had something in common—the

exclusive love for work." Their admiration for each other was un-
bounded; Meyer considered Cuccia "the best banker in Europe," and
Cuccia was similarly lavish in his praise for his French friend.

In early August 1969, Meyer, during his usual summer sojourn in
Crans, phoned his colleague in Milan. One of Lazard's clients, Meyer
explained, had a little problem, and he thought that Cuccia might be
able to help. The client, ITT, had to dispose of a large block of its
shares in the Hartford Insurance Company. Would Cuccia and
Mediobanca, by any chance, be interested in buying the block?

Cuccia replied that he might. But this was too big a deal to discuss
on the telephone; he wanted to negotiate with the principals in person. Quickly, he and Meyer decided to bring the two sides together at
Lazard's office in Paris at the end of the month. But Cuccia still had
one small qualm. "I don't know these people who will be present at
that meeting," he said.

That was all right, Meyer assured him. He, André Meyer, would
be there to *personally* make the introductions.

The Hartford takeover, for Harold Geneen and ITT, had been nothing but trouble almost from the beginning.

The idea of buying the insurance company had come about in the
same way so many of ITT's takeover ideas did: in the course of those
long, after-hours dialogues between Geneen and Felix Rohatyn. Rohatyn had become convinced—perhaps as a result of conversations
with Al Hettinger—that the purchase of a major insurance company
was an ideal move for cash-hungry conglomerates like ITT. Not only
would an insurer's premium income provide a steady flow of earnings, but the vast, untapped riches in an insurance company's investment portfolio could be a source of huge capital gains. At one point,
Rohatyn showed Geneen and other top ITT executives how those
capital gains could be translated into ITT income over a ten-year
period; how, in essence, they could provide ITT with a guaranteed
10 percent earnings growth per year. To Harold Geneen, obsessed
with reporting ever-increasing earnings, Rohatyn's arguments were
uniquely persuasive.

At around that time—the summer of 1968—a San Francisco mutual fund called ISI was reshaping its portfolio. ISI had specialized in
insurance stocks, but now it wanted to diversify, and so it was cleaning out its shelves to make way for its new holdings.

Lazard, as a key broker for ISI, was in a good position to know what would be unloaded next. And when Lazard learned that the mutual fund planned to dispose of a substantial investment in Hartford Insurance Group, it alerted Hal Geneen. The block for sale was hardly a controlling interest—it was 1.2 million shares, about 6 percent of the company—but it was a start. Geneen snapped up the shares.

Hartford was one of America's great old-line insurers (it was founded in 1810 and had insured both Robert E. Lee and Abraham Lincoln) and in 1968 was the country's fifth biggest property and casualty company, with premiums of $969 million and assets of nearly $2 billion. Eager to remain independent, Hartford directors and management had little taste for a merger. When Rohatyn approached the insurer's investment banker, Robert Baldwin of Morgan Stanley, about a possible Hartford-ITT deal, Baldwin stiffly replied that Hartford was not for sale.

Then André Meyer got into the act. He phoned Hartford's chairman, Harry Williams, to request a meeting. But instead of getting through to Williams, he was connected to one of the chairman's assistants; miffed, Meyer told an aide that if Mr. Williams was too busy to come to the phone, he would call him another time. The assistant mumbled a vague reply, and Meyer snapped that he was not accustomed to such treatment and he hoped the aide would pass *that* message on to Mr. Williams.

Meyer then got a call from a Hartford executive vice-president, who told the eminent investment banker that Mr. Williams was very busy. But if Meyer *insisted* on a meeting, they *could* get together—in the Hartford airport cafeteria. The cafeteria! Incensed, Meyer sputtered that he had never been treated this way, that he was the head of an important firm, that he was not accustomed to holding business discussions in airport cafeterias. What's more, this vice-president could tell Mr. Williams what André Meyer thought of him and his manners.

A half-hour later Williams himself finally called. He explained that he was reluctant to be seen with Geneen and Geneen's investment bankers in his office. Yes, answered Meyer, but isn't it stupid to meet in the cafeteria of the Hartford airport? Isn't it all very childish? Williams admitted that perhaps it was and agreed to see Meyer, Rohatyn, and Geneen that afternoon in his Hartford office.

The meeting was inconclusive. "Words and words and words," was the way Meyer would later describe it. "It was a kind of blah-

blah-blah." Williams did not bring up the subject of a merger, and neither did Geneen. But they agreed to talk some more. The ice was broken.

Soon Geneen was bringing the full force of his persuasive powers to bear on Hartford's directors. He hosted a series of getting-to-know-you lunches, at which he extolled the virtues of a merger and how well Hartford would fit into the burgeoning ITT empire. The insurance company's directors, however, were still unimpressed. In a last-ditch defense bid, Williams asked Morgan Stanley's Baldwin to come on board as chief executive officer and spearhead a diversification program that would insulate Hartford permanently from ITT's predations.

Alerted to Williams's plan, Geneen was so infuriated that he undertook what he was almost never willing to do: launch an unfriendly takeover attempt. On December 23, 1968, he fired off an angry letter announcing that ITT was now openly offering $1.5 billion (double the value of Hartford's shares) for the whole company.

During the next three months, Geneen launched an all-out arm-twisting campaign to bring the reluctant Hartford directors around. He told his people to use their "full panoply" of contacts to exert "inexorable pressure" on Hartford; in the meantime, ITT acquired over 500,000 more Hartford shares. By May, the last vestige of resistance had crumbled. The Hartford board approved the merger with ITT.

But any joy Geneen may have derived from this victory was deflated by rumblings of another, much bigger, battle that was taking shape. The new administration's assistant attorney general for antitrust, Richard McLaren, was making good on his tough words about conglomerates. In April, he took his first steps toward breaking up the most omniverous conglomerate of them all. He announced he would go to court to stop ITT's planned acquisition of Canteen Corporation (another Lazard deal). A troubled Geneen wrote Rohatyn on April 29, "Unfortunately, the terms 'raider' and 'conglomerate' seem to get confused and it has resulted, in our opinion, in McLaren's policy that they should attack all conglomerates without making this distinction."

Nevertheless, he pressed on with the Hartford takeover. He still had one small technical detail to attend to: ITT planned to pay for the acquisition not with cash but with newly issued ITT preferred stock, which it would exchange for the Hartford shares. But in order to make the swap attractive to Hartford stockholders, the exchange had to be considered tax-free by the Internal Revenue Service. And the IRS insisted that before it would issue such a ruling, ITT would have to dispose of the 1.7 million Hartford shares the company had acquired earlier.

Geneen took his problem to Rohatyn, and Rohatyn proceeded to shop the block around. But the banker found his efforts hampered by ITT's requirement that the shares be sold for at least $51 each—since that was what ITT paid for them, and Geneen didn't want to look foolish by selling the Hartford shares for less than $51 only to buy them back later, when the takeover was completed, for ITT stock worth more than $70. But with Hartford stock languishing then in the low 40s, finding someone willing to pay $51 for it was an impossible task.

After unsuccessfully canvassing several large American securities houses, Rohatyn concluded that the only possible buyer was someone overseas—perhaps one of the Swiss banks. He took his idea to André Meyer.

"Too slow," the old man responded. "The Swiss banks would probably be too slow in making up their minds." But Meyer told his protégé that he knew of someone who *could* do it, someone who was just as big as the Swiss banks they were talking about and who could move far more rapidly. The buyer he was thinking of, he told Rohatyn, was Mediobanca.

Rohatyn relayed the suggestion to Geneen. Fine, said the ITT boss, but how could they get in touch with this Mediobanca? Rohatyn told him that would not be a problem. André Meyer would arrange everything.

On November 10, 1969, a little over two months after Meyer brought the two sides together in a Lazard Paris conference room, the ITT board approved the sale of the 1.7 million Hartford shares to Mediobanca. The transaction was a complicated one, but ITT's directors were assured by the company lawyers that it complied with the tax authorities' principal requirement: that the sale be "unconditional," and to a third party totally independent of ITT and Hartford.

Now that the shares were disposed of, ITT had a clear path ahead of it—if only McLaren would get out of the way. The feisty antitrust chief, however, wasn't budging. In August 1969, he had broadened his campaign against the conglomerate by seeking injunctions to stop the Hartford merger as well as ITT's intended acquisition of the Grinnell Corporation, the country's leading manufacturer of fire alarms. And while ITT was busy battling McLaren in the courts, a second front was opened against the company. Connecticut's insurance commissioner, William Cotter, made it known that *he* wasn't going to allow the Hartford deal, either.

Cotter, though, was willing to hold hearings; and in the early spring of 1970, a succession of top ITT officers and directors trekked to Hartford to plead the company's case. The commissioner was unmoved—but just as Geneen's "inexorable pressure" had worn down the Hartford directors, so, too, did it have its effect on Cotter. After numerous private entreaties by intermediaries and by Geneen himself, and after ITT expressed its desire to make a "charitable contribution" to the city of Hartford's new civic center, Cotter reversed himself on May 23 and allowed the deal to go through.

ITT was now ready to begin the formal process of buying up the Hartford shares and exchanging them for the new issue of ITT series N preferred stock. Lazard set up a "war room" at ITT, manned by Ray Troubh and associate Melvin Heinemann, to monitor the tender offer's progress; and by the end of June, ITT had acquired more than 95 percent of the Hartford shares. Yet the transaction was meaningless as long as the Justice Department continued to fight the merger in court and McLaren resisted all entreaties for a settlement.

In the midst of this tug-of-war, hardly anyone noticed that Mediobanca was quietly disposing of its ITT series N preferred shares—the shares the Milan bank had received in exchange for its Hartford stock in ITT's May tender offer. Eight hundred thousand shares were sold to the Dreyfus Fund, and 400,000 shares to the leading investment-banking firm of Salomon Brothers. The rest of the block was purchased by two utterly obscure entities: 100,000 shares to a small Swiss bank, Les Fils Dreyfus (which had no relationship to the Dreyfus Fund) and 400,000 to something called International Investment Associates.

Nor was much attention paid to two more acquisitions ITT made around the same time. On December 12, ITT agreed to buy Way Assauto, an Italian auto-parts manufacturer. A little over two weeks later, the still-voracious conglomerate purchased Eurofund, an investment fund whose portfolio consisted solely of foreign securities. The amounts of money involved were relatively minuscule: $22 million for Way Assauto and approximately $26 million (in ITT stock) for Eurofund. By the standards of a company battling to complete a $1.5 billion takeover, the deals were barely worth mentioning.

In the early months of 1971, the prospect of any accommodation between the Justice Department and ITT seemed slimmer than ever. Geneen desperately wanted to hold on to Hartford, yet any ITT settlement offer that didn't include the disposal of that prized jewel, Hartford, was rejected out of hand. To McLaren, the Hartford takeover epitomized the worst aspects of the conglomerate movement, and he was determined to undo the merger.

But by June, mysteriously, he had changed his mind.

Suddenly and quite inexplicably, McLaren was mouthing the very same arguments that Geneen had put forward so ardently. Unloading Hartford, McLean told his superior, Deputy Attorney General Richard Kleindienst, would cripple ITT—an outcome he did not feel was in the country's best interest. Instead, McLaren proposed a settlement. ITT would be required to divest itself of Avis, Levitt, Canteen, and part of Grinnell, and would be prohibited from acquiring any corporation with assets of $100 million or more without special approval. The settlement was remarkably similar to an offer ITT's lawyers had made just seven months before. Not surprisingly, the company consented to it immediately. On July 31, the settlement was announced.

McLaren claimed the agreement—the biggest forced divestiture ever in an antitrust case—had stopped Geneen "dead in his tracks." But other commentators considered the victory a hollow one. Not only did the settlement allow ITT to keep its most prized plum, Hartford, but it deprived the Supreme Court of an opportunity to issue a landmark ruling in the case. McLaren had always described this ruling as his ultimate objective; why, on the eve of obtaining it, did he suddenly pull back?

The question intrigued the press, certain members of Congress, and corporate gadfly Ralph Nader, who had long been suspicious of ITT's motives and tactics. Twice now, public officials had done abrupt about-faces in their opposition to the Hartford deal, and Nader felt that McLaren's explanation was no more convincing than Cotter's was. Nader pressed his fabled "raiders"—the aggressive young lawyers in his employ—into a full-scale investigation of the Hartford takeover and the settlement.

Soon, one of those raiders, Reuben Robertson III, was wondering whether there was any connection between the settlement and a $400,000 contribution by ITT to the upcoming Republican National Convention in San Diego. On September 21, Robertson wrote to Kleindienst asking him about it; the reply came from McLaren. "There is no relationship whatsoever" between the two, McLaren assured him. But neither Nader nor Robertson nor a suspicious Washington press corps was convinced.

The SEC, meanwhile, was also taking another look at the Hartford deal. In September, SEC investigators began checking out evidence that certain ITT shareholders, in the days before the settlement was announced, had unloaded their shares—as if they knew something was about to happen. The trails the commission sleuths uncovered all led to one place: the investment-banking firm of Lazard Frères.

Lazard's ties to ITT—and both companies' links to the Justice Department—were now coming to be seen in a far more sinister light.

The first great revelation was the disclosure by columnist Jack Anderson of the soon-to-be celebrated Dita Beard memorandum. The memo, from ITT lobbyist Beard to the head of the company's Washington office, William Merriam, appeared to document a direct connection between the $400,000 gift and the Hartford settlement, even going so far as to implicate the president himself. It sent tremors throughout the capital when it came to light in February 1972. Among the most shaken was Kleindienst, who had just been nominated to take over as attorney general from Mitchell, recently departed to run the president's reelection campaign. Embarrassed by the revelation—which seemed to contradict his earlier denials that there was any connection between the gift and the settlement—Kleindienst asked the Senate to give him an opportunity to clear his name by reopening his confirmation hearings.

The hearings laid bare, for the first time, many of the machinations behind the Justice Department turnabout. And placed firmly at the center of the vast arm-twisting exercise was the man Geneen always relied on to get things done: Felix Rohatyn. Kleindienst admitted he had had several discussions with Rohatyn in the months preceding McLaren's change of heart. Those talks, Kleindienst insisted, were not "negotiations"; Rohatyn had merely impressed upon him the hardship ITT would suffer if it was forced to divest itself of Hartford. What's more, the hearings revealed that Rohatyn had made the same case to top presidential aide Peter Flanigan.

While no one ever accused Rohatyn of having anything to do with the big ITT convention contribution (he told a reporter that the Dita Beard memo was "absolute bullshit"), the disclosure of his behind-the-scenes role was enough to mark him, in the public eye, as a key figure in the mushrooming ITT scandal. Before long, the affair took on even more sinister dimensions, what with Dita Beard's mysterious disappearance in the midst of the hearings and the disclosure of ITT's efforts to overthrow Chile's leftist government. And bound up in it all, rightly or wrongly, was the master merger-maker from Lazard, Felix Rohatyn.

Increasingly, Rohatyn was characterized in the press as a shady financier, a back-room manipulator with a hypnotic hold on high administration officials. Some of the harshest characterizations came from influential *Washington Post* columnist Nicholas von Hoffman. Branding Rohatyn an "anemic little financier" and "a little narrow-tied man who doesn't look like a million dollars," von Hoffman lashed out at the Lazard partner repeatedly on the pages of Kay Graham's *Post*. In one of those columns, von Hoffman dealt Rohatyn the unkindest cut of all, bestowing upon the banker the sobriquet that would haunt him for years afterward. Felix Rohatyn became, to one and all, "Felix the Fixer."

The unwelcome spotlight soon shone not only on Rohatyn, but on Rohatyn's firm. In April, in the midst of the Senate hearings, "Nader raider" Reuben Robertson charged that Lazard had unloaded hundreds of thousands of ITT preferred shares in the weeks before the antitrust settlement was announced. (The substance of Robertson's allegations was precisely what the SEC had been investigating since September.) Lazard admitted that it had indeed sold the shares—but insisted it had acted strictly as a middleman.

Yet ironically, just as the insider trading charges were coming to public attention, the SEC was shifting its inquiry to a totally different tack. The agency's investigators were becoming less interested in what had happened in the spring of 1971 than in the events of the summer and fall of 1969. They were scrutinizing the one aspect of the Hartford deal that had thus far escaped the probers' microscopes: ITT's sale of its Hartford shares to the obscure Milanese bank called Mediobanca.

The SEC soon became convinced, as one of its investigators later put it, that "the IRS had committed a massive goof" in approving the transaction. The crux of the deal was that ITT had to sell the shares "unconditionally" to an "unrelated third party" in an "arm's-length" manner; in other words, with no strings attached. But after reading the sales contracts over and over, SEC officials realized that the transaction was anything *but* "unconditional" and "arm's-length." Recalled one investigator, "It was all done in such a complicated way that somebody looking at it quickly would not understand. But if you sat down and read through that contract, you understood."

What made the contract so bewildering to the unpracticed eye was that it did not spell out a fixed price for the shares; instead, Mediobanca was given three pricing options, any one of which it could select. The first option was straightforward enough: Mediobanca would pay ITT $51 a share or the market price of the shares on the day the sale was closed, whichever was higher. ITT would thus at least break even on the shares, while Mediobanca would bear a risk if the Hartford shares, at the time of closing, were selling in the open market for less than $51.

The other two options were far more puzzling, since both provided for delayed pricing of the shares. Under the second alternative, the stock's price would be its "fair market value" during a two-week period in May 1971—more than eighteen months after the shares were supposed to change hands. And the third option—the one eventually selected—allowed Mediobana to pay ITT whatever price the Milan bank received for the shares when it, in turn, resold them. Mediobanca, then, bore no risk at all. While the shares would officially come under the bank's control in November 1969, it would not have to pay for them until it knew what it was getting from another buyer.

The SEC concluded from all this that the "sale" had not actually been a "sale." ITT had merely "parked" the Hartford shares with Mediobanca until the tax questions were resolved, paying the bank a $2 million fee for its trouble. In a true unconditional sale, the buyer would bear the risk and gain the rewards of later price fluctuations. But in this case, because of the delayed pricing features, the risks and the rewards were all ITT's—even after the shares changed hands.

ITT, in short, stood accused of grossly deceiving the IRS—with Mediobanca and Lazard Frères as its active accomplices.

That was not the only aspect of the Mediobanca transaction coming under fire. In April 1972, a Dreyfus Fund shareholder sued the fund, Lazard, ITT, and others, charging that there was a connection between Dreyfus's purchase of the 800,000 ITT preferred shares from Mediobanca and Dreyfus's later selection as a manager of ITT's pension-fund assets. Lazard, Rohatyn, and André Meyer, the share-holder alleged, were parties to the scheme.

To Meyer, the buffeting he and his firm were taking was becoming intolerable. The suits, the Nader charges, the SEC investigation, the slurs against Rohatyn all seemed part of a vast plot to sully the hallowed name of Lazard. As one Lazard partner recalls, "Here was a situation where Johnson was gone, where the Kennedys were out of power, where you had Nixon reeling and caught up in the ITT mess, and André was simply afraid that his reputation and the reputation of the firm would be inexorably entwined with this scandal. For the first time in his life, he was confronted by a situation he couldn't control."

Not that Meyer didn't try. During the Senate hearings, he was visited by Frederick "Fritz" Beebe, Graham's right-hand man at the *Post*. Beebe often accompanied Graham to her lunches at Lazard, and he was accustomed to an avuncular Meyer, bubbling with gossip and kindly advice. This time, however, Beebe had an angry old man on his hands. What the *Post* was doing to Felix was *outrageous,* Meyer bellowed. This Felix the Fixer thing—Felix's children were being taunted mercilessly by their schoolmates about it. It was *awful.* And Felix hadn't done *anything* to deserve it.

His ears thoroughly seared, Beebe promptly phoned the intended recipient of these tidings: Kay Graham. "This is awful," Beebe groaned. "We have to do something." But Graham was unfazed. For one thing, von Hoffman was von Hoffman, and Graham was accustomed to the outrageous comments that spilled forth so profusely from his typewriter. She also was enough of a Meyer intimate to know that the banker had absolutely no understanding of the press; as far as he was concerned, if something couldn't be reported favorably and sympathetically, then it shouldn't be reported at all. As one of Meyer's partners once put it, "He had this mentality that you should not only read newspapers, you should write them."

Knowing all this, Graham told Beebe that she did not intend to do anything. She would not tell von Hoffman to lay off on Rohatyn. She would not apologize to André. "We'll have to learn to live with it," she said. But she had also gotten Meyer's message: he was holding her personally responsible for the comments about Felix and Lazard that appeared in her paper.

In June 1972, as the SEC was putting the finishing touches on its case against ITT, Lazard, and Mediobanca, the commission's chairman,

William Casey, was told that a U.S. senator wanted to speak to him. The senator was Edward Kennedy. Casey picked up the phone and listened, with some astonishment, as Kennedy made an impassioned plea on behalf of André Meyer. Kennedy told the SEC chairman that Meyer was a trustee of the Kennedy family's foundation, that he was a "man of high reputation" and "had been very helpful" to the Kennedy family. While Kennedy knew that Meyer himself would not be named in any SEC suit against ITT and Lazard, the senator expressed concern that Lazard would be named and thus indirectly besmirch André Meyer's reputation. Casey politely thanked Kennedy for his information and assured him the case would be considered on its merits.

That Kennedy did not make the call on his own initiative was only revealed a year later, after Casey reported the conversation as an example of "improper" interference in the ITT investigation. A spokesman for Kennedy said that the senator's recollection was that Meyer "apparently felt there was some question being raised about his reliability and trustworthiness."

Within days of the Kennedy call, despite Meyer's best efforts, the SEC filed suit against ITT, Mediobanca, and Lazard.

The charge was an arcane one, but it was the best the SEC could come up with. The three were accused of violating the Securities Act of 1933 by failing to register the ITT shares that Mediobanca sold between November 1970 and May 1971. Implicit—but unstated— was the conclusion that the shares still belonged to ITT, not Mediobanca. ITT was also charged with violating the Securities Act by failing to disclose the Justice Department settlement in a July 1971 prospectus. As for the insider trading allegations, only two people were charged—both senior executives at ITT.

Four days later, on June 20, 1972, the SEC announced it had settled the suit. The mechanism used was a common one in such cases: a consent decree, in which the defendants neither admit to nor deny their alleged misdeeds but nonetheless promise never to do them again in the future. With the signing of the decree, the case officially was closed.

Still, the charges stung, especially since they came hot on the heels of Eddie Gilbert's well-publicized suits against Meyer. Nonetheless, considering all the attention the ITT case had generated, Lazard and Meyer had come out of it relatively unscathed. The sanctions the SEC imposed were hardly more than a wrist-slap. The more damaging accusations—that Lazard had been guilty of trading on inside information on the eve of the settlement—never officially saw the light of day. And while Rohatyn was publicly pilloried as a fixer, Meyer himself remained an indistinct, shadowy figure, his name rarely surfacing in the reams of stories on the ITT scandal.

But the case, like a nagging head cold, refused to go away. A few months after the consent decree was signed, a former Hartford shareholder named Hilda Herbst filed a class-action suit against ITT on behalf of 17,000 other former Hartford shareholders. She charged that ITT had misled investors by not disclosing the tax liability they might be incurring because of the Mediobanca transaction.

Then, in March 1973, an embarrassed Internal Revenue Service reopened its inquiry into the Mediobanca deal and the tax exemption the IRS had granted three and a half years before. The first time the agency had studied the transaction, it had taken only a week to make up its mind. Now, the IRS intended to take its time. A year later, charging that it had been duped by ITT, the IRS revoked the tax ruling.

And far from closing their own books on the matter, the SEC staff still pored over the case, like medical examiners dissatisfied with their preliminary autopsy. So many loose ends still dangled; so many questions were still unanswered. There was, for instance, the question of the ITT share sales on the eve of the Justice Department settlement. A large number of the shares, they knew, were handled directly by André Meyer on behalf of someone named Gaetano Furlotti. Who was this Gaetano Furlotti? And what did he have to do with André Meyer?

CHAPTER TWENTY-FIVE

The Vise Tightens

The assorted ITT inquests—into the Chilean conspiracy, the Hartford settlement, the Republican convention contribution—were merely warm-ups for the main event. The country was rapidly immersing itself in investigation, engrossed in an unfolding drama of abuse of power and conspiratorial concealment. This time, though, the principal target was not a wayward conglomerate and its overreaching chairman, but the man who held the highest office in the land.

For André Meyer, this spectacle was not without a certain irony. Many of the bloodhounds were commanded by friends of his. The House Judiciary Committee investigation into Watergate, for example, was headed by John Doar, the attorney who had worked side by side with Meyer on Bobby Kennedy's Bedford-Stuyvesant project. And the godmother of the journalistic shock force that broke open the scandal was Kay Graham.

His friends' involvement, however, did not make it any easier for him to understand what was happening to the country. He had never been close to Nixon (although, like many other Wall Streeters, he made a substantial contribution to the 1972 campaign). But he respected the president and could not comprehend the seriousness of Nixon's crime. His old-world mentality could not see the injustice in secrecy, in eavesdropping, in plotting to confound one's enemies. To André Meyer, such tactics were sad but necessary facts of everyday life.

He worried about Kay Graham's safety, warning her not to be alone. But this personal concern did not stop him from seething about the way the *Post* revelations were bringing the American government to its knees. At one point he told Graham, "You tore it down. You now should be thinking about how to build it up. It's your responsibility to help reconstruct it." Remembers Graham, "I said to him that he really didn't understand the press, that we didn't tear it down, so

I didn't consider it was our responsibility to put it together again."

Meyer was also undoubtedly reacting to the striking similarities betwen Nixon's plight and his own. Both he and Nixon were being relentlessly investigated for what seemed to both men to be minor aberrations—minor in relation to all the great things they had done. The world, in its single-minded pursuit of the *truth,* was utterly ignoring their accomplishments. As far as Meyer was concerned, none of it made any sense.

And, by early 1974, the world was closing in on both Meyer and Nixon. In Washington, the Watergate special prosecutor, the House Judiciary Committee, and a federal grand jury were pulling together the strands that would soon cost Richard Nixon his presidency. Meanwhile, in New York, the lawyers in the Herbst case were pressing tor a conversation, under oath, with the senior partner of Lazard. They wanted to hear *his* version of the ITT-Mediobanca story.

On March 7, 1974, their wish was granted. In his office at One Rockefeller Plaza, at ten o'clock in the morning, André Meyer swore to tell the whole truth and nothing but, and began what would prove to be the first of three days of testimony in the case of Hilda Herbst versus ITT.

"I am afraid I am talking too much," Meyer told his interrogators early on, "but I am not afraid because I have nothing to hide."

Indeed, in what was probably the first full-scale deposition he had ever given, Meyer was positively chatty. He apologized for his poor command of English ("I have sometimes difficulties in my broken English to express myself as clearly as I should") and tried to point out that they were probably talking to the wrong person ("I still play rather a certain role at a certain level in this firm, but I am not as active as I was earlier because I am not very young"). But with those caveats out of the way, he freely described his role in the Hartford saga—such as it was.

No, ITT's acquisition of Hartford was not his idea, though he wholeheartedly approved of it. (Earlier, he had allowed as to how he didn't like some of ITT's other acquisitions, despite Lazard's active role in them. He would have argued against them "if I had been consulted—but when I am not consulted, I don't give advice.") His own involvement in the Hartford merger, according to Meyer, began when Geneen asked him to arrange a meeting with Harry Williams at Hartford. Meyer described the obstacle course he had had to run to set up the rendezvous: the assistants who insisted Williams was too busy to come to the phone, the suggestion that they meet in the cafeteria of the Hartford airport—"probably the worst airport of the United States," Meyer interjected. When the meeting finally took place, he recalled, "I did very little. Mr. Geneen is very articulate and he speaks for himself, and as a matter of fact, I had very little to say." After that, Meyer left the negotiations entirely in Rohatyn's hands, and Rohatyn advised him only periodically of their progress. As Meyer explained, "It was a matter essentially which was in the province of the board of ITT, and the directors of companies in which we are represented never kept me informed about anything."

Then he described the phone call from Rohatyn in early August 1969, advising him of ITT's little problem with the IRS. Meyer was vacationing in Crans at the time, and, he recalled, "I was not very keen on being five thousand feet in the mountains and dealing with a problem like that sometime in August." Rohatyn told him of ITT's need to dispose of 1.7 million of its Hartford shares, and its inability to find a buyer at the right price in the United States. "He asked me," recounted Meyer, "what I felt and if I think a big block could be placed in Europe and he asked me to think it over maybe for two days, and I said that I will inquire about it, because I still tried to follow the thing." It was Rohatyn, Meyer testified, who suggested a foreign buyer, and after ruling out a Swiss bank ("The Swiss are very expensive and very slow, and they operate generally through boards and committees"), the senior partner suggested Mediobanca.

"I spoke to Cuccia," Meyer testified, "and Cuccia told me, 'I know ITT is certainly a great company,' and I told him why I felt it was a great company with good potential and a lot of international ramifications." They arranged the meeting with ITT for the end of the month, and Meyer offered to be there to make the introductions. But that, Meyer insisted, was the extent of his participation in the ITT-Mediobanca talks; once he had brought the parties together in the Lazard Paris conference room, and stayed for a while out of politeness, he had left the room and his involvement with the deal had ceased.

"I had other things to do," Meyer maintained. "If it had not happened that I was on holiday in Switzerland and that I was coming to Paris on my way to New York, I would probably never had anything to do with the prenegotiation." He was "purely and simply and just by accident little more than a messenger boy."

Sidney Silverman, Hilda Herbst's attorney, found this "messenger boy" self-characterization a trifle hard to swallow. Didn't Meyer participate in two days of discussions in Paris, as an ITT memo indicates? No, Meyer replied, he was only present at the first. Did Meyer not participate in the exchange of views and ideas and solutions? No, sir, Meyer answered: "I was present. I might have opened my mouth. I might have said something. I would not tell you that I did not say anything, but I did not play a role in the negotiation. That," he saw fit to add, "is the honest answer."

Silverman then asked Meyer who else at the firm, besides himself, discussed the deal with Cuccia. "It was a matter," Meyer answered, "which was to be expedited by people who are familiar with the intricacies of putting a complicated deal in motion." You haven't answered my question, said Silverman. Who was it?

"Well," Meyer replied, "Mr. Walter Fried."

Walter Fried—the in-house worrier, the partner whom Meyer termed the firm's "housekeeper," its "watchdog," and its "tower of strength"—was responsible for putting the Mediobanca deal in motion. Not André Meyer, not Felix Rohatyn. The same Walter Fried, who, according to the accounts of his partners, was unable to push a paper clip across a desk without clearing it first with Meyer, was given total responsibility for one of Lazard's most sensitive deals.

So you relied on Mr. Fried to negotiate it? asked Silverman. "Yes." And you never checked with him and he never checked with you? "No." Can you tell me of any other contracts that Mr. Fried negotiated of the same magnitude? "I don't know."

The only problem with Meyer's answers was that there was no way Silverman could cross-check them with the other man in question—since Walter Fried had died only a few weeks before. "I can't speak of him except with tears in my eyes," Meyer blurted out at one point in his testimony.

Meyer's attempt to turn Walter Fried into the case's key figure did not catch Silverman unaware. The attorney began quizzing Meyer about Fried's mental condition at the time of the Mediobanca deal. Wasn't Mr. Fried institutionalized towards the end of 1969?

"It depends," answered Meyer. "Maybe then he needed some help. I have trouble with the word institutionalized. He went to rest. He was not mad. He was not in that condition."

Silverman also began hammering Meyer about the other end of the transaction: Mediobanca's sale of its shares to those two obscure entities, International Investment Associates and the small Basel, Switzerland, bank, Les Fils Dreyfus. Meyer admitted that Lazard at one time, had owned a "small interest" in Les Fils Dreyfus—but, he said, the interest had been sold, at the behest of the New York Stock Exchange, in the early 1950s. (He pointedly denied an assertion by a Dreyfus family member, Richard Dreyfus, that Lazard "owned" the Basel bank.) As far as Meyer was concerned, LFD was nothing more than a Lazard stockbrokerage customer of long standing.

Was LFD, asked Silverman, buying the ITT preferred shares for itself or on behalf of others? "They were acting on their own behalf," replied Meyer—adding that he only knew that fact after the event. And, Silverman went on, LFD resold the stock that it purchased, through Lazard, did it not? "Maybe," answered Meyer noncommittally. "I don't know. Maybe through Lazard, maybe through other brokers."

Meyer was far more forthcoming when questioned about Lazard's ties to IIA. He testified that IIA was, in fact, a Luxembourg investment company owned by the Agnelli group—and that IIA's president was none other than Lazard Paris partner Jean Guyot. What's more, Meyer admitted that Lazard was IIA's principal stockbroker in the United States. "They give us the orders," he said, "and we execute the orders, and they ask us from time to time about our judgment." Yet, strangely, this "judgment" had not been sought when IIA purchased the ITT preferred shares from Mediobanca; Meyer insisted that neither he nor anyone else at Lazard had been consulted about the transaction.

Meyer then volunteered a reason why Lazard had not been consulted: it seemed that IIA was not actually buying the shares for its own account but was acting as a middleman, purchasing the shares on behalf of parties Meyer described as "other corporations of that same group." Who were these other corporations? Meyer was asked.

"Liechtenstein companies," he replied.

Liechtenstein is a postage-stamp-sized country wedged between Switzerland and West Germany that serves as the nominal "headquarters" for numerous European companies. The headquarters, though, is usually nothing more than a file in the cramped office of a local lawyer. Liechtenstein companies are, for the most part, paper companies, created solely to mask the financial transactions of their owners.

The obvious question, then, was who owned these Lichtenstein companies. "I don't know," Meyer responded, "but they are all people of that group."

Of which group?

"The Italian group."

The Agnelli group?

"Yes. Also the Furlotti group."

Gaetano Furlotti was then identified by Meyer as "the managing director of or president of IFI," the Agnelli-owned holding company. Thus, when Meyer spoke of the "Agnelli group" and the "Furlotti group," he was actually talking about one and the same thing.

It was Furlotti, Meyer went on to say, "who negotiated that transaction in the ITT shares."

The mysterious Gaetano Furlotti, then, played a strangely multifaceted role. Not only was he acting as the middleman, buying the ITT shares through the Agnelli-controlled IIA, but somehow he was also involved with the end purchasers, those shadowy Liechtenstein companies. And this was the same Gaetano Furlotti who had swamped André Meyer with sell orders in July of 1971, on the brink of the Justice Department announcement.

Unfortunately, Furlotti had something in common with that other key figure in the case, Walter Fried: Furlotti, too, had died recently.

But what role did André Meyer play in the movement of these shares from Milan to Luxembourg to Liechtenstein? "Did you," Silverman asked, "participate in any aspect of the transaction pursuant to which Mediobanca sold ITT series N stock to IIA?"

The answer was a flat no.

Did Meyer participate in IIA's sale of the shares to the three Liechtenstein companies?

The answer again was no.

Did he know whether the Liechtenstein companies resold the shares?

This time, the answer was yes. "What is the basis of your knowledge?" Silverman asked. Replied Meyer: "Because I believe that product was sold through us."

"Were you consulted about that sale?" he was asked.

"No, not consulted, but informed, yes."

"By whom were you informed?"

"I believe by Mr. Furlotti."

Meyer went on to say that "much more than one-hundred-thousand shares" were sold, with Lazard acting as the broker; he was hazy about the date. "I believe it was June of 1971." But, once again, he insisted that he was not directly involved in the sale of those shares—or, for that matter, the sale, at almost the same time, of the shares owned by Les Fils Dreyfus. "I don't do that kind of thing, Mr. Silverman," said Meyer. "I am a broker because this firm is a brokerage firm, which it has been since I believe the creation of the stock exchange, but it is really not my occupation here. I am not a customer's man." The term "customer's man" was a Wall Street euphemism for the run-of-the-mill stockbroker; as so often in the past, Meyer sought to distance himself from that line of work. He was an *investment banker,* not a stockbroker. What he knew about the transactions, he had learned only after the fact.

The role Meyer attributed to himself in his testimony, viewed in its entirety, was a strangely passive one. Despite his well-known involvement as Gianni Agnelli's confidant and "periscope" in the United States, Meyer insisted he had had absolutely nothing to do with the complex series of purchases and sales of ITT shares by Agnelli-controlled companies. If his statements were taken at face value, Myer had not even been consulted. His role in the long chain of transactions had effectively begun and ended in August 1969, when he set up the meeting between Cuccia and ITT executives. After that point, it had been all Walter Fried's deal.

Silverman, though, plainly did not believe the assertions of the distinguished senior partner of Lazard. He repeatedly badgered Meyer about what he knew, and when. During the final day of testimony, Meyer finally let his weariness and impatience show.

"Mr. Silverman," he said, "I am an old man and I have taken three pills this morning to be able to be with you, to be able to do the job of trying to answer properly, but I am not going to speak of things that I don't know and which I have not been involved in. I had nothing to do with the preparation of that agreement. I had nothing to do with it and with its implementation.

"I want to stop the meeting today," Meyer continued. "I am too tired. I have a high regard for you for many reasons, and I assure you I am showing the maximum of goodwill, but you are asking me questions where I have told you at the outset I can't answer because I did not know and I did not prepare that agreement. I would never have made that agreement like that.

"I have never made an agreement so complicated like that, that you have to read it twenty times to understand it after the event."

And with that, André Meyer sought to close the books, once and for all, on his involvement in the ITT-Mediobanca affair.

By this point, the investigators were homing in on another curious aspect of the case. Mediobanca's sales of its shares to IIA and Les Fils Dreyfus were not outright sales; the contracts were, in fact, more like options to purchase the shares. The buyers had no ironclad commitment to purchase the stock, and could simply wait and see what happened to the market value of the shares before exercising those options. As it turned out, that was exactly what occurred. The shares were contracted for in December 1970 at $55 a share but did not actually change hands until four to six months later, when the stock price was in the 70s. (In the case of IIA, the stock was close to $80 a share when the option was exercised.) In other words, the buyers had made a quick killing—but, because they were not really obligated to buy the shares, bore no risk if the price fell below $55.

Exactly *who* benefited from this, however, was still an open question, and one that Sidney Silverman raised when he examined Felix Rohatyn on April 24, 1974.

"Do you have any knowledge at all," Silverman asked Rohatyn, "as to whether Dreyfus Basel was acting as a nominee for another or others?"

"I have no such knowledge," Rohatyn replied. "My understanding is to the contrary. That Dreyfus Basel was acting for their own account."

The SEC investigators plugging away at the case concluded that Rohatyn was technically correct: LFD did indeed buy the stock for its own account. But they also learned that when LFD signed its agreement with Mediobanca to buy the shares at $55, it signed an *identical* agreement to *sell* 30,000 of the shares, at the exact same price, to someone else. The pretense that LFD was totally acting on its own was, like so many other aspects of this bizarre transaction, a legal fiction.

The buyer who had hidden behind LFD, the SEC probers learned, was a wealthy and powerful man who had died within months of signing the agreement. His heart had given out, unable any longer to support a frame swollen to the grossest obesity by too many Hershey Kisses and six-packs of Coca-Cola. Charlie Engelhard was his name.

* * *

In the late 1960s, Engelhard—vastly enriched by the many deals André Meyer had engineered for his precious-metals empire—put some of his enormous wealth into an investment company called Eurofund International. In the fall of 1969, Meyer told Rohatyn that Engelhard was interested in selling his controlling 28 percent interest in the company. It occurred to Rohatyn that Eurofund might be an ideal investment for ITT. The conglomerate at the time was encountering problems with the new U.S. Office of Foreign Direct Investments (OFDI); to bolster the American balance of payments, OFDI was restricting the amount of U.S. funds that companies could invest overseas and the amount of earnings that their foreign affiliates could reinvest. The new rules threatened to greatly crimp ITT's foreign operations, but Rohatyn realized that Eurofund offered a way around the restrictions. Since Eurofund's portfolio consisted exclusively of foreign securities, ITT could liquidate them and reinvest the proceeds overseas without running afoul of OFDI rules. Rohatyn took the idea to Geneen, who was immensely intrigued. On December 29, 1970—three weeks after Mediobanca had told ITT it had lined up buyers for the ITT preferred shares—the conglomerate agreed to acquire Eurofund in exchange for ITT common stock.

When the SEC investigators probed deeper into the Eurofund deal, they learned once more that appearances were deceiving. The actual seller of Eurofund wasn't Charlie Engelhard himself, but a partnership called the Far Hills Securities Company. (Far Hills was the New Jersey town where Engelhard's estate was located.) The partnership had been formed on December 26, 1969, for the sole purpose of unloading the Eurofund shares. The majority partner was Charlie Engelhard. The minority partner in Far Hills was none other than the investment-banking firm of Lazard Frères.

Lazard's hidden interest in Eurofund wasn't the only aspect of the deal to catch the SEC's eye. There was the coincidence of certain dates. The agreement between Les Fils Dreyfus and Englehard was signed December 15, 1970, exactly two weeks before the Eurofund-ITT deal was finalized. Then there was the testimony of one of Engelhard's closest aides, Lawrence Hoguet. Hoguet revealed that the shares of Engelhard's holding company, Engelhard Hanovia, that he thought were held by Lazard one day turned up in the hands of Mediobanca. When Engelhard was asked about this, Hoguet said, he professed not to know how they got there.

But Hoguet saved his biggest bombshell for later in his testimony.

He disclosed that Charlie Engelhard had had extensive dealings with Les Fils Dreyfus in the past, primarily in the gold market. When asked who was Engelhard's principal contact at the Basel bank, Hoguet answered, "A man called Plessner there. Henry Plessner." The same Henry Plessner who was Felix Rohatyn's stepfather.

Rohatyn, who had spent the better part of six years fielding investigators' questions on everything from the conglomerate movement to Dita Beard, now found himself being queried by the SEC on, of all things, Henry Plessner.

He described his stepfather as "a semiretired, wealthy individual who looks after his own interests and shows up for a couple of hours and looks at the mail and the newspapers, and then goes off and plays bridge in the afternoon." Plessner, he said, had "affiliations" with LFD and with Samuel Montagu, a British merchant bank that was also prominent in the gold market. But Rohatyn insisted that Plessner had been "essentially self-employed" since the mid-1940s.

Rohatyn was then asked about Far Hills Securities. He testified that he became aware of the partnership, and Lazard's role in it, only *after* he began discussing an ITT-Eurofund merger. When he found out, Rohatyn added, he ruled himself out of any further role in the merger talks and decided he would not participate in any profit Lazard would make on the deal. Nevertheless, there was no question that Rohatyn's multiple allegiances had been strained to the breaking point by the transaction; not only was he on the board of ITT, but he was also a director of Engelhard Minerals & Chemicals (Meyer had arranged that appointment).

And what about Engelhard's purchase of 30,000 ITT shares from LFD? What did Rohatyn know about that? Virtually nothing, he replied; it was only after Charlie Engelhard's death that he had learned of the Engelhard-LFD agreement. And he didn't know why Engelhard had bought the shares.

Throughout his testimony, Rohatyn portrayed himself as a man in the dark, someone who, despite his pivotal roles at both ITT and Lazard, had had only the vaguest awareness of the bewildering movements of shares going on around him. He had reacted to the contracts between Mediobanca and LFD and Mediobanca and IIA the way any confused outsider would: "They looked pretty strange. They were written in a strange way, and it took me a while finally to understand who had a right to do what to whom." Rohatyn maintained he didn't even know what IIA was until December 1970, when he was informed of the Luxembourg investment company's agreement to purchase part of Mediobanca's ITT block. And who had told him of IIA then, he was asked? André Meyer, he answered. As for the sales by Lazard of ITT shares in June 1971—at the time Rohatyn was nailing down the settlement with the Justice Department—he testified that the "sales were identified to me as sales on behalf of the Italian group, without identifying the accounts in particular. The impression I had and still have was that they were sales on behalf of the Agnellis." And who had told him of the Italian group's sales? Rohatyn was asked. André Meyer, he answered.

The SEC investigators then dropped two more strange names in Rohatyn's lap: Quinedes Handels Anstalt and Establishment Salgesch. They were two companies in the principality of Liechtenstein. Again, Rohatyn pleaded ignorance. He didn't know anyone at either company.

If the names Quinedes and Salgesch drew a blank from Rohatyn, they were becoming household words among the handful of SEC staffers assigned to the case. The two Liechtenstein companies had been involved in the sale of the Italian auto-parts company, Way Assauto, to ITT in December 1970. And the SEC investigators strongly suspected that they had played another role: that they were the same Liechtenstein companies that had bought the much-traveled ITT preferred from the Agnelli-controlled IIA, which in turn had bought the stock from Mediobanca.

Agnelli, in fact, had been responsible for suggesting the purchase of Way Assauto to Geneen during a meeting arranged by Meyer and Rohatyn. ITT's acquisition experts studied the company but, in August 1970, decided against going ahead. Four months later, however, ITT changed its mind. On December 8, ITT agreed to purchase Way for $22 million in cash. The deal would be closed on April 30, 1971.

Just who were the owners of Way? ITT officials told the SEC that their understanding was that while the majority of the auto-parts company was owned by the Griffa family of Asti, Italy, a substantial minority—30 percent—was owned by Agnelli's holding company, IFI. IFI, these officials added, didn't hold the shares directly. It held them through an intermediary: a Liechtenstein company.

Again, the sparks of coincidence gleamed. First, the fact that Liechtenstein entities had been involved in both the Way deal and the purchase of shares from IIA. Then, the strange similarity of the closing dates: the option agreements signed by IIA, LFD, and Engelhard all were scheduled to expire May 1, exactly one day after the Way acquisition was slated to be closed. Furthermore, the amounts of money involved were exactly identical. ITT had agreed to purchase Way for $22 million; IIA's purchase of ITT preferred shares, which would then be resold to the Liechtenstein companies, was equal to exactly $22 million. And, finally, there was the one thing that both IIA and the sellers of Way Assauto had in common: the behind-the-scenes presence of Gianni Agnelli.

As these disparate pieces were connected by the SEC investigators, the shape of the complete puzzle started to emerge. It now seemed likely that while one Agnelli entity, IIA, acted as a middleman in the passage of the ITT shares, other Agnelli entities, the Liechtenstein companies, ended up actually owning the shares, selling them off a few months later at an enormous profit. The beneficiary of these moves, in any case, was Gianni Agnelli—just as Charlie Engelhard would have been the beneficiary of a similar arrangement via Les Fils Dreyfus.

Inexorably, all roads were once again leading to André Meyer's doorstep. Who else could have brought Agnelli, Engelhard, Mediobanca, and ITT together in a single grand design?

On December 30, 1974, eight months after Meyer thought he had washed his hands of the whole mess, the SEC's assistant director of enforcement, Theodore Altman, wrote to Simon Rifkind. Altman requested the presence of André Meyer and Felix Rohatyn in his office in Washington on January 13. He had some more questions to ask them.

This time, though, the quarry proved more elusive than anyone at the SEC could have imagined.

CHAPTER TWENTY-SIX

Fighting for His Life

The sad news was broken to André Meyer on January 17, 1975. After a long battle with cancer, his oldest and closest business partner, Pierre David-Weill, had died. Dropping everything, Meyer raced off to Paris for the funeral.

Those who attended the services couldn't help remarking how terrible Meyer looked: grayish, depleted, devoid of all his old sprightliness. Clearly, something was wrong with him, something more than grief at the loss of a colleague. Instead of returning to New York right after the funeral, which would have been his normal course, Meyer repaired to Crans. There, a local doctor was summoned by Bella to examine her husband. The doctor told Meyer he needed an operation but told Bella something more: her husband had cancer of the prostate.

Meyer and Bella flew back to New York, and on February 1, the Lazard senior partner underwent surgery. The operation was a success, and hope was voiced that the cancer had been arrested. But many months of rest and recuperation lay ahead. Meyer was confined to his Carlyle apartment, and, while he kept up with business via phone calls and visits by his partners, his activity was drastically reduced.

Yet his illness did not cause him to shrug off the ITT-Mediobanca affair. On the contrary, in his weakened state, the investigation became an obsession for him. One of the Lazard partners who was closest to him then, Robert Price, remarks, "Absent his health problem, I think he would have handled it as just another pain in the neck. But when it was compounded with his cancer, it really jangled him." Meyer would speak about the ITT situation daily with Price and with close friends such as Anna Rosenberg Hoffman. "The ITT thing disturbed him very much," recalls Hoffman. "He was unduly worried about it."

To be sure, the ITT probe wasn't the only intrusion on his recovery. As Meyer lay in his sickbed, another crisis took shape: the Arab boycott of Lazard and other prominent Jewish-owned banking houses. Arab banks were refusing to participate in financings organized or helped along by Lazard, Rothschild, S. G. Warburg, and others; and in view of the enormous resources the Arab banks commanded, the blacklist's implications were frightening. Already, a leading British merchant bank, Kleinwort Benson, had made it known it would exclude those houses from financings at the behest of the Arabs. And already, the French government had blocked Lazard from participating in financings for two state-owned companies.

The singling out of Lazard seemed especially incomprehensible in view of its senior partner's sympathies. True, Meyer had been a fervent supporter of the founding of the state of Israel and had given generously to such Israeli scientific endeavors as the Technion Institute. But he was hardly an ardent Zionist, and he was often privately critical of what he viewed as the undue intransigence of the Israeli government towards its neighbors.

Meyer's first reaction, after the initial shock of the boycott, was to grandly announce, "I see no reason why I should discuss this. I ignore it." But he soon realized that the threat was too great to simply walk away from. Lazard filed a formal protest with the French finance ministry, and Meyer phoned his contacts at the major non-Jewish houses urging them not to fall in line behind the boycott. By mid-February, Lazard was once again included in underwriting syndicates for French state-owned entities.

But the resolution of this crisis gave Meyer little peace. The SEC, after all, was still waiting in the wings.

The commission's enforcement division waited a decent interval before pressing Meyer again. Then on April 25, almost three months after his operation, it issued a subpoena.

This time, Meyer had no intention of playing the part of the cooperative witness. He had engaged another prominent attorney, former Nuremberg trial prosecutor Samuel Harris, to join Rifkind in representing him, and through Harris he made it known to the commission that he was too ill to testify. What's more, he was just about to leave for Switzerland to continue his recovery. To document Meyer's fragile state, Harris handed the skeptical SEC staffers a letter from Meyer's doctor spelling out Meyer's inability to bear up under cross-examination. And, just in case the SEC questioned *that,* Harris attached to the letter the doctor's five-page curriculum vitae, including citations of articles he had written for distinguished professional publications.

The upshot of all this documentation was unmistakable. Relates one former SEC investigator, "It was said that Sam Harris would rather deliver the entire firm of Lazard Frères in a freight car than produce André Meyer."

Nevertheless, the commission persisted. If Meyer was physically unable to appear before it, the least he could do was furnish written answers to the SEC's questions. Reluctantly, Meyer's attorneys agreed, and at the end of May the questions were sent to Meyer in Crans.

In the meantime, the SEC investigators heard the testimony of Harold Geneen. The ITT chairman's version of the events in question was perfectly consistent with Meyer's and Rohatyn's. He insisted, as Meyer and Rohatyn had, that it was ITT, not Lazard, that had structured the transaction. "We did our own negotiating," Geneen maintained. Yet, just as the two key Lazard partners had done in describing their own roles, Geneen sought to portray himself as a know-nothing manager, someone who took little interest in the mundane details of the deals he set in motion. It was hard to believe that the Harold Geneen who presented himself before the SEC was the same Geneen who roamed the world with six briefcases stuffed with several hundred pounds of reports, and who once had said, "You can't delegate anything you can't understand. If you read it all, you have an idea of the situation." This Geneen, the Geneen seen by the SEC, claimed to have been totally in the dark about what had happened to the shares after Mediobanca signed the agreement—"other than knowing, finally, the cash had come through on its normal date." Exactly who had bought the shares from Mediobanca, and the terms, had been, according to the ITT chief, a mystery to him until two years after the fact, when he had begun preparing for the shareholder suits.

He hadn't known, he said, of Les Fils Dreyfus's role. He hadn't known of an agreement between ITT and Lazard in which ITT agreed to indemnify the investment banker on any matters related to the ITT-Mediobanca contract and Lazard's role in arranging it. He hadn't known what IFI (the Agnelli holding company) was. He had never discussed the sale of Les Fils Dreyfus's ITT preferred shares to Charlie Engelhard. He had never met Charlie Engelhard. "The only thing I know about him," said Geneen, "is that he drank a case of Coca-Cola a day."

In their quest for someone who knew *something,* the SEC investigators turned next to the one-time Mother Superior of New York society, Jane Engelhard.

She described how she had uncovered the letter outlining the agreement between her late husband and LFD. The day after his death at their Florida home, she recalled, she and his secretary were going through his bedroom desk there. They found a letter. "I thought it was a little strange there was a business letter in his desk," she related. The letter, she recalled, said "something about the Swiss bank and that it was Dreyfus." But she did not read the letter through; rather, she simply instructed the secretary to turn the letter over to her lawyer. She also did not talk to Meyer about it, even though, as she herself put it, "I have met with Mr. Meyer a great deal of my life."

Then she was asked if she knew any of the other principals in the investigation. Gianni Agnelli? "I only met Mr. Agnelli once in my life on President Kennedy's destroyer when we were all up in Newport together. Mrs. Agnelli had been a close friend of my sister's for a long time; they went to school together. But that's all." Gaetano Furlotti? Leopoldi Furlotti? She drew a blank. "Who are these people?" she asked.

The written answers that Meyer furnished to the SEC's questions left a lot to be desired, as far as the commission's investigators were concerned. Now, more than ever, they wanted to confront the man himself, in the flesh. Meyer's lawyers, however, still balked. The senior partner of Lazard had returned to New York, but, they said, he remained quite ill.

This time, though, the commission was adamant. Meyer's personal testimony was essential. Eventually, a compromise was reached. Meyer would indeed allow himself to be deposed—but the testimony would take place in the friendly confines of the Carlyle.

And so, on October 31, 1975, André Meyer once again testified under oath in the matter of ITT-Mediobanca. The tone of this encounter, however, was far different from that of the session with Sidney Silverman a year and a half earlier. On that occasion, Meyer had been in fine form, regaling his listeners with snatches of his life story, tossing out catty jibes about Harry Williams's rudeness and the hor-

rors of the Hartford airport. Now, though, Meyer was very much the
weary old man, an impression that was reinforced at the outset by
Simon Rifkind when he asked the SEC interrogators to confine their
questions to those that could be answered "yes or no—to conserve the
energy of our witness," Rifkind explained. The SEC people, for their
part, were unusually deferential throughout the proceeding, concealing whatever skepticism they harbored behind a facade of utmost politeness.

Once more, Meyer was asked about his role in arranging the ITT-
Mediobanca deal. And, once more, he described it, after the initial
introductions, as negligible. He had, he said, "nothing to do" with
Mediobanca's subsequent sale of 100,000 of the shares to Les Fils
Dreyfus—and he knew of no relationship between that sale and ITT's
acquisition of Eurofund. Nor, "to the best of my knowledge," did he
know of any link between Mediobanca's sale of 400,000 shares to IIA
and the Way Assauto deal. (He described Lazard's position in the
Way acquisition as merely that of "messenger boys" who "never negotiated anything.")

What was your role, he was asked, in the dealings between Les
Fils Dreyfus and Charlie Engelhard? "Nil, zero, no role," was
Meyer's emphatic answer.

On the other hand, he had been aware that Engelhard had purchased the shares—because the metals magnate himself had told him
so at the end of 1970 during a rare Meyer visit to the Engelhard home
in Florida. As Meyer recounted the conversation, "He told me, 'I
bought thirty thousand shares of ITT recently.' I said, 'Why have you
done that? A queer idea.' 'Oh, I'm sure it's very good. I'm sure it's a
very good investment,' and I didn't care really. I didn't control the
market of ITT. I never look at it. I have nothing to do with it. I was
not struck by that. It's one of the many things that you hear during
one day."

But, as Meyer told the story, upon Engelhard's death three
months later, his widow showed him an inventory of Engelhard's
portfolio, and he noticed that the ITT shares were not listed. "Nobody found the shares for two days or five days or ten days," he
testified, "and then, finally, there were two or three people dealing
with that estate. Somebody found a letter by which he had bought
thirty thousand shares, which was these shares. And one of the executors wanted to sell them, and he saw that they had been bought
in Switzerland and he talked to me about it, and I said, 'We will see

if we can do something.' " He then "expedited the thing. . . . This is the role which I play, which was more the role of a friend than of an investment banker." But when Meyer was then asked by his SEC interrogators if he was aware that LFD had itself bought back the shares from the estate, he merely replied, "I have no idea. I don't know, and I didn't care, honestly."

The questioning then returned to the Way Assauto deal. Meyer was asked if Gianni Agnelli owned any interest in Way. "I don't know," was the reply. "He said that he had no interest. I have always trusted Mr. Agnelli." And what about the Agnelli-controlled International Investment Associates—did Meyer know what relationship there was between it and the two Liechtenstein companies, Quinedes and Salgesch? Meyer's first answer was "No," but he quickly amended it: "It's the Italian group. . . . The people represented by Mr. Furlotti." Did Meyer know who those people were? "No." Who, Meyer was asked, were the end purchasers of IIA's 400,000 ITT preferred shares? The Liechtenstein companies, he replied. Was he then aware of those purchases at the time they were made? "No," he answered, "I was not. It was not my province. I had nothing to do with it." Was the transfer of those 400,000 shares to the two Liechtenstein companies related to ITT's acquisition of Way? "I don't know," Meyer answered.

Then he was asked about another mysterious development in the case: a payment of $520,000 that LFD made to Lazard in June 1971. The entry in Lazard's ledger referred to the payment as "Settlement of fee—re Agnelli matter." Did this fee have anything to do with the ITT-Way deal? "No, not at all," Meyer answered. What, then, was the payment for? "They owed us money for a lot of services which were rendered over a period of years," he replied. The fee, in short, was for all the miscellaneous advice that Meyer and Lazard had given the Agnelli interests over the years.

On *that* point, at least, he was expansive. "We have rendered a lot of service," he told the SEC questioners. "In an article, and I don't like articles in the press, there was, years ago, an article about me— no, I'm not very publicity-minded—at which time they interviewed Mr. Agnelli, and Mr. Agnelli said, 'Mr. Meyer, I know him well. He's my periscope in the United States.' What that meant was that they ask dozens of questions." The fee, Meyer said, "was a kind of mish-mash in which certain apples and potatoes were added."

But if all that was the case, why was Les Fils Dreyfus paying the fee? Did Meyer know why? "I have no idea," was his response.

Unable to get any further with that line of questioning, the SEC staffers turned one last time to the central focus of their inquiry: Meyer's role. Did he, they asked, ever have any discussions with Geneen about the ITT preferred shares? "Never," Meyer answered.

Did he ever discuss with Rohatyn the purchases of the ITT preferred shares by IIA and Les Fils Dreyfus? "We learned of it at the same time, but I don't think that we had any conversation, to the best of my knowledge.

"You know," he added, "Mr. Rohatyn is my partner, my famous partner, but he has never been talkative about anything and especially about ITT."

Having arrived at that dead end, the commission investigators closed off their questioning. Meyer interjected that if they had any more questions later on, he would be happy to answer them: "I don't want you to feel that I'm not trying to be helpful." To that, SEC staffer Gary Sundick replied, "Let me say, Mr. Meyer, we certainly appreciate that you are going out of your way to be cooperative." And Rifkind then saw fit to remind the commission of the witness's delicate state: "I want to thank the commission and the staff for making it possible to have this examination here instead of being outside, because I think that has been a great convenience to Mr. Meyer and I think his health requires it."

If the commission had gotten practically nowhere with André Meyer, it had even worse luck in its examination a month later of Gianni Agnelli. All the Fiat boss would admit to was a long-standing link with Mediobanca; he had been a director of the bank for fifteen years. On everything else, he professed total ignorance. He was utterly unaware of the arrangement by his family-owned company, IIA, to purchase the ITT preferred shares; the agreement had been totally the doing of the late Mr. Furlotti, as was the "Fee Agnelli matter" paid to Lazard. What's more, he asserted that he had never heard of Les Fils Dreyfus, which had paid the fee on his behalf. "It rings no bell whatsoever," he said. And he denied holding any interest in Way Assauto—despite the assertions of ITT executives that he did.

Felix Rohatyn, however, was under a different impression. Called again before the SEC probers three months after Agnelli's appearance, Rohatyn told them it was his belief that Agnelli in fact owned a minority interest in Way. Asked how he knew that, Rohatyn answered that André Meyer had told him. Furthermore, Rohatyn for the first time was willing to admit that there probably was some connection between ITT's acquisition of Way and Mediobanca's sale of the ITT preferred. He told his questioners that he had come to the conclusion that the same Liechtenstein companies that sold Way Assauto to ITT had also bought the ITT preferred—although he hastened to add that his insight had only come about "very, very recently," and was based on "a review of the testimony or reading documents in connection with this examination." He was not, however, willing to make the same surmise about Engelhard's share purchases and ITT's acquisition of Eurofund. Nevertheless, coming on the heels of Meyer's resolute "I don't knows," Rohatyn's admission that all may not have been coincidental was something of a break through.

Two weeks later, Geneen appeared again. After confessing that the welter of transactions had become a blur to him—"I work twelve hours a day and we run a company, and I think at that time we were buying about a company a week"— the ITT chairman insisted he had no knowledge that the sellers of Way Assauto and the purchasers of the ITT preferred were one and the same. "I didn't know at the time anything except that we had bought the company we were trying to buy," he said. "Three years later, I heard what the rest of the transactions were." Why, he was asked, would the sellers of Way take the money they received and reinvest it in ITT stock? Geneen held fast: "I think it was a damn good buy at that point, and that's all I can see in it."

Geneen's protestations notwithstanding, the SEC staff was now coming close to establishing conclusively that some sort of grand design tying this maze of transactions together existed. The key was the link between ITT's acquisition of the Italian auto-parts company and the later purchase, by the sellers of that auto-parts company, of ITT preferred shares. Rohatyn conceded that there probably was a connection, and in March 1976 came further confirmation: the testimony of Lazard's in-house counsel, Thomas Mullarkey. "It's my present impression," Mullarkey told the SEC investigators, "that anybody, even of the meanest intellect, understands these transactions were linked." What's more, Mullarkey testified that he was told they were linked by Simon Rifkind.

Now that the SEC had that acknowledgment from Mullarkey, and indirectly from Rifkind, it pressed for more. Did André Meyer admit they were linked? On that score, however, Mullarkey backed off. He parroted Meyer's denials: "He has told me many times he didn't know who was behind those accounts with the funny names. . . . He described himself as an introducing factor in this transaction, that he didn't play a substantial role. He characterized himself as a messenger boy." Did Meyer ever express any surprise that the two transactions were being linked in the investigation? "I can't say Mr. Meyer has ever expressed any surprise to me of the linking of the transactions," commented Mullarkey.

The SEC probers then turned to the mysterious $520,000 "Fee re Agnelli matter." Mullarkey testified that Meyer had difficulty recalling exactly what specific services were covered by the fee: "His memory was faulty, and he was sick." When the investigators then asked Mullarkey if he was personally satisfied with Meyer's hazy answer, he snapped, "Are you, in effect, asking whether I'm going to impeach the integrity of my senior partner? Is that your question? My senior partner is a man of great integrity. If he told me this, I have no reason to dispute him."

By the time the SEC wound up its inquiry in the spring of 1976, it was clear that integrity—specifically the integrity and reputation of André Meyer and Lazard Frères—was a paramount issue in the case.

The theme was sounded throughout the extensive final briefs Sam Harris and Sy Rifkind submitted on their clients' behalf. After asserting Lazard's complete innocence from wrongdoing, Harris and Rifkind went on at length about the "tremendous accomplishments" of the firm and its partners over the years, attaching extensive biographies of each of the accused, including Meyer.

The attorneys pleaded with the SEC not to resort to legal action. "All of the proposed defendants," they said, "are decent men of impeccable reputation who do not deserve the humiliation of being named as defendants in a commission lawsuit." Moreover, they cited Meyer's fragile health as a reason for restraint. His very survival, they said, "could be jeopardized by the stress and torment of a lawsuit.

"Because of the enormous damage that the mere bringing of a lawsuit could inflict upon the reputations, the careers, and in some cases the very lives of the individuals involved," summed up Rifkind and Harris, "we urgently appeal to the commission's sense of fairness, restraint, and compassion."

Sam Harris struck the same chord in a personal note he sent to

SEC associate enforcement director Irwin Borowski on July 18. Writing from London, Harris said, "To me the most important matter on my business agenda is the Lazard investigation because it involves the reputations and careers of three fine human beings.

"I can't begin to emphasize how strongly I feel about the possibility of André Meyer ending an extraordinary career, which has involved conferring tremendous benefits on men and women in many nations—particularly in the U.S., France, and Israel—with a suit in which he is viewed by the Commission as a guilty defendant."

The SEC enforcement staff spent over a year sifting through some thirty-four cartons of documents, depositions, and filings. Then, on October 13, 1977, the commission made known its findings.

First, it concluded once again that ITT's sale of the Hartford shares to Mediobanca was not the unconditional, arm's-length transaction required by the IRS. Even after the supposed "sale," the risk of market fluctuations in the shares continued to be borne by ITT. Of the three pricing alternatives worked out between ITT and Mediobanca, only one was actually considered: the other two, in the SEC's view, were shams inserted in the contract to help ITT obtain its IRS ruling.

Instead of disposing of the shares unconditionally, ITT, the SEC found, later used them to acquire Way Assauto and Eurofund. Way Assauto had not been the straight cash acquisition ITT had made it out to be. Rather, ITT in effect had swapped the old Hartford shares, by then converted into ITT series N preferred, for the shares of the Italian auto-parts company. As for the Eurofund deal, the SEC concluded that ITT used the preferred shares to "confer a valuable benefit" upon Charlie Engelhard, Eurofund's controlling shareholder, as a sweetener in the deal.

Furthermore, the commission also concluded that by giving IIA, LFD, and Engelhard options to purchase the preferred shares, rather than selling them to them outright, Mediobanca—and, by inference, ITT—was allowing these purchasers to make a potential killing on the shares, while freeing them from any risk. In fact, that was exactly what had occurred, as ITT shares soared to almost $80 a share compared to the option price of $55. By surrendering the shares at the option price, ITT was also surrendering to these purchasers profits of at least $10 million on the stock.

The commission report was, for the first time, able to fully chart the migration of those shares and to demonstrate how, like beneficent wayfarers, they had enriched everyone with whom they had come into contact. The journey had begun with ITT, and its need to dispose of its old Hartford shares in order to obtain the IRS ruling. Unwilling to part with the stock for less than $51 a share, ITT had turned to Mediobanca. The Milan bank was not interested in buying the stock itself but was willing to have the shares "parked" with it long enough for the IRS ruling to be obtained. That was where Way Assauto had come in. ITT was able to pay for the auto-parts company by giving its owners options on the stock parked with Mediobanca: if the stock went up, the owners would make a killing; and if it didn't, they could drop the option and still be left with the $22 million in cash ITT had paid them. Similarly, Charlie Engelhard was given an option in connection with the Eurofund deal. Six months later, the price of the shares went up, just as everyone hoped they would; the options were exercised; and the stock then resold in the open market—through Lazard—for a fat profit.

In this manner, the owners of Way Assauto, including Gianni Agnelli (the SEC finally concluded that Agnelli's IFI holding company was indeed a 30 percent owner of Way), had made their promised killing. So had the estate of Engelhard, and Les Fils Dreyfus. As for Mediobanca, it had been handsomely rewarded for its middleman work, receiving some $1 million in fees from ITT.

But the most prodigious milker of the money machine, by far, had been Lazard Frères. Every twist and turn of the convoluted deal had yielded it a profit, in one way or another. To begin with, Lazard had received a $1 million fee from ITT for arranging the Hartford takeover. Then, because of a fifty–fifty fee-splitting agreement with Mediobanca, Lazard had earned another $1 million when ITT parked the Hartford shares with the Milan bank. It had received $250,000 from ITT in connection with the Eurofund acquisition and, on the other side, earned a profit of $1.2 million from its partnership interest in Charlie Engelhard's Far Hills Securities, which had sold Eurofund to ITT. Lazard also had been paid $150,000 from one of the Liechtenstein companies for introducing Way Assauto to ITT. And, finally, there had been that $520,000 for "settlement of fee— Agnelli." The SEC concluded that the payment was not for miscellaneous advice, as Meyer had claimed, but was a cut of the Way Assauto owners' (including Agnelli) profit on their ITT shares, possibly as further compensation for arranging the deal.

In all, then, Lazard's total receipts from the ITT-Hartford merger and its carefully choreographed aftermath was $4.1 million.

But as impressive as—perhaps more impressive than—the gross amounts involved was the sheer ingenuity of the whole operation. The scheme bound together a series of seemingly unrelated fragments—ITT's need to dispose of its Hartford stock, Engelhard's interest in selling Eurofund, Mediobanca's reluctance to accept any risk, among others—yet fit them so perfectly that every party to the deal could come away satisfied. And, from start to finish, the transaction was a masterpiece of concealment, with its multiple layers of intermediaries and its Liechtenstein companies—all of which may have been intended to obscure, from the IRS and other prying eyes, exactly where the wayward stock was going.

But while the SEC investigators saw through most of the subterfuges, they were unable to definitely answer the central question: just whose handiwork was this? Certainly, no one was stepping forward to take credit. In the thirty-four boxes of documents and depositions, not a single smoking gun could be found, and the latticework of denials by the principals involved offered little help. Yet, when viewed in its entirety, the evidence pointed inescapably in one direction. Who else could have brought Lazard, ITT, Giovanni Agnelli, Mediobanca, and Charlie Engelhard together in a grand scheme, one that solved ITT's tax problems and netted huge profits for everyone along the way? Who else could have pulled together the far-flung network of intermediaries and anonymous holding companies and used them to fashion an utterly impenetrable and well-nigh riskless chain of transactions? Who else could have been responsible for such an awesome display of financial engineering?

"It was brilliantly conceived, just brilliant," Tom Mullarkey would say years later. "There were a lot of minions involved—myself, Felix, and some other people. But the conception of it was André's."

It was, unquestionably, one of André Meyer's greatest deals.

On the face of it, the punishment meted out to Lazard for this exercise in deception was relatively light. Despite years of dogged pursuit of the case and the damning findings that were issued, the SEC declined to prosecute Lazard or ITT. Instead, it negotiated another settlement which was hardly more severe than the 1972 agreement. Lazard agreed to adopt better procedures for ascertaining and recording its fees, and agreed to provide those clients for whom a Lazard partner or employee served as a director with full and complete information on fees and other compensation Lazard derived in the service of the client. As for ITT, it agreed to set up a committee of independent ITT directors to review the commission's findings and come up with procedures that would prevent such misdeeds from happening again.

With the signing of this consent decree, however, ITT was hardly out of the woods. The company still was facing a possible $100 million tax liability—$100 million being the total amount of back taxes the former Hartford shareholders owed the government, now that the ITT-Hartford merger was no longer considered tax-free. (ITT had assumed the tax liability on the shareholders' behalf in settling the Herbst case in 1977.)

It was not until May 1981 that an accommodation was finally reached among ITT, the IRS, and the Justice Department. And once again, considering the possibilities, ITT got off relatively easy. The government agreed to accept $18.5 million from ITT in settlement of the tax liability. "We are very pleased to have this litigation behind us," commented ITT's new chairman, Rand Araskog, when the settlement was announced.

More than a decade after it began, ITT's long legal odyssey was finally over.

Despite the SEC's leniency, Lazard could hardly have been said to have come out of the ITT-Mediobanca affair unscathed. The firm had been branded in the public consciousness as the prime mover in a scheme to skirt the law; deceive the IRS; and, along the way, line its own pockets and those of a few favored friends. In the world that mattered most to Lazard and André Meyer, the world of corporate movers and shakers, the taint of ITT-Mediobanca lingered. "The stock maneuver was very hurtful," says a former Lazard hand. "It caused some people not to deal with the firm, because of the fear of association with untoward action."

Over the long haul, the firm could eventually ride out the storm. But for André Meyer, at the twilight of a distinguished career, the damage could not so easily be repaired. From his earliest days on the Paris Bourse he had labored to be known as an *haute banquier*, someone whose highmindedness and probity were beyond question. From the 1940s on, he had molded his firm in that image, spurning clients and businesses that would, if only by association, sully the snobbish reputation he so carefully cultivated. Now, in his last years, that reputation had been tarnished. It was not André Meyer, the *haute banquier*, the world saw now. It was André Meyer, the schemer. And the irony of it all was that the instrument of revelation had been that which he had prided himself upon most: his skill as a financial engineer. His genius had been his undoing.

CHAPTER TWENTY-SEVEN

Adrift

"I am a very old man, a very sick man," André Meyer told the *New York Times* in January 1977. "I'm completely out of business. I had a very serious operation two years ago, and just a year ago I was given forty-eight hours to live."

The article in the *Times* Sunday business section, titled "End of an Era at Lazard," portrayed a firm in transition, rudderless, as its senior partner moved with mincing steps toward the grave. "Meyer and his wife Bella live quietly at the Carlyle," it reported, "shuttling occasionally to their Swiss chalet for a change of scene. Mr. Meyer is visited almost daily by a physician who takes his blood pressure. Visitors say the Lazard senior partner often wears an old robe and bedroom slippers, and sips tea with his toast and jelly."

But the picture the *Times* painted—the one Meyer chose to present to the world—didn't fully correspond to the reality of the situation. True, Meyer was every bit the recluse the newspaper made him out to be. He had not appeared in the office since his departure for Pierre David-Weill's funeral, two years before; he was too weak to come in, he explained to associates, and he did not want the people at Lazard to see him in his debilitated state. But he remained a spectral force hovering over the firm, thanks to his unshakable grip on the one lifeline to power he had left: the telephone. Whether he was at the Carlyle or in Crans, he would phone his partners constantly, demanding the same incessant flow of information that they had accorded him when he was a real, physical presence at One Rockefeller Plaza. His Swiss phone bills alone were said to be the highest racked up by any private individual in the country. And what he couldn't obtain on the phone, he would get in person, by summoning various partners to the Carlyle for private audiences. "Things really hadn't changed," remembers partner Frank Pizzitola. "The locus just moved to the Carlyle. The only thing different was that we would go to the Carlyle and not the corner office."

To be sure, there was some inevitable weakening of his iron hold on his minions. Some partners simply ignored the old man, neglecting to keep him abreast of what they were up to. Says Felix Rohatyn: "It was the perfectly normal reaction of people who say to themselves, 'Well, now at last we're free.'" Meyer's awareness of this brought out the worst aspects of his latent insecurity. He would loudly complain that not only his partners but many of his friends had abandoned him in his old age and had thrown him away. The griping led one man who did visit him often, attorney Ben Bartel, to lash back. "What do you expect?" he told Meyer. "They come here, you say they want something out of you. They don't, you say they don't come anymore. It's your own fault."

Many undoubtedly stayed away because of the pervasive state of gloom that draped him like a shroud. The ITT-Mediobanca investigation, of course, obsessed him, but his worries hardly ended there. He became preoccupied with random news events, regaling his visitors with horror stories about the Italian terrorist group, the Red Brigades; about kidnappings; about the theft of Charlie Chaplin's body from a Swiss cemetery. He was convinced that the world was heading for an economic apocalypse, that capitalism was dying, that government deficits and inflation were out of hand, and that *nothing* was a safe investment any longer. "I remember once talking to him about investments," says former Morgan Guaranty Trust Company chairman Ellmore Patterson. "Should you buy gold? Stocks? Art? Bonds? And he didn't want to buy *anything*. I said to him, 'This is perfectly amazing for a man of your experience and knowledge of investments. It's just amazing and discouraging that absolutely nothing looks attractive to you.'"

Occasionally, associates would try to snap him out of it. Lazard partner Robert Price, who grew especially close to Meyer in those last years, would regularly phone him in Switzerland early in the morning and tell Meyer to take out a yellow pad. "OK, Bob," Meyer would say, "I have here the pad. What do I write on it?" And Price would tell him to draw two columns, one for potential problems and one for make-believe ones. Invariably, Meyer would interrupt. "Ah, they are not make-believe," the old man would say. "Gold, it is going too high. It is real. People fear a war." Nothing Price could say would convince him otherwise.

The only consolation he had in this state of depression—about the world, about ITT-Hartford, about his health, about Lazard—was the presence of Bella.

With the onset of his illness, the spiritual and physical separation between Meyer and his wife ended. She was constantly at his side, caring for him, ministering to his every need. Recalls Anna Rosenberg Hoffman, "She stayed in the house with him all the time. I would say to her, 'Bella, get the hell out of the house, go and see somebody; I'm going to be here for an hour at least.' But André would be very selfish about it. If she did go out, he would say, 'Where's Bella? Why did she go out?' He was like a child clinging to her.

"He would say to me, 'See, Bella's an angel.' And I'd laugh and say, 'I've told you that for thirty years.' "

The wear and tear never showed on Bella. In fact, many of their friends thought she looked more radiant than ever. She seemed positively aglow in his presence; probably, these friends concluded, because now, at last, André finally needed her and reached out for her. "In many respects," says Andrea Wilson, "I thought the last years were the happiest years for Bella."

His reconciliation with Bella, however, did not mean Meyer was totally at peace with his family. He now had to deal with the problem of his grandchildren.

André Meyer had always been a doting grandparent—but, in his case, a combination of family circumstances and his own overwhelming personality caused the term "doting" to take on a far more sweeping meaning. This was not as much true for Philippe's son, Vincent, who grew up in Paris, a city Meyer only occasionally visited, as it was for Francine's three children. The Gerschels lived in Manhattan, not far from the Carlyle; and if that wasn't reason enough for Meyer's presence to be constantly felt, there was also the domestic situation. The children's father, Marc, was far away in France, and Francine's fragile psyche made it difficult for her to cope with the life of a single parent. Inevitably, she turned to her father for support. This became even more true after 1963, when Francine married a French diplomat and moved to Morocco with him. By that time, the two older children, Patrick and Laurent, were away at boarding school, while the third, Marianne, was about to be enrolled in one. Coming home for the holidays, to them, meant coming to the Carlyle.

As a grandfather *cum* foster parent, Meyer was affectionate, tender, and fiercely protective. "He sort of viewed his children and his grandchildren as his creations," comments Marianne, "and no one was going to wreck that creation—no one." The children all reacted differently to this sort of smothering attention. Laurent, the most free and easy of the trio, took it most in stride. Patrick, the oldest, basked in his grandfather's attentiveness and soon became spoiled by it. And Marianne, the youngest, sought to break away.

A special bond had always existed between Marianne and her grandfather. As a small child she wrote him poems; other people in the family would read the poems and say, "Isn't this nice? Isn't this sweet?" but Meyer himself would never talk about them. He took her under his wing and taught her lessons she would never learn in the classroom. Once, in Paris, he told her, "Marianne, we're going to go to one store, and you can have anything you want." They walked into a department store, and she immediately picked a blue scarf. Meyer beamed. "Good," he said. "You decided quickly." Recalls Marianne, "The question was, did I have the confidence and guts to tell him what I wanted? That's how he would teach me."

"Marianne," he would say to her, "business, real business, is not numbers and it's not money. It's people. You have to be able to know and to judge people." And she learned from him that the best way to judge people was to simply watch and listen to them; if you sat with a person long enough, listening for the offhand remarks as well as the calculated ones, you could figure out where they were coming from. She absorbed the lesson so well that soon she turned the tables on the master, staring at *him* for minutes on end. He would have to pretend he was asleep or hold a newspaper in front of his face to ward off the stare.

But no matter how subtle their relationship was, Meyer's leonine protectiveness was never far from the surface. Marianne would tell him she really was uncertain about a boy she was going out with, and he would say, "Let me check him out." He would look bewildered when she turned the offer down. "It was all very confusing for him because it wasn't something he could control," she points out. "His granddaughter's emotions for somebody else—he couldn't really control that."

As she grew older, her impatience with him began to show through. She told him once that she was hoping to get into a certain college, and he replied, "I'll buy them a swimming pool." "No, Grandfather," she snapped. "You've had the chance to do it on your own. Let me have the same chance."

She also came to realize that while she may have been the apple of her grandfather's eye, it was Patrick who was, in her words, the "Crown Prince," the member of the family whom Meyer sought to make his heir apparent in the business. Uncertain about what she was going to do with her life, she drifted from one course of study to another, moving from Russian studies to economics to political science to law to psychology to art. (Along the way she failed a course in, of all things, money and financial markets.) Marianne became, in short, a professional student, to the utter exasperation of her grandfather.

"Well, here she comes," he would say when she walked into the room. "Marianne wants to be czarina of Russia, queen of England and president of the United States, all at the same time. Which is it today?"

Eventually, Marianne drifted into a marriage that both André and Bella were adamantly against. The marriage lasted only slightly longer than one of Marianne's majors. She remained in school, a melancholy woman who in her late twenties still had no idea what she wanted to do with her life. She adored her grandfather, yet would have violent arguments with him; in that respect, at least, she took after her mother. "Get out and don't come back," Meyer would yell at her, waving the cane that he used after his illness to get around.

"Marianne," he would say to her plaintively in his last years, "what can I give you?"

"Grandfather," she would reply, "you can give me peace of mind."

"But," he would say, "I *can't* give that to you."

Marianne may have struggled to find herself, but there seemed no doubt at all in Patrick's mind who *he* was. He was, quite simply, André Meyer's heir apparent.

As Patrick grew up, his grandfather did everything in his power to buttress that notion. Patrick's wedding in Paris in 1968, for example, was a rare instance for Meyer of outright ostentatiousness. It seemed more like a coronation than a marriage ceremony, what with touches such as matching Guy Laroche gowns for the bridesmaids and singers from the Paris Opera, whose appearance was arranged by Madeleine Malraux. (The wedding also caused another violent falling-out between Meyer and his granddaughter, who felt that staging such a sumptuous affair while Paris was in the midst of student rioting was in questionable taste. "Don't you care, Grandfather?" she pleaded.

"Well, yes," he replied, "but now I want you to be a good girl for Patrick's wedding.")

Soon after his graduation from Cornell, Patrick joined Lazard and almost immediately was made a full partner. It was a shocking breach of investment-banking etiquette. Customarily, even the best-connected aspirants went through *some* period of apprenticeship before being anointed with a partnership. But Meyer made an exception for Patrick, and it was apparent to everyone at Lazard why he did so. He saw in Patrick his last chance to perpetuate his family's influence in Lazard, to create a dynasty that would counterbalance the David-Weills' influence at the firm.

Soon Patrick became known, among the Lazard Paris partners, as *le petit fils de Dieu*—the grandson of God. And Patrick acted every bit the part. His arrogance was overwhelming. Frank Pizzitola, who worked with him for about two years in an attempt to give the young man a crash course in the business world, once asked Patrick to do something, and Patrick retorted, "Do it yourself." After that, Pizzitola would have nothing to do with him. "Poor Patrick," Meyer sighed when he heard about the incident. "Nobody will work with him. You refuse to work with him." Answered Pizzitola: "No, I don't. He refuses to work with *me.*"

"At first, Patrick was just a nuisance," recalls a former Lazard hand, "but then he became a pain in the neck. André kept pushing him into the middle of conversations with business people about their problems, and Patrick wasn't capable of handling it. The clients rejected the premise that Patrick was a proper lead man for their business. He lost us at least two clients that I'm familiar with."

By the time Meyer fell ill, Patrick was a virtual outcast at Lazard; no one wanted to have anything to do with him. In desperation, Meyer turned to his old colleague, Ned Herzog. Herzog, who describes himself as "one of Patrick's best friends at the firm," recalls, "André used to beg me all the time, 'Do something with Patrick.' I said, 'Do something? I'm his best friend, and you're his grandfather, and neither one of us can do anything with him.' André said, 'Ned, do something to make him less crazy.' And I'd say, 'What can I do?' God knows, André used to occasionally fly off the handle, but this boy's off the handle all the time, all day long."

Yet, almost to the end, Meyer stubbornly believed that Patrick would straighten himself out. Remarks one intimate of Meyer's, "What is unbelievable is that he would not or could not see Patrick's weaknesses until the last few years. When André wanted something to be, he had trouble accepting that it wasn't going to be. He didn't see it until very late."

What led Meyer, at the very end, to come to his senses was Patrick's estrangement from the person at Lazard Meyer respected most: Felix Rohatyn. He and Patrick had never really gotten along—not surprisingly, in view of the long apprenticeship Rohatyn had had to go through before becoming a partner—but as the years went by, their relationship became marked by open, bitter acrimony. Patrick would snipe at Rohatyn's preference for fame over fortune, and in a November 1977 *Fortune* magazine article on Lazard he was quoted as saying he would like to see Lazard attract more "avaricious" people. "Most Lazard partners would rather be like Felix Rohatyn than Daniel Ludwig," he lamented, referring to the publicity-shy billionaire shipowner.

When Rohatyn was asked later about Patrick's comment, he seethed. "I thought that was an asinine remark, and still do," he told this writer in February 1979. "If I'm setting an example, I think I'm egotistical enough to believe that I'm not that bad an example. And I think people who spend some of their time not just grubbing around doing business are better people. And ultimately they become better businessmen than rich young kids who think that the world is nothing but money."

He and Meyer engaged in what Rohatyn termed "long and painful discussions" about Patrick's future. And while Rohatyn refuses to talk about the outcome of those discussions, there was no question that with Rohatyn dead set against him, Patrick's days at Lazard New York were numbered. Eventually, Meyer found a place for him elsewhere in the Lazard empire, installing him at Corporate Property Investors, the real estate investment trust Disque Deane had started. Deane, at least, was sympathetic to Patrick's plight. Says Deane: "He was terribly wronged by many of his Lazard partners because they didn't have enough warmth themselves to understand the problems the grandson of a mogul like André Meyer had trying to get along with people. In other words, they didn't have heart. But I always had a lot of sympathy and heart for Patrick. I thought he was a very lovable young fellow." Under Deane's tutelage, Patrick began to learn the real estate business.

Patrick's failure to make it at Lazard was, by all accounts, a source of enormous anguish for Meyer in his last years. He had been denied what he had wanted most: an heir. He would have to look outside the family to find one.

For a long time, it seemed that the obvious candidate was Felix Rohatyn.

Rohatyn, after all, had always been the closest thing to a protégé, an alter ego, that Meyer ever had. "He can negotiate anything," Meyer once said admiringly. But the relationship was always a complicated one. Kay Graham, who knew both men well, remarks, "Felix behaved like a son. He both loved André and resented the fact that André wanted to dominate him and wanted him to do things that he just didn't want to do."

From the late 1960s on, Rohatyn sought to distance himself from the old man's suffocating grip and carve out a measure of independence for himself. He lived simply and avoided being caught up in the money machine that had made so many other Lazard partners utterly dependent upon Meyer. "André always thought I was extravagant in not wanting to make more money," Rohatyn once joked. He began taking an interest in affairs outside the Lazard orbit. In 1970, Rohatyn chaired the crisis committee the New York Stock Exchange formed to head off the collapse of several large brokerage firms. Then, in 1975, came MAC.

New York City was heading straight for bankruptcy, and governor Hugh Carey was in dire need of a financial wizard to stave off what many regarded as the inevitable. He turned to Rohatyn, asking the Lazard partner to head the new rescue vehicle, the Municipal Assistance Corporation. From the outset, Meyer was adamantly against Rohatyn's involvement in the city's fiscal crisis. "He equated it with some sort of mid-life madness, not unlike falling in love with a stripteaser," Rohatyn once said. "I told him, 'You have weaknesses for beautiful paintings and beautiful women. Consider this of that order.' "

It fell to Simon Rifkind, who would also play a role in the crisis as counsel to MAC, to try to persuade Meyer that Rohatyn was doing the right thing. "André kept saying to Felix, 'Why do you need it? What good will it do you? It'll only interfere with your affairs,' " remembers Rifkind. "I persuaded André that it was a good thing for Felix to do, and he yielded to me on that."

So Rohatyn stepped into the spotlight, and Meyer gradually became reconciled to his partner's public role. Says Rohatyn: "I think he finally concluded two things—(a), that I wasn't really aiming to leave the firm to run for mayor or governor or become secretary of the treasury; and (b), that it was probably good for our business, that it added something to me and it added something to our firm. And, in any case," Rohatyn adds, "he had no choice." Meyer even came to feel a twinge of jealousy. Recalls Rohatyn, "He said to me, 'You know, I would have loved to do it, but I don't think I could have,' and then I said, 'Of course you could have.' And then he came back to the issue of his speaking English with an accent and being a foreigner and not being able to take public criticism."

True to his word, Rohatyn returned to the fold after the worst of the New York City crisis was over. But when he returned, it was as a celebrated public figure; MAC had allowed Rohatyn to establish, once and for all, his independence from André Meyer. He made it clear to the old man that while he would go on masterminding deals for the firm, he had no interest in filling Meyer's shoes as senior partner and resident "garbageman." In his last years, Meyer would privately put Rohatyn down for his decision. "Felix Rohatyn?" Meyer told a fellow septuagenarian financier. "He's a very able man in making deals, but he's no good in dealing with garbage. And a good banker must, above all, be good at dealing with garbage."

Reflects Kay Graham, "He adored Felix, but he would have wanted Felix to do just what he wanted him to do, and he resented the fact that Felix was independent. It was a sort of love-hate thing with both of them."

In the end, Meyer had no more luck controlling his professional son than his real one.

There was one other Lazard partner who was seriously mentioned, for a time, as a possible successor to Meyer: Disque Deane, the real estate whiz. If Rohatyn represented one side of Meyer's business personality—the smooth, well-connected negotiator—Deane represented the other—the fast-moving, money-hungry deal-maker. But Deane, like Rohatyn, had little interest in running an investment-banking firm (and, even if he did, his combative personality probably would have ruled him out). Deane, like Rohatyn, wanted to carve out an independent position for himself—except that in Deane's case, the independence he was talking about was largely financial.

In 1971, a vehicle emerged that would give him that. It was Corporate Property Investors, a real estate investment trust. The impetus for CPI came from Morgan Guaranty, which wanted to set up and sponsor a real estate investment trust that would specialize in leveraged net leases. Knowing of Deane's expertise in the area, Morgan asked him if Lazard's real estate investment arm, Peerage Properties, would serve as CPI's investment adviser. Deane agreed, and soon CPI was attracting major investments by the Ford Foundation, the General Electric pension fund, and the U.S. Steel pension fund.

While Deane saw the seeds of an empire in CPI, Meyer regarded the new entity as an ideal way to liquidate many of his real estate holdings. Already preoccupied with putting his estate in order, Meyer, in George Ames's words, "wanted to get things into as liquid a form as he possibly could." CPI offered him the chance to translate his real estate investments into readily marketable shares of a real estate investment trust.

The transfer was arranged in 1973. Peerage Properties, which held many of the real estate investments of Meyer and other Lazard partners, was merged into CPI. Both Meyer and Deane came out ahead. Meyer had the liquidity he was after, while Deane was given an enormous springboard for the growth of CPI, since the Peerage portfolio included such choice properties as Roosevelt Field.

Shortly afterward, however, a rift developed between Deane and Meyer. "Mr. Meyer," asserts Deane, "didn't want me to have a separate power base." As Deane tells the story, Meyer was also advised by another Lazard partner involved in CPI that the CPI stock was overpriced and Deane was incompetent to run the real estate trust. Meyer began pressing for the liquidation and dismantlement of CPI, and lobbied Morgan Guaranty chairman Ellmore Patterson in the hope of getting Morgan's backing. The bank's trust department, though, was against scuttling CPI, and Meyer's plan was thwarted.

So Meyer, instead, sold the $26 million in CPI stock that he and a group of coinvestors (including Jane Engelhard) held. And Deane went on to build his empire. Not only did CPI steer clear of the woes that plagued most other real estate investment trusts in the mid-seventies, but it went on to become one of the nation's most successful real estate investors, with assets of close to $2 billion. By dint of his own substantial CPI holdings, as well as other investments, Deane's dreams of wealth—wealth independent of André Meyer—were realized.

"You may ask," Deane says today, "why I wasn't more interested in Lazard? Why I didn't bow down to André Meyer and do his bidding and run the firm? The answer is *money*. When I came to Lazard in 1964 I had a cash net worth of two million dollars. What do you think my net worth is today? Take a guess. It's *seventy million dollars*. Felix's, I'd say, is five million dollars.

"Felix and I were six percent partners of Lazard for many years. But I wanted more. I wanted one hundred percent."

And so Meyer had one less heir apparent.

With Meyer out of the office, Rohatyn preoccupied with MAC, and no clear line of succession in place, Lazard began to drift. The firm's corporate clientele became increasingly restless, now that Meyer was no longer the omnipresent force keeping them in line. The clients were also fed up with Lazard's unwillingness to pay attention to them during periods when deals weren't in the works. "The firm didn't really cultivate and stay with and massage its clients. It only serviced them when they had a deal coming," notes a former Lazard partner. "You still have to take flowers to the girl, even if you aren't going to marry her."

The crowning blow was when Salomon Brothers supplanted Lazard as one of Chase Manhattan's lead underwriters. "Maybe Meyer's illness vitiated his ability to work on David Rockefeller," comments a former top Chase executive, "but the fact is the dissatisfaction with Lazard there goes way back. People at Chase were always complaining that Lazard was only interested when we had a piece of business."

While Meyer had often remarked, with a touch of pride, that "my life is a series of improvisations," it became increasingly apparent that in opting for spontaneity and rejecting long-range planning he had blown some lucrative opportunities. When the Eurodollar bond market began blossoming in the early seventies, for example, Lazard was nowhere to be seen—even though Meyer played a part in creating that market through his work on various presidential committees. Meyer had definitely been caught unawares; a former Lazard Paris partner recalls Meyer telling him in 1967, "Don't waste your time with the Euromarket. It's such a stupid business that anybody can do it. And, anyway, it's not going to last." Laments another former partner, "With Lazard in Paris and Lazard in London, there shouldn't have been any firm in the world that came close to them in the Eurodollar bond-underwriting business. They should have owned it."

Part of the problem was Meyer's faulty instincts, but part of it also was his reluctance to lay on the extra manpower and trading ability needed to exploit the new market. His phobia about size and overhead had never waned; the notion of building Lazard into a global powerhouse like Goldman, Sachs and Salomon Brothers was totally alien to him. The dictum that Lazard remain small and maneuverable was, as far as he was concerned, carved in stone.

Unable to come up with a clear-cut answer to the succession problem, Meyer opted for a patchwork solution. Just before Christmas 1975 he brought Donald Cook, former chairman of the Securities and Exchange Commission and the American Electric Power Company, into the firm and named Cook "managing partner." "I am not the boss," Meyer told the *New York Times.* "The new boss is Mr. Cook." Cook, who was sixty-eight, had no experience in the investment-banking business and talked of running Lazard as though he was chairman of the board of a large corporation. What he soon discovered, however, was that the temperamental partners of Lazard wanted no part of such a management structure, or *any* management structure, for that matter. "Some of the other partners simply cut his balls off," says someone who worked with Cook then. "He fizzled from day one." Lazard came to be governed by a nebulous "management committee," which consisted of Cook, Tom Mullarkey, the frequently absent Felix Rohatyn, and Howard Kniffin, whose emphysema kept him out of the office much of the time.

Meyer, it seemed, was finally reaping the harvest of his impromptu management methods and his emphasis on ruling the firm through the sheer force of his personality. As one observer of this sorry spectacle points out, "He didn't do what an institution builder has to do, which was to put in place a plan for pulling out. He didn't do it but kept talking about doing it, which was even *worse.*"

By late 1977, Lazard was virtually written off by its Wall Street competitors. The firm still made money, but it totally lacked any sense of purpose. The merger business was dormant. The venture-capital area had long since been shuttered because of Meyer's aversion to taking new risks. Stockbrokerage and money management remained little more than sidelines. The firm's underwriting clients were unhappy and pondering shifts of allegiance. The ITT-Mediobanca investigation had, in the public eye, tainted Lazard and its key partners.

"Your firm," Don Petrie was told by a Wall Street friend, "is a has-been."

Desperate to do *something,* Meyer turned to the only viable alternative he had left. He reached out to Lazard Paris and, in effect, asked history to repeat itself. Once again, a French partner would be called upon to restore the great name of Lazard.

CHAPTER TWENTY-EIGHT

The Torch Passes

Succession had never been a problem at Lazard Paris. Running that firm was the David-Weills' birthright, and upon his father's death in 1975, Michel David-Weill settled comfortably into the role of senior partner. In outward manner, at least, he was a double for his father: jovial and unassuming, he had the air of a man totally at ease with his wealth and position. But unlike Pierre, whose natural inclination was toward lethargy, Michel worked hard and enjoyed working hard. Furthermore, Michel's geniality concealed an inner toughness, even coldness, at the core.

He had kept a discreet distance from the chaotic situation in New York; deferring to Meyer had long been second nature to the David-Weills, and Lazard New York was *still* Meyer's firm. But by the summer of 1977, the vacuum yawned too wide for David-Weill to ignore. He and Meyer agreed that the only solution for the firm was to have David-Weill assume the senior partner's reins in both New York and Paris. As David-Weill put it, "I had the feeling, and Mr. André Meyer had the feeling, that the time had come."

David-Weill trod very lightly upon his arrival (the plan was for him to spend three weeks a month in New York and one week in Paris). He wanted at all costs to avoid ruffling the old man. He shared Meyer's office, just as his father before him had shared offices with Meyer; and Meyer's desk was kept ready and waiting for the old senior partner, as though he were about to emerge from seclusion any day. It sat in the middle of the room, while David-Weill's was off to the side, and on Meyer's desk was a simple gold Tiffany clock that testified to the influence of David-Weill's absent roommate. It was a gift to Meyer from the Kennedys, and it was inscribed: "To André— with deep appreciation and affection—Rose, Eunice, Jean, Pat, Ted."

But as deferential as he was, David-Weill also knew he had to act. He came to the conclusion that one of the firm's problems was that there were too many partners who didn't, for one reason or another, deserve their partnerships. The indiscriminate swelling of the partnership ranks was a legacy of Meyer's policy of "garaging" people—bringing new people who caught his eye into the firm, giving them fancy titles, and *then* figuring out what to do with them. But in David-Weill's opinion, "Being a partner is not an honor. It is either a fact or not a fact."

In 1978, then, he took the unusual step of "departnerizing" seven partners—making them either limited partners, with a capital stake in the firm but no influence on its activities, or senior vice-presidents. In some cases, such as Disque Deane's, departnerization simply ratified their lessened involvement in the day-to-day affairs of Lazard. But in other cases, the move reflected David-Weill's judgment that the individuals involved did not make a contribution to Lazard that was worthy of a partnership. He handled the situation as tactfully as possible, assuring those people that their income would not suffer because of their change in status, and making sure to consult Meyer every step of the way. But once he committed himself to the course, he did not back down.

Then, in a bid to bring fresh blood into the firm, David-Weill made another gutsy decision: he raided Lazard's oldest and closest associate on Wall Street, Lehman Brothers. The lightning strike was a shattering one, from Lehman's point of view; Lazard snapped up two of its best-connected, most prestigious partners, James Glanville and Ian MacGregor, and two of its hottest up-and-coming stars, Alan McFarland and Ward Woods. Once again, David-Weill did his best to keep the former senior partner in the mainstream, dispatching the four recruits to Crans for an on-site inspection before formally bringing them on board.

David-Weill also took steps to mend relations with the long-lost cousin, Lazard Brothers of London. He brought Lazard Brothers in as a limited partner of the New York firm—the first time the London house had had any kind of ownership position in Lazard New York. As he put it, "It is a little different if you are a partner of the owner than if you are just a cousin of his." For the first time in years, Lazard Brothers began working jointly on projects with the New York and Paris firms, and Lazard New York people felt free to call their London counterparts without fearing the senior partner's wrath.

Lazard partners also took to David-Weill's style of management, which was far less paternalistic and smothering than his predecessor's. "Mr. Meyer wanted to know every time a pebble turned over," said partner David Supino, "but not Michel." On the other hand, the firm's underlying business philosophy remained much the same under the new regime—not because of undue deference by David-Weill, but because the new senior partner firmly believed in the same basic tenets. Like Meyer, David-Weill was committed to keeping Lazard small and maneuverable; he shared the old man's aversion to expansion and high-volume business, such as retail brokerage, that required excessive overhead. Under David-Weill, Lazard's offices would remain as drab as ever. "Luxury helps at home, not in the office," David-Weill said, echoing the master. The new chief also perpetuated Meyer's doctrine of availability. David-Weill never went anywhere that was out of reach of a phone and continued Meyer's practice of distributing a "weekend list" every Friday, indicating where partners could be reached on Saturday and Sunday. "You don't have to say with whom," said David-Weill with a Gallic twinkle in his eye, "but you have to say where."

His partners, however, proved far more resistant to such disciplines than the Lazard partners of old. Glanville, for instance, couldn't get over the fact that "the secretaries have to go outside to buy typewriter ribbons. We don't stock them here." He was willing to accept that, but the weekend list was another matter. "Do you want to know what I do with it?" he asked a visitor. "I put it right there," he said—pointing to his wastepaper basket.

For the most part, though, David-Weill proved remarkably successful in maintaining a measure of continuity while putting the wayward firm back on course. Not long after David-Weill's arrival, the head of one of Wall Street's most important firms appraised his performance this way: "Michel has taken a firm that was on the brink of extinction and brought it back into being a really first-class organization." The hemorrhaging of Lazard's client base was stanched, and the firm once again began adding new clients. It moved forcefully into such burgeoning businesses as advising needy countries on their balance-of-payments problems. When corporate mergers and acquisitions picked up, Lazard was once again an important factor (although by no means as dominant as it was in the sixties). The firm was even talking about getting back into the venture-capital business. Little more than a year after David-Weill arrived on the scene, Lazard regained the vital element it had lost: a sense of purpose.

Through all this, Meyer remained in the background. Yet he still was an omnipresent force who was consulted whenever any critical move was being considered. He phoned David-Weill and other key partners constantly, leading some at Lazard to conclude that perhaps the patriarch hadn't given up the reins, after all. David-Weill, however, was very firm on that point. "André Meyer enjoys being kept abreast of what is happening," he said in early 1979. "He is and can be quite useful in introducing perspectives and bringing in client relationships. But he is not operating in any way, shape, or form the life of this place."

A few months before, Meyer had emerged from his seclusion and started showing up at the Rockefeller Center office for the first time since January 1975. The Meyer who appeared, however, was a far different specimen from the one who had walked out the door almost four years earlier. He was now a shuffling old man who walked slowly and deliberately with the aid of a cane and had difficulty getting up from his seat. His routine had also changed. Instead of arriving at 8:00 A.M. or before, he now would merely appear for lunch, chat with David-Weill and a few other partners, and leave by mid-afternoon. The cancer had been arrested, but the battle, compounded by the accumulated wear and tear of old age, had taken its toll.

Yet, despite Meyer's physical frailty, his mind and his curiosity about the world around him remained as sharp as ever. He still held court at the Carlyle, entertaining an endless procession of the high and mighty, and he still displayed an elephantine memory as to who came and who didn't. From time to time, he even ventured out to see clients. When Edgar Griffiths became chief executive of RCA, Meyer expressed a desire to get to know him better. Griffiths was willing to come up to the Carlyle for lunch, but Meyer dismissed the idea out of hand. "Oh no," he said. "He's the chief executive of RCA. I will go down to see him." So Meyer, along with Rohatyn and Don Petrie, trundled over to RCA headquarters at Rockefeller Plaza to lunch with Griffiths. "He was not well, and he was very tired at the end of the lunch," remembers former RCA counsel Robert Werner, who was there, "but he was very impressive talking about the present financial scene and his association with RCA. He was just as sharp mentally the last time I saw him as the first time I met him."

To some who knew him, it seemed a shame that Meyer did not employ his still-lucid mind to write his memoirs. When the subject was broached, Meyer would grunt, "Aah!" and wave his hand as if to shoo the notion away. But then he would add, "You know, Mrs. Onassis told me *she* wants to write my memoirs."

The closest he came to waxing reflective about his life and career was in the infrequent interviews he gave. His last one, and the one in which he was probably at his most reflective, was granted to this writer in February 1979, in connection with an article for *Institutional Investor* magazine on Meyer's legacy and the changing of the guard at Lazard. Meyer was in Crans at the time, and the interview was conducted by phone; the writer was told to call him early in the morning, Swiss time, because by the afternoon Meyer was heavily drugged. "About the past I can talk," Meyer warned at the outset. "About the present I can't say very much." His voice cracked occasionally, but his answers were concise and to the point.

Which of the many deals in your career, he was asked, are you proudest of?

"I have done a number of things," Meyer replied, "but I would have a certain amount of difficulty telling you which one was better than the other. And, you know, you should never take yourself too seriously."

Would it be fair to say that you had little interest in aspects of the investment-banking business other than deal making?

"That's absolutely true. The person who said that to you knew me. I've never been an unusual investment banker. There have been many who were at least as good. But I was certainly very much interested in deals and creating things. Underwriting was the bread-and-butter business, especially in the past, and it was very, very important. But certainly for years I've been a believer in the business of creating."

Why didn't you want to build Lazard into a larger firm, along the lines of a Goldman, Sachs or a Morgan Stanley?

"I thought we were more financial engineers. I was always very much afraid of big organizations. I was always afraid of large overhead expense, and I must say that in the kind of world I saw coming it was much more reasonable not to be a big organization and to remain master of your destiny. You know that when I started in New York we had two hundred forty employees; now I believe we only have two hundred fifty or two hundred sixty."

Will that smallish structure still make sense in the future?

"Despite the competition of the big brokers and the fact that the big banks are trying more and more to get into the investment-banking business, I think there will always be a place for a firm like Lazard with outstanding people and not too big an organization. But

I can't tell you what my younger partners will do in the future."

What is your impression of the recent changes made by your younger partners?

"It seems to me that the principles with which I guided the firm have remained the same. The group that came from Lehman Brothers are very competent people. I have met them. They were kind enough to visit me here, and I was very well impressed by their perfect manners. And Michel David-Weill is certainly a very intelligent boy; he has worked with me for many years, and he has up to now followed the principles that have been mine."

Is he capable of running both the Paris and New York firms?

"That will be very difficult. But he has good men in Paris and very good men in New York, and if he doesn't want to do everything I'm certain that he can adjust himself."

But when you ran the firm, you wanted to do everything, didn't you?

"Yes, but that was in another world, and years ago. That's why I decided to get out—because I thought I was not strong enough to continue what I was doing twenty years ago."

Looking back, is there anything you would have done differently?

"I would have worked much less, because I've certainly exhausted myself. But altogether it has worked well; we have developed our position enormously, and many partners have made a great deal of money. And we have never had one year in the red, in fifty years. I'm very proud of that because there have been a lot of ups and downs during that period. And I have seen a lot of people become rich and a lot of people lose their position. When you tell me that our people work a great deal, it's absolutely true. But they have been very well paid, and many have made fortunes."

Is it true that you did not approve of vacations?

"No, that's not true. Certainly I have always been very allergic to overhead expenses, and to achieve that, people have to work. I didn't approve of too much vacation, but I have never been accused of having chained down anybody."

Many people say that one of your greatest disappointments was Felix Rohatyn's refusal to succeed you as senior partner.

"It's true. I believe that eight or ten years ago, when I was seventy and I felt it was time to prepare for my retirement, my idea was for Felix to take the job. Of all the people I've seen in my very long career, I think Felix has always been the best, and I would have liked to have him take the full job and the responsibility. And at certain moments I had the hope, the illusion that he would. But he has never expressed any desire for doing that."

How is your health?

"When you have had a cancer, even though it is completely cured, you have to take all kinds of precautions. We take some drugs every day, and I see a doctor very often. I can go from time to time to the office, but if I had to work a great deal I would be absolutely unable to do it."

But you call New York every day?

"Yes, because New York is the place in the world where a lot of things are happening and because most of my friends are there. I call the office every day because when you have been in that business for so many years, even if you are not active at all, you like to know what's going on."

How often do you visit the office when you are in New York?

"I come to the office twice a week and have lunch with some of my partners. But after two or three hours, I'm glad to go home. They make me tired. Maybe I've made them tired in the past, but now they do it to me."

Two weeks after that interview, Meyer returned to New York. It was a time for reminiscences, and for summing up. "Did I ever trust anyone?" he said to his granddaughter Marianne. "No. But I wish I could have."

He visited Marianne's new apartment in a luxury East Side high rise. The panorama of New York City from her windows—the dramatic views in every direction of a city scraping the sky and brimming with life—touched some chord of him. The old fire, for one brief moment, flickered again. He pounded his cane on the floor. "New York is at your feet," he told his granddaughter. "*Do* something with it.

"Work hard," he admonished her. "And dream big dreams."

In early July 1979, the Meyers prepared to return to Crans. A few days before their departure, Fred and Andrea Wilson came to the Carlyle to say good-bye. Andrea brought André a cheesecake, the same cheesecake he had raved about during a dinner at the Wilsons' Soho apartment a few years before. "We ate the cheesecake and joked about it," Andrea Wilson recalls. "We reminisced about the old days, because there had been so much bantering and teasing each other back and forth in that Carlyle study where we sat." The mood was that of a cheerful bon voyage party.

At around the same time, attorney Ben Bartel also called on Meyer to wish him a safe trip. The encounter was far less bubbly. "Mr. Bartel," said Meyer, "this is the last time you will see me."

Meyer booked a Swissair night flight for Bella and himself, to the great distress of one close friend, who worried about the effects of the night flight on the old man's fragile constitution. This friend, with Bella's concurrence, tried to talk Meyer into chartering a plane for a day flight instead. Meyer, however, was not interested. It was the second time the friend had seen Meyer subordinate his health to his compulsive frugality. A short while earlier, the friend had tried to convince Meyer that he should buy a country home in the New York area rather than stay at the Carlyle all the time. "So you'll have four hundred thousand dollars less to give to your heirs," the friend said to Meyer. "What difference does it make?" But Meyer wouldn't be moved.

So Meyer took his night flight. And as his friend had feared, the fatigue of the journey loosened the last cords tethering the old banker to life. Soon after his arrival at Crans, he fell gravely ill and was admitted to the Nestlé Hospital in Lausanne. He was suffering from a circulatory problem, the doctors told his family, and from sheer old age. He was barely conscious much of the time and spoke very little. When he did speak, he rambled. A few visitors were allowed into the sickroom, including Madeleine Malraux, who brought with her her daughter-in-law Priscilla and Priscilla's two-year-old son Laurent. When Meyer caught sight of the boy, he smiled.

Meyer's eighty-first birthday came on September 3, and with it arrived the usual raft of congratulatory cables from well-wishers around the world. For the first time, he was unable to answer them himself; Bella responded on her husband's behalf. By then, his conscious moments were fewer and farther between. During one of them, his doctor asked him if he wanted anything.

"Yes," Meyer answered. "I want to work again."

On Sunday, September 9, 1979, in the Nestlé Hospital at Lausanne, André Meyer died.

Upon his death, André Meyer was paid homage befitting a world figure.

His demise was reported on the front page of the *New York Times*, and he was given the rare honor of a tribute on the paper's editorial page. "Many thriving conglomerates owe their existence to his genius at corporate mergers," the editorial declared. The article's greatest praise, however, was reserved not for his business dealings, but for his work on Robert Kennedy's Bedford-Stuyvesant redevelopment project. The paper described it as "one of his toughest mergers, bringing together the barons of Wall Street and the people of Fulton Street."

In France, *Le Monde* described him as "one of the great figures of international banking," someone who had "incontestably dominated the international financial scene for the past thirty years." The paper hailed his "fecund imagination and incomparable flair" in deal making, as well as his efforts on behalf of France.

He was eulogized at two memorial services. The first was in France, following his burial in Montparnasse Cemetery. The second was at New York's Temple Emanu-El on October 12. The Emanu-El service was an especially stellar gathering, a convocation of the power elite whose lives and fortunes had been influenced by the master financier of Lazard. Simon Rifkind eulogized Meyer as "a giant whose extraordinary career made him a man of renown to a worldwide generation." David Rockefeller paid tribute to Meyer, the financial engineer. "He was fascinated by the most complex business and financial problems," said Rockefeller. "The more difficult they were to solve, the more he accepted them as a challenge. He handled them with the skill and finesse of a concert violinist playing before an audience of sophisticated music lovers."

And Rockefeller hailed, in equal measure, Meyer, the counselor. "Throughout his life and even after his retirement from the active management of Lazard," he said, "André's advice was sought out by the thoughtful, the discerning, and wielders of power in many sectors of society. For myself, I can say there have been few people in my life to whom I could go, as I felt I could go to André, with personal dilemmas and be sure of receiving thoughtful, objective, and sympathetic advice."

But the most emotional of the eulogies came from the usually unflappable Felix Rohatyn. Rohatyn's voice cracked as he recounted how he still instinctively reached for the phone to call his mentor. "Sometimes I imagine what the conversations would be like, what he would say, but I can't be sure—it's left a terrible void," he said. And, of all the speakers, Rohatyn came the closest to summing up André Meyer, the man. "Behind that stern, forbidding, and sometimes theatrical facade," he said, "lay a man who was really yearning for affection.

"In my youth," commented the MAC chairman, "he was an Olympian figure: Zeus hurling thunderbolts. Then he was my teacher. He taught me not only to achieve perfection, but to do it in style."

That same day, Senator Charles Percy rose on the Senate floor to deliver his own encomium to the departed investment banker. "He was," said Percy, "without question one of the most brilliant investment bankers of our time. We shall all sorely miss him, but the governments of France and the United States, the free world and all of their citizens are the better for his long and productive lifetime."

Jackie Onassis was at the New York memorial service, and afterwards she walked a few blocks with Roswell Gilpatric. So many people she had relied on in her life were gone, she wistfully told Gilpatric. Now another major bulwark had been removed.

"She was very sad," remembers Gilpatric. "She felt that in her life there was nobody else to take his place."

CHAPTER TWENTY-NINE

The Final Tally

Her husband's death devastated Bella Meyer. Despite their long periods of separation from one another, he had always been the centerpiece of her life, and in his last years that bond had become again a tangible one. André's passing had left a void that nothing could fill. Her nephew François Voss, a Lazard Paris partner, remarks, "You read it all the time in books, but in this case it was true: she no longer had any reason to live."

During her husband's long illness, Bella had felt unwell herself, but in her zealous preoccupation with André, she shrugged off the symptoms and refused to be examined by a doctor. Now that he was gone, she no longer had the strength or the will to fight the disease, and it began to take its toll. Jaundiced-looking, she flew from Crans to Paris on January 22 and was immediately admitted to a hospital. The doctors operated and discovered the worst: Bella had cancer and was given a year to live. "She was not told what it was," her son recalls, "but I would say she suspected it." She returned to her apartment on the Quai des Orfèvres, where she had so often repaired while André was engrossed in his New York wheeling and dealing. There she continued to waste away. Five weeks after she left the hospital, Bella was dead.

The last links between André Meyer and the firm he had built eroded quickly.

After his death, Meyer's family had retained his partnership interest in Lazard. But the family's percentage was far less than it had been in his lifetime, and by the end of 1982, the firm was in negotiation with the family as to whether they would continue to retain any interest at all. The firm did not need their capital, and Lazard no longer wanted to give them so great a share of the firm's soaring profits. "It's obvious that a given percentage means a different sum of money than it used to," says Michel David-Weill, "so it's o the percentage which was fixed in the past cannot apply in the future." But David-Weill did not want the Meyers totally out of the picture. "In part for sentimental reasons," he would welcome their staying in.

Not that a continued involvement in Lazard would matter much to Meyer's heirs. All were set for life, and all were going off in directions that had little to do with the investment-banking firm. Philippe's son Vincent was an airline pilot. Marianne Gerschel, still struggling to find herself, now had settled on a career in clinical psychiatry. She also was coming to grips with the vast wealth that had been left her and had formed her own small foundation: the Spunk Fund. "It's a way for me to be creative with money," she says. "The fun part is to take a little amount of money when you're somebody my age and fortunate enough to have it fall in your lap and say, 'How can I watch it really be useful, and how can the thing that I'm giving it to grow as I'm growing?' " The Spunk Fund was her way of turning the money—a burden for so much of her life—into an opportunity.

The self-doubts that tormented Marianne had never seemed to afflict her brother Laurent, who moved confidently into a career in medicine. In early 1982, however, a peculiar rumor began circulating among those at Lazard who still followed the Meyers' comings and goings, a rumor that Laurent had dropped out of the medical profession. The gossip was well founded. Laurent, indeed, was no longer practicing medicine. Instead, he had gone into business with his brother Patrick, in a partnership called simply G & Company.

G & Company represents Patrick's attempt to finally make it on his own in the financial world, free of the withering glances of his partners at Lazard. Located on the fifty-third floor of the Chanin Building, across the street from Grand Central Station, G & Company is in the real estate business—although exactly what it does in that business is a mystery to many at Lazard and, indeed, to most of Patrick's family.

An encounter with Patrick is often a shock to anyone who was familiar with his grandfather's emphasis on style and elegance. A pudgy little man stuffed into a three-piece suit, Patrick speaks in a New York-accented whine and usually has a fat cigar jutting from his mouth.

Sitting in a conference room at the G & Company office not long ago, Patrick assessed his grandfather's accomplishments, and his own. What, he was asked, was his grandfather's greatest achievement?

"He made a lot of money, OK?" answered Patrick. "That's difficult to do, OK? Did he leave behind a U.S. Steel? No."

What about all the friends he had?

"Friends? What friends?"

Jackie Onassis, the Agnellis, the Rockefellers?

"Those aren't friends. Those are business acquaintances."

Would you say you've inherited any of your grandfather's traits?

"None."

The acquisitiveness, the desire for influence, the attention to detail?

"I pay great attention to detail. I'm a workaholic, OK? I try to do the best job I can, and I want to be left alone."

Does it bother you when people mention your grandfather's name in conversation?

"Indifferent."

So his success and reputation don't represent a weight over your head?

"Not at all. I like doing a good job and making money," said Gerschel, chomping on a mid-morning cigar. "It's the game I play."

André Meyer had long been an habitué of the Sotheby Parke Bernet Gallery on Madison Avenue, just across the street from the Carlyle. So it was only proper and fitting that the auction of his collection would take place there.

The scene at the auction, on the evening of October 22, 1980, would have awed and startled even Meyer. It was not so much a sale as a social event. The hall was jammed to a point of suffocation with both old money and new (among the latter was *Penthouse* publisher Bob Guccione, who bought one of Meyer's prized Picassos). So many people crowded into the room that some bidders had to stand on the steps leading to the stage, and a path had to be cleared for Sotheby chairman John Marion, who was acting as auctioneer.

When the auction started, another surprise was in store. The vaunted Meyer collection was worth considerably less than anyone who had gazed in awe at the walls of the Carlyle apartment would have imagined. The assorted Rembrandts, Renoirs, Picassos, and Van Goghs fetched only $16.4 million, some $2 million less than their appraised value in the estate. (The auction did not include Picasso's

Homme à la Guitare, valued at $1.9 million, the painting which Meyer had agreed, at the time of the Gertrude Stein auction, to donate to the Museum of Modern Art upon his death.) And the Sotheby people, it turned out, were overjoyed that the collection brought even that much. "It was a typical rich man's collection," one art expert who had sized up the works would later say. "He had the names, but he didn't have the best examples of those names. People were stunned that such second-rate pictures brought that kind of money." The verdict afterward was that if the glamour of the Meyer name had not been attached to the collection it would have brought 30 to 40 percent less.

The prized André Meyer collection, in short, had been a glorious triumph of mystique over substance.

If André Meyer is remembered at all in the art world, it is as the donor of the magnificent André Meyer wing of the Metropolitan Museum of Art in New York. Here again, however, illusion overtook reality. The impressive array of nineteenth-century European paintings in the wing were not, in fact, Meyer's; Meyer simply donated $2.6 million for the construction of the gallery. As museum chairman Douglas Dillon tells the story, Dillon had asked Meyer for the contribution in 1971, as part of a major capital-raising campaign. "It seemed to me that a fair amount for a trustee to give was two million dollars, so I asked him for it, and he gave it," Dillon recalls. "Later on when the costs went higher I went back to him and asked him for another six hundred fifty thousand for the installation, and he said sure, and he gave that in two installments." According to Dillon, the idea of using the donation for the construction of the nineteenth-century European wing and naming it after Meyer had been his brainchild, not Meyer's. "I thought everyone who gave two million dollars ought to have something that they could call theirs," he says, "and I suggested to him that that particular gallery would be appropriate because he liked impressionist paintings. He loved that idea."

These nuances, however, will not be known by the thousands who visit the wing each year. All that will be apparent to them is that one of the world's most lustrous collections of nineteenth-century art bears André Meyer's name. By his generosity, Meyer had finally assured himself of a measure of immortality in the art world.

As might be expected, the estate of André Meyer was a fearsomely complicated affair, made even more complicated by Meyer's obsessive concern with the Internal Revenue Service. Before Bella's death, for instance, her share of the estate was put in the hands of a Bermuda holding company, Woodstock Ltd. Even though by law her inheritance would go to her untaxed, Meyer apparently wanted to ensure that any further income Bella received would remain untaxed as well. Thus, the Bermuda company. (After Bella died, her interest in Woodstock Ltd. was passed on to her heirs.) In death, André Meyer was still doing his best to evade the taxman.

When the last will and testament of André Meyer was filed in Manhattan surrogate court, the general public—or at least those who were willing to plow through the thick file in the courthouse—was given its first real glimpse of the nature and extent of the financier's fortune. But the will and the estate were as enigmatic as the man. Meyer left half his U.S. estate to Bella and the other half, in equal shares, in trusts for the benefit of his four grandchildren. (Excluded from this was his art collection, which was bequeathed to the André and Bella Meyer Foundation, Inc.) Meyer's French assets were split between his two children—the New York documents gave no indication as to how large those assets were—but Philippe and Francine were not given any share of the American estate, undoubtedly far larger than the French holdings.

The contents of the estate itself were even more puzzling. The total amount of marketable stocks, for example, was a mere $13 million. The list of securities gave a good indication of the sort of investment Meyer was interested in, in his old age—most of the holdings were in oil and natural-resource stocks and Hettinger's beloved Japanese insurance companies—but the total cash value of each holding was meager. (The largest was $2.3 million worth of stock in Amerada Hess, the oil company.)

Under the heading "Miscellaneous Property" were Meyer's interests in various real estate partnerships and Lazard Frères. But, here again, the amounts were astonishingly small. None of the real estate partnership investments totaled more than $1 million, and Meyer's interest in Lazard, including profits that were due him, was a mere $8.3 million. Dwarfing them all was Meyer's art collection, valued in his estate at $20.3 million.

By far the largest segment of the portfolio was made up of bonds: $38 million in all. And the bulk of the bonds were U.S. Treasury securities, so-called "flower bonds" which were bought at a discount and could later be redeemed at face value to pay off estate taxes.

In all, then, the total value of André Meyer's estate was $89.5 million. For almost anyone else, the sum would be so staggering as to be beyond question. But for André Meyer, the total was disappointing and bewildering. To those who worked closely with him over the years, it was inconceivable that his total fortune was *only* $90 million.

Where could the rest of the money have gone? No one outside Meyer's immediate family will ever know for sure, but there is little doubt that considerable sums must have been transferred to trusts for his children and grandchildren over the years. In addition, Meyer customarily put significant chunks of his deals into the family trusts. In Avis, for example, a little less than a quarter of Meyer's shares was purchased on behalf of his grandchildren's trusts. A fair share of Meyer's wealth, in other words, may have been deliberately diverted into the hands of his dependents from the beginning.

The true extent of Meyer's fortune is a secret probably known by only one man, André's son Philippe. And on that subject, Philippe is absolutely mum. "The secretive part of my father I will respect," explains Philippe. "If he had wanted to put his fortune in a public place, he would have done it. But since he didn't want to do it, and didn't like to do it, and was very keen on *not* doing it, I will respect that."

While a number of Meyer's associates over the years have made guesses as to his fortune—the figures range anywhere from $300 million to $800 million—the only one who claims to do so on the basis of inside knowledge is Disque Deane. "I know the amount of money that he contributed to the trusts for his two children and his four grandchildren," Deane says. "And if you add all those numbers up, you get into some pretty big numbers. I think Patrick's trust has a residual value which he will admit to of thirty million dollars. You multiply that by four and that's a hundred twenty million dollars. And each of his children, many, many years ago got fifty million dollars. Even at eight percent compound interest, that has to have grown to a hundred fifty million each. So that's four hundred twenty million dollars."

When the $90 million in Meyer's estate is added to that, then, the grand total would be in excess of $500 million.

But no one, save Philippe Meyer, will ever know for sure. André Meyer's estate was the final masterstroke of the secretive, magnificent financier.

The business world, in the years since André Meyer's death, has come alive again. Giant mergers once more dominate the corporate landscape. The venture-capital arena is undergoing a renaissance. Huge real estate fortunes have been made.

In so many of these areas, André Meyer had been a forerunner. In many respects, long ago, he had helped set these forces in motion.

It is a world, once again, of deal-makers. A world in which André Meyer would have felt right at home.

Notes on Sources

One of the safest assumptions one can make about André Meyer is that he would not have wanted this book—or any book about himself, for that matter—to be written. Nearly his entire life was played out behind a curtain of secrecy. Not only did he consider such secrecy an essential element of investment banking, but it also satisfied some elemental part of his makeup. He preferred to remain an enigma, even to those closest to him.

For that reason, the researching of this book posed some unique challenges. As is noted early on, Meyer did not leave a trail of paper behind him; he was careful *not* to put into writing his ideas and reflections. A letter or memo of substance for him was a rare event. Usually, he preferred to respond to other people's memos, dashing something across them in a virtually illegible scrawl. Most of the time, he dealt with people either face to face or on the phone.

Hence, this biography was, to a large extent, an oral-history project. In all, 147 people were interviewed, many several times. Nearly all the interviews took place between June 1, 1981, and February 28, 1982.

Many more potential interviewees were approached but declined to cooperate. Some, such as Jacqueline Onassis, said no because they were not in the habit of giving such interviews. Others refused because they did not feel Meyer would have wanted them to talk. (Even a few people who agreed to sit down with the author suggested that Meyer's specter was hovering over the discussion, inhibiting what they said.) Despite these difficulties, the author feels that he spoke to a sufficient number of people, in every aspect of André Meyer's life, to give a full and accurate portrait of his career.

Some of the interviewees deserve special mention because of the extraordinary help and encouragement they provided. At the top of the list are Meyer's son, Philippe, and granddaughter, Marianne Gerschel, both of whom not only served as invaluable sources but also helped renew and strengthen the author's conviction that this project was worth pursuing, despite the many moments of frustration along the way. Michel David-Weill, Meyer's successor as Lazard senior partner, gave unstintingly of his time; his perceptions were consistently frank, incisive, and astute. The chapter on Meyer's 1950s deals would not have been possible without the generous cooperation of Ferdinand Eberstadt's long-time aide, Nelson Loud. Similarly, Meyer's involvement in real estate as well as other ventures could not have been reconstructed without the assistance of George Ames and Disque Deane, and his adventures (and misadventures) with Avis and Allied Concord would have been impossible to recount fully without Donald Petrie's aid.

For various reasons, some individuals who were of critical importance in the researching of this book preferred to remain anonymous. The author is grateful for their information and advice.

Despite the great reliance on interviews, some written documentation was available. The progress of some of Meyer's early deals could be followed through prospectuses and other old public documents on file at Cahill, Gordon & Reindel, one of Lazard's principal law firms in those years. The author is indebted to Arnold Daum, Dudley Tenney, and others at Cahill, Gordon for their help in locating these documents. Meyer's relationship with Lyndon Johnson could be reconstructed with various memorandums, letters, and other materials at the LBJ Library in Austin, Texas. The House antitrust subcommittee's investigation of conglomerates in 1969 was especially useful in detailing Lazard and Meyer's role in the merger mania of the 1960s.

The greatest single treasure trove, however, was the Securities and Exchange Commission's investigative file on the ITT-Hartford-Mediobanca affair. The complete contents of that file were obtained for inspection by the author under the Freedom of Information Act. (The file also contained depositions and other materials in the related *Herbst* v. *ITT* case.) Considering the reluctance of many of the principals to talk about these events, even years afterwards, the investigative file was a unique and indispensable resource.

Finally, one other source should be singled out: *The Journals of David E. Lilienthal,* published in six volumes by Harper & Row during the sixties and seventies. These diaries by the first head of the Tennessee Valley Authority and the Atomic Energy Commission offer some rare glimpses of Meyer in his heyday. In the source notes that follow, they are simply referred to as *Lilienthal.*

Interviews

Of the 147 people interviewed for this book, 114 agreed to go on the record, although occasionally they would ask that some comment not be used for attribution. Those interviewed on the record are listed below; they are identified by their capacities at the time of their relationship with André Meyer.

Agnelli, Giovanni (Fiat chairman)

Alphand, Hervé (French ambassador to the U.S.)

Altschul, Arthur (Goldman, Sachs partner, Frank Altschul's son)

Ames, George (Lazard partner)

Baker, Edward (Lazard oil and gas specialist)

Bartel, Benjamin (counsel to Meyer)

Bernbach, William (Doyle, Dane & Bernbach chairman)

Bernheim, Antoine (Lazard Paris partner)

Bernstein, Arthur (Allied Concord chairman)

Bilbey, Kenneth (RCA executive)

Black, Eugene (World Bank president)

Bliss, Richard (Bankers Trust executive)

Boël, René (Solvay chief)

Cannell, Peter (Ferdinand Eberstadt's son-in-law)

Colin, Justin (Lazard partner)

Connor, John (Allied Chemical Co. chairman)

Corcoran, Peter (Lazard partner)

David-Weill, Michel (Lazard partner)

Deane, Disque (Lazard partner)

De Kamouleria, Claude (French civil servant)

Dillon, C. Douglas (U.S. treasury secretary)

Dilworth, Richardson (Rockefeller aide)

Ellsworth, Robert (Lazard partner)

Engelhardt, Herbert (Lazard associate)

Fabre, Francis (Chargeurs Réunis head)

Fowler, Henry (U.S. treasury secretary)

Fraser, Ian (Lazard Brothers London chairman)

Gabetti, Gianluigi (Agnelli aide, Olivetti chief)

Geisser, Andrea (Lazard associate)

Gerschel, Marianne (AM's granddaughter)

Gerschel, Patrick (AM's grandson)

Gilbert, Edward (E. L. Bruce Co. president)

Gilpatric, Roswell (deputy U.S. defense secretary, attorney)

Glanville, James (Lazard partner)

Graham, Katharine (*Washington Post* chairman)

Gut, Rainer (Lazard partner)

Guyot, Jean (Lazard Paris partner)

Haas, Jean-Claude (Lazard Paris partner)

Hall, Perry (Morgan Stanley senior partner)

Herzog, Edwin (Lazard partner)

Hettinger, Albert (Lazard partner)

Hoffman, Anna Rosenberg (public-relations executive, AM's friend)

Hoffman, Peter (RCA Corp. executive)

Howard, Leonard (Lazard partner)

Javits, Jacob (U.S. senator)

Jesselson, Ludwig (Philipp Brothers chief)

Kahn, Herman (Lehman Brothers partner)

Kenney, Thomas (Lazard partner)

Kindersley, Hugo (Lazard Brothers director)

Klein, Louis (Lazard associate)

Krim, Arthur (United Artists chief, Democratic party fund-raiser)

Leonard, James (Lehman Brothers associate)

Satterthwaite, James (Lazard associate)

Savage, Robert (ITT executive)

Shumway, Forrest (Signal Companies president)

Shriver, R. Sargent (Kennedy family member, U.S. ambassador to France)

Simon, William (Salomon Brothers partner)

Smith, Stephen (overseer of Kennedy family finances)

Stein, Howard (Dreyfus Corp. chairman)

Supino, David (Lazard partner)

Sykes, Walter (Allied Chemical chief financial officer)

Thomas, Franklin (Bedford-Stuyvesant Renewal and Rehabilitation Corp. chief)

Tisch, Laurence (Loews Corp. chairman)

Tree, Marietta (socialite)

Troubh, Raymond (Lazard partner)

Valensi, Christian (Lazard Paris partner)

Vogelstein, John (Lazard partner)

Voss, François (Lazard Paris partner)

Weill, Michel (AM's nephew)

Werner, Robert (RCA Corp. executive)

Wilson, Andrea (AM's friend, Lazard executive)

Wilson, Fred (Lazard partner)

Wilson, Kemmons (Holiday Inn founder)

Woods, George (First Boston chairman)

Wriston, Walter (Citibank executive)

Wylie, Vern (Lazard Brothers London director)

Zarb, Frank (Lazard partner)

Zeckendorf, William, Jr. (real estate executive)

Zeller, Robert (F. Eberstadt & Co. partner)

Sources

1. A TALE OF TWO FINANCIERS
    Interviews: Gilbert.
    Details of Gilbert's life-style, crimes, flight came from news accounts, especially articles by Murray Rossant and McCandlish Phillips, *New York Times*, June 24, 1962. Additional material from court documents in *Gilbert v. Meyer*, U.S. District Court, Southern District of N.Y., 1972, 72 Civ 2302.

2. THE PICASSO OF BANKING
    Interviews: Lewis, A. Wilson, McNamara, Rockefeller, Rohatyn, P. Meyer, David-Weill, anonymous sources.

3. UP AND COMING
    AM's family, childhood, courtship: David-Weill, P. Meyer, M. Gerschel.
    School records: archives of Collège Rollin, Paris, France.
    French financial market, economy: "French Money, Banking and Finance During the Great War," *Quarterly Journal of Economics*, November 1915. Also, Tom Kemp, *The French Economy 1913–39*, New York: St. Martin's Press, 1972.
    Lazard background: Various accounts of Lazard over the years, especially "In Trinity There Is Strength" by Thomas Wise, *Fortune*, August 1968.
    David-Weill: F. Wilson, Gay, David-Weill.
    SOVAC: Gay.
    Citroën: Contemporary news accounts, and Silvain Reiner, *La Tragedie d'André Citroën*, Paris: Amiot-Dumont, 1954.
    AM's prewar friendships: P. Meyer, Fabre.
    Exodus from France: P. Meyer.
    Stripped of his honors: news accounts, P. Meyer, Fabre.

4. STARTING OVER
    Meyer's depression: P. Meyer.
    Setting up shop: Rosen.
    Altschul's Lazard: *Newsweek* profile of Altschul and Lazard, October 6, 1934. Also Satterthwaite. Altschul's marriage: Stephen Birmingham, *Our*

Crowd, New York: Harper & Row, 1967. Altschul's help to AM: P. Meyer.
AM's takeover: Altschul, David-Weill.
Murnane: Murnane, Jr., Boël. Also, Jean Monnet, *Memoirs*, New York:
Doubleday, 1978.
Utility plays: F. Wilson.

5. GOLD UNDER THE ASPHALT
Postwar Wall Street: Various contemporary news and magazine accounts.
Wall Street and AM: Satterthwaite, F. Wilson, Herzog.
AM and Hall: Hall.
AM and Lehman: Kahn, Manheim, anonymous Lehman sources.
AM and visiting French officials: De Kamouleria, Also, *Lilienthal.*
AM's Jewish feeling: Weill, Jesselson, Rosen.
AM and Israel: P. Meyer, Rosen.
Jean Lambert: Tree, Ames, Rosen.
Matador: Ames; news accounts, especially "Matador: Last Big British-Owned Ranch Sold," *Business Week*, August 4, 1951.

6. ANDRÉ AND FERD
Eberstadt background: Eberstadt obituary, New York *Times*, November 13, 1969. *Fortune* profile of Eberstadt, April 1939. Also, *Lilienthal.* Interviews: Loud, Zeller, Porter, Cannell.
AM and Green: Colin.
AM and Ross: Ross.
Building of Engelhard Minerals and Chemicals: prospectuses, news accounts, *Lilienthal.* Interviews: Rosenthal, Loud, Zeller, Jesselson.
Building of Warner-Lambert: prospectuses, news accounts. Interviews: Loud, Zeller, Porter, Markoe. Also, Elmer Bobst, *The Autobiography of a Pharmaceutical Pioneer*, New York: David McKay Co., 1973.
Haiti: Loud.
Ziv: Loud, Krim, news accounts.

7. FRIENDS
AM and Albert Lasker: *Lilienthal.*
AM and Mary Lasker: Hoffman.
Sarnoff: Werner, Bilbey, news accounts.
Paley: Paley.
Rockefeller: Rockefeller, anonymous Chase sources.
Monnet: Guyot.
Agnelli: Agnelli, Ellsworth, news accounts.
Graham: Graham, Paget, Gilpatric.

Engelhard: Pat Ryan, "The Walking Conglomerate," *Sports Illustrated*, April 28, 1969. Also, *Forbes* feature on Engelhards, August 1, 1965. Interviews: F. Wilson, Zeller.

Javits: Javits.

Percy: Percy.

8. THE WOMEN IN HIS LIFE

Bella: A. Wilson, Graham, P. Meyer, F. Wilson.

Claude Alphand: M. Gerschel, Tree. Also Thomas J. Hamilton, "New Friend from Paris in Washington," *New York Times Sunday Magazine*, September 23, 1956.

Philippe Meyer: P. Meyer, Fabre.

Francine Meyer: M. Gerschel, anonymous sources.

9. THE AVIS SAGA

Interviews: Petrie, Mackey, Rohatyn, Hoffman, Porter. Also, Robert Townsend, *Up the Organization*, New York: Knopf, 1970.

Holiday Inns: K. Wilson, Howard.

10. SINS OF PRIDE

Interviews: Petrie, Vogelstein, Bernstein, David-Weill.

11. ZECKENDORF

William Zeckendorf, *The Autobiography of William Zeckendorf*, New York: Holt, Rinehart & Winston, 1970.

Interviews: Ames, Deane, Phelan, Nicholson, Zeckendorf, Jr., Petrie.

12. THE INCOMPARABLE INVESTOR

AM's investment philosophy and strategies: Deane, Baker, Ainsworth, David-Weill, Murnane, Agnelli, Colin, Guyot, Lewis, Corcoran, Howard, Hettinger, Herzog, anonymous sources. Also, *Lilienthal*.

Lazard Fund: Howard, contemporary news accounts.

Real estate: Deane, Ames, anonymous sources, news accounts.

13. MONEY HUNGRY

Life-style: F. Wilson, Deane, Hoffman, Ellsworth, David-Weill, Manheim, Herzog.

Gertrude Stein auction: Paley, Rockefeller.

The description of Crans comes from personal inspection by the author, August 1981. The description of the Carlyle comes from the report by AM's estate appraisers.

AM and charity: Ames, Werner. AM's comments come from *New York Times* "Man in the News" story, October 28, 1965.

14. MADELEINE MALRAUX
Interviews: Malraux, M. Gerschel, Deane.
Biographical material on Madeleine and André Malraux comes from Alain Malraux, *Les Marroniers de Boulogne*, Paris: Plon, 1978.

15. LIFE AT LAZARD
Atmosphere and anecdotes: Gut, Bernstein, David-Weill, Pizzitola, Colin, Troubh, Lewis, F. Wilson, Petrie, Rohatyn, Ames, Corcoran.
AM's comments on the Rockefeller Center offices come from "The Remarkable Felix Rohatyn," *Business Week*, March 10, 1973.
AM and government officials: Ellsworth. Offer to Vance confirmed by Vance.
Financial arrangements: Colin, Manheim, Deane, Ainsworth, Mullarkey.
Shean: News accounts, Simon, anonymous sources.
Gut fishing trip: Gut, Murnane.

16. PIERRE THE DUKE
Pierre David-Weill: Herzog, David-Weill, Rifkind, Agnelli, F. Wilson.
Lazard Paris: Haas, Guyot, Bernheim.
Lazard London: Wylie, Norman, Fraser, Kindersley, anonymous sources.

17. THE SAGE OF THE CARLYLE
Howard Hughes and AM: Ames.
AM the adviser: Rohatyn, Gabetti, Pizzitola, Rifkind, Malozemoff (Newmont), Conner, Sykes (Allied Chemical), Gilpatric (General Dynamics), Samuels (Sofina), Plescoff.
Additional material on Newmont from Robert H. Ramsey, *Men & Mines at Newmont*, Octagon Books, 1973.

18. MERGER MAKING
Background on 1960s merger activity and historical comparisons: Raymond Anthony Piccini, *An Analysis of the Merger Activity of Large Industrial Firms 1948-1965*, Ph.D. Thesis, Columbia University, 1970; André-Paul Weber, *Les Concentrations Industrielles dans la France Contemporaine*, Paris: Bordas, 1971; Lewis Beman, "What We Learned from the Great Merger-Frenzy," *Fortune*, April, 1973; The Editors of *Fortune*, *The Conglomerate Commotion*, New York: Viking, 1970.
Rohatyn: "The Remarkable Felix G. Rohatyn," *Business Week*, March 10, 1973; Peter Hellman, "The Wizard of Lazard," *New York Times Sunday Magazine*, March 21, 1976; "The Cities' Mr. Fixit," *Newsweek*, May 4, 1981; Everett Mattlin, "Felix Rohatyn: The M&A Man's M&A Man,"

Corporate Financing, February, 1970; "John Callaway Interviews Felix Rohatyn," WTTW Chicago, December 10, 1981. Interviews: Porter, Rohatyn, Mackey.

Geneen and ITT: Anthony Sampson, *The Sovereign State of ITT*, New York: Stein & Day, 1973; Carol Loomis, "Harold Geneen's Moneymaking Machine Is Still Humming," *Fortune*, September, 1972. Interviews: Perry, Rohatyn, anonymous sources.

Additional material on Geneen and Lazard merger techniques comes from the House antitrust subcommittee's *Hearings on Conglomerates*, 1969. (This includes the hearings themselves and documents submitted for the record.)

Merger making at Lazard: Osborne, Gabetti, anonymous sources.

Robert Sarnoff: Werner, Rohatyn, Manheim, anonymous sources.

19. CASHING IN
Lazard fee figures: House hearings.
Franco Wyoming: David-Weill, Troubh, Lewis, Guyot, Osborne.
AM and merger era: Rohatyn, Guyot, Klein, Colin, Lewis.

20. JACKIE O.
AM and JFK: *Lilienthal*, Smith, Shriver, Krim, Dillon, Fowler.
AM and Kennedys: Shriver, Smith, Agnelli.
Kennedy finances: Michael Jensen, "Managing the Kennedy Millions," *New York Times*, June 12, 1977.
AM and RFK: Agnelli, Smith, Gilpatric, Johnston. Also, *Lilienthal*.
AM and Jacqueline Kennedy Onassis: Stephen Birmingham, *Jacqueline Bouvier Kennedy Onassis*, New York: Grossett & Dunlap, 1978; Kitty Kelley, *Jackie Oh!*, New York: Lyle Stuart, 1978; Fred Sparks, *The $20 Million Honeymoon*, New York: Geis, 1970; Frank Brady, *Onassis: An Extravagant Life*, New York: Prentice Hall, 1977. Interviews: Smith, Black, Gilpatric, A. Wilson, Hoffman, M. Gerschel, Malraux, Rifkind, Graham, McNamara, Hall, anonymous sources.

21. A RENDEZVOUS WITH LBJ
Memos, letters referred to are from the LBJ Library, Austin, Texas. Interviews: Krim, Fowler, Rosen, Dillon, Ellsworth, Plescoff.
Johnson summarized the battle with the French and the work of the Dillon committee in his memoirs, *The Vantage Point*, New York: Holt, Rinehart, 1971.
Bedford-Stuyvesant: Johnston, Dillon, Thomas. Also, Arthur Schlesinger, Jr., *RFK and His Times*, New York: Houghton Mifflin, 1978.
Vietnam: *Lilienthal*, M. Gerschel, Krim, McNamara, Fowler, A. Wilson, anonymous sources, Johnston.

22. TIDYING UP

AM's early-1970s mood: Bliss, David-Weill, Pizzitola, Perkins, anonymous sources.

Iranian Development Bank: *Lilienthal,* anonymous sources.

Mountain Park: Ames, Nicholson, Bartel. Also, *Zeckendorf* autobiography.

23. EDDIE GILBERT ... AGAIN

Most of the material for this chapter comes from testimony and court documents in *Gilbert* v. *Meyer,* U.S. District Court, Southern District of N.Y., 1972, 72 Civ 2302.

Interviews: Mullarkey, Gilbert, Supino, Rifkind, David-Weill, Price.

24. A DEAL UNDER FIRE

Cuccia: Guyot, Agnelli, *Lilienthal.*

Hartford takeover chronology: news accounts. Also, Sampson, *Sovereign State of ITT.*

AM's involvement in Hartford takeover: AM deposition in *Herbst* vs. *ITT,* U.S. District Court, District of Connecticut, 1972.

Movement of Hartford shares, details on Way Assauto and Eurofund shares: SEC investigative file HO-536.

AM's reaction to investigation: Graham, anonymous sources, Mullarkey.

Kennedy intervention: news accounts of Casey testimony.

25. THE VISE TIGHTENS

All testimony is from *Herbst* vs. *ITT* and SEC investigative file. Also, interviews with SEC investigators.

AM and Watergate: Graham, anonymous sources.

26. FIGHTING FOR HIS LIFE

AM's illness: P. Meyer, Rosen, Price.

Boycott: Guyot, news accounts.

Testimony from SEC investigative file.

Letters; appeals from Harris, Rifkind; SEC investigative file.

SEC findings: *In the matter of International Telephone and Telegraph Corporation, Lazard Frères,* Release no. 14049, October 13, 1977.

27. ADRIFT

Image of waning AM: Robert Cole, "End of an Era at Lazard," *New York Times,* January 30, 1977.

AM's influence on firm and mood: David-Weill, Pizzitola, Bartel, Rohatyn, Patterson, Agnelli, Price.

AM and grandchildren: Hoffman, M. Gerschel, Malraux, Pizzitola, Herzog, Rohatyn, Deane, anonymous sources.

Rohatyn: Rohatyn, Rifkind, Graham, anonymous sources.

Deane: Deane, Ames. Also CPI-Peerage merger documents.

28. THE TORCH PASSES

David-Weill's arrival and changes: David-Weill, Rohatyn, Supino, Petrie, Glanville. Also, Wyndham Robertson, "Passing the Baton at Lazard Frères," *Fortune*, November, 1977; and author's piece, "The Legacy of André Meyer," *Institutional Investor*, April, 1979.

The André Meyer interview is excerpted from "The Legacy of André Meyer."

AM and RCA: Werner.

AM's final days: M. Gerschel, A. Wilson, Malraux, P. Meyer, anonymous sources.

29. THE FINAL TALLY

Bella: Hoffman, Rosen, Voss, P. Meyer.

Gerschels: M. Gerschel, P. Gerschel, anonymous sources.

Art auction: Sotheby Parke Bernet officials, eyewitnesses.

Metropolitan Museum gift: Dillon.

The accounting of AM's estate is available at the New York County Surrogate Court, 31 Chambers Street, New York City.

Index

E

F